HEAVEN AND EARTH ARE NOT HUMANE

WORLD PHILOSOPHIES

Bret W. Davis, D. A. Masolo, and Alejandro Vallega, *editors*

HEAVEN AND EARTH ARE NOT HUMANE
The Problem of Evil in Classical Chinese Philosophy

Franklin Perkins

Indiana University Press

Bloomington & Indianapolis

This book is a publication of

Indiana University Press
Office of Scholarly Publishing
Herman B Wells Library 350
1320 East 10th Street
Bloomington, Indiana 47405 USA

iupress.indiana.edu

Telephone orders   800-842-6796
Fax orders   812-855-7931

© 2014 by Franklin Perkins

All rights reserved

No part of this book may be reproduced or utilized in any form or by any means, electronic or mechanical, including photocopying and recording, or by any information storage and retrieval system, without permission in writing from the publisher. The Association of American University Presses' Resolution on Permissions constitutes the only exception to this prohibition.

♾ The paper used in this publication meets the minimum requirements of the American National Standard for Information Sciences—Permanence of Paper for Printed Library Materials, ANSI Z39.48-1992.

Manufactured in the United States of America

Library of Congress Cataloging-in-Publication Data

Perkins, Franklin.
  Heaven and earth are not humane : the problem of evil in classical Chinese philosophy / Franklin Perkins.
    pages cm. — (World philosophies)
  Includes bibliographical references and index.
  ISBN 978-0-253-01168-8 (cloth) — ISBN 978-0-253-01172-5 (pbk.) — ISBN (ebook) 978-0-253-01176-3 (ebook) 1. Philosophy, Chinese—To 221 B.C. 2. Good and evil. I. Title.
  B126.P54 2014
  170.931—dc23

2013043038

1 2 3 4 5   19 18 17 16 15 14

Dedicated to JoAnn Perkins
1947–2004

天地不仁，以萬物為芻狗。
聖人不仁，以百姓為芻狗。

Heaven and earth are not humane,
They take the myriad things as straw dogs.
Sagely people are not humane,
They take the people as straw dogs.

—*Dàodéjīng*

Contents

Acknowledgments — *xi*
Note on Abbreviated Citations — *xiii*

Introduction: Philosophy in a Cross-Cultural Contex — 1

1 Formations of the Problem of Evil — 10

2 The Efficacy of Human Action and the Mohist Opposition to Fate — 45

3 Efficacy and Following Nature in the *Dàodéjīng* — 82

4 Reproaching Heaven and Serving Heaven in the *Mèngzǐ* — 116

5 Beyond the Human in the *Zhuāngzǐ* — 151

6 Xúnzǐ and the Fragility of the Human — 184

Conclusion — 219

Notes — 227
Bibliography — 271
Index — 285

Acknowledgments

I NEVER FORMALLY STUDIED Chinese philosophy or Sinology, so I have accumulated many, many teachers over the past dozen years. A list of everyone who has given me some crucial bits of guidance, feedback, or assistance would encompass almost everyone working on any related topics. I can only single out a few who have had the most profound effect on the work presented here. On-cho Ng was the first scholar of Chinese thought I had the chance to work with, and he has been helping me ever since he served on my dissertation committee on Leibniz and China. The person most responsible for my move into Chinese philosophy is Bryan W. Van Norden, who took a chance and hired me as a sabbatical replacement and then generously spent time getting me oriented in the field. My occasional disagreements with his readings here should not obscure how deeply he shaped my whole approach to early Chinese philosophy. Hans-Georg Moeller also has been a guide and a friend since I was a complete beginner, and many of my views took shape through discussions with him. More recently, my interpretations of many texts have been deeply influenced by years of discussions with Chris Fraser and Dan Robins, and even more recently by many long talks with Brook Ziporyn. Roger T. Ames and Henry Rosemont Jr. have given me generous support at several crucial points. My teacher on the Sinology side has been Esther Klein, who helped me develop the skills needed for this book and who carefully corrected many of its mistakes. I am deeply grateful to all of you for your guidance and friendship.

A number of people read earlier (even longer!) versions of this manuscript, and gave me crucial feedback and encouragement: Roger T. Ames, David Jones, Colin Klein, Esther Klein, Hans-Georg Moeller, Graham Parkes, Michael W. Pelczar, Michael J. Puett, Aaron Stalnaker, Robin R. Wang, and Brook Ziporyn. Others gave me important feedback on individual chapters, or articles that developed into chapters: Chung-ying Cheng, Kelly James Clark, Chris Fraser, David Farrell Krell, Philip J. Ivanhoe, and Liu Xiaogan. This book would not be what is without their suggestions. I have also benefited from presenting versions of many parts of this book at conferences, particularly years of attending the Midwest Conference on Chinese Thought and the Comparative and Continental Philosophy Circle. I owe a great debt to my colleagues, not only for supporting me in such a radical change in research areas but also for their philosophical insights, many of which appear in this book. I am particularly grateful to Sean D. Kirkland for his assistance with various Greek terms. My students also have allowed me to refine my ideas, and to absorb some of theirs. Finally, I would like to thank

Indiana University Press, particularly Nancy Lightfoot and Dee Mortensen for guiding me through the whole process; Dawn Ollila for her careful copyediting; and Bret Davis, the Asia editor for the World Philosophy Series, for encouraging me to submit the manuscript in the first place. I am grateful to Cyndy Brown for creating the index.

One of the most important elements of support throughout the writing of this book has been my friendship with Robin R. Wang, whose magical powers have helped me in almost every possible way—from initially attaining the Fulbright grant that got this started to correcting the Chinese in the final version of the manuscript—but most of all by being a constant source of support and joy. I will always be grateful. On a personal level, I owe the greatest debt to my parents, who encouraged me to pursue whatever I was most interested in, whether that led me to philosophy or to China or both.

This research would not have been possible without generous financial support from a number of sources. Two grants from the Blakemore Foundation allowed me to develop the necessary language abilities. A paid research leave from DePaul University allowed me to lay some of the foundations for this work, and I began the actual writing with a Fulbright research grant that enabled me to spend a year in affiliation with the Philosophy Department at Peking University. An earlier version of the project began through an NEH summer fellowship for the seminar "Individual, State, and Law in Ancient China, Greece, and Rome," held at University of California Berkeley. Finally, I could not be where I am now without generous help in financing my college education, particularly with a Dean's Select scholarship from Vanderbilt University and scholarships from the Richardson Foundation and the Citizens Foundation. I will always be grateful for the opportunities those scholarships made possible.

Parts of two previously published articles have been incorporated into various chapters of this book: "Wandering beyond Tragedy with Zhuangzi," published in *Comparative and Continental Philosophy* 3.1 (Spring 2011): 79–98, and, "The Moist Criticism of the Confucian Use of Fate," published in *Journal of Chinese Philosophy*, 35.3 (September 2008): 421–36. I am grateful for permission to include parts of these articles.

Note on Abbreviated Citations

All translations from the Chinese are my own. I have used standard Pinyin romanization throughout, and have converted other forms of romanization into Pinyin except in published titles and author names. For citations of classical texts, in general, I have cited the chapter number and the page number in a standard Chinese edition, along with some way of locating the passage in a readily available English translation. Frequently used Chinese texts are cited according to the following abbreviated format:

Dàodéjīng 道德經. Cited by chapter number according to the order of the received text. I have followed the Mǎwángduī text in Liú Xiàogǎn 2006, unless otherwise noted.

Hánfēizǐ 韓非子. Cited by chapter number and page in Chén Qíyóu 2000.

Lùnhéng 論衡 (Wáng Chōng). Cited by chapter number and page in Huāng 1990.

Lúnyǔ 論語. Cited by chapter and passage, using the numbering system of Yáng 2002 (which is followed by most recent translations), based on the text in Liú Bǎonán 1990.

Lǚshì chūnqiū 呂氏春秋. Cited by book/section and page number in Chén Qíyóu 1984. The book and section numbers correspond to those in the English translation by Knoblock and Reigel 2000.

Mèngzǐ. 孟子. Cited by book (1–7), part (A or B), and passage number, following the numbering of passages in Yáng 2003 (which is followed by most recent translations), based on the text in Jiāo 1987.

Mòzǐ 墨子. Cited by chapter number and page in Sūn Yíràng 2001.

Shǐ jì 史記 (Sīmǎ Qiān). Cited by chapter number and page in Sīmǎ Qiān 1959.

Shī jīng 詩經. Cited by the traditional Mao numbers, following the text in Zhōu Zhènfǔ 2002.

Xúnzǐ 荀子. Cited by chapter number and page in Wáng Xiānqiān 1988.

Zhuāngzǐ 莊子. Cited by chapter number and page in Guō Qìngfán 1978.

HEAVEN AND EARTH ARE NOT HUMANE

Introduction
Philosophy in a Cross-Cultural Context

Bad things happen to good people. This sad fact was at least as true in early China as it was for Leibniz or Voltaire and still is today. This book takes this simple observation as a thread by which to trace the tensions and reconciliations between human beings and nature or the divine (in Chinese terms, *tiān* 天). While focusing on Chinese thought, it is ultimately an attempt to do philosophy by bringing together ideas from different traditions and cultures, particularly ideas rooted in Warring States China and early modern Europe. It could thus be labeled as a work in "comparative philosophy," "world philosophy," or "intercultural philosophy."

Intercultural approaches to philosophy are by no means new. What we call Western philosophy originated in the mixing of cultures around the Mediterranean. Medieval philosophy largely arose from the introduction of Christianity into classical Mediterranean thought, and the development and end of medieval philosophy was driven by the introduction or reintroduction of Arabic, Greek, and Roman philosophy. On a global level, one of the most fruitful and consequential examples of intercultural philosophy was the introduction of Buddhism from India into China, which generated hybrid forms of Buddhism and of Confucianism. We can even say that the twentieth century was an age of intercultural philosophy, with the leading philosophers across most of the world bringing European philosophy into dialogue with their own traditions, from Móu Zōngsān 牟宗三 and Táng Jūnyì 唐君毅 in China and Nishida and Nishitani in Japan to Vivekanda and Bhattacharya in India and Hountondji and Wiredu in Africa. From a global and historical perspective, then, contemporary philosophers in Europe and North America are unusual in their general refusal to engage ideas outside their own traditions and cultures. Although this exceptional status reveals the absurdity of attempts to characterize Europe in terms of openness to the Other, it follows from relations of power more than from inherent cultural traits.[1] Imperialism and its legacy have allowed philosophers in Europe and North America to ignore the rest of the world in a way that the rest of the world has not been able to ignore them. This ignorance is a privilege and a curse, not unlike the privilege Americans have of not needing to learn another language.

If only because of shifts in global power, this exclusion of other cultures is unlikely to last much longer. In fact, philosophical engagement with cultures outside the "West" has made rapid progress in the past several decades, generating a wide range of approaches and methodologies. Such work is still experimental enough, though, that some brief reflections on methodology are required. Like any work in the history of philosophy, this book is structured by the tension between two goals. On the one side, it aims to produce something philosophically insightful or revealing for contemporary readers. On the other side, it seeks to present an accurate understanding and explication of various Chinese texts in their own terms and on their own grounds. As J. D. Schneewind puts it, the challenge is to avoid the dangers of "anachronism" and "antiquarianism" (2005, 178). The tension can be negotiated in many ways, and valuable work is to be done at various points of the continuum, with philosophers tending toward anachronism and Sinologists toward antiquarianism. This book may annoy both sides, as I have tried to bring Chinese philosophy to bear on European philosophy without bringing it into its orbit or onto its terrain. It is not an attempt to do European philosophy while drawing resources from classical Chinese texts, nor does it look to China for answers to European questions. Such approaches are necessary and have already proven fruitful.[2] They have the obvious advantage of making Chinese philosophy relevant and intelligible to contemporary (Western) philosophers. Nonetheless, bringing Chinese philosophy onto the terrain of European categories puts that terrain itself fundamentally out of question. The greatest value of another perspective, though, is often precisely in the different ways it plots out this basic terrain. Furthermore, one is always at a disadvantage on foreign terrain. If we approach Chinese texts with distinctions and issues foreign to them, they are unlikely to deal with them as well as European philosophers have done. Similarly, if we look for answers to questions that were not asked, the answers are not likely to be as sophisticated as those given by philosophers who did ask them. Thus, even when Chinese thinkers can be shown to provide interesting and important insights, they often come off as poor philosophers.

My strategy here has two sides. The discussions of the Chinese texts are as much as possible structured according to their own terms, distinctions, and categories. Although I have provided English stand-ins for all Chinese terms, the reader must try to keep these at a distance, and allow them to take on something of the breadth and nuance of the original Chinese term. A broad study of Chinese thought meant to show both continuity and development can work in English only if the English itself is modified to fit the Chinese discourses. Standard terms from European philosophy are introduced only by way of contrast, and I make no attempts to apply terms such as "transcendence," "free will," or "virtue ethics," nor to place Chinese philosophers on one side or the other of various familiar dichotomies, determining in which of our folders their positions should be filed. This orientation comes from a belief that the world can be carved up, labeled, categorized, and problematized in many different yet viable ways. My hope is that the plausibility and coherence of Chinese philosophy will come out better in its own terms than in ours, and that explicating Chinese philosophy according to its own ways of carving up the world will help illuminate the strangeness and peculiarity of its own categories and assumptions.[3] The danger in comparative philosophy is putting one's own words into the mouth of the other, ending up with a monologue or, more often, a dialogue between elements of one's own tradition, an approach that goes at least back to Nicholas Malebranche's 1707 *Dialogue between a Christian Philosopher and a Chinese Philosopher on the Existence and Nature of God*, in which the Chinese philosopher speaks for Spinoza and the Christian for Malebranche. Of course, it is true that wherever you go, there you are: we never escape ourselves or our own perspectives. We will never see the world as Mèngzǐ or Zhuāngzǐ did. Yet, at the same time, we are always in a process of becoming. Our perspectives change, largely through what we immerse ourselves in.[4] As Mòzǐ puts it, if the dye which one enters changes, one's color also changes (*Lǚshì chūnqiū* 2/4: 96–97). If my work here has been successful, it has produced a kind of hybrid between European philosophy and Chinese philosophy, generating something that would not have been possible without both.

Avoiding bringing Chinese philosophy into the orbit of Europe must operate even on the level of questions and problems. The work of philosophy encompasses both the raising and answering of questions, the posing and solving of problems.[5] The answers always depend on the questions we ask, and to formulate a question is already to have moved from tensions in experience to particular conceptualizations of them. There may be some perennial questions, but the questions elaborated on by philosophers usually are not. There is a real sense in which there was no mind-body problem before Descartes, just as there were no problems around the causality of a free will before Augustine. This is not to say that our questions are arbitrary or merely conventional. Philosophical problems reflect genuine tensions in experience, but they also embody contingent cultural assumptions, political pressures, technological developments, and so on. My goal is to follow questions and problems raised out of classical Chinese philosophy itself, although the choice of questions also reflects the dialogical goal of the project.

The severity of the tension mentioned earlier should now be clear: Without using European concepts or even questions, how will there be any dialogue? This question can be addressed only through the work itself. Assumptions of radical otherness and incommensurability can be maintained only by those who have not seriously attempted to understand another culture. These classical Chinese texts often speak to our concerns, and such intersections would not be possible if our philosophical questions and concepts did not have some basis in common (although not necessarily universal) human experiences. My goal is to examine how common *tensions* in experience become different *problems* in China and Europe, leading to different kinds of answers.⁶ Comparative philosophy can work only if we turn back toward these basic tensions in experience—toward, to take a phrase from Susan Neiman, "the real roots of philosophical questioning" (2002, 13). Yet it is doubtful that we have access to pure experience itself. Intercultural dialogue would be easier if it were really a trialogue among one culture, another culture, and objective reality. Unfortunately, that is not the situation in which we find ourselves. We must rely on a method of triangulation, taking questions and concepts from European and Chinese philosophy and using those two points to project a third point in experience itself. My hope is to use differing perspectives to gesture toward certain tensions in human experience and thereby to better understand the various ways in which those tensions can be taken up and theorized. Ultimately, the negotiation between similarity and difference can be addressed only in practice. On that level, I follow Lee H. Yearley's suggestion "to chart similarities within differences and differences within similarities" (1990, 3). That is, when texts seem to say the same thing, I attend to the ways the contexts make them different, and when they raise different issues, I look toward analogies that might link them.

This study is already long and it would naturally be longer. The limits of time and pages force the drawing of certain limits in scope. The historical limits are not so problematic. While giving some earlier background, this study begins in chapter two with the conflict between the Ru (Confucians) and Mohists on the role of fate (*mìng* 命) starting around the fifth century BCE.⁷ Whatever may have been happening earlier, the Mohists provide the first systematic discussions that we have concerning heaven and fate, so they make a natural starting point. This study concludes with the *Xúnzǐ*, which comes near the end of the Warring States Period (475–222 BCE). Discussions of the problem of evil of course continue into the Hàn dynasty. The most famous statement of the problem comes in a comment from Sīmǎ Qiān 司馬遷 at the end of the biographies of Bó Yí 伯夷 and Shū Qí 叔齊, and Sīmǎ Qiān is supposed to have said that one purpose of his history, the *Shǐ jì* (史記), was "to investigate the boundary between heaven and human" (*Hàn shū* 62.2735). The most systematic early investigation of the problem of evil comes from Wáng Chōng 王充. A central point of his *Lùnhéng* 論衡 is that worthiness and ability have little correlation with success and long life. Nonetheless, the shift from a condition of warring states to that of unified empire makes the end of the Warring States period a natural boundary for this study.

A more problematic limit is in approaching Warring States texts as *philosophy*, an approach that already brings Chinese thought onto a terrain formed in

Europe. The question of whether it is proper to label Warring States thought as philosophy is more a question about philosophy than about the Warring States. In practice, it is a question about institutions and the power of exclusion or inclusion. Such issues cannot be adequately addressed here. What is important to note is that although there remains disagreement on what counts as philosophy, certain boundaries are accepted in practice by almost all academic philosophers. First, while we hope that our students will become good people, it would be strange if not illegal to require ethical action as part of a philosophy major. While many contemporary philosophers would maintain that being a good philosopher contributes to being a good person, most would agree that these are distinct pursuits. Second, direct involvement of the body is excluded. It would be controversial in almost any philosophy department to have students meditate in class, as suggested by the *Zhuāngzǐ*'s "sitting and forgetting," or to have them dance, as Xúnzǐ might recommend. Third, explicit appeals to authority are excluded from philosophy and taken as fallacious. Even when considering thinkers as great as Aristotle or Kant, it would be unacceptable for me to tell my students to trust what they say.

These boundaries are definitive of what (academic) philosophy now is, regardless of what it may have once been. By this definition, the thinkers considered here are certainly not philosophers. Ignoring this difference fundamentally distorts what they were doing and brings them onto a foreign ground where they are at a considerable disadvantage.[8] The problem, however, is not that these thinkers would fit better in some other academic discipline. Many of their concerns and practices fall most naturally into our discipline of philosophy. The disjunction between them and us lies not so much in the boundaries of *philosophy* as in the boundaries of *academia*, which make it impossible for professors in any discipline to do what Zhuāngzǐ or Mèngzǐ themselves were trying to do. For better or worse, the boundaries of modern academia seem firmly set, not just in Europe but throughout the world, including contemporary China. Our options are either to ignore early China or to approach it through our own fields, all the while admitting the distortion this involves. Inevitably, this produces a hybrid thought distant from what was happening in the Warring States period. This result, however, is better than refusing to engage early Chinese thought at all.

This orientation toward philosophy means that I am primarily concerned with theoretically coherent, perceptive, and interesting responses to the fact that bad things happen to good people. In practice, this study follows what has taken shape as the "canon" of classical Chinese philosophy: the *Lúnyǔ*, *Mòzǐ*, *Dàodéjīng*, *Mèngzǐ*, *Zhuāngzǐ*, and *Xúnzǐ*. As is standard for the "history of philosophy," I have not attempted to reconstruct common beliefs and practices at that time. It would be odd to argue that a study of medieval philosophy would have to include an analysis of the beliefs and practices of non-intellectuals, and

I have tried to follow the same standard. Nonetheless, this approach risks two dangers. First, these texts cannot be taken as representative of the general views of people in the Warring States period (let alone something like the "Chinese spirit"). The question of the efficacy of good actions was bound up with beliefs about conscious ghosts and spirits, sacrificial rituals, and divination practices, beliefs that extended across all levels of society. In contrast, none of the texts considered here, aside from the *Mòzǐ*, give any significant role to spirits or ghosts, and several explicitly distance themselves from or oppose reliance on spirits. Similarly, none of the texts considered here give any explicit role to divination, and the *Mòzǐ*, *Zhuāngzǐ*, and *Xúnzǐ* all have passages limiting it.[9] That is not to say that the authors and compilers of these texts disbelieved in the existence of spirits—most of them probably did not—or that they denied the power of divination. That points to the second danger. A philosophical approach may obscure the ways in which the marginalization and reinterpretation of beliefs in spirits and divination actually reflect a deep level of concern with such beliefs. In other words, this marginalization should not be taken as merely reflecting common assumptions but rather as deliberate attempts to grapple with them.[10] This concern is most apparent in the appropriation of language associated with divination and the various extensions of the term "spirits" (*shén* 神), as we will see. Finally, any philosophical approach to early China has to remain open to the fact that among those European dichotomies that must be resisted is the very dichotomy between philosophy and religion. The greatest value of a comparative study of early Chinese "philosophy" may be in the way it forces us to rethink the limits of how philosophy has been defined in European thought.

In terms of texts, it is an exciting time to research Warring States thought but a dangerous time to write a book on it. The archeological discovery of more and more texts, particularly ones buried at the end of the fourth century BCE, has thrown our knowledge of that time into flux. I have tried as much as possible to take account of recently excavated texts. Two of those texts—*Qióng dá yǐ shí* 窮達以時 (Failure and success are by timing) from a tomb at Guōdiàn 郭店, and *Guǐshén zhī míng* 鬼神之明 (Discernment of ghosts and spirits) published in the Shanghai Museum collection—were decisive for the formation of this project. Both contain explicit discussions of the fact that bad things happen to good people. My readings of several traditional texts have also been shaped by recent discoveries, particularly my readings of the *Dàodéjīng* and the *Mèngzǐ*. Other excavated texts appear peripherally throughout this book. Of course, other texts were either not yet available or not yet intelligible enough to incorporate, and more will surely be found. My hope is that my positions are grounded well enough that new texts will not overturn them, even if new discoveries inevitably make them less complete.

These newly discovered texts raise deeper questions about how we relate texts and positions, both in terms of so-called schools of thought and in terms of dates and authorship. The texts further problematize the division of Warring States thinkers into distinct schools, on the one hand by revealing a greater diversity of positions within schools, while on the other hand showing a greater amount of hybridity between positions we might have taken as distinct.[11] In terms of the dating of texts, much has been learned by comparing texts for which we now have multiple copies.[12] In comparing versions of these texts, three elements can be seen to change in transmission.[13] First, the order and grouping of passages, even in apparently coherent texts like the *Xìng zì mìng chū* 性自命出 frequently change. Second, there seems to have been a concern with transmitting the ideas of a passage but not so much with preserving the exact words, which frequently change. Third, texts were expanded over time, with other materials working their way in. The most obvious example is the integration of a commentary into the *Wǔ xíng* 五行 (Five actions) text, but each version of the *Xìng zì mìng chū* contains passages not found in the other, suggesting they are two different expansions from one original. These points obviously problematize our access to the "original" texts, but the news is not all bad. The excavated texts at least let us know with some certainty what ideas were active in the late fourth century. We also know that written records of philosophical discussions circulated by the mid- to late fourth century BCE, so that anyone from that time on would be aware that their ideas might spread in written form. We can assume, then, that someone like Mèngzǐ would be concerned with having his ideas put into writing, and that the ideas of earlier philosophers like Kǒngzǐ and Mòzǐ would have been written down by this time. Finally, in spite of the changes that occur, the meaning of passages is generally (but not always) maintained in transmission.

These findings force us to fundamentally rethink our approach to Warring States thought. In spite of the trend toward skepticism of traditional dates, most critics remain centered on authors with individual positions that can be firmly dated. Debates focus on which passages are authentic and which are interpolations. Such an approach is so natural that it hardly appears as an assumption, but it does not fit the evidence we have, which is that texts and passages were modified gradually over time, having no single date or author. If a clever saying was uttered by Kǒngzǐ, passed orally through a few disciples, recorded on bamboo strips by one or two of them, copied with minor modifications over several generations, and finally collected and "corrected" by an editor in the Hàn dynasty, then what is its proper date? Is it "authentic"? The question makes little sense. There is no evidence to support a view that any sentences attributed to Kǒngzǐ or Mòzǐ or Mèngzǐ were said in just that way by those people. On the contrary, there is much evidence that the specific wording of passages was fluid. At the same time, there is good reason to think that passages recorded in the discourses of a later time period may reflect, incorporate, and convey ideas from earlier times.

If we take this archeological evidence seriously, we must develop some way of writing the history of philosophy that is compatible with evolving, aggregate texts. It will take more time to figure out how to do that properly, but I hope here to have made some steps in that direction. Overall, my goal has been to make this account depend as little as possible on specific dates and authors. I have tried to do that by focusing on the dialogue and interplay between positions and problems, without insisting on firm dates. For example, chapter 2 analyzes early debates around fatalism over a span of a century or two. Although the two main positions can be distinguished as those of the Mohists and those of the early Ru, I make no claim about what either Mòzǐ or Kǒngzǐ themselves thought, nor that either group held one single position. Other chapters are primarily organized according to the texts in which certain positions appear most centrally and explicitly, but in each chapter, I have drawn in other materials (whether later or earlier) if they seem to be variations on the same basic position. I have not approached any text with the assumption that it represents a single viewpoint. Rather, I make the more minimal claim that a certain position is present in the text. For example, in reading the *Zhuāngzǐ*, I have not attempted to argue for a position that fits everything in the Inner Chapters, but have just given evidence for one position that is central to those chapters. Other texts seem to articulate one core position, but the way texts were transmitted means that we cannot place too much weight on a single term or even a single passage in any text. This approach has the most significance for reading the *Xúnzǐ*, in which several isolated passages would require significant modifications to the system developed coherently across other chapters. This approach will become clearer as it is carried out, and when more problematic texts are taken up, I have included a brief discussion of my approach.

The chapters herein are generally each focused on a particular text and position. Chapter 2 examines debates about heaven and fatalism among the early Ru and the Mohists. Chapter 3 discusses the shift away from morality toward a focus on efficacious human action in the *Dàodéjīng*. Chapter 4 considers the attempt to break from emulating the patterns of nature through a shift toward natural human emotions, centering on the *Mèngzǐ*. Chapter 5 discusses the overcoming of categories of good and bad in the *Zhuāngzǐ*. The final chapter examines Xúnzǐ's account of how accumulated human effort can shape the world into a sustainable and ethical order. Chapter 1 consists of four sections meant to introduce the necessary context and background for readers coming from a variety of perspectives and interests. The first section discusses the ways in which the concept of "the problem of evil" can and cannot be applied in an early Chinese context, pointing toward the tension between two influential mottoes: the unity of heaven and human and the division of heaven and human. This is then applied to the problematic description of early Chinese thought as "humanistic." The second section turns to the concrete historical events that came to symbolize the fact that bad things happen to good people, describing the suffering and disorder of the time and introducing the figures that became exemplars for the problem of evil. The third section sets these exemplars against the earlier belief that the Mandate of Heaven supports the people. The fourth and final section outlines various formulations of the problem of evil in European philosophy, setting them in a comparative context.

1 Formations of the Problem of Evil

Problems of Evil

This project originated out of reflections on Susan Neiman's *Evil in Modern Thought: An Alternative History of Philosophy.* Neiman's book brilliantly integrates careful historical studies with a broad narrative of the development of modern European thought. What made it so interesting to me was its ability to present philosophical discussions specific to particular places and times in a way that appeared to illuminate *human* issues beyond that historical context. This broader relevance is what enables the history of philosophy to be philosophy. Of course, few would now openly claim that a study of *European* philosophy suffices as a method of addressing the *human* condition, a phrase that itself sounds outdated. Neiman evades the problem by invoking a vaguely bounded "we," suggesting significance for "us" while avoiding universalistic claims about human beings.[1] The "we" for whom only Europe is relevant, however, probably no longer exists.

The history of philosophy gains its philosophical value in part from its comparative dimension, at least implicitly laying out a contrast between past ways of thinking and current forms of thought. This contrast helps illuminate the limits of contemporary thinking and to open up other possibilities. In this context, one can see that a contrastive approach restricted to alternatives within one lineage or tradition—even one as diverse and polyvocal as that of the West—is restricted both in its ability to reveal limits and to open up new possibilities. With no point of reference outside Europe, we cannot even recognize what might be peculiarly European. Imagine someone whose goal was to understand the city of Chicago as well as possible, and so spent his or her entire life residing only in Chicago and learning only about Chicago. Such a person would develop a kind of expertise, but would not even make a great tour guide, being unable to know what features were most distinctive. On a theoretical level, such a person would have a limited understanding of cities and of Chicago, precisely because he or she would have no way to distinguish the two.

My original intention was to write a paper to raise these points, to argue that there is no problem of evil in Chinese philosophy, and thus to show that the relevance of the problem of evil is largely limited to peculiarities of Europe. Indeed, if we take evil to be ontologically distinct from bad, and we take the problem to be reconciling that evil with an omnipotent and benevolent God that creates everything ex nihilo, then this problem of evil is absent in Chinese philosophy. But the problem of evil proved harder to evade than I initially assumed. One finds a persistent concern among classical Chinese philosophers with the fact that bad things happen to good people and with what this means for our relationship with the world, with nature, and with the divine. The link between shifting ideas of the divine in Warring States China and the European problem of evil has been noted by a wide variety of interpreters. Perhaps the first one to make an explicit connection is Max Weber, who in 1915 briefly mentioned that Confucians faced the "eternal problem of theodicy" (1964, 206). Homer Dubs ends his book on the philosophy of Xúnzǐ with a chapter called "Idealism and the Problem of Evil" (1927, 275-94). Lee Yearley, Robert Eno, Chen Ning, and Mark Csikszentmihalyi all claim an early Chinese concern with "theodicy," a term invented by Leibniz for the attempt to justify God's goodness in the face of the world's evil.[2] Robert Eno, for example, attributes the emergence of philosophy from religion in China to an attempt to address the problem of "theodicy," arguing that the decisive question was this: "[H]ow can a deity prescriptively good allow a world descriptively evil?" (1990a, 27). A. C. Graham does not invoke theodicy or the problem of evil explicitly, but takes the fourth century as a transition from a social crisis to a metaphysical crisis characterized by a "profound metaphysical doubt, as to whether Heaven is after all on the side of human morality" (1989, 107). This "metaphysical doubt" can be traced back to the collapse of the Western Zhōu in the eighth century BCE, which initiated five centuries of conflict and war, known as the Spring and Autumn (770-481 BCE) and the Warring States (475-222 BCE) periods. Yuri Pines thus begins his account of the thought of the Spring and Autumn Period with the chapter "Heaven and Man Part Ways" (2002, 55-88).

As is often the case in comparative studies, we must refuse a simple dichotomy between difference and identity. It is as true to say that the problem of evil is present in Chinese thought as it is to say there is no problem of evil there.[3] Rather than argue about the cross-cultural applicability of this problem, I will trace out the various problems that emerge in China around the observation that bad things happen to good people. The point may seem trite. We have all heard that life is not fair. Yet this truism is inherently problematic. If most people are motivated by hopes for reward and fear of punishment, then a series of ethical problems follows: Why should I be good if it is not rewarded? Are there more efficacious ways of ensuring success? There are also questions about the purpose of life: Should we struggle against the world or retreat from it and cultivate acceptance? What kind of success does a good life require? Another series of problems centers on the psychological challenges of dealing with uncertainty and failure: How do we remain committed to virtue in the face of failure? Can we cultivate ourselves so as to attain some level of peace of mind or even joy? All of these are practical questions in ethics, politics, psychology, and so on, but they also are philosophical questions. They are the kinds of questions that classical Chinese philosophers took as most central to the problem of evil.

The remarkable thing about the fact that bad things happen to good people is that so many traditions have been built on denying it. Some try to explain away appearances of unfairness, as some Christian ministers explained Hurricane Katrina as a just response to the decadence of New Orleans. More often, the suffering of this life is excused by pointing beyond it, to eternal life in heaven and hell or to karma in past or future lives. Why would so many traditions insist on denying the obvious? There are always limits to the actions society and government can monitor and control, so there is always the temptation to act badly with the hope of escaping punishment. But, in the words of the *Mòzǐ*, heaven sees what you do even in the "forests and valleys, in dark and distant places where no one lives" (26: 192–93; cf. Johnston 2010, 26.1). The denial of the problem of evil, however, goes beyond what we might call the "Santa Claus effect" (making a list, checking it twice . . .). At stake is not just the existence and nature of God. Nor is it simply a matter of satisfying a desire for justice. Neiman explains the foundations of the problem thus:

> Every time we make the judgment *this ought not to have happened,* we are stepping onto a path that leads straight to the problem of evil. Note that it is as little a moral problem, strictly speaking, as it is a theological one. One can call it the point at which ethics and metaphysics, epistemology and aesthetics meet, collide, and throw up their hands. At issue are questions about what the structure of the world must be like for us to think and act within it. (2002, 5)

What is ultimately at stake in the problem of evil is the status of human beings. *Theo*-dicy is always *anthropo*-dicy. If the basis of the universe resembles us—sharing our concepts and values—then we are radically different from other natural things. It makes us special and gives our concepts and values an objective foundation. The problem of evil fractures this alignment. Seeing that bad things happen to good people reveals that the universe is not ordered according to our values. It suggests the world (or its creator or divine force) is neither human nor humane, leaving a sense that our values and concepts are merely *ours*. As Heidegger says, the tragic condition in which we find ourselves illuminates the way in which we are "uncanny" (*unheimlich*) in the sense of being not at home (*unheimisch*) in the world (1996, 71).

This rupture seems to leave two unappealing choices—we side with the human or we side with the world/the divine. There is an obvious absurdity in railing against the universe or cursing God. The *Zhuāngzǐ* tells us that "things do not conquer heaven" (6: 260; cf. Mair 1994, 58), and gives this story: "Don't you know about the praying mantis? It brandished its arms to block the chariot wheel, not knowing that it could not be victorious in bearing it, affirming the fineness of its own ability" (4: 167; cf. Mair 1994, 36). It is not just that resisting the world is futile and dangerous. If we are products of the universe or creatures of God, what possible ground could we stand on to turn back and decry it? The ability to label the world as bad requires the objective status of good, but if the basis of the world is bad or amoral, where could the good get this status? Labeling the world as bad or evil is probably ultimately incoherent. The difficulty is compounded by the fact that different people consider different things good, so that the unity of "the human" itself is in question. All of this suggests that we give up our labels and, as the *Zhuāngzǐ* recommends, just go along with things. Yet such resolve overturns all conceptions of morality. There is something reprehensible about accepting or affirming the kind of world that appears before us, as we see if we take seriously Alexander Pope's famous statement in the "Essay on Man": "Whatever IS, is RIGHT." Once we say that children being washed away in a tsunami or chopped apart by machetes is *right,* can we claim to have morality at all?[4]

The connection between the problem of evil and the status of the human lies at the heart of this book. My claim is that in China as in Europe, the recognition that bad things happen to good people disrupted the mutual support between a divine force that grounded and enforced human values and the confidence human beings placed in those values. While it would be going too far to take this realization as the birth of philosophy, it marks a fundamental shift in philosophical reflection, precisely because it throws philosophy itself into question, shaking the groundwork that allows us to take our understanding of the world for granted. This book is a study of that shaking and the responses to it. This focus explains the juxtaposition of ancient China and early modern Europe. A comparative project must take up analogous tensions and movements of thought. Given the contingencies of human history, there is little reason to expect these analogies to arise in the same time periods across different cultures. The intellectual and political dominance of Christianity in European thought delayed a confrontation with the problem of evil until a remarkably late period. In fact, if we look at Western philosophy, we see discussions of the problem of evil arising twice, once in the classical Mediterranean world and then again following the breakdown of the Church's political authority in early modern Europe. While a comparison between classical China and classical Greece might be more natural and in some ways easier, it would also be less relevant in bringing out the peculiarities of modern European thought. Thus it would be less relevant for *us.*

Although this project began from questions in European philosophy, it came to center on two issues arising from the Chinese context itself, both prominent as ways of situating Chinese thought in relation to Europe. In that context, the fundamental problem can be expressed through the tensions between "the unity of heaven and human" (*tiānrén héyī* 天人合一), and, "the division between heaven and human" (*tiānrén zhīfēn* 天人之分).⁵ More specifically, this book traces the conflict and division between heaven and human in order to problematize their unification. This emphasis on conflict, suffering, and the failures of goodness contradicts a lingering stereotype about Chinese thought, that it is all about accommodation and harmony. Such a view goes at least back to Hegel, and it is applied to China in detail by Max Weber. Weber writes, "Completely absent in Confucian ethics was any tension between nature and deity, between ethical demand and human short-coming, consciousness of sin and need for salvation, conduct on earth and compensation in the beyond, religious duty and socio-political reality" (1964, 235–36). Although Hegel and Weber took this lack of tension as a negative trait blocking progress, Sinophiles have frequently taken up the same view as positive. This tradition of reading Chinese thought has been well summarized and critiqued by Michael Puett and need not be repeated here (2001, 3–21; 2002, 1–26).

The image of Chinese thought as assuming harmony and unity is not so much false as it is unilluminating. The phrase "the unity of heaven and human" arises most often as a way of situating Chinese philosophy in relation to Europe. In that context, it is true that classical Chinese philosophy had no concept of radical discontinuity or transcendence.⁶ While there were gods and spirits that transcended the limits of the human, there was nothing super-natural in the strong sense of being totally *independent* of the natural world. From this lack of radical transcendence, it follows that the line between human beings and nature or human beings and heaven will be difficult to draw in any definitive way. Thus, if we take our orientation from European philosophy, we can indeed say that all of classical Chinese metaphysics falls on the side of immanence and continuity. The problem is that if all of Chinese thought falls on one side of a dichotomy, that dichotomy is obviously useless for understanding the singularity and complexity of Chinese philosophy itself. It becomes, to take a phrase from Hegel, a night in which all cows are black. Such an orientation further requires one to be deeply ungenerous to either Europe or China. That is, one must either assume that the various dualisms that emerged in European philosophy are baseless, or that they express genuine tensions in human experience that the Chinese failed to notice. Neither conclusion is likely. To respond by reimposing Western dichotomies—to argue, for example, that there is transcendence or dualism in early Chinese thought—would be exactly wrong. This is precisely the point at which we need to shift to Chinese terms and distinctions, to see how common tensions were theorized in different ways.

As a general contrast, we might point out opposite orientations toward such tensions. If one approaches the tensions through ontological dualisms and radical discontinuities, the challenge becomes how to reconcile what has been divided, particularly in accounting for the apparent integrity of our experience. Thus, in European philosophy, topics on the more integrated side of human experience—such as embodiment, emotion, and even family—tend to be ignored, and the most difficult philosophical problems lie in reconciling kinds of reality: free will and natural causality, mind and body, reason and emotion. Such *problems of reconciliation* rarely arise in classical Chinese philosophy, and as we might expect, Chinese philosophers emphasize those very aspects of our naturalness that tend to be neglected in Europe. In a Chinese context without radical dualisms, the challenge is rather in *problems of distinction*. The difficulties lie in explaining how we differ from other things, the fact that we use words, act deliberately, go against the sustainable natural order, generate massive wars, and so on. Such questions are much more central in classical Chinese philosophy than they were in medieval or early modern Europe, where the separation of human beings from nature was taken for granted.

The emphasis on the unity of heaven and human draws support from the philosopher's bias toward theoretical results rather than the messier problems that drive them. Early Chinese philosophers did not take harmony for granted. They would have to have been fools or propagandists to not recognize the massive level of conflict among human beings and between human beings and the world. Nonetheless, all of the thinkers considered here attempted to find ways of reconciling human beings with heaven. If we look only at the resulting philosophical systems, we will naturally emphasize claims for the alignment of heaven and human. Another way to put it is that, while the unity of heaven and human may be more central to philosophical systems, the division between heaven and human is more fundamental in human life. An orientation toward that division better fits the general emphasis of Chinese philosophy on practice—on philosophy as a way of life. The problem of evil was not fundamentally a problem of philosophical theology or metaphysics but rather a practical problem of negotiating various existential needs—for example, avoiding the anxiety and absurdity that comes with defying the way the world actually is, while also striving for a human good in a world that does not support it.

The second problem of central importance to this book is the idea of "Chinese humanism." The description of the Chinese tradition (and more specifically the Ru) as a kind of "humanism" (*rénwén zhǔyì* 人文主義) has been dominant among Chinese intellectuals of the twentieth century and is central to many accounts of the history of Chinese philosophy. For example, Wing-Tsit Chan labeled the first section of his highly influential *A Sourcebook in Chinese Philosophy* "The Rise of Chinese Humanism" (1963a). Xú Fùguān 徐復觀 also began his history of Chinese conceptions of human nature by characterizing the Zhōu dynasty as a progressive transition toward humanism and a "humanistic spirit" (*rénwén jīngshén* 人文精神) (1969, 15). This emphasis on humanism continues to the present—seen, for example, in the works of Chén Lái 陳來, whose collection of essays on twentieth-century Chinese thought is titled *Tradition and Modernity: A Humanist View* (2009a), and more recently in Péng Guóxiáng's study, *Confucianism: Between Religion and Humanism* (2007). Like the phrase *tiānrén héyī* (the unity of heaven and human), the term *rénwén* (humanism) has a long history but rose to prominence in the attempt to situate Chinese thought in relation to Europe, where it is meant to mark a general contrast between Chinese philosophy and the ontotheological orientation of European thought. One might trace this contrast all the way back to Leibniz, who said that just as Europe was sending missionaries of "revealed theology" to China, the Chinese should send their own missionaries to Europe, to teach "the greatest use of practical philosophy and a more perfect manner of living."[7]

More precisely, the label "humanism" rose to prominence as a way of thinking through the specificity of China's experience of what Karl Jaspers called the "Axial Age." Chén Lái articulates this position well, beginning with the claim that the Axial Age in China showed more continuity with the past than it did elsewhere. He explains,

> The whole Axial Age in China, if we start to count from 800 BCE, was not because the recognition of individual limits turned toward a limitless transcendent existence. The progress of rationality was not through the initiation of an ethical reaction to the many spirits of mythology, let alone a move toward monotheist faith. In China, this process was more like the recognition of the limits of gods and divinity, so that it tended more toward this world and the human sphere. Thus calling this process a "transcendental" breakthrough is not as good as calling it a "humanistic" turn. (2009a, 5)

Chén Lái is working with modern European terms, but the characterization of the Zhōu transition as moving toward something like humanism goes back to the early Ru. The "Record on Standards" ("Biǎo jì" 表記) chapter of the *Lǐ jì* contrasts the Yīn and the Zhōu dynasties with regard to their relationship to spirits:

> The leaders of Yīn respected spirits and led the people to serve spirits, putting ghosts first and rituals after, penalties first and rewards after. They were respected but not cherished.... The leaders of Zhōu respected ritual and elevated action, they served ghosts and revered spirits but kept them at a distance. They were close to the people and there was loyalty among them. Their rewards and punishments were applied according to rank. They were cherished but not respected. (Sūn Xīdàn 1988, 1310–11)

The phrase "respect them but keep them at a distance" derives from words attributed to Kǒngzǐ (*Lúnyǔ* 6.22), and it is commonly cited as evidence for the orientation of the Ru away from the divine and toward the human.

Characterizing Chinese thought as humanistic mistakenly conflates the Ru tradition with all of Chinese thought. Thus, Táng Jūnyì begins his book on the Chinese humanistic spirit by analyzing the ways humanism was *contested* in Warring States philosophy, taking the Ru as "humanistic," but characterizing other positions as "non-humanistic," "transcending humanism," "secondary humanism," or "anti-humanism."[8] The status of the human was one of the most hotly debated issues. Even for the Ru, humanism was fragile and problematic. The early Zhōu confidence in the ability of human beings to determine their own future rested on the belief that heaven consistently responds to human virtue. Once we admit that heaven does not follow our ethics—as most Ru agreed—what basis do we have for the status of the human? The Mohist support for an anthropomorphic heaven against the fatalistic elements of the early Ru was precisely driven by a concern for maintaining the centrality of human beings. While the Ru consistently maintain positions we could adequately label "humanistic," its weak foundations press it into forms quite different from those it took in Europe, making it less confident, less individualistic, and less secular.

Bad Things Happening to Good People

In European thought, the fact that bad things happen to good people has coalesced around great events, most of all the Lisbon earthquake of 1755 and the Holocaust in the twentieth century. The two events raise different problems, the first around the "natural evil" that God allows, and the second on the "moral evil" we inflict on ourselves. The first undermines the optimistic belief that God is good and all-powerful; the second undermines the optimism of Enlightenment humanism and its faith in human progress. As Neiman puts it, "Lisbon revealed how remote the world is from the human; Auschwitz revealed the remoteness of humans from themselves" (2002, 240).[9] In early China, the problem of evil rose to prominence with the collapse of the Zhōu dynasty and the descent into five centuries of civil war and upheaval, but the symbols of the problem were prominent individuals rather than specific events.[10] This section will introduce the main characters who became symbols of the problem of evil and some of the debates their lives provoked. These stories will also serve as a vivid introduction to the dismal conditions to which Chinese philosophers were responding.

We can begin with the story of Wǔ Zǐxū 伍子胥 (526–484 BCE), who lived and died within the lifetime of Kǒngzǐ (Confucius).[11] Wǔ Zǐxū was from a long line of ministers and his father was a minister to King Píng 平 of Chǔ 楚 (r. 528–516 BCE) and the primary tutor to the royal heir, Jiàn 建. The story begins when a rival minister (Fèi Wújì 費無忌) was sent to the state of Qín to get a wife for Jiàn. When he saw how beautiful she was, he persuaded the king himself to take her. As one might expect, this action opened a rift between the king and his son. The minister eventually convinced the king that his son would rebel, and the king sent someone to assassinate him. Jiàn escaped into exile. When Wǔ Zǐxū's father denounced these actions, the king had him imprisoned. He then tried to lure Wǔ Zǐxū and his brother (Wǔ Shàng) back using their father as a hostage. The brothers knew that if they returned, the king would kill them all. Even so, Wǔ Shàng insisted that as a filial son, he had to return. He was executed together with his father. Wǔ Zǐxū chose instead to live and seek revenge, fleeing to the neighboring state of Sòng 宋 to join the royal heir in exile. The state of Sòng was itself in the midst of a rebellion, so the two fled further, to the state of Zhèng 鄭, where they were given shelter. The royal heir, Jiàn, though, joined with another nearby state (Jìn 晉) to plot a rebellion. Jiàn was executed and Wǔ Zǐxū fled again, this time taking Jiàn's son. Wǔ Zǐxū ended up sick and starving, dependent on the kindness of strangers for survival. Eventually, the two made their way to the state of Wú 吳, where Wǔ Zǐxū served as a minister until his death.

Wú was a growing power to the southeast of what were then the central states. Soon after Wǔ Zǐxū's arrival, a minor conflict on the border of Wú and Chǔ spun out of control, leading to a war between the two powerful states. When the king of Chǔ died, Wú took advantage of the period of mourning to launch a surprise attack, but Chǔ responded and trapped two of Wú's armies. With his troops delayed in Chǔ, the king of Wú was assassinated by his cousin, who took power as King Hé Lú 闔廬. Wǔ Zǐxū became one of his main ministers. There followed a series of battles, guided by Wǔ Zǐxū and Sūn Wǔ 孫武 (the famed military strategist), culminating in the fall of the Chǔ capitol. Wǔ Zǐxū entered the capitol where his ancestors had served as loyal ministers and his father and brother had been executed. Since King Píng had already died, Wǔ Zǐxū had the king's body dug up, and he whipped the rotting corpse with three hundred strokes. Wú's control of Chǔ was short-lived. As the state of Qín sent troops to the rescue, the younger brother of King Hé Lú rebelled and enthroned himself in Wú, forcing Hé Lú to return and secure his power.

The conflict now shifted to Wú's southern neighbor, Yuè 越, and its famous king Gōu Jiàn 句踐. King Hé Lú was fatally wounded in battle, and his son, Fū Chāi 夫差, became the new king. Two years later, Wú nearly destroyed Yuè, but Gōu Jiàn sent gifts to another minister, who helped convince King Fū Chāi to accept his surrender. Soon after, a third series of conflicts opened up, this time between Wú and the great state of Qí in the north, and eventually Gōu Jiàn was allowed to send troops to assist in the battle. Wǔ Zǐxū always saw Gōu Jiàn as a threat, but his vehement arguments were ignored. Finally King Fū Chāi lost trust in him, sending him a sword with which to kill himself. Wǔ Zǐxū's defiant last words are legendary: "Be sure to plant catalpa on my grave, so that they can be made into instruments [for coffins], and pluck out my eyes and hang them above the eastern gate of Wú, so that I can watch the Yuè invaders when they enter and destroy it."[12] Wǔ Zǐxū then killed himself. King Fū Chāi was so enraged by this message that he stuffed Wǔ Zǐxū's body into a leather wineskin and threw it into a river. According to the version in the *Lǚshì chūnqiū*, he did gouge out Wǔ Zǐxū's eyes and hung them above the city gate (23/3: 1563). In the end, things played out as Wǔ Xíxū had predicted. The king of Wú successfully attacked Qí but then decided to attack the state of Jìn. He was defeated. King Gōu Jiàn took advantage of the moment to launch a surprise attack on Wú, eliminating the state of Wú entirely (in 473 BCE).[13]

We can see why the problem of evil would become prominent. In the span of one person's life, we hear of three major series of wars: between Wú and Chǔ, between Wú and Yuè, and between Wú and Qí. Other states were drawn in as well—Qín, Lǔ, Jìn, and Zhèng. According to Hú Shì 胡适, in the three-hundred-year period from 800–500 BCE, not a single year passed without a war (2003, 24). These wars involved the worst treachery, as when the heir of Chǔ betrays the state that has given him shelter, or when Wú uses Chǔ's period of mourning to launch a surprise attack. The situation within states is just as bleak. Almost every state mentioned has a civil war during the course of the story; some have several. These rebellions follow the breakdown of two key relations, those of the family and those among ministers and sovereign. King Píng first steals his son's bride and later attempts to have him killed. In the state of Wú, Hé Lú takes the throne by killing his cousin, only to later have his younger brother rebel against him. The relations within Wǔ Zǐxū's family reflect this breakdown in a different way—in such times, the sons must choose between dying alongside their father or betraying their father but getting revenge. They split on the decision, showing its difficulty. We also see bad ministers, as the whole story arises through a minister's manipulation of King Píng's vices: his desire for beauty and tendency toward suspicion. In this context, we can appreciate Mèngzǐ's sad description, "The age was one of decline, and the way became faint. Unrestrained words and oppressive actions arose again. There were ministers who killed their sovereigns. There were sons who killed their fathers" (3B9). Mèngzǐ gives this as the reason Kǒngzǐ was compelled to write a history of the Spring and Autumn period, to illuminate the bad actions that had taken place.

The story follows the elite and powerful, but it is easy to imagine the suffering inflicted on all levels of society. Some of the most powerful descriptions come in passages of the *Mòzǐ*, as in this description of what the leaders of powerful states do:

> Thus they enter the borders, mow down their grains, chop down their trees, topple their city walls to fill in their moats and ponds, burn down their ancestral temples, and kill their sacrificial animals. Those of the people who resist are killed; those who do not resist are bound and brought back, the men used to care for livestock or serve in chains, the women used to pound grain and pour drinks. (28: 214–16; cf. Johnston 2010, 28.9)

The direct effects of the battles were not the worst of it. Mòzǐ points out that since the summer is too hot for moving troops and the winter is too cold, wars are conducted at the times most crucial for agriculture (18: 130; Johnston 2010, 18.1). He describes the results: the corpses of those who have starved or frozen lie strewn about in ditches, in numbers greater than can be counted (19: 145; Johnston 2010, 19.3). All of the philosophers considered in this book were concerned with opposing or reducing war, and the continual state of war was one of the factors that prompted a shift in views of nature and the divine. As Mèngzǐ concludes, "Heaven does not yet desire peace and order in the world" (2B13).

We do find virtuous characters in the story of Wǔ Zǐxū, but they meet tragic ends. Wǔ Zǐxū's father bravely performed his duties as a devoted minister; Wǔ Zǐxū's older brother acts heroically by returning to Chǔ when his father is threatened. They die together. The ruler of Zhèng shows some kindness in taking in Jiàn, the displaced heir of Chǔ, but Jiàn plots a rebellion against him. Then there is Wǔ Zǐxū himself. He is clearly a man of great talent, fierce will, and deep loyalty, but Yuri Pines takes him to be representative of a new kind of statesman in the Spring and Autumn Period, one without regard for morality or ritual (2002, 131). For example, when Yuè, in the midst of a famine, asked Wú to lend food, Wǔ Zǐxū argued against it and instead pressed for an invasion.[14] His refusal to return when his father was held hostage and his whipping of King Píng's decaying body both show a shocking willingness to violate custom. Whatever the truth about Wǔ Zǐxū's character, Sīmǎ Qiān notes that after his body was thrown into the river, the local people built a shrine in his honor, and by the Hàn dynasty there were various legends of supernatural occurrences around his death.[15] Wǔ Zǐxū also became a spokesperson for various theories. There are records of a book attributed to him, and a recently excavated text entitled *Hé Lú* portrays a dialogue between Wǔ Zǐxū and the king.[16] It consists of policy advice for a variety of general governmental concerns, particularly military affairs. This advice is set in the context of a claim for the efficacy of ability and virtue: "Heaven in generating the people is without any constant favorites [*qīn* 親]. Those who benefit each other have good fortune. Those who harm each other are wiped out. If I want to eliminate those who harm the people, how is it to be done?" (Shào 2007, strip 46). The king needs good policy because success and failure depend on it.

Ironically, by the late fourth century, Wǔ Zǐxū had become a symbol of the opposite point—that good fortune can elude even the most worthy and talented. One recently excavated text from that time, *Qióng dá yǐ shí* (Failure and success are by timing), observes simply: "Wǔ Zǐxū first accomplished much but then later he was executed. It was not because his wisdom declined" (Liú Zhāo 2003, strips 9–10). The comment is meant to demonstrate the claim that virtue and ability do *not* determine success and failure, which depend instead on timing (*shí* 時). This term, *shí*, originally referred to the seasons or acting according to the seasons, but then extended to the demands or opportunities of the particular moment, to acting according to those demands, and to the ability to act in that way. In this sense, Kǒngzǐ was called the "sage of timing" (*Mèngzǐ* 5B1). The concept of *shí* became one of the most important Ru terms for dealing with the arrival of good and bad events, emphasizing both our dependence on forces outside our control and the proper way of dealing with this dependence. The terms "failure" and "success" do not adequately capture the dynamic sense of the Chinese terms, *qióng* 窮 and *dá* 達. *Qióng* often means extreme poverty or destitution, but it also has a sense of reaching a limit. Thus, "failure" means to be pushed to extremes but also to be blocked or thwarted. Similarly, *dá* means to reach, pass through successfully, or to progress. As a contrast with *qióng*, *dá* is sometimes replaced by *tōng* 通, which means "pass along smoothly," "penetrate," "master," or "commune." The point of *Qióng dá yǐ shí*, then, is that whether we progress smoothly or are thwarted and pushed to the limit depends not on our actions and ability but on timing. Wǔ Zǐxū is given as an example.

Another recently discovered text, *Guǐshén zhī míng* (Discernment of ghosts and spirits), uses Wǔ Zǐxū in a similar way. It begins by listing virtuous people who succeeded and vicious people who suffered, but then changes course: "When it comes to Wǔ Zǐxū, one of the world's sagely people, he was tied in a leather bag and died. Róng Yígōng, one of the world's creators of disorder, lived many years and then died" (Mǎ 2005, strips 3–4). This leads into a formulation of the problem of evil, addressing why in these cases the ghosts did not punish or reward:

> Is it that their strength could reach it but they do not do it? I do not know this. Or is it that their strength cannot reach it? I do not know this. These two diverge. I thus [say ghosts and spirits have] what they discern [*míng* 明] and have what they do not discern. (Mǎ 2005, strips 4–5)

This statement is worth comparing to that attributed to Epicurus:

> God either wants to eliminate bad things and cannot, or can but does not want to, or neither wishes to nor can, or both wants to and can. If he wants to and cannot, then he is weak—and this does not apply to god. If he can but does not want to, then he is spiteful—which is equally foreign to a god's nature. If he neither wants to nor can, he is both weak and spiteful and so not a god. If he wants to and can, which is the only thing fitting for a god, where then do bad things come from? Or why does he not eliminate them?[17]

The similarity in the basic arguments of the two passages is striking.

The connection between Wǔ Zǐxū and the problem of evil continued into the Hàn dynasty. Wáng Chōng (first century CE) frequently raises him as an example, as in this passage:

> As for those like Qū Píng and Wǔ Zǐxū, they were fully loyal in assisting their superiors and exhaustively fulfilling the regulations of minister and sovereign. But the state of Chǔ discarded Qū's body and the state of Wú boiled Wǔ Zǐxū's

corpse. These two enacted the good and should have attained good fortune from a compliant fate [*suìmìng* 隨命], but instead they hit the misfortune of an adverse fate [*zāomìng* 遭命]. Why? (6: 52)[18]

Qū Píng 屈平, better known as Qū Yuán 屈原, was a famous poet and minister in the state of Chǔ in the fourth century BCE. He fell out of favor with the king and drowned himself, an event commemorated still by the Dragonboat Festival. Wǔ Zǐxū was also commonly paired with another loyal minister who met with a bad end, Bǐ Gān 比干. Bǐ Gān was an uncle and minister to the evil King Zhòu 紂, the last king of the Shàng dynasty. Being loyal, he was unwilling to rebel; being virtuous, he could not condone the king's behavior. After he repeatedly admonished the king, the king ordered his heart to be cut out. King Zhòu explained that he had heard that virtuous people have hearts that are different from those of regular people. He wanted to see for himself.[19]

Although Wǔ Zǐxū is the most interesting and complex example of a good person who suffers, the most common exemplars were the brothers Bó Yí and Shū Qí.[20] Legend has it that when their father died, he chose Shū Qí to become the next king. Shū Qí refused, since power should normally go to the eldest brother, Bó Yí. Bó Yí also refused, since it would go against his father's wishes. They went into exile instead. This event took place in the last days of the Shàng dynasty, around the time of Bǐ Gān. The two were unwilling to serve the evil King Zhòu, but they heard of the virtue of a lord in the west and went to support him. By the time they arrived, King Wén 文 (whose name means "cultured") had died and his son, King Wǔ 武 (whose name means "warlike" or "martial") was already in open rebellion. Bó Yí and Shū Qí admonished him for rebelling. When King Wǔ defeated the Shàng and founded the Zhōu dynasty, Bó Yí and Shū Qí refused any support from the new state. They fled into the mountains, where they died of starvation.

Like Wǔ Zǐxū, Bó Yí and Shū Qí face dilemmas we might call tragic. Within the family, they are torn between their father's command and the rule that the eldest brother should become ruler. Politically, they can neither support the virtuous rebel King Wǔ nor defend the evil King Zhòu. All choices seem incorrect, so much so that they ultimately choose death by starvation. Their virtue is praised in a number of Ru texts—Mèngzǐ even refers to Bó Yí as a sage (7B24). Their miserable fate was commonly raised to dispute the claim that virtue is rewarded, most famously by Sīmǎ Qiān, who quotes a line appearing in *Dàodéjīng* 79:

> Some say, "The way of heaven has no favorites; it is constantly with good people." Now Bó Yí and Shū Qí can be called good people, can't they? They accumulated such humaneness and acted so purely, yet they starved to death like this![21]

Sīmǎ Qiān mentions other prominent examples and continues,

> When it comes to the present age, there are those acting recklessly off the track, focused only on violating taboos, but they live out their lives in ease and joy, enjoying abundant prosperity lasting for generations without being cut off. Others choose their ground carefully and tread there, speaking only in a timely way, their actions not following deviant paths, indignant only at what is not fair or correct, but they meet misfortune and disaster. Such people are more than can be counted. So I am deeply perplexed by this. What we call the way of heaven—is right? is it wrong? (*Shǐ jì* 61.2125; cf. Nienhauser 1995, VII.4)

Sīmǎ Qiān's expressions of doubt echo the tone of *Guǐshén zhī míng*.[22] It may also express his own life experience—he had been punished with castration after defending a general who had surrendered to the enemy.

While Warring States texts generally agree on how these characters died, the meaning of their deaths could be disputed. They are most often used to argue that goodness is not rewarded, but a passage in the *Zhuāngzǐ* gives a different view:

> Thus those who delight in succeeding with things [*tōng wù* 通物] are not sagely people. Those who have familial cherishing are not humane. Those who calculate heaven's timing are not worthies. Those who disconnect benefit and harm are not gentlemen. Those who enact a name and lose themselves are not scholars [*shì* 士].[23] Those who destroy their selves and are not genuine do not get people to serve. Those like Hú Bùjiē, Wù Guāng, Bó Yí, Shū Qí, Jīzǐ, Xū Yú, Jì Tān, and Shēn Túdí had the service of serving other people and the pleasure of pleasing other people, but did not have the pleasure of pleasing themselves. (6: 232; cf. Mair 1994, 394)[24]

Here, Bó Yí and Shū Qí are held responsible for their own actions. As Táng dynasty commentator Chéng Xuányīng 成玄英 explains it, all of these people violated natural feelings and coerced themselves based on external things (Guō Qìngfān 1978, 234). Guō Xiàng says simply that they abandoned themselves to imitate others (Guō Qìngfān 1978, 233). A passage from the first chapter of the *Mòzǐ* takes a similar approach to the case of Bǐ Gān:

> Now if there are five spears, the sharpest is surely first to be blunted. If there are five knives, the keenest is surely first to be ground down. Thus sweet wells run dry first, tall trees are felled first, numinous tortoises are burnt first, spirit-like snakes are scorched first. Thus Bǐ Gān's being killed was because of his directness, Mèng Bēn's death was because of his bravery, Xī Shī's drowning was because of her beauty, Wú Qǐ's being torn apart was because of his work. Of such people, few do not die from what they are strong in. Thus it is said: what is too flourishing is hard to protect. (1: 4–5; Johnston 2010, 1.4)[25]

In these interpretations, characters such as Bǐ Gān are converted from good people who inexplicably suffer to foolish people who bring harm upon themselves. The belief that our actions determine success and failure is maintained by shifting the meaning of proper action, often by rejecting ideals based on conventional morality.

Examples of evil people who escaped punishment were less frequent, probably because times were such that almost everyone suffered. The only consistent example is Robber Zhí.[26] Sīmǎ Qiān mentions him in his comments on Bó Yí and Shū Qí: "Robber Zhí daily killed the innocent, snacked on human flesh, was oppressive, ruthless, willful, and fierce, but he gathered followers in the thousands to rampage throughout the world, ultimately living out a long life. This is according to what virtue [*dé* 德]?" (*Shǐ jì* 61.2125; Nienhauser 1995, VII.4). Robber Zhí was not only a symbol in debates about the efficacy of virtue—in the *Zhuāngzǐ*, he gives his own response. The passage records a long discussion in which Kǒngzǐ attempts to persuade Robber Zhí that he would benefit more by becoming virtuous. Robber Zhí responds with a list of virtuous people who had miserable lives, including Bó Yí, Shū Qí, Bǐ Gān, and Wǔ Zǐxū (29: 998–99; Mair 1994, 304). He then draws a radical conclusion:

> Now let me tell you about natural human feelings [*qíng* 情]. The eyes desire to see good looks, the ears desire to hear sounds, the mouth desires to explore flavors, and the will and vital energies [*qì* 氣] desire to flourish. At the most people live a hundred years, in the middle they live eighty, and at the lowest they live sixty. If we set aside times of illness, mourning, anxiety, and trouble, in a month there are no more than four or five days in which we open our mouths and laugh. Heaven and earth have no limit [*qióng*] but people's death has its time [*shí*]. To grasp a tool that has limited time and put it into a space that has no limit—this is no different from a good horse galloping past a crack in the wall. If one cannot enjoy their will and nourish the fate of a long life, then they have not succeeded [*tōng* 通] in the way. (29: 1000; cf. Mair 1994, 304)

Robber Zhí makes this speech while snacking on human livers.

We see here yet another response to the problem of evil. The future is uncertain and the end is always near. Enjoy yourself while you can. There are traces of this position in another dialogue in the same chapter of the *Zhuāngzǐ*, and such a view is developed in the "Yáng Zhū" (楊朱) chapter of the *Lièzǐ*. Similar views go back to songs such as "On the Mountain is the Thorn-Elm" ("Shān yǒu shū" 山有樞), in the *Shī jīng* (Book of Odes), which says,

> On the mountains are the varnish trees, in the lowlands are the chestnuts.
> You have liquor and foods—why not daily strike your zither,
> To take pleasure in your joy, to prolong the day.
> When you have withered and died, other people will enter your home. (115)[27]

The meaning of Robber Zhí, however, also could be contested. Another chapter of the *Zhuāngzǐ* pairs Robber Zhí with Bó Yí:

> Bó Yí died for a name under Shǒu Yáng mountain; Robber Zhí died for benefit on top of Dōng Líng. Regarding these two—what they died for was not the

same, but in damaging life and harming their nature, they were equal. Why must one affirm Bó Yí and oppose Robber Zhí? (8: 323; cf. Mair 1994, 78)

This passage contradicts the claim that Robber Zhí lived a long and happy life. In this passage, he brings suffering on himself in just the same way as Bó Yí. By positing both good and evil as harmful, the passage points toward an amoral ideal of efficacious behavior, a view that will be examined in chapter 3 in the context of the *Dàodéjīng*.

As the Ru became famous moralizers, they also became exemplars for the limited efficacy of virtue. The most prominent example was Kǒngzǐ's favorite disciple, Yán Huí 顏回, who lived in poverty and died young. Kǒngzǐ places responsibility for Huí's death on the divine, lamenting that heaven has caused him this loss (*Lúnyǔ* 11.9), and saying that Huí unluckily (*búxìng* 不幸) was given a short fate (*mìng* 命) (*Lúnyǔ* 11.7). Kǒngzǐ's disciple Zǐlù 子路 provided a different example. He seems to have been daring by nature and he held several high-level political positions. Eventually, he was caught up with a rebellion in the state of Wèi 衛 and died attempting to protect his sovereign.[28] Robber Zhí says that Zǐlù's corpse was pickled and suspended above the eastern gate (*Zhuāngzǐ* 29: 997; Mair 1994, 302–303).

Kǒngzǐ himself also became an exemplar. Kǒngzǐ was twice forced to flee his home state of Lǔ. In Wèi, he was forced to cover over his own tracks as he fled, in order to avoid pursuit. In that story, he was surrounded and besieged for several days in the town of Kuāng 匡 after being mistaken for a rebel leader. He was put into desperate conditions in the state of Qí, was nearly killed in the state of Sòng when someone cut down a tree under which he and his disciples were practicing rituals, and he was surrounded and starved between the states of Chén and Cài. Robber Zhí gives this list and concludes, "There is nowhere in the world that will tolerate your presence!" (*Zhuāngzǐ* 29: 997; cf. Mair 1994, 303).[29]

The story of Kǒngzǐ and his disciples in trouble between the small states of Chén and Cài was particularly popular, appearing in many texts with a variety of meanings.[30] After fleeing the state of Sòng, Kǒngzǐ and his disciples got caught up in the battles between the states of Wú and Chǔ. He and his disciples went so long without food that they nearly died, and there is some evidence that Kǒngzǐ afterward lost followers.[31] The story was often raised to illustrate the failure of virtue to bring success, sometimes merging with versions of *Qióng dá yǐ shí*.[32] One of the more touching versions begins with Zǐlù lamenting their suffering. Kǒngzǐ responds,

> Kǒngzǐ said, "What words are these! Succeeding [*tōng* 通] in the way is what gentlemen call success. Failing [*qióng* 窮] in the way is what they call failing. Now, I, Qiū, embrace the way of humaneness and rightness to meet the troubles of a disordered age. How can that be called failure! Thus examine the internal and do not fail in the way, and in approaching difficulties, do not lose this virtue [*dé* 德]. When great cold is at the utmost and frost and snow

fall, this is how we know the vigor of the pine and cypress. Being confined between Chén and Cài is for me lucky [xìng 幸]!" Kǒngzǐ calmly returned to his zither, strumming and singing. Zǐlù joyously grabbed a branch and danced. Zǐgòng said, "I did not know the height of heaven or the depth of the earth!" (Zhuāngzǐ 28: 982; cf. Mair 1994, 293–94)

Although this passage is found in the Zhuāngzǐ, it is consistent with Ru views, and the reference to the pine and cypress is attributed to Kǒngzǐ in Lúnyǔ 9.28. We must remember that "failure" (qióng) has a more specific sense of being thwarted or blocked, as tōng, the term here used for "success," means to penetrate, advance, or go smoothly along. This passage illustrates another common response to the problem of evil, which is to shift the meaning of progressing smoothly and being thwarted away from worldly success and onto the way itself. This shift closely connects to another function of the story, to show that even in desperate situations, gentlemen (jūnzǐ 君子) do not compromise their values (Zhuāngzǐ 20: 690–94; Mair 1994, 194–96).[33]

In contrast to this interpretation, other passages in the Zhuāngzǐ blame Kǒngzǐ: for clinging to an outdated past, for making himself too prominent, for trying to force external things, and for promoting what is beneficial rather than what is natural.[34] Although it does not mention this specific story, the Hánfēizǐ points out that in spite of his great virtue, Kǒngzǐ had only seventy disciples and had to serve the much less virtuous Duke Āi of Lǔ (49: 1097). The lesson is that success depends on power, not virtue. The Mòzǐ instead disputes the basic facts, claiming that Zǐlù got some pork and wine, which Kǒngzǐ ate without regard for how it was attained (3: 303–304; Johnston 2010, 3.12). When questioned, Kǒngzǐ explains that with the lords he is anxious about rightness but now he is anxious about staying alive. This is more than an ad hominem attack on Kǒngzǐ. It eliminates the function of the story in showing that good people sometimes fail, thus allowing the Mohists to maintain their claim that heaven always rewards the good.

The Mandate of Heaven and the Rewards of Virtue

These stories suffice to dispel any lingering view that classical Chinese thinkers took the harmony of heaven and human for granted, or that they lacked awareness of the possibilities for tragic conflict between human beings and the world. The prominence of these stories across a variety of texts shows that the otherwise obvious fact that bad things happen to good people had become a *problem*. They also show a widespread recognition that things do not always work out as they would if the world were good or fair. Absent an afterlife as a place for happy endings, it would be difficult for a reasonable person to hold a more optimistic view, although the Mohists try.[35] These stories of good people who meet bad ends, though, would not have been so significant were they not raised against a more optimistic view. To understand the problem of evil as it arose in early China, we must consider the earlier worldview that these stories disrupted.

Thinkers of the Warring States period already saw themselves as part of a tradition going back several millennia. This history was divided into three dynasties, the Xià, the Shàng or Yīn, and the Zhōu. They saw themselves as living during the breakdown of the Zhōu (approximately 1050–256 BCE), a period of turmoil that would end only with the unification of China by the state of Qín in 221 BCE, around the time of the death of Xúnzǐ, the last philosopher discussed here. Given the authority of traditional figures, this history was a point of contention, but in general, the exemplars of wisdom, ability, and goodness were the sagely kings who founded the three dynasties, and the exemplars of evil were those wicked kings who brought about the ends of their dynasties.

The key event is the overthrow of the Shàng dynasty in the middle of the eleventh century BCE. The last Shàng king, Zhòu, was notoriously evil—we have seen him as the one who cut out the heart of Bǐ Gān. The *Lǚshì chūnqiū*, compiled around 240 BCE, gives a vivid example of how King Zhòu was portrayed:

> A hill of liquor dregs and a lake of wine, a garden of meat with racks for roasting, and a "roasting pillar" to torture the feudal lords—these were not proper. Executing the woman of the Marquis of Guì to take her jade amulet, cutting open the calf of a man who forded cold streams to look at his marrow, murdering the Earl of Méi and sending a meat pie made from him to King Wén as a gift—these were improper. (King Wén politely received it and then reported it to the feudal lords.) Building a jade chamber and constructing a jade tower, cutting open a pregnant woman's womb to see the fetus, killing Bǐ Gān to look at his heart—these were not proper. (23/4: 1568–69)[36]

During this time of misrule, King Wén steadily cultivated his virtue in a state on the western edges of the Shàng, gradually drawing more and more support. The "Kāng Announcement" ("Kāng gào" 康誥) in the *Shàng shū* 尚書 (*Book of Documents*), which supposedly goes back to the founding of the Zhōu dynasty, describes this thus:

> Your great illustrious father King Wén was able to illuminate virtue [*míngdé* 明德] and be conscientious in punishments. He did not dare slight the widows or widowers. He used what should be used, revered those who should be revered, and awed those who needed to be awed, thus becoming illustrious among the people.[37]

It was King Wén's son, King Wǔ, who led the revolution that ended the Shàng and founded the Zhōu dynasty.

We can already see a narrative of virtue triumphing over vice. The Zhōu faced the challenge of justifying their own revolution without justifying the next one. Like many revolutionaries, they appealed to their moral superiority and care for the people. This triumph of virtue over vice was projected back through Chinese history. Tāng Chīn—the legendary founder of the Shàng dynasty—became another paradigm of virtue, and the evil last Xià emperor, Jié Chīn, was presented in terms similar to that of the Shàng king Zhòu. The founders of the Xià dynasty—Yáo Chīn, Shùn Chīn, and Yǔ Chīn—also were portrayed as great sage kings who ruled through their virtue. This history naturally led to claims that good people are rewarded while bad people are punished. The above description of the wicked King Zhòu from the *Lǚshì chūnqiū* is introduced to illustrate a general claim about the efficacy of human action, for better or worse: "The leaders of lost states are like one thread. Although the timing from heaven differed and their affairs varied, that by which they were destroyed was the same: what they found joy in was improper. If joys are not proper then one cannot survive" (23/4: 1568). Characters such as Jié and Zhòu (who were justly punished), and Tāng, Wén, and Wǔ (justly rewarded) were the exemplars against which Wǔ Zǐxū, Bó Yí, and Robber Zhí were raised as challenges.

The importance of the triumph of the virtuous kings over the evil ones was partly in the way it was theorized into a broader religious context. It is impossible to reconstruct ancient Chinese views of the divine with much certainty, but we can draw out a few widely accepted points in order to set the context for later developments.[38] Based on sources from the Shàng dynasty, there was a common belief in a variety of spirits, including spirits of ancestors and spirits of natural phenomena such as rivers, rain, and the wind. These spirits received sacrifices and provided information through divination. Given their power over many aspects of human life, they inspired both fear and reverence. The spirits were more or less organized under a highest god or spirit, known as the Dì 帝 or Shàngdì 上帝 (High Lord). The Dì was anthropomorphic, having a will and ministers, and exceptional ancestors could ascend to join the Dì, as one of the odes says: "King Wén ascends and descends, at the left and the right of the Dì" (235). The Dì and the other spirits, though, were not primarily ethical. Shàng sources contain no appeals to spirits based on what is right, nor do they present ethical human behavior as a reason for divine favor (Chén Lái 2009a, 126). As Chén Lái puts it,

> From oracle bone inscriptions, it can be seen that for the Yīn people, Shàngdì fundamentally is not a compassionate spirit that takes care of people or spreads love in the human realm, but rather is a god high above with inconstant pleasure and anger. All human beings can do is struggle every day to divine and sacrifice, to flatter and ingratiate themselves to seek assistance and prosperity from the spirits. (2009a, 126)[39]

In this world, bad things happening to good people poses no deep philosophical problem.

Early Zhōu religious views were largely continuous with those of the Shàng, but the Zhōu introduced several concepts that became fundamental for later discussions of the problem of evil. The first is *tiān* 天 (heaven), which largely displaced Shàngdì as a name for the highest divine force. Most of this book will examine how the meaning and significance of *tiān* shifted when confronted with the fact that good people sometimes fail. In the early Zhōu context, *tiān* names an anthropomorphic god, largely interchangeable with Shàngdì. At the same time, *tiān* also referred to the sky, with several resonances—a sense of *tiān* as a sky god, a reference to a place above us where the divine is located, and an appeal to the ordered patterns of the movement of the heavens.[40] The classical Chinese word for "the world" or "the realm" is literally what is "under heaven," *tiānxià* 天下. I will follow convention in translating *tiān* as "heaven," and the nuances and developments of its meaning will be considered as they arise. A second key concept is *mìng*. The meaning of *mìng* eventually shifts to refer to negative events we cannot control, and I will generally translate it as "fate," but its original meaning is simply a "command" and it is closely linked to the terms *lìng* 令 (to command), and *míng* 名, (to name). In the early Zhōu context, *tiān*, like an earthly ruler, issues commands, *mìng*, and the phrase *tiānmìng* is now widely known as the "Mandate of Heaven."

Heaven promotes virtue and punishes vice. The early parts of the *Shàng shū* associate heaven's concerns with several areas of morality and governing. For example, sons who do not serve their fathers, fathers who do not care for their sons, and younger brothers who do not follow their elders are said "not to consider what heaven makes manifest."[41] Some passages are quite specific, as "The Announcement about Drunkenness" ("Jiǔ gào" 酒誥) says that when heaven sends down its might, the cause usually involves excesses in liquor.[42] Heaven's judgment is also associated with specific aspects of governing, particularly the fair and restrained use of punishments and the selection of worthy ministers. Most fundamentally, heaven shows concern for the people, displacing rulers who make them suffer.[43] This concern appears most clearly in the "Great Declaration" ("Tài shì" 泰誓), which famously says, "Heaven sees from where my people see; heaven hears from where my people hear," and that "Heaven takes pity on the people: what the people desire, heaven surely follows."[44]

The Mandate of Heaven became the way of explaining the success of good rulers: Wén and Wǔ succeeded because heaven responded to their virtue and gave them its mandate or command. This way of rationalizing the Zhōu conquest had profound consequences. One might imagine a fundamentally different route, in which the Zhōu people appealed to their inherent superiority or the superiority of their gods. Instead, they presented themselves as essentially the same as the peoples who came before them, differing not by their essence but by their virtue. Like the Zhōu, the Shàng had been founded by illustrious ancestors, and like the Shàng, the Zhōu would lose the mandate if they did not keep their virtue. In the fall of the Shàng, the Zhōu ruler should see what could happen to him. The "King Wén" ("Wén Wáng" 文王) ode says,

> Always match [*pèi* 配] the mandate, and seek good fortune from yourselves.
> Before Yīn lost the multitudes, they were able to match Shàngdì.
> Look to Yīn as a mirror—the great mandate is not easy. (235)

One consequence of this view was a deep historical consciousness, as the Zhōu thought of themselves not as instituting something new but rather as following an already established pattern. The equality of the Shàng and Zhōu also points toward a view of human beings as fundamentally the same in their ability to become virtuous, a common point among Warring States philosophers. This sense of equality was linked with the elevation of heaven as a universal divinity not bound to any particular ancestry, leading toward the common claim in the Warring States period that heaven is impartial and without familial bias.[45]

One remarkable aspect of the early speeches in the *Shàng shū* is their sense of anxiety. There is none of the gloating we might expect from new conquerors. Heaven's mandate is difficult to keep, not because heaven is willful or inconstant but because it is so hard to sustain the required level of virtue. The Duke of Zhōu warns,

> If our later sons and grandsons are greatly unable to respect those above and below, cutting off and losing the glory of our predecessors in the house, not knowing that the mandate of heaven is not easy and heaven is difficult to rely on, then their mandate will be dropped and they will not be able to go through the years or inherit and continue the respect and luminous virtue [*dé*] of our predecessors.... Heaven cannot be trusted. Our way is only to extend the virtue of the Pacifying King, so that heaven does not let go the mandate King Wén received.[46]

The "King Wén" ode echoes this by saying, "the mandate of heaven is not constant [*tiānmìng mí cháng* 天命靡常]" (235). These claims that heaven cannot be trusted or is not constant are ambiguous. The position rejected is one in which a single lineage would have constant or eternal possession of the mandate. The Shàng are criticized for holding such a view: as his kingdom was falling apart, King Zhòu was said to have arrogantly laughed off his troubles, saying "I have the mandate [*mìng*]."[47] The constancy linked to one ruler, family, or people was given up, but it was replaced by a different constancy, one based on the possession of virtue.

Although this anxious concern in the face of the mandate may prompt us to think of fear and trembling before the divine, the anxiety follows not directly from awe of the divine but from a realization of human responsibility. Xú Fùguān calls this sense of responsibility and anxious concern *yōuhuàn yìshí* 憂患意識, drawing on a phrase from the "Xìcí" ("Attached Verbalizations" 繫辭) commentary to the *Zhōu yì* 周易 (Book of Changes).[48] The term *yōu* means "anxious concern," or "worry"; *huàn* means "trouble" or "harm," but also has a subjective sense of being troubled. In the Ru tradition, *yōu* took on a central role, going back to Kǒngzǐ's claim that one should be anxious about (*yōu*) the way but not anxious about poverty (*Lúnyǔ* 15.31). One of the most famous statements of the sense of responsibility and anxiety was made in the Sòng dynasty by Fàn Zhòngyān 范仲淹: "Go first in being concerned (*yōu*) for the world's concerns; go last in enjoying the world's joys."⁴⁹

This feeling of anxious concern is commonly linked to the "humanism" of the Chinese tradition. Xú Fùguān explains,

> Thereupon, the mandate of heaven (divine intent [*shényì* 神意]) no longer gave unconditional support for certain rulers but made choices based on human actions. In this way, the mandate of heaven gradually moved out from a spirit of mystery and darkness and became something that could be understood and grasped through human beings' own actions (1969, 24).

In a similar way, Chén Lái claims that the fall of the Shàng led to the following realization:

> Human beings cannot attribute all worldly events to the necessity of heaven's commands. History is not entirely determined by heaven (Shàngdì) but human actions genuinely participate in historical processes, so that human beings should seek the causality of historical change within human action itself. (2009a, 191)

By making heaven consistently and predictably responsive to human actions, the responsibility for order moves to human beings themselves. We see this shift in the *Shàng shū*, as in the "Announcement on Drunkenness," which says, "It is not that heaven is cruelly oppressive; it is just that people bring guilt upon themselves."⁵⁰ Another chapter, probably from the Spring and Autumn period, says, "Be always in awe of the punishments of heaven. It is not that heaven is not correct [*bùzhōng* 不中], but that people bring their fate [*mìng*] on themselves."⁵¹ It is tempting to place this shift toward human responsibility and control into a narrative of secularization, taking this humanism as marking a break from religion. Xú Fùguān says it allowed a move from reliance on spirits to trust in the power of one's own actions (1969, 21). Such a claim, though, is misleading, if not wrong. The power of human actions depended entirely on the regularity and humaneness of heaven: the power of heaven as a humanlike deity functions to guarantee human responsibility. This guarantee, though, depends on a denial of the problem of evil. This denial sets human beings firmly in control of their own destinies, but the resulting humanism could only be as reliable as heaven itself. As the goodness of heaven was thrown into doubt, so, too, was the status of human action and virtue.

If we look in the Chinese context for something like the classical problem of evil, *tiān* plays the role corresponding to European conceptions of God. It is important to note, though, the limits of this conception of heaven. First, there are no claims that heaven is either omnipotent or perfectly good. The early chapters of the *Shàng shū* attribute various harms to heaven; for example, the fatal illness of King Chéng is said to have been sent down from heaven, without any implication that he did something wrong.[52] Second, the discussions of the rewards and punishments of heaven are limited to the actions of rulers. There is no general claim that good is always rewarded and bad always punished. In fact, that cannot be the view, because it was primarily the people—whether innocent or guilty—who suffered when the ruler was bad.[53] Heaven follows the logic of economic sanctions, where the suffering of the people is pushed to such an extreme that they have no choice but to enact "regime change" for themselves. Since the suffering heaven lays on the people is never treated as a *problem*, the Mandate of Heaven must have been seen in terms of establishing political legitimacy rather than being a thorough principle of divine justice. The role of the people points toward a third crucial point, which is the difficulty in isolating heaven's activity. While heaven is conceived as willful and anthropomorphic, its actions are causally regular and enacted through the natural world, blurring the line between heaven and nature. Moreover, the main expression of heaven's mandate is through the people: the sign that the mandate has shifted is that people resist the emperor and welcome the rebel. The mutual implication of heaven and world would later provide an easy route for what we might call the "naturalization" of heaven, shifting from a personal deity to the patterns of nature or the natural reactions of the people.

We have no way to know how dominant or widespread these views of heaven were. Our records are limited, of questionable authenticity, and reflect the views of elites. Belief in the need to supplicate divine forces through sacrifices and pleas continued. Such practices imply that divine forces might not help you, even if you are good.[54] Earlier views of the divine as more frightening and irregular likely continued alongside the view of heaven as ethical and constant.[55] In any case, doubts about the mandate of heaven arose as the power and virtue of the Zhōu rulers declined. We have exemplars of evil from that time, but not the virtuous man that heaven would elevate to rescue the people. The frequency with which good people met harm made it difficult to believe heaven cared. The *Shī jīng* includes many laments, several of which explicitly portray heaven as a negative force. One the most eloquent is "Rain without Regularity" ("Yǔ wú zhèng" 雨無正), which begins,

> Vast heaven, great and mighty, does not extend its virtue
> Sending down bereavement and starvation, spreading destruction throughout the states.
> Expansive heaven, brutal and cruel, does not consider, does not plan,
> Leaving aside those with offenses, fully concealing their guilt.
> But as for these without offense, all are immersed in suffering. (194)[56]

"Gazing Upward" ("Zhānyǎng" 瞻卬), supposedly written during the reign of King Yōu, the last king of the Western Zhōu and another common exemplar of wickedness, begins in a similar way:

> I gaze up toward vast heaven, but it shows us no kindness.
> Very long has there been no peace, sending down these great disasters.
> In the state, nothing is stable, the officers and people are diseased.
> Insects stealing grain and causing sickness, there is no limit.
> Those who offend are not caught in the net, there is no cure. (264)

In both odes, suffering comes from aberrations in nature and from human actions, mixing what we might distinguish as "natural" and "moral" evil, but heaven is blamed for both. If the rulers were bad, heaven should have taken away their mandate and given it to someone more worthy. On a deeper level, heaven may have been seen as influencing the moral qualities of rulers. Such a view is suggested in parts of the *Shàng shū*, as when the "Shào Announcement" ("Shào gào" 召誥) says that whether the new king will be wise (*zhé* 哲) cannot yet be known but is mandated by heaven.[57] This willingness to attribute actions of individuals to heaven continues through the Warring States period, contributing to the difficulty of distinguishing heaven and human.

Another moving example singles out a paradigm of natural evil—a drought. It begins,

> The great and distant milky way is luminous, revolving in the heavens [*tiān*].
> The king said, Oh! What guilt is now on us people?
> Heaven sends down bereavement and disorder, famines come one after another.
> No spirit is not revered, no sacrificial offering is grudged.
> Our jade ornaments and disks are used up—could it be there are none that hear us?
>
> The drought is already too deep, searing heat and thunder.
> We have not ceased sacrificial offerings, from suburban altars to the ancestral temple.
> Making offerings to those above and below, no spirit is not honored.
> Hòu Jì is insufficient, Shàngdì does not approach.
> Withering and ruining the land below, thus falling directly on me!
>
> The drought is already too deep, thus it cannot be pushed away.
> Terrible and frightening, like thunder, like lightning.
> Of these black-haired remnants of Zhōu, none will be left.
> Vast heaven, Shàngdì, then leave us nothing.
> Shall we not be in awe of it, lest the ancestors be cut off? (258)[58]

While the emphasis is on the inefficacy of sacrifices rather than morality, the speaker's claim that he and his people are without guilt shows that he takes the disasters as undeserved, and his deep concern for the suffering of the people suggests he is indeed a good leader. The fear and sorrow of the king are clear, but his attitude toward the divine is less so. He seems perplexed: We have done all that we were supposed to do, so how is it that this disaster still comes? The speaker assumes that the drought has come from the gods rather than by chance or by blind patterns of nature, and we can see how the failure of the gods to respond would lead toward skepticism—"could it be there are none that hear us?"

In considering Zhōu views of heaven, we must again keep in mind the limitations of our sources and avoid overgeneralization. The period leading directly up to Kǒngzǐ and Mòzǐ contained diverse views of the relationship between heaven and human, and we have no way to know which were dominant.[59] Views of heaven as good and as protecting the people surely persisted, as we see in the fact that both Kǒngzǐ and Mòzǐ took them up to varying degrees. Some of the odes suggest a contrary view—of a heaven that is, in the words of Yuri Pines, a "sentient, though probably malevolent deity" (2002, 59). A view in between these also emerged, in which heaven more neutrally meant something like "the way things are."[60] This final use of heaven has come to be called "descriptive," in contrast to its "prescriptive" function.[61] This descriptive function was taken up by a new sense of the term *mìng*, the "command," which took on a meaning closer to "blind fate."[62]

Skepticism about heaven's support for the good and its protection of the people is commonly associated with an acceleration of the humanism of the early Zhōu period.[63] This connection, however, is more complex than it might initially appear. We must avoid misleading analogies with the history of European thought, where the rejection of a good God transitioned immediately into a confidence in human power over nature. Europe had lived in denial of the problem of evil for most of its history. The problem of evil began to generate real doubts about the goodness of God only at a time when discourses of human power over nature were already thoroughly established. Human beings remained as the "image of God" even after God faded into the background. It took several more centuries for this confidence in the human to breakdown. If we follow Neiman in taking "modernity" as beginning with the Lisbon earthquake and ending with Auschwitz, then modernity is precisely that lag time during which confidence in the human remained after its divine foundations had fallen away (Neiman 2002, 250–51, 255, 288). The situation of China during the Spring and Autumn period was fundamentally different. Consider Xú Fùguān's claim that in the early Zhōu, "the mandate of heaven gradually moved out from a spirit of mystery and darkness and became something that could be understood and grasped through human beings' own actions" (1969, 24). The breakdown of confidence in the Mandate of Heaven came early enough that this "mystery and darkness" had not yet been forgotten. It continued to haunt claims for the status of human beings. There were, of course, many who tried to maintain confidence in the power of human action, whether efficacious action was taken to lie in virtue, power, cleverness, or spontaneity. Just as likely, though, one might conclude that human life is dominated by mysterious forces that cannot be grasped or controlled. One might then cling to virtue while calmly accepting fate, as some of the Ru did, or try to enjoy as much as our short fragile lives allow, as Robber Zhí recommends. One of the main divides in Warring States thought is around this question of the efficacy of human action, a question that was never separated from the relationship of human beings to heaven.

Problems of Evil in European Thought

We have now seen the context in which Chinese philosophers approached the fact that bad things happen to good people, and some of the ways it became problematic. Before turning to these problems in detail, we can briefly sketch how the same fact was problematized on the terrain of European thought. This explanation will serve as a point of reference in making comparisons later, but it will also help to clarify the specificity of the Chinese positions considered. That is, we can better see the specificity of the various Chinese discussions if we first draw into our awareness some assumptions that conditioned the formation of the problem of evil in Europe. Many different problems emerge, but we can consider three that are particularly central. The first is the classical problem of evil, a theological problem about the nature and existence of God. The second is the problem of moral or human evil—in particular, how human beings are capable of "radical evil." The third encompasses a number of issues grouped under philosophical reflections on tragedy. In each case, I will briefly describe the problem and then gesture toward contrasts to help orient the discussions of Chinese philosophy that follow.

The Classical Problem of Evil

In European thought, the fact that bad things happen to good people was primarily taken up through the classical problem of evil—how can a good, omnipotent God allow evil and injustice to exist in the world?[64] We can take our initial formulation from David Hume's *Dialogues Concerning Natural Religion*, where Philo echoes Epicurus in asking of God: "Is he willing to prevent evil, but not able? then is he impotent. Is he able, but not willing? then is he malevolent. Is he both able and willing? Whence then is evil?" (Part X; Hume 2007, 74). Scholars have since defined the problem more precisely, but for comparative purposes it is more helpful to broaden the formulation.[65] We can distinguish three elements forming the problem. First, given that we are human, we see the world in our own terms. Ethics is almost necessarily anthropocentric in the sense of *centering* on human beings (which is, of course, quite compatible with valuing other things as well). It is difficult to imagine an ethics that would not give greater value to human beings than to mice or grass. Moreover, death and destruction appear to be bad only from our perspective. Whatever happens here, the solar system will go on. The second element is the world we live in, which does not appear to be ordered according to these ethical categories. The insecurity caused by this divergence between the world and our ethics may itself inspire the third element of the problem, a divine being who is responsible for the order of the world and who acts according to our ethical categories. The fact that bad things happen to good people becomes a metaphysical or theological problem, the classical problem of evil, only when it is observed to happen in a world supposedly ordered according to the categories of human ethics. Such a belief is common, but not universal. In the context of the early Greeks, for example, the massacre at Troy poses no fundamental philosophical problem; it is what we would expect in a world run by gods who are jealous, vain, and possessive, like us.[66]

Based on this discussion, we might reformulate the problem of evil as the difficulty of simultaneously maintaining three points:

1. An ethics that defines the good in anthropocentric terms;
2. The recognition that the world itself is not good in those same terms;
3. The belief in a being that is responsible for the world and is good in those same terms.

Since any two of the three points are easily maintained together, the problem can be resolved by abandoning any one of the three commitments. In Europe, those who raise the problem have concentrated on disputing (3), the commitment to a good being responsible for the world. In general, this entails the denial of God's existence rather than God's goodness. While the rejection of the existence of a good God is the simplest way out of the problem, it triggers further problems. If the world itself is not good, to what can we appeal in justifying our ethics? Abandoning a good God threatens the very foundations of goodness. To avoid these conclusions, one seems compelled to give up (2) by making the implausible claim that, in spite of appearances, this is the best possible world. Many thinkers approach the problem by compromising several principles. For example, although Leibniz denies (2) by claiming that this world is the best possible, he also weakens (1) by saying that human beings are not God's only consideration and weakens (3) by restricting God's power to the realm of possibility.[67]

The problem is most acute when God is taken as perfectly good and absolutely powerful, totally responsible for all that exists. Chinese philosophers never shared these assumptions and thus the problem was not strictly a matter of logical contradiction. Nonetheless, I will argue that the breakdown of the Zhōu dynasty generated an intense crisis around these same three points. For the sake of comparison, we could situate various early Chinese philosophers within this configuration of assumptions. The Mohists could be positioned as denying (2), claiming that heaven and other spirits consistently reward the good and punish the bad; the *Zhuāngzǐ* would reject (1), overcoming our ethical labels in order to affirm the world as it is. Most of the philosophers considered here would take some complex middle ground. Although such an analysis might be interesting, my intention is not to arrange these Chinese philosophers on the terrain of European problems. Rather, we can note two initial contrasts.

The most important contrast is in the relationship between the divine and the world. The problem of evil in Europe operates on a complex mix of connection and separation. The causal connection between the divine and the world is what makes the problem of evil effective, allowing the apparent moral indifference of nature to throw doubt on the goodness of God. The radical transcendence of God, however, allows us to maintain a foundation for the world that is much more anthropomorphic than the world itself appears to be. In early China, heaven and the world were not clearly separated. Thus, while the problem of evil in the European context is primarily about the *existence* of God, in the early Chinese context it is exclusively a problem about the *nature* of heaven. To deny the existence of heaven would be as incomprehensible as denying the sky above us. This basic difference has several crucial consequences. In Europe one finds a sudden break from trust in a perfectly good God to a radically disenchanted world operating on amoral causal principles. In the Chinese context, there never was a "death of God." At most, "heaven" gradually becomes more and more naturalistic and less and less anthropomorphic. What follows is a difference in human attitudes toward nature. The split between God and the natural world meant that reverence and obedience were directed toward God. Any reverence toward nature was derivative. Thus, the death of God is the death of religion. In contrast, the gradual shift in the nature of heaven in early Chinese thought allowed for continued reverence toward it, even in texts recognizing that heaven does not act according to what we consider right. Much more than in Europe, one key dimension to the problem of evil in early China was how to reconcile this sense of reverence with the seeming amorality of the world we inhabit.

This leads into the other broad point of contrast. If the problem of evil introduces a rift between our concepts and values and the way the world is, European reactions to the problem tended to throw the world into question, whereas Chinese reactions tended to throw the human into question. These are general tendencies, with exceptions on both sides, but consider the position given to Philo in the *Dialogues Concerning Natural Religion*. Echoing King Alfonso of Castile's legendary claim that if God had consulted him on designing the world, he could have told him how to improve it, Philo lists four ways in which the world could be made better. For example, we might be guided only by gradations of pleasure rather than both pleasure and pain, or we might have been made more diligent and energetic (Part XI; Hume 2007, 81–85).[68] Philo's absolute confidence in human values and his willingness to condemn nature based on them is striking in its hubris. It points clearly toward the project of taking control of nature and "improving" it to better suit our needs. This confidence in the human eventually broke down, but only much later, under the pressure of the wars and genocides in the twentieth century. Chinese philosophers *immediately* took the conclusion that heaven might not be good as a threat to the status of human beings. Some, like the *Zhuāngzǐ*, push this realization toward a radical overcoming of the human. Most, though, struggle to reconcile some form of humanism with heaven. Facing nature, all maintain a humility and reverence that was largely absent in the wake of the classical problem of evil in early modern Europe.

The Problem of Human Evil

Leibniz distinguished three kinds of evil—metaphysical evil, which refers to the inherent limitation in anything created; physical (or natural) evil, referring to suffering; moral evil, which refers to the evil done by human beings themselves (*Theodicy* §21; Gerhardt 1978, VI.115). God appears most directly responsible for natural evil, which is why the classical problem of evil most often appeals to it. Moral evil might be attributed to God, who creates the people who do the evil, but it is more commonly attributed to free will and thus removed from God's direct responsibility.[69] If we separate moral evil in this way, then it poses a different set of philosophical problems, which we could gather under the term "radical evil." "Radical evil" is sometimes used loosely to label human actions so horrible as to make the term "bad" seem inadequate, but as a philosophical problem it has a technical sense going back to Immanuel Kant's *Religion within the Bounds of Mere Reason*. The root of the problem is Kant's claim that actions can only be considered moral (or evil) if they are free, which means that the ultimate causes of good and evil must lie outside the causally determined realm of nature. To explain evil actions by appeal to social conditions, poor upbringing, or available temptations is to place those actions into the causally determined phenomenal realm, making them not truly free. Such actions could be harmful or bad, but not evil.[70] Kant cannot even accept sensory desires as an ultimate cause of evil, since the submission of the will to sensory desire would mean the will was not free. To be free (and thus capable of evil), the will must of itself freely choose to follow desire.[71] Given that evil actions are also not random or uncaused, good and evil can exist only if they are in some sense self-caused. It is this self-causation that makes us *totally* responsible for our actions and, thus, subject to justice. Augustine makes this connection to punishment and reward in what may be the first philosophical account of a radically free will:

> And as for the goodness that we so admired in God's justice—his punishing sins and rewarding good deeds—how could it even exist if human beings lacked the free choice of the will? No action would be either a sin or a good

deed if it were not performed by the will, so both punishment and reward would be unjust if human beings had no free will (Augustine 1993, 30).

If human beings were not *fully* responsible for their actions, then it would be unjust to punish anyone, let alone condemn them to eternal hell.

Since any actual explanation for why a given person chooses evil would appeal to influences excluded as belonging to the causal realm of nature, radical evil must be in some sense inexplicable. This inexplicability conforms to a common intuition—there are some actions so evil that the attempt to explain them in terms of historical and social forces might itself appear immoral, as if one were making excuses. In a sense, the difficulty of explaining evil is just the difficulty of explaining a free will whose causality is independent of the rest of the world. At the same time, it seems easier to explain freely choosing good than to explain freely choosing evil. In particular, if evil cannot be explained through a desire for some particular thing, then it seems that evil itself must be a motive. Moreover, because moral evil is freely chosen, it lurks as an ever-present danger. Habits, dispositions, and self-cultivation ultimately cannot *determine* the will, which remains free at any time. As Kant puts it, every act of evil must be thought of "as if the human being had fallen into it directly from the state of innocence."[72]

Radical evil as a philosophical problem depends on demands particular to the European tradition: to separate evil action from the God who creates us, to maintain the status of human beings as supernatural, and to ground an idea of responsibility that can justify eternal torture as a punishment. Insofar as radical evil is inseparable from concerns about free will, it appears only with the assumption of two fundamentally different kinds of causality—the causality we find between things and events in the world and the causality of a free will. The very idea of radical evil depends on a non-naturalistic account of human beings, a point first articulated critically by Spinoza:

> Indeed they seem to conceive man in Nature as a dominion within a dominion [*imperium in imperio*]. For they believe that man disturbs, rather than follows, the order of Nature, that he has absolute power over his actions, and that he is determined only by himself. And they attribute the cause of human impotence and inconstancy, not to the common power of Nature, but to I know not what vice of human nature, which they therefore bewail, or laugh at, or disdain, or (as usually happens) curse.[73]

This idea of radical evil is particularly difficult to apply in an early Chinese context. Explaining why human beings do bad things is a common topic, but not different in kind from explaining any other complex phenomena. Evil does not arise mysteriously from a free will but is rather, as Aaron Stalnaker puts it in relation to Xúnzǐ, "a contingent matter of bad tendencies allowed to grow under the pressure of violent, chaotic circumstances" (2006, 147). As this suggests, human choice and responsibility was not seen as isolatable from broader social forces, which is why it was common to put responsibility for the misdeeds of the people on the ruler rather than the people themselves. In fact, if we make a distinction between bad and evil, the Chinese lack the latter concept, which is one of the most problematic aspects of even using the phrase "problem of evil" in a Chinese context. Without a distinct conception of evil, the distinction between moral and nonmoral values also is blurred (as it was for the Greeks).[74] The main term for "good" (shàn 善), could just as well be translated as "excellent"; the main word for "bad" (è 惡), means to be repulsive and could just as well be applied to what is considered ugly. This continuity helps explain why debates about the rewards of (morally) good actions so easily became questions about efficacious action in general.

Although the problem of radical evil in European philosophy is determined most of all by theological concerns, it is implausible to assume it has no basis in human experience. We must again be careful of the problem of reversal, letting a blanket naturalism obscure all tensions. Whether taken as signs of a radically divided ontology or as tensions within an interconnected whole, human actions do seem different from the movements of other natural things. The strangeness of being human was remarked on in early China. A line from a recently excavated text, Yǔ cóng 語叢 I (Collected sayings I) says positively, "Heaven generates the hundreds of things, and human beings are most noble" (Liú Zhāo 2003, strip 18). Human beings are not different in kind—they are just one of the many kinds of things generated by heaven—but they are the most noble or precious. In contrast, another excavated text from around the same time, Héng xiān 恆先 (Constancy first), says, "At first there is good, there is order, and there is no disorder. When there are people, there is what is not good. Disorder comes out from people" (Jì 2005, strip 8). If we put these contrasting passages together, we get something like the ambiguous sense of deinon in the famous line from Antigone: "Many things are wonderful-terrible [deinon], but none is more wonderful-terrible than human beings."[75]

Several points of difference are singled out in the early Chinese context. The most distinctive thing about human beings is the degree of harm that we are capable of. This potential for causing harm relates to another key point, our greater variability. The Zhuāngzǐ takes this point the furthest, affirming the singularity of each person and taking our perspectives as almost infinitely flexible, but we see this among the Ru as well. The Xìng zì mìng chū says, "Within the four seas, their natural dispositions are the same. It is in using their hearts that each becomes different. Education makes it so" (Liú Zhāo 2003, strip 9). The roots of these differences are rarely addressed explicitly, but while natural forces operate spontaneously and of themselves (by zìrán 自然), human beings deviate into deliberate actions, for better or worse. The unique propensity of human beings to act deliberately suggests a different mode of causality for human actions. Of course, the distinction between deliberate and spontaneous action differs radically from the distinction between free will and causal determinism. While the latter two are mutually exclusive, one can be more or less spontaneous or deliberate. Moreover, the distinction between spontaneous and deliberate does not map entirely onto the distinction between the natural and the human. Human beings can act spontaneously like nature itself—in fact, almost all the texts considered here take this kind of spontaneous action to be the highest ideal. Even so, the strangeness of human action lingers through early Chinese texts while rarely being explicitly addressed. The question of how to explain this strangeness is a good example of the opposite orientation of problems in early China and in Europe. European philosophers have traditionally begun with the assumption that human beings are unique (with an eternal soul, and a free will and rationality made in the image of God), with the challenge then being to explain how we find ourselves integrated in the world around us. For early Chinese philosophers, the difficulty is the opposite—to explain how one of the myriad things ends up so different and troublesome.

The Tragic Condition

The third set of problems that arose in Europe from the fact that bad things happen to good people can be clustered together as philosophical reflections on tragedy. The philosophical significance of tragedy goes back to Aristotle's *Poetics*, but its modern form comes primarily as a reaction against the optimistic view that, in the end, everything works out fairly. Leibniz is the exemplar for this optimism, writing in the *Principles of Nature and Grace According to Reason*,

> Here there is no crime without punishment, no good action without proportionate reward, and finally, as much virtue and happiness as possible. And this is accomplished without disordering nature (as if what God prepared for souls disturbed the laws of bodies), but through the very order of natural things, in virtue of the harmony pre-established between the kingdoms of nature and grace, between God as architect and God as monarch.[76]

This optimism about divine justice manifests a deeper optimism—that human categories, judgments, and values are commensurable with the structure of the universe itself, that we are fundamentally at home in the world, or that the world is ultimately coherent and intelligible in both epistemological and ethical terms.

In contrast, what we might (following Nietzsche) call "the tragic worldview" (*die tragische Weltbetrachtung*) claims that things do not always work out, and that we should confront rather than deny this fact.[77] Tragedy involves recognition of the problem of evil: Aristotle takes the core of tragedy to be the pity and fear "occasioned by undeserved misfortune."[78] Unlike the classical problem of evil, however, the primary issue is not the existence of a good God. On the contrary, modern tragic views often appear as mourning for a lost God, and they cannot be separated from a Christian lineage that defined human beings as longing for the infinite. This view has its modern start in Descartes, who takes awareness of the infinite as constitutive of human consciousness:

> When I turn my mind's eye upon myself, I understand that I am a thing which is incomplete and dependent on another and which aspires without limit to ever greater and better things; but I also understand at the same time that he on whom I depend has within him all those greater things, not just indefinitely and potentially but actually and infinitely, and hence that he is God.[79]

Descartes' position reformulates ideas found in Augustine, whose youthful restlessness described in the *Confessions* is driven by an unrecognized longing for the infinite, and could be traced back to Plato's *Symposium*, where the motivating force of philosophy (the love in the love of wisdom) derives from a felt gap between ourselves and the pure, divine, forms of beauty and goodness. Taking human self-awareness as constituted by a sense of *lack* already holds a certain tragic tone, but the real tragedy—or absurdity—comes if we lose the belief in this infinite being. This is "the death of God," leaving what David Farrell Krell brilliantly calls, with reference to Ahab, "the phantom limb of the absolute" (2005, 14).

While this element of the modern tragic viewpoint remains under the spell of theism, it confronts the problematic status of human life in a world that is not good. Human beings are sometimes forced into choices that are unavoidably wrong. As Martha Nussbaum writes, what is most troubling about tragedy is that "it shows good people doing bad things, things otherwise repugnant to their ethical character and commitments, because of circumstances whose origin does not lie with them" (1986, 25). Tragedy results from a double bind, the conflict between values such that acting on one requires violating the other, best represented in the conflict between family and state in *Antigone*. This pessimism can extend to the human capacity to grasp and understand the world, as Nietzsche sees the Dionysian spirit of tragedy appearing in the "monstrous" or "uncanny dread" (*ungeheure Grausen*) we feel when events appear to defy the principle of sufficient reason.[80] Oedipus, unknowingly in bed with his mother, symbolizes this epistemological pessimism. The fullest pessimism would see our very existence as tragic, as Nietzsche appeals to the "the necessity of sacrilege imperative upon the titanically striving individual."[81] Even the optimistic Hegel says that the only way a human being can entirely avoid guilt is by "non-action," *Nichttun*.[82]

What distinguishes a *tragic* view from a merely *pessimistic* one is an element of affirmation. This affirmation and defiance is brought out most clearly by Nietzsche, through the central position he gives to Prometheus as revealing the "magnificent 'ability' of the great genius, for which even eternal suffering is too small a price to pay."⁸³ This element of affirmation is most important when we consider the function of tragedy as a form of art—witnessing a tragic drama is enjoyable, even if it involves what Nietzsche calls a "wondrous self-splitting" in which we feel both horror and joy.⁸⁴ That joy involves some defiant affirmation or even ecstatic celebration of human striving and suffering. At the very least, as Martha Nussbaum puts it, tragedy maintains "a vivid sense of the special beauty of the contingent and the mutable, that love for the riskiness and openness of empirical humanity" (1986, 3).

Of the various problems that emerge in Europe around the fact that bad things happen to good people, those concerned with the tragic condition are most relevant in approaching early Chinese thought. Like Chinese philosophers, the concerns of tragedy are primarily existential, reflecting the concrete challenges that come with contingency, unjustified suffering, and the failure of goodness. A tragic viewpoint is haunted by doubts about the significance of human beings, the status of our ethics, knowledge, and power. Perhaps the first person to apply the concept of tragedy to Chinese thought was the great Chinese scholar Wáng Guówéi 王國維 (1877-1927), who described the *Dream of the Red Chamber* as "a tragedy among tragedies" (1997, 12). Wáng traced the linking of human life with anxiety, suffering, and exhaustion back to early China, supporting it with a line from the *Zhuāngzǐ*: "The great clod burdens me with form and labors me with life" (1997, 1).⁸⁵ More recently, Michael Puett has emphasized a tragic sensibility in early China, for example, pointing out the analogies between the Greek myth of Prometheus and the story of the birth of Hòu Jì 后稷, Lord Millet, as described in the *Shī jīng*.⁸⁶

As with most European concepts, the claim that early Chinese thinkers had a tragic viewpoint is both true and false. We have seen a list of well-known characters whose lives could easily be described as tragic, even as falling into a double bind. When Wǔ Zǐxū is called to return for his father, he cannot avoid acting wrongly—to go is to allow evil to win; not to go is to violate his filial duty. Wǔ Zǐxū's obsession with revenge against all odds and obstacles even bears comparison with Ahab's relentless pursuit of the whale. Such stories clearly show a conflictual view of life far from the negation of individuality through absorption into a "universal substance," which Hegel uses to explain why tragedy never developed in the "Orient."⁸⁷ Nonetheless stories like that of Wǔ Zǐxū do not *feel* like tragedies. Early Chinese thinkers saw little in human finitude, suffering, or defiance that should be celebrated. If tragedy is absent in classical China, it is not due to a lack of pessimism but rather the missing valorization of Nietzsche's "titanically striving individual." Instead of defiance, one finds anxious concern (*yōuhuàn*).⁸⁸ This difference follows partly from differences with regard to the importance of the individual, but it is rooted in the place of human beings in nature. For those in the European tradition who emphasize tragedy, the human is defined by will and freedom (in some sense). This freedom is part of an orientation toward transcending our immediate conditions and is what makes us responsible for our own being. Even without God, the tragic celebration of the human will clings to a sense of our divinity. Chinese philosophers were much more willing to give up the exceptional status of human beings, making tragedy not that different from any other sad and violent conflict between forces of nature. The tragic hero resembles the *Zhuāngzǐ*'s praying mantis, foolishly waving its arms to fend off the oncoming chariot.

2 The Efficacy of Human Action and the Mohist Opposition to Fate

THE VIEW OF heaven associated with the rationalization of the Zhōu conquest—that the Mandate of Heaven (*tiānmìng* 天命) protects the people and ensures good rulers—began to break down in the turmoil that followed the disintegration of the Zhōu political order. Some questioned the goodness or reliability of heaven, blaming the current injustices of the world on the divine. Others elevated an altered conception of *mìng* as something like blind fate to label events that were beyond human control and occurred without regard for right or wrong. The Mohists are the first philosophers we know of to explicitly react against these trends, to argue that good people are rewarded and the bad suffer. More specifically, the "Will of Heaven" ("Tiān zhì" 天志) chapters of the *Mòzǐ* can be seen as responding to charges of heaven's indifference, whereas the "Against Fate" ("Fēi mìng" 非命) chapters respond to the trend toward fatalism.

The Mohist position on heaven and ghosts tends to be dismissed as a legacy of popular religion. On this view, their arguments reflect a conservative reaction to religious skepticism, a reaction rooted in older religious views still widespread among common people. This reaction, in turn, is often explained by appeal to Mòzǐ's own class background.[1] This view has some support. The Mohists themselves claim that their views were shared by past sages, and in arguing for the power of ghosts and spirits, they appeal to the testimony of ordinary people. But this kind of explanation misses how Mohist views of heaven form an integral part of their philosophical system. Even if they align with traditional and popular views, we must still ask this: Why did the Mohists incorporate those views into their thought? Surely the Mohists display enough critical thinking and radicalism to make an appeal to Mòzǐ's personal background insufficient as an answer. The promotion of a heaven that cares inclusively for human beings plays a crucial role in justifying the efficacy of human action, which underlies the Mohist commitment to activism. The loss of this anthropomorphic and anthropocentric divinity threatened not only the early Zhōu "humanist" view that human beings are ultimately responsible for their conditions, but also the very possibility of defending a humanistic ethics. While the Mohists react against what were probably general trends among the educated elite, their one explicit target is the Ru (Confucians). Thus, to grasp the stakes of the debate, we can begin with early Ru discussions of heaven and fate.

Tiān and Mìng in Early Ru Thought

The Ru were a diverse group that held a variety of views. Chapters 4 and 6 will consider the positions of two Ru philosophers in detail, those of Mèngzǐ and Xúnzǐ. This section will focus on views of heaven, fate, and the efficacy of human action, showing that at least some of the Ru held views close to those criticized by the Mohists. I will concentrate primarily on the *Lúnyǔ*, commonly known as the *Analects,* while drawing on other Ru texts as they address the same issues.[2] Early Ru views of the divine are notoriously difficult to determine and provide an excellent illustration of the Chinese saying that the humane see humaneness while the wise see wisdom.[3] In this case, theists tend to find God while atheists find agnostic humanism. This split goes back to the first European encounters with Confucianism: Leibniz praises a "rational theology" like his own, whereas Christian Wolff finds the virtuous atheists he seeks.[4] Although not as extreme, one finds similar alternations among Chinese interpreters, particularly between the more supernaturally oriented interpretations of the Hàn dynasty and the more naturalistic readings of the Sòng.[5]

Part of the problem is that Kǒngzǐ's attitude toward the divine resembles what he says about ghosts and spirits: revere them but keep them at a distance (6.22). Among the terms listed that Kǒngzǐ reportedly did not speak of were "the way of heaven" (*tiāndào* 天道) (5.13), "fate" (*mìng* 命) (9.1), "strange omens" (*guài* 怪), and "spirits" (*shén* 神) (7.21).[6] This reluctance to talk about the divine reflects an orientation toward caring for human life in the present. In a passage that might remind us of the Buddhist parable of the poisoned arrow, Kǒngzǐ redirects a set of questions from his disciple Zǐlù:

> Zǐlù asked about serving ghost and spirits. The Master said, "Not yet able to serve people—how could you be able to serve ghosts?" "May I ask about death?" "Not yet knowing life—how could you know death?" (11.12)

Kǒngzǐ does not claim that ghosts do not exist, but that serving ghosts and dealing with death must be extensions of our work for the living.[7] Kǒngzǐ's focus on the living and the human not only takes discussions of the divine out of the center, but also shapes how those discussions appear and function. In other words, we cannot consider his views of heaven and fate without considering the human context in which such appeals function.[8]

The real difficulty is that the claims attributed to Kǒngzǐ support two distinct and even contradictory positions. On one side, there is clear evidence that

Kǒngzǐ took heaven as a moral authority. When Zǐlù accuses Kǒngzǐ of some impropriety, Kǒngzǐ appeals to heaven as a higher judge—"If I have done wrong, may heaven reject me! May heaven reject me!" (6.28) Wáng Chōng, in one of the oldest extant discussions of this passage, takes it as a strong claim in support of heaven's justice (28: 410–12).[9] Another passage says that if one offends heaven, then one has no where to pray for good fortune (3.13). The term for "offend" (*zuì* 罪) connects to punishments, as it means both to offend or to receive punishment for offending; the term for "pray for benefit" is *dǎo* 禱, which contains a radical indicating spirits and is explained in the *Shuōwén jiězì* 說文解字 (Explaining and analyzing characters) as a way of "seeking good fortune."[10] These terms place heaven as the highest power in a context of issuing rewards and punishments—if you offend it, you have nowhere else to turn. Praying for benefits, though, should not be taken too narrowly. Another dialogue addresses prayer thus:

> The master was gravely ill and Zǐlù asked to pray [*dǎo*]. The master said, "Is there such a thing?" Zǐlù answered, "There is. The *Eulogies* says, 'Pray to spirits above and below.'" The master said, "Then I have been praying for a long time!" (7.35)

Kǒngzǐ's skepticism of direct prayers for help does not necessarily mean he gives up the idea that some actions gain favor with heaven. Kǒngzǐ is linked to heaven not by prayers but by his virtue (*dé* 德) and his role in preserving Zhōu culture. In another instance, when Kǒngzǐ is extremely ill, Zǐlù has the other disciples serve him as if they were his ministers. When Kǒngzǐ awakens, he criticizes them, "Whom would I fool? Would I fool heaven?" (9.12). Heaven here is contrasted with human beings, who can be fooled. This contrast functions in a different way when Kǒngzǐ takes comfort in the fact that, while other people do not recognize him, at least heaven knows him (14.35).

The *Lúnyǔ* tells us little about what heaven wants, but heaven is concerned with human culture. Kǒngzǐ appeals to this concern when he is besieged in the town of Kuāng, one of the stories mentioned earlier. In the *Lúnyǔ* version, Kǒngzǐ confidently claims that heaven will protect him: "Since King Wén [文] is gone, is not this culture [*wén* 文] here in me? If heaven would have this culture lost, those coming after King Wén's death would not have attained it. Since heaven has not made this culture lost, what can the people of Kuāng do to me?" (9.5). In this passage, Kǒngzǐ takes historical events as revelatory of heaven's will. Since heaven has maintained the continuation of the cultural patterns established by King Wén, Kǒngzǐ infers that it will continue to do so and thus will protect him. He makes a similar claim when nearly killed in Sòng: since heaven has given birth to his virtue, nothing can harm him (7.23). In another passage concerned with enduring difficulties, a gatekeeper tells Kǒngzǐ's disciples not to be troubled by his loss of official position; he explains that heaven will use Kǒngzǐ like the wooden clapper for a bell (3.24). The mission given to Kǒngzǐ by heaven is not to take political office but to set a model for the future through his teachings.

Taken at face value, these passages make one wonder how anyone could claim that Kǒngzǐ is agnostic, but such passages are rare and all occur in contexts in which the appeals to heaven are means toward some further point.[11] The real difficulty comes in passages suggesting that the forces of the universe do not always help the good, passages recognizing the problem of evil. The most powerful example comes in a discussion of the dangers facing his disciple Zǐlù, who was serving in the state of Lǔ:

> Gōng Bóliáo made false accusations against Zǐlù to the head of the Jì family. Zǐfú Jǐngbó reported it, saying, "My master [Jì Kāngzǐ] certainly has had his resolve confused by Gōng Bóliáo, but my power still suffices to have his corpse displayed in the marketplace." The master said, "If the way will be enacted, that is fate; if the way will be abandoned, that is fate. What can Gōng Bóliáo do about fate?" (14.36)

The term translated here as "fate" is *mìng* 命, which we have encountered already as the "command" or "mandate" of heaven. Gōng Bóliáo and Zǐfú Jǐngbó were both ministers to the powerful Jì family that controlled the state of Lǔ. Kǒngzǐ essentially says that neither has any influence on what will happen to Zǐlù, which will be determined by fate alone. Thus, Kǒngzǐ tells Zǐfú Jǐngbó that he need not interfere. The fact that both the enacting and abandoning of the way is determined by *mìng* indicates that *mìng* itself does not particularly align with the good. At times, the chaos of the world is determined by fate, and human effort to reverse that might be futile. This claim, which one finds explicitly in other Ru texts, is directly criticized by the Mohists. We should recall Zǐlù's future death in the line of duty, his pickled corpse hung above the east gate of Wèi. Although his death is unrelated to the incident in this passage, the compilers of the *Lúnyǔ* would have known how severely Zǐlù was treated by fate.

The injustice of the forces of the world appears in a more personal form around the life and death of Yán Huí, who, as mentioned in the last chapter, became a common figure for the problem of evil. His early death traumatized Kǒngzǐ, whose disciples accuse him of letting his heart be moved too deeply (11.10). Yán Huí's death is rendered all the more poignant by a story from when Kǒngzǐ was surrounded in Kuāng. Yán Huí had fallen behind and Kǒngzǐ feared he had been killed. When he finally reunites with the group, Yán Huí reassures him, "While the master is alive, how could I dare to die?" (11.23). This was a promise that Yán Huí was not able to keep. Kǒngzǐ attributes Yán Huí's death to his having a short *mìng* (6.3, 11.7), just as he says of the deadly and deforming illness of another disciple, Bó Niú: "What destroys him is *mìng*" (6.10). Regarding Yán Huí, Kǒngzǐ also laments, "Alas! Heaven has bereft me! Heaven has bereft me!"

(11.9). The phrase is complex, because *sàng* 喪 means "to lose" or "to cause to be lost," but also "to mourn" or even "to conduct a funeral." The character itself combines the character for "gone," "lost," or "destroyed" (*wáng* 亡) and the character for "crying" or "tears" (*kū* 哭). It could mean that heaven has caused this loss to him or made him mourn, but it could mean more directly that heaven is destroying him—implying that in losing Yán Huí, he loses part of himself.[12] Given Yán Huí's high character, the effects of fate and heaven here are clearly separated from rewards and punishments. Thus Zhū Xī 朱熹 explains *mìng*: "It says that this person should not have this illness but now he does have it, so it must be what heaven commands/fates."[13]

Xú Fùguān has argued that the best way to make sense of the tension between these two sides of the divine is through a distinction between *tiān* (including *tiānmìng*, the "Mandate of Heaven," and *tiāndào*, "the way of heaven") and *mìng* (fate), where the former has ethical meaning and the latter does not (Xú 1969, 80–90).[14] The Mohists make such a division, and it largely holds through the *Lúnyǔ*, although Kǒngzǐ's lament to heaven for Yán Huí's death shows that the lines are not so clear. Even if we could separate these prescriptive and descriptive dimensions according to a terminological distinction between *tiān* and *mìng*, the problem of how to reconcile these two sides would remain. I suspect that there is no single Ru resolution to this problem. Different Ru held different views and these differences appear in the *Lúnyǔ*, sometimes in the words of Kǒngzǐ himself. As we will see in later chapters, Mèngzǐ and Xúnzǐ approach the same issue in very different ways. Even the views of the historical Kǒngzǐ may even have changed over time, perhaps after the death of Yán Huí and his own political failures. We must also consider that coherence in the *Lúnyǔ* must be sought not just on the theoretical level but also in terms of practice. It is quite possible that various individuals, including Kǒngzǐ, did not have a theoretically unified view of the divine and thus maintained what Lee Yearley calls "irresolvable but revelatory and productive tensions" between contradictory views, each of which was useful in different contexts.[15]

If we follow the contours of the problem of evil and look for a position that is theoretically coherent, three possibilities appear. One would be to compromise heaven's goodness. Kǒngzǐ never says that heaven *always* rewards the good and punishes the bad. But weakening heaven's goodness would force a wedge between what heaven does and what we consider right, undermining heaven as a moral authority.[16] A second option would be to lessen heaven's power. Heaven might be a force for the good, but it would not have power over *mìng*. One might read the gatekeeper's comments in this way: it is fate that the world lacks the way and thus Kǒngzǐ cannot take office, but heaven works around this by setting up Kǒngzǐ as a teacher for the future (3.24). The third possibility would be to deny the problem of evil, claiming that apparently bad things actually correspond to a broader plan for the good. Since this is a common interpretation for both the *Lúnyǔ* and the *Mèngzǐ*, we can address both here. Regarding the *Lúnyǔ*, Robert Eno has the most thorough account, claiming that the Ru address the gap between the prescriptive and descriptive aspects of heaven through belief in "a teleological plan." He explains, "This notion shifts the evaluative standard against which events are judged from the present into the distant future, and, in essence, subordinates the descriptive values of experience to prescriptive dogma. Regardless of the evidence, all must be for the good" (1990a, 88). Similarly, Bryan Van Norden writes that the Ru ability to calmly accept fate is "born of the confidence that, whether one succeeds in the short term or not, Heaven has an ethical purpose that will prevail in the long run" (2007, 152).[17]

On these views, Kǒngzǐ's position would be close to that of Leibniz, who tells us that although it may seem that bad things happen, this "is based only on the inadequate knowledge we have of the general harmony of the universe and of the hidden reasons for God's conduct."[18] We have seen that two passages in the *Lúnyǔ* explicitly read heaven's ethical purposes into events, but these far from establish that all events reflect heaven's ethical plans or that all bad things are actually good. On the contrary, many Ru statements are difficult to reconcile with Leibnizian optimism. If the way (*dào* 道) refers to what is good, how could it be good for the way to be discarded (*Lúnyǔ* 14.36)? Or how could it be good for human beings to go through perpetual five-hundred-year cycles of goodness and chaos, as Mèngzǐ says (2B13)? Of course, Leibniz himself shows that—with the proper mix of skepticism, creativity, and logical subtlety—pretty much any event can be interpreted as good. Leibniz could explain why the best possible world required that Yán Huí die young, Bó Niú get leprosy, and Zǐlù end up pickled. The Ru offer no such explanations.[19] Although an argument from silence cannot be decisive, it is almost inconceivable that a view so theoretically central and practically useful would never be mentioned. Similarly, it is difficult to believe that such a counterintuitive view would never have been criticized by enemies of the Ru. The Mohists attack them only for *denying* that the world works on ethical principles. Finally, such a view would have led the Ru in philosophically different directions. For example, explaining the deaths of innocents and the suffering of the masses as serving some ultimate good requires a radical split between appearance and reality. To be successful, it also requires very sophisticated logical maneuvers. Leibniz is a paradigm for both. Ru thinkers made little effort in either direction.

If we rely on the sayings attributed to Kǒngzǐ in the *Lúnyǔ*, then he seems to accept both a morally indifferent fate and an ethically concerned heaven, but the latter element is stronger. In this sense, the gap between the thought of Kǒngzǐ himself and that of Mòzǐ may not be as large as is commonly assumed.[20] Even if both believe in a providential heaven, there are important differences in how this is used. The passages in the *Lúnyǔ* read most naturally as claiming that Kǒngzǐ has something like a personal relation to heaven. Heaven knows him and, because of his importance in maintaining the tradition, will protect him. Kǒngzǐ never articulates a general principle that heaven rewards or protects the good. In contrast, Mòzǐ claims no special relationship with heaven, only taking heaven as setting broad, generally accessible criteria. Heaven sets the basic standard of inclusive care.[21] Concrete policies and cultural forms are left to us. For Kǒngzǐ, specific cultural forms have the direct sanction of heaven.

We see further evidence of a more theistic Ru view in some of the Guōdiàn texts, which appear to generally be Ru but integrate appeals to heaven now associated more with the Mohists.[22] For example, *Chéngzhī wènzhī* 成之聞之 (Completing it, hearing it) says that gentlemen follow along or comply with (*shùn* 順) heaven's constancy (*tiāncháng* 天常) and heaven's virtue (*tiāndé* 天德), doing so through the natural relations between husband and wife, father and son, and sovereign and minister (Liú Zhāo 2003, strips 31–33). Through these relations, they make offerings to (*sì* 祀) heaven's constancy (Liú Zhāo 2003, strips 38–40). The text even says that gentlemen measure by the heart of heaven (*tiānxīn* 天心) (Liú Zhāo 2003, strips 33), a phrase that echoes the Mohist use of the "will of heaven" (*tiānzhì* 天志 or *tiānyì* 天意) as a standard.[23] Another excavated text, the *Táng Yú zhī dào* 唐虞之道 (Way of Táng and Yú), says that sagely people serve heaven, earth, and various spirits by teaching the people proper relations (Liú Zhāo 2003, strips 4–5). The same text says that Yáo was assisted by heaven and earth (strips 15), although it also says that success depends on fate and timing (strips 14–15). In a dialogue between Kǒngzǐ and Zǐgāo in another excavated text, Kǒngzǐ presents the progenitors of the three dynasties as descending from the divine, literally as sons of heaven (Jì 2003, 25–39).[24]

In contrast to these texts, received Ru texts from the Warring States period give much less evidence for anthropomorphic or providential views of heaven.[25] In one passage in the *Lúnyǔ*, Zǐgòng says that heaven intends Kǒngzǐ to be a sage (9.6). A dialogue in the *Xúnzǐ* begins with Zǐlù, when stuck between Chén and Cài, saying he has heard that "heaven will repay those who enact goodness with good fortune, and heaven will repay those who enact badness with misfortune" (8: 526; cf. Knoblock 1988, 28.8). Kǒngzǐ, however, rejects Zǐlù's claim and responds with a fatalistic passage incorporating parts of *Qióng dá yǐ shí* (Failure and success are by timing). This more fatalistic view appears to have become dominant, and the Mohists only criticize the Ru for fatalism and skepticism of heaven's will. One of the most fatalistic claims in the *Lúnyǔ* comes from Kǒngzǐ's disciple, Zǐxià:

> Sīmǎ Niú said anxiously, "People all have brothers; only I have none!" Zǐxià said to him, "I have heard this: 'Death and life have *mìng*; prosperity and honor are with *tiān*.' Gentlemen are reverent and have no errors, they are respectful and have ritual. Within the four seas, all are their brothers. How can gentlemen be troubled by having no brothers?" (12.5)[26]

Zǐxià may be invoking a common saying, but he clearly approves it, and a similar line is attributed to a representative of the Ru in the *Mòzǐ* (48: 455; Johnston 2010, 48.5). Wáng Chōng takes the saying as originating from Kǒngzǐ himself (28: 411). This passage fits other *Lúnyǔ* passages on *mìng*, but here *tiān* plays the same role, with no sense that long or short life, prosperity or honor are distributed according to any ethical purpose.

This element of fatalism and its connection with heaven appears most clearly in the Guōdiàn text *Qióng dá yǐ shí*, which was buried around 300 BCE. It must have been a significant text, because versions of it (or its mother text) appear in several later Ru texts, most notably in the *Xúnzǐ*, where it is put into the mouth of Kǒngzǐ (28: 526–27; Knoblock 1988, 28.8).[27] The Guōdiàn text begins thus:

> There is heaven and there is human; heaven and human have a division. By examining the division between heaven and human, one knows what to do. If there is the right person but not the right age, then even if he is worthy, he cannot enact it. If it is the right age, what difficulty can there be? (Liú Zhāo 2003, strips 1–2)

This is the first known reference to the division between heaven and human. The term for division, *fēn* 分, has a particular sense of the division of roles, thus separating the realm of human action from the movements of heaven. The passage continues by describing historical figures—such as the sage king Shùn, who went from difficulties to success by meeting a ruler who employed him—but then draws a general conclusion invoking Wǔ Zǐxū: "In the beginning they were sunk in obscurity, but later their names spread far. It was not that their virtue increased. Wǔ Zǐxū first accomplished much and then was executed. It was not that his wisdom declined" (Liú Zhāo 2003, strips 9–10). While the text does not use the term *mìng*, timing functions in the same way. The text uses two different words in relation to timing. The first few lines use *shì* 世, which refers to a generation or something like "the times," suggesting the broader situation of the world. The remainder of the text uses *shí* 時, which refers more to the timing of particular events—in this case, whether or not one meets an opportunity. Another significant term is *yù* 遇, which means "to meet" or "to encounter," particularly by chance or luck; here it means to meet an opportunity, more specifically, meeting a ruler who will give one responsibility.[28] Whether or not one meets an opportunity is determined by heaven without regard for wisdom or virtue (Liú Zhāo 2003, strip 11). The claim that "their virtue did not increase" is significant because in earlier texts, such as the *Shàng shū*, (*Book of Documents*), virtue (*dé* 德), is a kind of power that influences heaven and guarantees success. Such a view is explicitly rejected here.

The use of fate (whether labeled *mìng*, *tiān*, *shí*, or *shì*) in these Ru texts is a reasonable recognition of the limits of human power and the fact that good actions do not guarantee success. The appeals to fate, however, must be approached within a horizon of practical concerns. One central Ru worry was the temptation of acting for material gains rather than according to what was right. We see this in numerous passages in the *Lúnyǔ*, such as these:

> The master said, "Prosperity and honor—these are what people desire, but if you cannot use the way to attain then, do not dwell in them. Poverty and dishonor—these are what people hate, but if you cannot use the way to avoid them, do not leave them." (4.5)

> The master said, "Gentlemen plot for the way; they do not plot for food. There is plowing—starvation may be in its midst. There is learning—a salary may be in its midst. Gentlemen are anxious about the way. They are not anxious about poverty." (15.32)

Such passages assume it is best to be both virtuous and successful, but they recognize that these goals often diverge, forcing a choice between doing what is right and doing what is beneficial.

To grasp the role of fate, it is crucial to see how this early Ru position differs from the position later advocated by another Ru, Xúnzǐ. Xúnzǐ aligns motivations toward virtue and toward worldly benefits by arguing that virtue is the most reliable way to achieve success. Success is never guaranteed, but the occasional intervention of fate does not alter the fact that the most prudential course in life is to cultivate the Ru way. While the *Lúnyǔ* and *Mèngzǐ* make similar arguments to the rulers of states, their view of virtue in the lives of individuals is much more pessimistic. For an individual, the Ru way is *not* the most likely route to worldly success. Thus, one must sharply distinguish between the two kinds of motivation, which are often presented through the contrast between a concern for rightness (*yì* 義) and a concern for benefit (*lì* 利). This contrast is drawn through the role of fate. Holding onto rightness and humaneness depends only on our own effort; worldly benefits depend on a multitude of other factors. Thus, even if we dedicate ourselves directly to growing food, we might still starve. External goods depend on fate, as the *Mèngzǐ* says explicitly: "If seeking it has the way but attaining it has fate, then this seeking is of no benefit to attaining. This is seeking in the external" (7A3). If we recognize the dominance of fate over external things, we will realize there is no point in putting our effort into pursuing them. We see the improper response to fate in a passage in which Kǒngzǐ contrasts Yán Huí with another disciple, Zǐgòng: "There is Huí! He has nearly attained it, but he often has nothing. Zǐgòng does not accept fate and multiplies his wealth, but his estimations often hit the mark" (11.19). In itself, having estimations hit the mark is good, but Zǐgòng dedicates his effort toward attaining wealth. We might expect not accepting fate to mean becoming sad and resentful when bad things happen, but Zǐgòng's efforts to get richer actually succeed. Not accepting fate, then, must mean not setting aside concern for the whole realm of things susceptible to fate.

A second Ru concern was with how to deal with failure, a likely prospect for anyone dedicated to reform at that time. Many passages concern peace of mind in the face of loss or danger. What distinguished Yán Huí was not just that he did not strive for wealth but also that he was happy being poor (6.11). This ability to find joy in poverty comes from the cultivation of simple tastes, such as pleasure in coarse rice and clear water (7.16), and social pleasures, such as friendship and music, but its roots lie in confidence in one's own goodness:

> Sīmǎ Niú asked about gentlemen. The master said, "Gentlemen are not anxious or afraid." "Not anxious and not afraid—is this all it takes to be called a gentleman?" The master said, "If you examine inside and have no defects, what is there to be anxious about? What is there to fear?" (12.4)

We have already seen the term translated here as "anxious," *yōu* 憂, as part of what Xú Fùguān calls *yōuhuàn yìshí*, a sense of anxious concern and responsibility. Two passages repeat what must have been a slogan: the humane are not anxious (9.29). This freedom from worry, though, extends only to external things, which are outside of our control. Turned inward, worry is required for all but the most sagely. Gentlemen are not anxious about poverty, but they are anxious about the way (15.32). The tension in these two senses of worry appears in Kǒngzǐ's self-descriptions: he is one who in his joy forgets worries (7.19), but also one with four worries: not cultivating virtue, not discussing what he learns, hearing what is right but being unable to follow it, and not being able to correct what is wrong (7.3).[29] The connection between appeals to fate and the acceptance of trouble is familiar, as when we comfort someone by saying, "There was nothing you could do about it," or "It was meant to be." That seems to be Zǐxià's purpose when he tells Sīmǎ Niú that his having no brothers is a matter of fate. Spinoza generalizes this function into a psychological law: "Insofar as the mind understands all things as necessary, it has a greater power over the affects, or is less acted on by them."[30] This connection between fatalism and peace of mind appears in the conclusion of *Qióng dá yǐ shí*: "If action is not for success, then one can be in failure yet without [resentment. If acting is not] for a name, then one can be unknown yet without regrets" (Liú Zhāo 2003, strips 11–12).[31] If we attribute wealth and recognition to heaven or fate, then poverty and obscurity will not upset us.

These two uses of *mìng*—to redirect our motivation and to bring comfort when in trouble—are mutually supporting. The ability to remain happy in poverty decreases our motivation for seeking wealth, while realizing that pursuing wealth is useless helps us be content without it. The centrality of fate in this process probably explains why the *Lúnyǔ* would go so far as to say, "If one does not know fate, there is nothing by which to become a gentleman" (20.3). If one cannot be content with worldly failure, then one cannot resist the temptation to sacrifice what is right for the sake of success, and one cannot become a gentleman. These points come together in another passage on Kǒngzǐ in trouble between Chén and Cái:

> When [Kǒngzǐ] was cut off from food in Chén, his followers became so ill they could not get up. Zǐlù, with evident anger, said, "Do even gentlemen have this kind of failure [*qióng*]?" The master said, "Gentlemen are firm in failure, but petty people are swept away by it." (15.2)

The Critique of Fate in the *Mòzǐ*

The *Mòzǐ* is best understood as a toolbox for activists whose primary goal was to persuade rulers and their advisors to introduce reforms that would benefit the people.[32] They put forward a platform consisting of ten planks, and then gather a variety of arguments that might be used to support each of them.[33] The best known and most fundamental is "inclusive caring" (*jiān ài* 兼愛). The term *jiān* is generally a grammatical particle marking the inclusion of multiple actions or things at the same time. The term *ài* has a broad range, at a minimum referring to care in the sense of "taking care of," but frequently including an emotive dimension that at its strongest could be translated as "love." The root meaning of *jiān ài* is incorporating others into the sphere of one's care. The *Mòzǐ* explains it thus:

> See other people's states as you see your own state, see other people's families as you see your own family, and see other people's body as you see your own body. Thus, if the feudal lords care for each other then they do not fight in the wilds, if family chiefs care for each other then they do not coerce each other, if people care for each other then they do not rob each other, if sovereigns and ministers care for each other then they are kind and loyal, if fathers and sons care for each other then they are nurturing and filial, if older and younger brothers care for each other then they harmonize, and if the world's people all care for each other, then the strong do not seize the weak, the many do not oppress the few, the prosperous do not demean the poor, the noble do not lord it over the lowly, and the clever do not deceive the simple. (15: 103; cf. Johnston 2010, 15.3)

The Mohists do not take "inclusive care" as eliminating the particularities of roles and social relations.[34] The first "Inclusive Caring" ("Jiān ài" 兼愛) chapter begins by defining disorder as the absence of filial piety (14: 99; Johnston 2010, 14.2), and the third version ends by saying that inclusive caring allows one to be "a kind sovereign, a conscientious minister, a nurturing father, a filial son, a friendly older brother, and a respectful younger brother" (16: 127; Johnston 2010, 16.15). The Mohists assume that we will put our efforts primarily into our particular roles and relationships.[35] Caring inclusively functions primarily as a restriction—we cannot harm others in order to benefit ourselves, our families, or our states. Three positive duties also appear consistently in explaining inclusive caring: to assist those who have fallen through the cracks of the family-based care system (such as orphans and the childless elderly); to contribute what one has in excess to those who need it; to work toward peace and order in the world.[36]

Other Mohist planks offer specific policies. "Elevating Worthies" ("Shàngxián" 尚賢) and "Conforming Upward" ("Shàngtóng" 尚同) lay out the need for a meritocratic government reliant on rewards and punishments and open to those of ability without regard for class or family connection. Several planks center on reducing the wastefulness of the upper classes: "Restraining Expenses" ("Jiéyòng" 節用), "Restraining Funerals" ("Jiézàng" 節葬), and "Against Orchestras" ("Fēiyuè" 非樂). The "Against Invasions" ("Fēigōng" 非攻) chapters appeal both to reducing waste and to inclusively caring for the people, including the people of other states.

The immediate basis for the Mohist arguments is benefit (*lì* 利), taken primarily as what is required for life: food for the hungry, clothes for the cold, rest for the weary, and order where there is chaos. The connection to basic human needs is visible in the roots of the character, which shows grain (禾) and a blade used for harvesting (刂). For groups, the goals are often given as wealth, orderliness, and greater population. Benefit in these senses is taken as obviously good:

> The standard of the humane toward the world is not different from the standard filial sons use toward their parents. Now what is the standard filial sons use toward their parents? If parents are poor then they work to make them prosperous; if their people are few then they work to increase them; if their masses are disordered then they work to order them. In doing this, they will stop only when their strength is not sufficient, their resources are not enough, and their wisdom does not understand. They do not dare spare any remaining strength, conceal any plans or neglect any benefits and not do them for their parents. In these three tasks, the standard for filial sons toward parents is like this. The standard of the humane toward the world also is like this. (25: 169; cf. Johnston 2010, 25.1)

To determine what we consider good, the Mohists examine what we do for those we care deeply about, like our parents. With that standard, we can know what humane people—those who care inclusively—want for whole world.

The Mohists took skepticism about heaven and the belief in blind fate as among the greatest dangers to inclusively promoting benefit. Three of the planks of the Mohist platform address these issues: "Will of Heaven" ("Tiānzhì" 天志), "Against Fate" ("Fēimìng" 非命), and "Clarifying Ghosts" ("Mínggǔi" 明鬼). They saw the Ru as one of their most dangerous foes. In a passage in the "Gōng Mèng" (公孟) chapter, Mòzǐ lists four policies of the Ru that could destroy the world. One is that they take heaven and spirits as not discerning (*míng* 明) or numinous (*shén* 神). Another is that they take fate (*mìng*) as existing and thus failure and success, order and disorder, as being outside human control (48: 459–

460; Johnston 2010, 48.14).³⁷ In fact, the Mohist concern is not so much with a superhuman realm as with human power and responsibility. The Mohists seek to preserve the view that human beings are primarily responsible for the condition of the world, and thus to encourage a commitment to changing the material conditions of human life, in particular, to ending war and poverty. In this view, the Mohists are the direct inheritors of the early Zhōu "humanism" founded on the Mandate of Heaven (*tiānmìng*), but they draw a sharp separation between the two terms, taking *tiān* (heaven) as a force for the good and *mìng* (fate) as morally indifferent. This chapter will follow that distinction, first discussing fate and then turning toward heaven.

We can begin by examining the view of fate that the Mohists oppose. The clearest statement of this position is in the "Against Ru" ("Fēi Rú" 非儒) chapter, which says,

> Those who insistently hold that there is fate promote it by saying: "Long life and short life, poverty and prosperity, safety and danger, order and disorder, certainly have *tiānmìng* and cannot be reduced or increased. Failure and success, punishment and reward, luck and harm are ultimately set. Human wisdom and effort cannot make them." (39: 290–91; cf. Johnston 2010, 39.3)

A version in the "Gōng Mèng" chapter is briefer: "Poverty and prosperity, long life or short life, certainly lie with heaven and cannot be decreased or increased" (48: 455; cf. Johnston 2010, 48.5). The phrasing is similar enough to *Lúnyǔ* 12.5 that they probably reflect a common source. The Mohist formulations add that these things cannot be decreased or increased, but the passage quoted above from the *Mèngzǐ* uses the same term, saying that for external things determined by fate, seeking is of no benefit or increase (*yì* 益) to attaining (7A3). In this case, then, the position attributed to the Ru by the Mohists appears to be a fair statement of what at least some Ru actually advocated.

The Mohists offer a variety of arguments against fate. Some appeal to historical authorities, either to the words of the sagely kings or to what is implied by their practices. Historical precedents for fatalism are acknowledged but dismissed as excuses developed by brutal and incompetent kings unwilling to admit their own failure (37: 279; Johnston 2010, 37.4).³⁸ The main argument the Mohists use against the existence of fate is the empirical evidence that hard work brings success, contrasting the sagely kings with the brutal kings who lost their dynasties. The most detailed formulation appears in the third of the "Against Fate" chapters. It begins by saying that the sagely kings of the former dynasties desired to encourage good people, so they set up teachings and systems of rewards and punishments. In this way, they thought they could bring order and safety. The Mohists take this trust in education and rewards and punishments already to be an implicit denial of fatalism. The argument continues:

> At those times [shí 時], the age [shì 世] did not shift and the people did not alter. The government above changed and so the people reformed their practices. Existing under Jié and Zhòu, the world was disordered. Existing under Tāng and Wǔ, the world was ordered. The world being ordered was from the work of Tāng and Wǔ. The world being disordered was from the crimes of Jié and Zhòu. Looking at it in this way, then safety and danger, order and disorder all exist from the governing of those above. So how can one say that there is fate? (37: 278–79; cf. Johnston 2010, 37.2)

This argument is directed against claims that order, safety, and honor are determined by fate rather than effort. More specifically, it attacks claims to the importance of having the right time, echoing *Qióng dá yǐ shí* in using both *shí* 時 and *shì* 世. The comparison between Jié and Tāng sets up a controlled experiment, where the external conditions (the timing and the people) remain the same yet the results diverge. The only difference in causes that explains the difference in effects is that Tāng worked hard for the good while Jié was lazy and bad.[39] Implicit in the argument is that the time of Jié was one of the most extreme cases of the world abandoning the way—and yet even at that time, Tāng was able to bring order to the whole world.

While the Mohists argue that fatalism is *false*, they emphasize that it is *dangerous*. The passage in the "Gōng Mèng" chapter that lists the disastrous policies of the Ru explains that if people believe external results are determined by fate, they surely will not work hard (48: 459; Johnston 2010, 48.14). A more developed formulation of this argument appears in the third "Against Fate" chapter:

> Why is it that kings, dukes, and great men go to court early and retire late, listening to the counsels of government, dividing things in the court evenly, not daring to be lazy or negligent? We say, because they think that if they work hard it will all be well managed and if they do not work hard it must be disordered; if they work hard there will be safety and if they do not work hard there must be danger. Thus they do not dare be lazy and negligent. (37: 283–85; cf. Johnston 2010, 37.7–8)

The passage makes parallel claims that ministers attend to their offices with dedication because they believe they can thus attain honor and glory, that farmers work hard in the fields to be prosperous and full, and that women work hard in weaving to become prosperous and warm. The passage concludes that if all of these people accepted fate, they would cease to work so hard. The result would be disorder, poverty, and—ultimately—the collapse of the state. It was precisely this belief in fate that destroyed the Xià and Shàng dynasties.

The Mohists are often taken as unfairly representing the position of the Ru, so it is important to recognize the structure of their argument. They do not accuse the Ru of advocating laziness and opposing hard work. On the contrary, a passage in the "Gōng Mèng" chapter accuses the Ru of contradicting themselves because they promote diligent study but also say that success depends on fate (48: 455; Johnston 2010, 48.5). The argument is not that the Ru *advocate* a passive response to fatalism, but that their doctrine leads to that result. The power of this claim depends on one's views of human motivation. The Mohists do not articulate a theory of human nature or motivation, and they mention a number of motives for action, including a desire to emulate superiors and a tendency to reciprocate the way we are treated.[40] Several passages appeal to ethical motivations, such as the desire to benefit one's parents or the sense that stealing is wrong, and two passages state in more general terms that people act on what they consider to be right.[41] The Mohists also believe that we can be motivated by arguments.[42] Nonetheless, the Mohists assume that people generally act for the sake of rewards and benefits.[43] One finds this in explicit claims about motivation, such as "What the people most deeply desire is life and what they most deeply hate is death" (9: 65; cf. Johnston 2010, 9.11), or that without the basic necessities of life, even fathers and sons will turn against each other (25: 177–78; Johnston 2010, 25.7). More convincing, however, is that half of the Mohist platform is concerned with aligning rewards with good actions, and the large majority of their arguments are based on showing that benefits will follow from the actions they recommend. Rewards and punishments remain fundamental in the ideal state described in the "Conforming Upward" chapters, and even the worthy are attracted primarily by rewards (10: 65–66; Johnston 2010, 10.1). This follows because "the world's officials and gentlemen all desire prosperity and honor and all hate poverty and lowliness" (10: 71; cf. Johnston 2010, 10.5). In this view, the Mohists diverge from the emphasis of the Ru on virtue and role models as the basis for political order. This motivation toward benefit is crucial for understanding the Mohist opposition to fatalism—if most people act for the sake of benefit, then teaching them that order, wealth, and honor follow from fate rather than effort will necessarily lead them to stop working hard. In making this point, the Mohists do not, and need not, say that *all* people necessarily act *only* for benefits. They themselves were famous for their willingness to forsake personal benefit and comfort in order to promote the common good.[44] The Mohists need only argue that it is unrealistic to expect most people to reach this level of dedication.

We have seen that the Ru use of *mìng* is primarily directed toward encouraging certain reactions in particular contexts. The Mohists point out the incoherencies, problems, and dangers that arise from thinking consistently through these pragmatic and contextual uses.[45] The basis for these criticisms is in the Ru distinction between the external and internal. One can, of course, have a consistent philosophical position based on achieving peace of mind through a distinction between the internal and external, as we see in the Stoic tradition.[46] In a Chinese context, Sòngzǐ was said to have such a position, unaffected by praise and blame because he firmly set the division between internal and external (*Zhuāngzǐ* 1: 16–17; Mair 1994, 5). Such a position, however, is problematic for the Ru, because of their emphasis on the relationality of the self and the importance of genuine feelings (*qíng* 情). Can one really be a filial son yet be unperturbed by a mother's early death? Can one be truly humane but look with an unmoved heart upon poverty, starvation, and warfare? Yet poverty and death are external, controlled by fate rather than ourselves. We see here one of the most significant tensions in early Ru thought, one that has drawn little attention but can be generalized as between the concepts of anxious concern (*yōu* 憂), and what Mèngzǐ calls an "unmoved heart" (*búdòngxīn* 不動心) (2A2). At the same time that "the humane have no anxieties," Kǒngzǐ criticizes someone who feels upset for only one year after the death of a parent (*Lúnyǔ* 17.21). Mèngzǐ develops the role of emotional sensitivity further, praising the feeling of distress we feel at seeing a child in danger (2A6) or a panicked animal about to die (1A7), taking such feelings as the basis for being human and for being humane.[47] Yet death—of the child or the ox or a parent—is surely within the domain of fate. Should we calmly accept it, or not?

More precisely, the Mohists take advantage of two contradictions in the Ru use of fate. The first cuts along lines of class. It may be admirable to teach some so-called gentlemen not to be concerned with material things—to say as Kǒngzǐ does, that even if you dedicate your life to farming, you may not end up with food. That same advice is not so good for farmers. Some people need to work for material things and need to believe their efforts will bear fruit. The second cuts between personal and common interest—a gentleman should not be concerned about his own suffering or poverty but should be concerned about the suffering and poverty of other people. The Ru would accept both distinctions. Their appeals to fate occur only in discussions with other gentlemen, and there is no evidence that they thought it should be taught to the people in general. They rarely appeal to fate when it comes to the suffering of the people, although personal political failure—failure to have the way enacted—obviously affects the people as well as oneself. The Mohists would not object to these distinctions either. They promote a division of labor based on ability, in which some are concerned with governing while others dedicate themselves directly to production, and their ideal is inclusive care for all rather than partial concern for one's own benefit. The problem is that neither distinction can be made through a coherent account of fate. If we say that poverty is due to fate and is not worth struggling against, we will help redirect gentlemen toward self-cultivation—but we also must admit that the poverty of the people is fated and not worth struggling against. If instead we say that poverty can be reduced through human effort, then we encourage social action on behalf of the common people—but we also tell gentlemen that they could become rich if they worked at it. The Mohist criticisms show a greater concern with coherent, defensible claims, but their worries are still practical. Psychologically, the acceptance that follows from convincing a person that they have no control over the material conditions of their own lives too easily leads toward complacency about the conditions of the people in general.

I suspect there is no unified view of fate in the *Lúnyǔ* as a whole (and certainly not among the Ru in general), but we could articulate two possible coherent positions, both of which have textual support. One would be to affirm the fatalist position that the Mohists accuse the Ru of advocating. The response would focus instead on motivation.[48] This position would allow that a good person strives to change the external world, from alleviating poverty to providing a fancy coffin for a parent, but these would not be of *direct* concern. Our motivation would be entirely internal, coming from a concern for acting ethically. For this reason, failure to succeed in these external endeavors would not upset us, while failure to make our greatest effort in them would. This position would fit passages that advocate struggling for change even when it is impossible. In one passage in the *Lúnyǔ*, Zǐlù encounters a recluse, whom he then criticizes:

> Not to take office is to lack rightness. The regulations between old and young cannot be abandoned—so then how can the rightness between sovereign and minister be abandoned? Desiring to purify his person, he disrupts the great relations. Gentlemen in taking office enact what is right. As for the way not being enacted—they already know that! (18.7)

D. C. Lau translates the final line less literally: "As for putting the Way into practice, he knows all along that it is hopeless" (1979, 13). Even when it is hopeless to do so, gentlemen strive to take office and enact rightness. They do so because political relations are just as inescapable as familial relations.

Another passage involving Zǐlù and two recluses develops this point in explicitly humanistic terms. In the midst of farming, the recluses make this criticism of Zǐlù and his master: "Flooding! Flooding!—all the world is like this! Who has the means to change it? Rather than follow a scholar who flees one person after another, how about following scholars who flee the whole age?" (18.6). The term translated as "whole age" is *shì*, 世, which we have seen in *Qióng dá yǐ shí*. In an age that is bad, rather than flee from one ruler to another hoping for success, wouldn't it make more sense to withdraw entirely? Kǒngzǐ does not respond by claiming he can make a difference. He simply says, "One cannot flock together with birds and beasts. If I associate not with people like these, with whom shall I associate? If the world had the way, I would not have to alter it" (18.6). Whether or not one can succeed, we human beings have no choice but to be human and associate with each other. Kǒngzǐ says this disconsolately or with a sigh: the term is *wǔrán* 憮然, which ranges in shades of meaning from "regretful" to "hopeless," combining the radical for the heart (忄/心) with the character meaning "lack," "emptiness," or "nonbeing" (*wú* 無).[49] In this sigh, we see the tragic element in early Ru thought. In another passage, Kǒngzǐ says simply, "There are sprouts that fail to flower! There are flowers that fail to fruit!" (9.22).

A position of dedication to changing the external world even though success and failure are fated would fit most of what the Ru say. As a position, though, it has at least two problems, both of which the Mohists highlight. First, it is empirically false. Human effort does contribute to attaining external things, even if it does not guarantee them. The contrast between Tāng and Jié demonstrates this point well enough. Second, this position assumes that people will make full effort toward a goal while believing this effort is of no use—completely separating consequences from motivation, the external from the internal. Such dedication to an unattainable goal is surely possible. In many ways, Mèngzǐ's argument that human beings naturally tend toward the good is an attempt to articulate an account of human motivation that would justify acting for the good without regard to consequences, as we will see in chapter 4. Nonetheless, the Mohists are reasonable in doubting that most people will be like Kǒngzǐ, described as one who "knows it cannot be done but still does it" (*Lúnyǔ* 14.38). To make matters worse, the Ru themselves use the connection between fate and de-motivation. As we have seen, the main function of saying that external things are determined by fate is that it reduces our desire to seek them.

These difficulties make this strong fatalist position implausible, so one might suspect that the Mohists exaggerate the Ru position. A more plausible view would be to admit that human effort is one of the many factors that determine events.[50] Many Ru passages do claim that humaneness brings benefits, particularly at the political level.[51] Conversely, bad people usually end up harmed: "The master said, 'People live through being upright. To live without it, one escapes only by luck'" (6.19).[52] In general, good people succeed and bad people are punished, but there are no guarantees. Sometimes we get lucky, or unlucky. Since the complexity of things makes this impossible to know beforehand, we can only strive to do our best. Once we fail, then we can console ourselves by appeal to fate. As an account of fate, this view is quite reasonable, and if Mèngzǐ or Kǒngzǐ had a coherent view, I suspect this was it. The problem is that such a position contradicts the actual *function* of *mìng* in a variety of Ru texts, including the *Lúnyǔ* and *Mèngzǐ*. Their appeals to fate rely on the following assumption: if we recognize that a thing cannot be attained by our own effort, then our desire for it will be weakened. Fate can only function in this way, though, if external things are significantly outside our control. The more one allows for the efficacy of human action in attaining external goods, the less one can use fate to exclude them as legitimate objects of concern.

Heaven as a Standard

We can now turn from *mìng* to *tiān*. The Mohists argue that the will of heaven favors inclusive caring. The term translated here as "will," *zhì* 志, depicts an officer, general, or scholar (*shì* 士) above the heart (*xīn* 心). It refers to the direction of the heart, not momentary choices or a faculty for making choices but rather a settled tendency, something like "commitment" or "resolve." Some passages instead use the term *yì* 意, a term corresponding better to "intention." Although the Mohists are the only philosophers we know of to have explicitly defended the goodness of heaven, this view must have held historical and popular authority in the Warring States period. We have seen that Kǒngzǐ warns against offending heaven and calls on heaven to punish him if he has done wrong. While the *Dàodéjīng* generally reacts against anthropomorphic views of heaven, several passages explicitly claim that heaven helps the good (e.g., 79, 81). One recently excavated text, *Sān dé* 三德 (Three virtues), gives us a glimpse of other views of divine retribution. The text mixes a variety of rules, from moderation in desires to ritual prescriptions to guides for sustainable agriculture, that are enforced by divine forces, mentioning both *tiān* (heaven) and Shàngdì. Both are described in anthropomorphic terms as being angry or pleased. This position is summarized thus: "If one does not avoid what should be avoided, heaven will then send down disasters. If one does not stop where one should stop, heaven will then send down anomalies. Even if one's own body is not destroyed, it will reach to sons and grandsons."[53] Although the emphasis on divine retribution might seem Mohist, the focus on specific rules is contrary to the Mohist approach. The text seems to represent an entirely different pattern of thinking about divine rewards and punishments, one probably closer to the views of popular religion.[54]

The central Mohist claim about heaven is given in simple anthropomorphic terms: "If I do what heaven desires, heaven also will do what I desire" (26: 193; cf. Johnston 2010, 26.2). What do I desire? I desire good fortune (*fú* 福) and prosperity (*lù* 祿), and I hate misfortune (*huò* 禍) and afflictions (*suì* 祟). All four terms were connected with the supernatural (marked by the 示/礻 radical) but also were frequently connected with fatalism and events outside our control.[55] The Mohists keep the supernatural but remove the element of contingency—fortune and misfortune depend entirely on whether or not you do what heaven wants. What is it that heaven wants? All three versions of the "Will of Heaven" chapter give the direct answer as rightness (*yì* 義). They then explicate rightness to say that heaven likes us to "inclusively care for each other and interact to benefit each other" (26: 195; cf. Johnston 2010, 26.4). This claim is detailed further:

> Heaven's intention does not desire for big states to invade small states, for great families to disrupt small families, for the strong to oppress the weak, for the clever to swindle the simple, or for the noble to lord over the humble. These are what heaven does not desire, but it does not stop just with these. Heaven desires people who have strength to work with others, those who have a way [*dào* 道] to teach others, and those who have wealth to distribute it to others. It also desires those above to vigorously attend to governing and those below to vigorously deal with their work. (27: 199; cf. Johnston 2010, 27.3)

What heaven wants is just what Mohist ethics requires. If we do these things then heaven will reward us; if we do not do them then heaven will punish us.

This image of a Mohist god laying down the law may seem too familiar, but two factors disrupt any attempt to equate heaven with a law-giving god.[56] First, the Mohists did not believe anyone had direct access to heaven as an anthropomorphic being.[57] Heaven gives no explicit commandments, scriptures, or revelation. While heaven sometimes uses aberrations in nature to convey its punishments, heaven also encompasses the regular natural patterns by which the world works, including social patterns.[58] Thus, our relationship to heaven is effectively identical to our relationship to the world, and the claim that heaven rewards the good amounts to saying that the world is structured so that people who care for and benefit others will succeed. The Mohists give historical examples to support this view, contrasting the success of Yǔ, Tāng, Wén, and Wǔ with the bitter ends of Jié and Zhòu. Specific arguments for the rewards of good actions are scattered through almost every chapter of the *Mòzǐ*, rarely invoking heaven directly. The "Inclusive Caring" chapters argue that someone who cares for other people will attract friends and assistance, and someone who harms people will draw enemies and hostility. The "Against Invasions" chapters argue that a state that invades others will bring harm on itself through waste of resources, loss of lives, disruptions to the cycles of farming, and the hostility of states that feel threatened. Extravagance in funerals, music, or expenses all deplete the resources of the state and require making oppressive demands on the people, ultimately weakening the state's defenses and leading to chaos. These chapters argue in detail for natural connections between good actions and success. Since heaven encompasses these connections, the success of the sagely kings can be attributed to heaven in one place but attributed to their elevating the worthy, minimizing wasteful expenses, or caring inclusively for the people in others. Considering that heaven also encompasses human patterns makes more plausible the Mohist claim that anyone who kills an innocent person will be punished by heaven (26: 196; Johnston 2010, 26.6). Murderers really do tend to be harmed, not directly by the divine, but either by the state or by the friends and family of the murder victim. Mèngzǐ, for example, also claims that anyone who kills an innocent person will be killed, but explains this as a result of revenge (7B7). The Mohists likely have such human reactions in mind.

The second important qualification for identifying heaven with "God" is that heaven serves only to increase human efficacy. It is striking that the historical events used to argue for the assistance of heaven are the very same examples used to argue that success depends on us rather than fate. This focus on efficacy qualifies the goodness of heaven:

> So then how do I know that heaven desires rightness and hates non-rightness?
> I say: when the world has rightness there is life; when the world lacks rightness

there is death. With rightness, there is prosperity; without rightness, there is poverty. With rightness, there is order; without rightness, there is disorder. (26: 193; cf. Johnston 2010, 26.2)

This passage simply claims that when people cooperate in peace, they will live in prosperity and order. When they rob each other to benefit themselves, life will be nasty, brutish, and short. Heaven only ensures that if we try to benefit each other, we will succeed. The agency of heaven is reduced to amplifying the power of human beings. In this context, the Mohist position is not as implausible as their rhetoric sometimes suggests: if we really did all work to help each other, we probably would all be able to lead decent lives.

The role of heaven, though, cannot be limited to the patterns of nature, precisely because those patterns seem too loose to guarantee that the good always succeed. The Mohists confront a basic problem in attempting to control a populace through reward and punishment—the rewards and punishments can never be quite thorough enough. Without justice in an afterlife, the Mohists fill the gap with ghost stories. As they say, one might plausibly escape the will of the ruler, but if one commits a crime against heaven one has no place to flee. Heaven's discernment or clear-sightedness penetrates even the darkest forests and valleys (26: 192–93; Johnston 2010, 26.1). We see here a fundamental tension in the Mohist position. Their emphasis on the efficacy of human action leads them to use heaven and ghosts to ensure justice, but the same concern for action also requires them to oppose relying on the divine to do our work for us. One passage, for example, criticizes the use of what were commonly accepted practices of divination (47: 447–48; Johnston 2010, 47.18).[59] In another passage, Mòzǐ ridicules two ministers who sacrificed at a forest altar, asking the spirits to help them to get along harmoniously. Mòzǐ says this is as ridiculous as covering your eyes and then asking the spirits to make you see (46: 437; Johnston 2010, 46.21). Such passages align Mòzǐ with more skeptical trends and problematize claims that he simply follows the views of the common people. The basis for the Mohist position, though, is practical—reliance on divine intervention would run counter to the very purpose of introducing the divine, which is to increase human agency and responsibility.

The attempt to enforce social order through appeal to divine retribution is familiar, but the Mohists develop a "religion" stripped of every element that cannot be demonstrated to benefit the living. Moreover, it is a religion entirely directed toward the good of the common people in this life—there is no pie in the sky when you die. The only possible exception to the alignment between the divine will and human good is the desire that heaven and spirits have for sacrifices, as a number of passages say that spirits will become angry and hostile if not given sacrifices. Every appeal to the importance of sacrifices, however, comes in arguments for making the people prosperous and numerous enough be able to sacrifice well (e.g., 25: 179–80; Johnston 2010, 25.9). Moreover, the sacrifices themselves must serve the human good. In one passage, a person tells Mòzǐ that although he sacrifices more and more to the spirits, members of his family have died, his cattle do not thrive, and he himself is ill. Mòzǐ explains that while spirits like sacrifices, what they like most is for us to take care of each (49: 476–77; Johnston 2010, 49.16). In making ghosts and spirits care about rightness rather than their own interests, the Mohists again diverge from popular religion.[60] The conclusion of the "Clarifying Ghosts" chapter adds one more important point: regardless of the existence of spirits, sacrifices benefit human beings by bringing them together and promoting mutual affection (31: 249; Johnston 2010, 31.20). Although this passage is sometimes taken to imply skepticism toward ghosts and spirits, it makes more sense as an attempt to align the divine with the human, showing that divine forces ask for nothing that is not already good for us.[61]

For the Mohists, heaven functions as an enforcer of morality and as its standard. The first "Will of Heaven" chapter quotes Mòzǐ:

> I have heaven's intention like wheelwrights have the compass and woodworkers have the square. The wheelwright and woodworker hold their compass and square in order to measure what is rectangular and circular in the world, saying, "What fits is right, what doesn't fit is wrong." Now the writings of the world's scholar-officials and gentlemen are more than can be listed, and their sayings are more than can be counted. Above they persuade feudal lords; below they persuade outstanding scholar-officials. Yet in their rightness and humaneness, they are very far apart.[62] How do I know this? I say: I have attained the world's clearest standard to measure them. (26: 197; cf. Johnston 2010, 26.8)

The Mohist position can again be best approached from the context of the early Ru. Although Kǒngzǐ took his ethical project as having the support of heaven, the *Lúnyǔ* does not appeal to heaven as a *standard*. This contrast between Kǒngzǐ and Mòzǐ is perhaps clearest in a passage that might at first seem to link them. When Kǒngzǐ calls on heaven to punish him if he has done wrong, he does not explain to Zǐlù what heaven wants, producing a principle by which actions could then be measured. The appeal to heaven does not yield a publicly accessible criterion. The Ru have little choice. While they occasionally appeal to heaven to illustrate elements of sageliness, they can point only to the general sense that heaven is constant, subtle, and all-encompassing.[63] As norms, these traits support the Mohist position much more than the Ru. Moreover, the shift toward fatalism in response to the problem of evil made the patterns of nature less and less plausible as a standard. While Kǒngzǐ appeals to heaven in justifying his mission, both *Qióng dá yǐ shí* and the *Mèngzǐ* posit some degree of division between heaven and their own humanistic ethics.

Kǒngzǐ and his earliest disciples show little concern for justifying the way. They take some things as obviously good and they explicitly rely on tradition. Among Kǒngzǐ's most famous self-descriptions is the following: "A transmitter and not a maker, trusting and loving the ancients, I might compare myself to Old Péng" (7.1). He also says, "I am not one who is born and knows it; loving the ancients, I am one who is diligent in seeking it" (7.20). We have already seen that Kǒngzǐ's mission—guaranteed by heaven—was to preserve and transmit ancient culture. It is tradition, rather than the patterns of nature, that serves as his standard. Thus Mèngzǐ tells us explicitly that the "compass and square" are the sages (4A1, 4A2), and Xúnzǐ says the standard is ritual (19: 356; Knoblock 1988, 19.2d). This attachment to the past remained definitive of Ru thought, something often pointed out by their opponents, from Mòzǐ and Hánfēizǐ to Chinese intellectuals of the early twentieth century.[64] Of course one cannot simply repeat the past. Tradition must be interpreted, adapted, and internalized, which requires creativity and individuality.[65] Nonetheless, Kǒngzǐ adequately states his position: "The Zhōu looked to the two earlier dynasties—so rich and plentiful in cultural patterns! I follow the Zhōu" (3.14).

This conservatism could not serve the Mohists, whose radicality as cultural critics required a foothold beyond culture from which to evaluate cultural practices. Furthermore, as relative outsiders, the Mohists would be reluctant to rely on a tradition accessible only to the highly educated, seeking instead a standard equally accessible to all.[66] Heaven served these functions. The Mohist shift toward heaven as a standard includes a positive argument for the role of heaven and a negative argument against the reliability of convention and authority. We see both in a passage from the "Models and Standards" ("Fǎyí" 法儀) chapter:

> So then what is it that can be a model for bringing order? Should people all take their fathers and mothers as models? The world's fathers and mothers are many but the humane are few; if people take their fathers and mothers as models, the model is not humane. A model which is not humane cannot be a model.

The same argument is applied to teachers and to political leaders and then concludes,

> So then what can be a model for bringing order? We say, there is no model like heaven. The actions of heaven are broad and without private concern, its extension is generous and does not cease, its illumination lasts long and does not wane. Thus sagely kings model themselves after it. (4: 21–22; cf. Johnston 2010, 4.2)[67]

The core of this passage is the unreliability of appeals to authority. Not all parents or sovereigns are good, so we cannot rely on what they say.[68] The Mohists essentially raise a skeptical argument against reliance on authority and then suggest a solution—heaven. The same point is raised in the passage quoted above, which emphasizes that the people now teaching and writing are so numerous that one cannot adequately take account of all of them (26: 197; Johnston 2010, 26.8). Facing these conflicting viewpoints, the only alternative to skepticism would be some independent criterion. Similar concerns underlie Mohist discussions of criteria in other chapters as well. The argument in "Restraining Funerals" is particularly significant. The chapter begins by listing as criteria the three benefits of enriching the people, increasing their numbers, and making them orderly. It then notes that historical precedent cannot resolve questions about funerals, since all sides of the dispute claim to follow the way of the ancient sage kings (25: 169–70; Johnston 2010, 25.2). Later in that chapter, Mòzǐ draws a key distinction between rightness or morality (*yì* 義), and custom (*sú* 俗). He points out that different cultures consider different practices correct, mentioning one in which the bodies of the dead are burned on a pile of wood and another in which the flesh of the corpse is discarded and only the bones are buried (25: 187–190; Johnston 2010, 25.14–15). If customs vary like this, then one cannot justify a practice by appeal to custom or tradition. One needs criteria that transcend and thus can decide between cultural practices.

Since the standard provided by heaven stands above worldly political authorities, it also grounds the possibility of political critique and resistance. The "Will of Heaven" chapters each contain an argument that begins by claiming that rightness functions by bringing order, but to do so it must come from those above to those below. Thus the common people are ordered by the rightness of officials, but officials need someone to order them, and these need someone to order them, leading up to the son of heaven as the final human authority. The key to the argument, though, is what follows it:

> Now the world's officials and gentlemen all see that the son of heaven corrects the world but they do not see that heaven corrects the son of heaven. Ancient sagely people understood this and explained to the people, "If the son of heaven has goodness, heaven can reward him. If the son of heaven has errors, heaven can punish him." If the son of heaven's punishments and rewards are not appropriate or his attending to counsels is not centered, heaven sends down sickness and misfortune, and the frost and dew are not timely. (28.4: 210; cf. Johnston 2010, 28.4)

This may seem like a fantasy invented to control the one person beyond the power of the state, but if we consider that rewards and punishments are based in the structure of the world itself, then the Mohists really claim that rulers are subject to the laws of the world. They are constrained by consequences (rewards and punishments) just like everyone else. Although the passage mentions irregular weather, heaven's punishments include regular patterns as well—a ruler who spends on lavish parties will deplete the state's resources and alienate the people; a ruler who invades neighboring states will end up having his own state invaded. These count as punishments from heaven. In this sense, earthly rulers cannot act arbitrarily; they must follow the way the world itself works. Positing the objective structure of the world as a higher authority is precisely what allows a Mohist to measure the kings, ministers, and great men who are politically above him. The addition of heaven as highest authority radically inverts the "Conforming Upward" chapters, qualifying a system of absolute obedience to political authority by subjecting that authority to the judgment or measurement of the individual who wields the will of heaven as his compass.

Knowing Heaven and Following Nature

The use of heaven as a ground for cultural and political critique naturally suggests positions in the European tradition, which long relied on a connection to the divine to justify an a-cultural standpoint from which to evaluate cultural practices. This goes at least back to Plato's Socrates, who projects divine ideas that exist independently of the order of any particular culture.[69] Plato imagines a critique of the shadows in the cave based on an analysis of the shadows themselves, but he rejects this enterprise; the philosopher ascends from the cave, enters into "the intelligible realm [*noêton topon*]," and then returns to the cave with an independent perspective (*Republic*, 514a–517b; translation from Cooper 1997, 1132–34). The obvious modern example is Descartes, who, like Mòzǐ, emphasizes the unreliability of authority and cultural practices. Descartes' ability to reach a truth beyond culture depends doubly on God: God's goodness guarantees he would not create us as hopelessly deceived—and, more fundamentally, we are able to reach truth through the analogy between our minds and that of God. There is a certain similarity between Descartes and Mòzǐ. Both recognize the skeptical problems that come from reliance on authority and culture, and both reconstruct traditional religious views as a means of avoiding these problems. Nonetheless, the critical standpoint granted by appeal to heaven is relatively weak. For both Plato and Descartes, the universe is structured according to the same categories in which we human beings think. Heidegger puts the point well in saying that the conception of truth as the adequation of ideas to things depends on a prior adequation of things with ideas.[70] In other words, human knowledge fits the world because the world itself is a product of a knowing being. There is no evidence that the Mohists held such a view, nor that they took seriously any analogy between something like innate ideas in our minds and those in the mind of heaven.[71] In spite of their theistic language, the position of the Mohists is closer to the attempt to reform culture by appeal to natural laws than it is a direct appeal to the divine. Following Descartes, we might say that Mòzǐ lacks the "the natural light [*lumine naturali*]" and so can only rely on what he is "taught by nature [*doceri a natura*]."[72]

These differences reveal the relatively weak foundations for humanism in the classical Chinese context.[73] It is much more difficult to distill patterns of nature and apply them to social and political problems than it is to appeal to God's ideas as recorded in books or inscribed in our own minds. Individual judgment is more difficult to justify without divine foundations. The limits of individual judgment best appear in Mòzǐ's description of the state of nature, which describes a war of all against all based on the fact that every person has their own norms or sense of rightness (*yì* 義) (11: 74–75; Johnston 2010, 11.1).[74] The crucial point is that the Mohists do not believe human beings could *think* their way out of this disagreement, for example, by direct appeal to the will of heaven.[75] The only solution is the imposition of some common standard and culture.[76] This inability to reach consensus follows only if human beings in nature lack a sufficient ability to reason and evaluate the world, if the ability of the individual to appeal to independent standards itself depends on some level of culture. It is striking that when the Mohists talk about debate, they begin not by saying that one *uses* or *finds* standards, but that one must first *establish* them, using the word that literally means "to stand," *lì* 立. Their metaphors for standards are all human artifacts: the compass and square, the gnomen (*yí* 儀, *biǎo* 表) used to measure the position of the sun, or signposts (*biǎo*) set up to mark the way.[77] Even in setting up benefit as a criterion, the Mohists begin with convention, asking what we would want for our family, just as in opposing war they begin with agreement that stealing is wrong. This does not mean that the Mohists saw their standards as arbitrary or merely conventional, but discovering and establishing the standards requires cumulative human effort. In short, placed in the context of the European Enlightenment, the Mohists would still appear to be conservatives skeptical of individual judgment. In comparison to their early Chinese peers, however, the Mohists look almost like rationalists, placing more confidence in individual human judgment and power than any other major Warring States philosophers. Ultimately, this position lost out in the Chinese battle of ideas, showing that even the limited humanism of the Mohists was difficult to justify in that context.

Most of the Mohist arguments for what heaven wants are indirect, and infer what heaven desires based on what succeeds in the world. A few arguments rely on an analogy between heaven and human rulers. The "Models and Standards" chapter explains, "Now the world has no small or big states—all are heaven's cities. Human beings have no young or old, noble or lowly—all are servants of heaven" (4: 22; cf. Johnston 2010, 4.4). All people are generated by heaven, sustained by heaven, and belong to heaven. Several passages explain this relationship in terms of offering and accepting sacrifices. The "Will of Heaven I" sets up this progression:

> So then how do I know heaven cares for the common people of the world? By its inclusively illuminating them [*míngzhī* 明之].[78] How do I know its inclusively illuminating them? By its inclusively possessing them [*yǒuzhī* 有之]. How do I know its inclusively possessing them? By its inclusively accepting their sacrifices [*shízhī* 食之]. How do I know its inclusively accepting their

sacrifices? Within the four seas, of grain-eating peoples, none do not feed their cattle and sheep, raise their dogs and pigs, and purify their offerings of grain and sweet wine, using them to sacrifice to Shàngdì and the ghosts and spirits. Heaven has cities and people—what would be the use of not caring for them? (26: 196; cf. Johnston 2010, 26.6)

Another version emphasizes that all people, in the past and in the present and even in distant barbarian (*yí* 夷) lands, have their sacrifices accepted (28: 210–11; Johnston 2010, 28.5).[79] These sacrifices express a mutual bond—all people recognize their belonging to heaven and thus sacrifice—and in accepting these sacrifices, divine forces recognize this belonging. The reciprocity is captured in the term used for the consummation of the sacrifices, *shí* 食, which means "food" or "grain" but as a verb can mean either "to eat" or to "feed." Thus the line could mean that heaven inclusively accepts their offerings ("eats them") or that heaven receives nourishment from all inclusively ("is fed by them"); it might even mean that heaven feeds the people.[80] This mutual support establishes feelings of care, particularly if we consider the background belief that the acceptance of sacrifices creates an obligation to provide benefits.[81]

This bond is compared to that between a king and his people, and the Mohists use this analogy to project what heaven would want. The "Questions of Lǔ" ("Lǔ wèn" 魯問) chapter provides a nice example, in which Mòzǐ attempts to discourage Prince Wén of Lǔyáng from invading the state of Zhèng:

Now suppose that within the four borders of Lǔ, large cities invade small cities and large families attack small families, killing their people and taking their cattle, horses, dogs, pigs, money, clothes, rice, grain, and resources. How would that be?" Prince Wén said, "Within the four borders of Lǔ, all are my subjects. If a big city invades a small city or a big family attacks a small family, seizing their resources, then I certainly will punish them heavily." Master Mòzǐ said, "Now heaven's inclusively having the world is like your having the area within your four borders. If you raise troops to invade Zhèng—will not the punishments of heaven arrive?" (49: 468; cf. Johnston 2010, 49.4)

In the "Against Invasions" chapter, Mòzǐ draws on the same analogy to describe wars between states as using heaven's people to attack heaven's cities (19: 142–43; Johnston 2010, 19.3).

These arguments appeal to the analogy between what a human being would want and what heaven wants, but we cannot forget that our relationship to heaven is through the natural world. To say that all people are sustained by and belong to heaven is to say that we equally belong to and live from the natural world. Consider the following line, quoted earlier: "The actions of heaven are broad and without private concern, its extension is generous and does not cease, its illumination is long lasting and does not wane. Thus sagely kings model themselves after it" (4: 22; Johnston 2010, 4.3). The passage is beautifully ambiguous: *xíng*

(行) could mean "actions" but commonly refers to the cyclical movement of the celestial bodies; *míng* (明) could mean "to discern" but also could mean "to illuminate impartially" like the sun (*rì* 日) and moon (*yuè* 月), the two elements composing the character. The *Zhuāngzǐ* will take up the same term *míng* as an ability to look on things as they are, without categorizing or judging. The phrase translated as "does not cease" follows an emendation; the original text says, literally, "does not virtue [*bùdé* 不德]"—the same phrase used in the *Dàodéjīng* to say that the greatest virtue is not enacted deliberately as virtue (38).[82] Underlying these ambiguities is the fact that *tiān* could refer to an anthropomorphic deity or to the impartial, all-encompassing, never-ceasing sky above us. Only that all-embracing impartiality can serve as a model.[83]

These passages already suggest how the natural world might serve as a model for inclusive caring. Nature is impartial—the sun and moon shine on all alike, and the benefits of nature are equally accessible to all people. Heaven does not discriminate, reaching even to the people beyond the cultures of the middle states. These arguments point toward something like a conception of natural equality. In the context of nature, all human beings are the same and of equal value. Distinctions between my family and your family, my state and your state, and even my body and your body are human impositions on this more basic reality. We are all heaven's people, dwelling under and possessed by heaven/sky. The basis of *jiān ài* is the recognition of this equality. To see the people of another state as one sees one's own is to look on things as heaven sees them, but it also is to see things as they really are.

Heaven's care is shown in the way nature generates things and the resources they need to survive. The care of heaven expressed in the generation of the natural world appears most fully in the "Will of Heaven II" chapter:

> Moreover, there is something by which I know the generosity of heaven's caring for the people. I say: it arrays the sun, moon, and stars with brightness to lead them; it arranges the four seasons, spring, fall, winter, and summer, in order to regulate and link them; it sends down snow and frost, rain and dew, in order to grow the five grains, hemp, and silk, having the people attain materials to benefit them. It lays out the mountains, rivers, streams, and valleys, and distributes the hundred offices, in order to look down and examine the good and bad of the people. It makes kings, dukes, and lords, having them reward the worthy and punish the brutal, to gather metal, wood, birds, and beasts, and to dedicate themselves to the affairs of the five grains, hemp, and silk, all in order to provide the people materials for clothing and food. From the ancients down to today, it has always been like this.

After comparing heaven to a parent, the passage concludes,

> Now heaven is inclusive toward [the people of] the world and cares for them, bringing to fruition the myriad things in order to benefit them. Even the tip

of a hair is something heaven has made. The people attain benefit from heaven and thus it can be called generous. (27: 202–204; Johnston 2010, 27.6)

Caring for and benefiting other people simply continues the process by which heaven naturally generates and sustains us.

These aspects of the Mohist position are fundamental to views of nature in the Warring States period, and in particular to how nature can be considered good and worthy of reverence. The Mohist claim that nature cares for things inclusively continues in less anthropomorphic forms. The more teleological concept of benefit will be replaced by the generative forces of nature as *shēng* 生—growing, generating, birthing, or living. The Mohists gesture in this direction when they say that heaven loves life (*shēng*) and hates death (26: 193; Johnston 2010, 26.2), and that the way taught by the first sages is that by which the world lives, grows, or generates (46: 429; Johnston 2010, 46.8). The Mohists themselves, though, remain bound to an anthropocentric conception of nature. The difficulty for them is that the generative aspects of nature points toward a more radical inclusivity—if heaven cares inclusively for what it generates, should it not care equally for all of nature? Are not the sun, moon, and seasons there to benefit *all* things that live? This conclusion is reached a century or so later by the philosopher and friend of Zhuāngzǐ, Huì Shī, who is supposed to have said: "Care overflowingly for all the myriad things [*fàn ài wànwù* 汎愛萬物]; heaven and earth form one body" (*Zhuāngzǐ* 33: 1102; cf. Mair 1994, 344). Huì Shī's position may be a direct projection of Mohist views to their radical conclusion, as the chapter of the *Zhuāngzǐ* quoting Huì Shī uses the same phrase to describe the position of the Mohists as "care overflowingly and benefit inclusively" (33: 1072; cf. Mair 1994, 336).[84] The best example of this progression toward more and more radical inclusivity appears in the *Lǔshì chūnqiū*. It begins with a famous statement of nature's impartiality (using the term *gōng* 公): "The world is not one person's world but the world's world. The harmony of *yīnyáng* does not grow just one type. Sweet dew and timely rain are not partial to one thing. The birth of the myriad peoples does not favor one person" (1/4: 45). The statement is followed by a well-known story about losing a bow:

> A person of Jīng lost a bow and was not willing to search for it, saying, "A person of Jīng lost it, a person of Jīng will find it, so why search?" Kǒngzǐ heard this and said, "If you leave out 'Jīng,' then it is acceptable." Lǎo Dān heard it and said, "If you leave out 'person,' then it is acceptable." Thus it was Lǎo Dān who reached the utmost impartiality. (1/4: 45)

Kǒngzǐ's statement is more Mohist than Ru (the Ru might prefer that a family member find the lost bow), but if we take our orientation from nature as a whole, it is the position given to Lǎozǐ (Lǎo Dān) that seems to follow. Lǎozǐ's view, however, eliminates the concept of loss entirely, since the bow belongs to nature no matter what happens to it. The *Zhuāngzǐ* pushes this inclusivity even further, arguing that since nature encompasses never-ending cycles of life and death, generation and destruction, we cannot even say that life and benefit are good. This shift leads toward a radical antihumanism extending to both human ethics and judgment, as we will see in chapter 5. This progression reflects the fundamental difficulty (if not impossibility) of deriving a humanistic ethics from the tendencies of nature itself.

Talking about the Problem of Evil

Insofar as the Mohists claim that all bad actions are punished and good actions rewarded, they seem too obviously wrong. Any adult has witnessed enough to know that divine justice, if restricted to this world, is incomplete. A charitable reading must question whether the Mohists really believed the justice of heaven to be so thorough. Of course, a hermeneutic principle of charity can easily lead a philosopher to underestimate the human ability to make bad inductive arguments. Even today, we find football players thanking God for helping them win games, people believing they recovered from illnesses because of prayer, and prominent preachers claiming that great disasters came as God's punishment. It is possible that the Mohists interpreted events in similar ways. Furthermore, the Ru believed that good actions are generally, but not always, rewarded. If the Mohist position ends up close to the same view, then we must explain the vehemence with which they oppose it from the Ru.

The core chapters of the *Mòzǐ* never acknowledge this difficulty, but four passages in the dialogue chapters raise something like the problem of evil. In two of them, Mòzǐ evades the problem by saying that the person involved does not fully enact Mohist doctrines and thus is not actually good (48: 462–63; 49: 476–77; Johnston 2010, 48.18, 49.16). The other two passages are more challenging, because they take Mòzǐ himself as an example. The first is in the "Gēng Zhù" (耕柱) chapter:

> Wūmǎzǐ 巫馬子 said to Master Mòzǐ, "You enact rightness, but people do not see it and serve you and ghosts do not see it and make you prosper. Yet you do it—that's crazy!" Master Mòzǐ said, "Now suppose you have two servants here. One person works if he sees you but if he doesn't see you, he does not work. The other person works if he sees you and if he doesn't see you, he still works. Which of these two people do you honor?" Wūmǎzǐ said, "I honor the one who works whether or not he sees me." Master Mòzǐ said, "So then, even you honor those who are crazy." (46: 428; cf. Johnston 2010, 46.6)

Mòzǐ's response is perplexing, because what we would want in a servant is not necessarily what we would want if we were that servant. One point may be that even an egoist like Wūmǎzǐ would agree that we should *teach* other people to work hard, a point emphasized in another dialogue with Wūmǎzǐ (46: 435–36;

Johnston 2010, 46.18). The argument, though, might be more sophisticated if Wūmǎzǐ as master is being compared to the observing ghosts, and Mòzǐ and Wūmǎzǐ are compared to the two kinds of servants. The point would be that, like any master, the ghosts are not constantly watching and rewarding, and so sometimes the good servant will not get rewarded. The most plausible way to take the metaphor is that the master (heaven or the ghosts) will eventually differentiate the good servant from the deceptive one, but that there could be exceptions.

The second passage focuses on the problem of evil more directly:

> Master Mòzǐ was sick. Diē Bí approached and asked, "Master, you consider ghosts and spirits as discerning and able to make fortune and misfortune, rewarding those who do good and punishing those who do bad. Now, master, you are a sagely person, for what reason are you sick? Could it be that there is something not good in your teachings? Or is it that ghosts and spirits are not discerning?" Master Mòzǐ said, "Even though I am sick, how could they not be discerning? There are many ways by which people become sick: some attain it from cold and heat, some attain it from suffering and labor. To have a hundred gates and block one of them—how can that stop thieves from getting in?" (48: 463–64; cf. Johnston 2010, 48.20)

This passage significantly moderates the Mohist position on ghosts and spirits—rewards from ghosts and spirits are indeed one factor in the world and they have a significant causal role, but they are not the only causes. They do not guarantee results.

One other text gives a more radical response, but it is not from the *Mòzǐ*. A brief text found in the Shanghai Museum bamboo strips, *Guǐshén zhī míng* (Discernment of ghosts and spirits), begins with a familiar Mohist argument, that we know ghosts and spirits have discernment, insight, or clear-sightedness because we have the examples of the sagely kings being rewarded and the brutal kings being punished. It concludes, however, in a different tone:

> When it comes to Wǔ Zǐxū, one of the world's sagely people, he was tied in a leather bag and died. Róng Yígōng, one of the world's creators of disorder, lived many years and then died. If you use this to interrogate it, then of the good some are not rewarded and of the bad [some are not punished]—should we rely on this? For the ghosts and spirits not discerning, there must be a reason. Is it that their strength could reach it but they do not do it? I do not know this. Or is it that their strength cannot reach it? I do not know this. These two diverge. I thus [say ghosts and spirits have] what they discern and have what they do not discern. (Mǎ 2005, strips 3–5)[85]

As we have seen, this passage contains the most explicit statement of the problem of evil that we have from Warring States China. Remarkably, it leaves unresolved whether the ghosts are not perfectly good or just have limited powers. The initial argument in favor of the discernment of ghosts could easily come from the *Mòzǐ*.

The use of *míng* 明 (to discern or see clearly) to encompass the ability of ghosts to see *and* to reward or punish fits Mohist uses of the term, particularly in related discussions in the dialogue chapters.[86] The tendency to use the discernment of ghosts and spirits to refer to all forms of divine justice also fits the Mohists. These connections led Cáo Jǐnyán 曹錦炎 to take this text as Mohist, even claiming it may be part of one of the lost "Clarifying Ghosts" chapters (Mǎ 2005, 306–307). Its style and expressions of doubt, though, make that unlikely.[87] At the same time, the passage goes only a small step beyond Mòzǐ's admission that ghosts do not control all forms of sickness, which could very well be explained as a case of the strength of the ghosts "not being able to reach it."[88]

These passages suggest that at least some of the Mohists may have backed away from claims that good is always rewarded and bad is always punished. Their significance, however, may be doubted because none are found in the core chapters of the *Mòzǐ*. A stronger reason to believe the Mohists did not consider the fairness of the universe to be perfect appears in their political philosophy, which assumes that without an effective human government, bad people will indeed escape punishment. One of the most fundamental principles of Mohist political thought is the need to establish and accurately administer rewards and punishments, most central in the "Elevating Worthies" and "Conforming Upward" chapters. The latter lays out a thorough system in which the ruler sets clear standards by which he evaluates the ministers directly under him, rewarding and punishing them. Those ministers then apply the standards to those below them, who apply them below, all the way down to the village and the individual. At the same time, each person also examines and remonstrates with those above them in the hierarchy. In such a system, every murderer would be punished, and every caring person would be rewarded. In fact, the ideal political system takes on qualities of heaven, reaching more than a thousand miles away. But we are told it is not *shén* 神—magical, numinous, by spirits—but rather comes through human agency (12: 88; Johnston 2010, 12.11). If divine forces always rewarded the good and punished the bad, human beings would have no need to establish such political systems. The Mohists would end up close to the *Dàodéjīng*, according to which human beings can engage in non-action because *dào* naturally works things out.[89]

If the Mohists believed that we sometimes do escape the consequences of our actions, how do we explain the vehemence of their opposition to Ru uses of fate? Even if the Ru and the Mohists both recognize limits to human efficacy, their attitudes toward these limits vary significantly. As we have just seen, when Mòzǐ is ill, he lists possible causes—excessive heat, cold, or labor. There is nothing mysterious or divine about his illness, and nothing that requires acquiescence. His response points toward investigating and controlling those causes, and it is no coincidence that the Mohists tended toward developing science and technology. Kǒngzǐ would label all these factors "fate" (*mìng*). This orientation remains passive: saying it is *mìng* is saying that it is mysterious, impenetrable, irresistible.[90] The *Lǚshì chūnqiū* explains *mìng* thus: "We do not know that by which it is so but it is so" (20/3: 1356). While the Mohists never claim that the Ru explicitly advocate passively waiting for fate or timing, they believed the Ru attitude toward obstacles erred in this direction. Some of their statements seem more like slander, but their concern is that the Ru are not activist enough, that they are too willing to accept failure as due to fate or to timing.[91] We find this view in Mohist criticisms of what appears to be a Ru claim: "A gentleman folds his hands and waits. If asked, then he answers, and if not asked, then he stops. It is like a bell: if struck, then it rings out, and if not struck, then it does not ring out" (48: 449–51; Johnston 2010, 48.1).[92] Mòzǐ responds that in some cases, one must speak out even if not asked. While the Mohists do not directly tie this claim to fatalism, it comes close to the position seen in *Qióng dá yǐ shí*, which holds a strikingly passive attitude toward opportunities. The claim is not that they are difficult to find and so one should spend their lives seeking them out, but rather that they cannot be controlled and so one should cultivate oneself and wait.[93] This passivity reflects how early Ru thinkers remain in a tradition of reverence for heaven. Attributing an event to heaven or its commands (*mìng*) grants it a kind of final authority, even if it has no ethical purpose. In this context, we can see how a contrast between the Mohists as more "religious" and the Ru as more "philosophical" or "humanist" makes sense only on a simplistic equation of religion and theism. If one were to characterize the dispute around *mìng* as a conflict between the forces of rationalistic humanism and the forces of religion, the Mohists would align more with the former and the Ru with the latter.[94] On the Ru account, events are largely determined by inexplicable divine forces that cannot be explained, cannot be resisted, and cannot be blamed. In contrast, the Mohists argue for a world in which the fate of human beings depends entirely on human effort, a world in which obstacles are to be analyzed and resisted and opportunities are to be sought out.

Even if the Mohists and the Ru similarly recognized some limits to human action, the differences in what they say are significant. It is what the Ru *teach*, not what they *believe*, that the Mohists attack. The Mohists were concerned above all with reforming society. Their writings are made for this purpose.[95] Consider the following saying attributed twice to Mòzǐ: "Words that suffice to motivate actions should constantly be said. Those that do not suffice to motivate actions should never be said. To constantly say what does not suffice to motivate actions—this is to waste a mouth" (47: 432; Johnston 2010, 47.5). A philosopher might prefer *true* words, but for Mòzǐ the most important aspect of speaking is motivating actions. Similar phrasing appears in a discussion between Mòzǐ and Wūmǎzǐ, which begins with Wūmǎzǐ declaring that he cares more for himself than for his parents, more for his parents than for the people of his district, and so on

(46: 435–36; Johnston 2010, 46.18). Mòzǐ does not attempt to refute this position, but asks Wūmǎzǐ if he plans to keep this view hidden or to announce it to other people. He then points out that if Wūmǎzǐ announces this doctrine, those who accept his view will seek to harm him for their own benefit, and those who reject his view will seek to harm him to stop his influence. The dialogue ends with another version of the line above: "To insist on talking when there is no benefit—this is to waste a mouth."

The Mohists apply this concern with action and consequences directly to the question of fate, as all three of the "Against Fate" chapters begin by setting up criteria that include the consequences of believing a claim. We can take the first version as an example.[96] It begins by noting disagreements on *mìng* and then says that to settle the debate one must first set up (*lì* 立) a standard (*yí* 儀). To do otherwise would be like trying to determine east and west on a spinning pottery wheel. Mòzǐ then explains that there are three standards or markers (*biǎo* 表):

> There is rooting [*běn* 本] it, there is originating [*yuán* 原] it, there is using [*yòng* 用] it. What is rooting it? Root it above in the work of the sagely kings. What is originating it? Originate it below in the evidence [*shí* 實] of the eyes and ears of the hundred families. What is using it? Issue it as governing policy and see if it benefits the middle states and the people. These are what are called the three markers. (35: 266; cf. Johnston 2010, 35.3)

As the rest of the chapter makes clear, "using it" does not mean evaluating a claim by empirically testing it, as a pragmatist would. Rather, it means seeing what would happen if people *believed* the claim. In other words, if people believe events are determined by fate, will this have good or bad consequences? If we take these criteria as standards by which to judge what is *true*, then this third element is puzzling. Why would the Mohists assume that teaching the truth always has good consequences? It seems there are many false things that we would be better off believing—for example, that hard work ensures success and that virtue is rewarded.[97] If these criteria, though, are about how activists decide what to *teach*, they are quite reasonable.[98] Teachings must cohere sufficiently with the tradition and they must be plausible in relation to people's experience. These set limits on what can become a live option for belief. Within those constraints, though, we teach what will bring the most benefits.[99] For example, one might believe that those born rich usually end up rich and those born poor usually end up poor—yet still promote the American Dream—because it fits our tradition, has some empirical support, and makes people hopeful and hardworking. The Mohist denial of fate functions in just this way.

This issue of criteria raises questions about how the *Mòzǐ* should be read and about the nature of debate in the early Warring States period. Two passages in the dialogue chapters of the *Mòzǐ* give guidance on how to read the text itself. In one, a student asks Mòzǐ what one should discuss first when meeting with a sovereign. Mòzǐ responds that it depends on the particular state:

> If a state is confused and disorderly, then speak of elevating the worthy and conforming to those above. If a state is poor, then speak of restraining expenses and restraining funerals. If the state delights in music and debauchery, then speak of opposing music and opposing fate. If a state is crooked and without ritual, then speak of honoring heaven and serving ghosts. If the state works to oppress and invade others, then speak of inclusive caring and opposing invasions. (49: 475–76; cf. Johnston 2010, 49.15)

The various Mohist doctrines are meant to serve different purposes. If the ruler of the state has good intentions but lacks the skills or policies to manage it well, then teach him how to create order, emphasizing the institution of a fair justice system. If the ruler is lazy and indulgent, then tell him that there is no fate and that success depends on him. If the ruler is bad, then tell him that heaven and the ghosts will punish him. The varying purposes of the doctrines partly explain why they are not fully coherent on a theoretical level. Bad rulers need to hear about divine punishments and the revenge of ghosts; good rulers need to hear that if they do not establish a fair system of rewards and punishments, then worthies will not be promoted and the bad will escape punishment. Although written in absolute terms, the doctrines are meant primarily as correctives, not utopian plans. That is, the point of "conforming upward" is to encourage a ruler to make the system of justice more reliable, and the purpose of the will of heaven is to warn bad rulers that their power does not guarantee they will escape justice. This helps explain some of the tensions between the various planks.

The second passage begins with Mòzǐ promising a person that if he studies, he will be made into an official. After a year of study, the student asks Mòzǐ to promote him, but Mòzǐ refuses and tells a story of five brothers. The eldest brother had a love of drinking and when their father died he refused to lead the funeral. The other brothers bribe him by offering to buy him liquor, but after the funeral they refuse to do it, explaining that they only got him to do what he was supposed to do anyway. The story clearly allows motivating someone with the promise of reward, even if the rewards will not arrive. We should not go so far as to say the Mohists did not believe that heaven was good or that ghosts and spirits enacted revenge, but the implications of the passage are obvious enough that it can be taken as a justification for exaggerating the efficacy of human actions in order to encourage good behavior.

This way of using language and doctrine with a focus on shaping behavior is of course not unique to the Mohists, and it would be a mistake to see the Ru as just objectively reporting the sad truth that life is not always fair. A. C. Graham insightfully refers to both their conceptions of *mìng* as "fictions," one meant to discourage interest in material things and the other meant to stimulate hard work (Graham 1989, 50). This shared focus on the practical effects of doctrine complicates any attempt to compare or contrast the Ru and the Mohists, as it leads into questions of audience. Consider a famous example from the *Lúnyǔ*:

> Zǐlù asked, "On hearing it, should it be immediately enacted?" The master said, "There are you father and elder brothers—how could you immediately enact what you hear?" Rǎn Qiú asked, "On hearing it, should it be immediately enacted?" The master said, "On hearing it, it should be immediately enacted." Gōngxī Huá said, "Zǐlù asked whether he should immediately practice what he heard, and you said, 'There are you father and elder brothers.' Rǎn Qiú asked whether he should immediately practice what he heard, and you said, 'Practice it immediately.' I am perplexed—may I ask about it?" The master said, "Rǎn Qiú holds himself back, so I push him forward; Zǐlù is daring, so I hold him back." (11.22)

Kǒngzǐ said different things to different people, depending on what they needed to hear. This personalized approach has important consequences for how one speaks of fate and heaven. It makes sense to emphasize effort to someone contemplating action and then to emphasize fate to a good person whose grand attempts at reform have just failed. One might even invoke a slogan such as "Death and life are fate; prosperity and honor are with heaven."[100] Such statements take on a different meaning when, in Plato's words, they "roam about everywhere, reaching indiscriminately those with understanding no less than those who have no business with it."[101] Kǒngzǐ would surely recognize the problem: "With people above the middle, one can discuss the highest. With those below the middle, one cannot discuss the highest" (6.21). Qīng dynasty commentator Liú Bǎonán 劉寶楠 explicitly connects this passage with the fact that Kǒngzǐ rarely spoke of fate or the way of heaven, topics reserved only for higher students (1990, 236).

Kǒngzǐ, like Socrates, probably taught only face to face. With such a restriction, many of the practical problems the Mohists point out with Ru fatalism would be avoided. Kǒngzǐ's method, though, requires personal knowledge of one's students and strict control over what is disseminated.[102] The spread of writing would make such control impossible. At what time the circulation of philosophical ideas on bamboo strips began, we do not yet know, but by the late fourth century, multiple copies of Ru texts were buried in the distant state of Chǔ. Mòzǐ himself is described as traveling with a mass of documents (*shū* 書), and there are records of his presenting written texts to King Huì of Chǔ.[103] The *Mòzǐ* seems to place particular importance on writing, often stressing that in order to pass on their ideas, sages had them "recorded on bamboo and silk and engraved in metal and stone" (47: 444; Johnston 2010, 47.12).[104] This emphasis on writing may again connect to concerns with accessibility, moving from private transmission between master and disciple toward a more inclusive dissemination of doctrines.

As Derrida points out, Plato's criticisms of writing are closely linked to his criticisms of democracy (1981, 144–45).

The Mohist criticisms of *míng* may point out the failures of the Ru to negotiate the transition from teaching in private conversations to the spreading of public doctrines, or at least the dangers and inconsistencies that arise when personal contact is lost. Ultimately, though, the way that writing spreads freely cannot be fully reconciled with the shared concern of early Chinese philosophers for the effects of words in specific contexts. The Mohists choose the safest route, advocating those policies that are most consistently beneficial while avoiding claims that might be counterproductive. Although such an approach may have best suited their purpose, it works less well when read now as philosophy. Claims that may have been inspiring guidelines for activists out to change the world end up either implausible (as in their denial of the problem of evil) or unappealing (as in the totalitarianism of the "conforming upward" system). For philosophy, the Ru approach may work better. The Ru may have begun by simply recording bits of conversation they recalled or were orally taught, but the insertion of passages such as *Lúnyǔ* 11.22 shows a deliberate attempt to address the problem of writing by drawing attention to its limits, warning readers that every statement is meant for a particular context. The short dialogic form may have become a deliberate tactic for negotiating the limits of writing, resembling Plato's choice to write dialogues in response to the same problem.

This concern with the effects of what one says brings us back to a key point of this chapter. The problem of evil—the fact that bad things happen to good people—was seen by both Ru and Mo as a problem of practice. Although the problem encompasses questions of philosophical theology, these are driven by questions about motivation, responsibility, and peace of mind. While the problem of evil in early China remained primarily practical rather than theoretical, the gap between coherent theory and what was said eventually narrowed. The styles of both the core chapters of the *Mòzǐ* and the mini-dialogues of the *Lúnyǔ* were partly superseded by the rise of essays articulating and defending coherent theories, as we already find in the *Xìng zì mìng chū* and the *Wǔ xíng* (Five actions) texts from Guōdiàn. This shift probably follows the fact that the philosophical debates initiated by the Mohists began to attract people who enjoyed such debates for their own sake, people closer to those we would now consider philosophers. At the same time, it would be natural that as philosophy was refined through the debates of the Hundred Schools of Thought, what could be plausibly defended as a practice was narrowed. In other words, if we take the Mohist criteria as claiming that one should promote what is most beneficial within the limits of what can be plausibly believed, the realm of plausibility became more restrictive as debates became more sophisticated. What should be *taught* converged more and more with what could be defended as *true*.

3 Efficacy and Following Nature in the *Dàodéjīng*

WE HAVE SEEN the vehement opposition between the Ru and the Mohists. The *Mòzǐ* includes a whole chapter called "Against Ru" ("Fēi Rú" 非儒), and Mèngzǐ goes so far as to say that if Mohist ideas came to dominate, human beings would descend into cannibalism (*Mèngzǐ* 3B9)! In the broader context of Warring States thought, however, the opposition between the Ru and Mo looks more like sibling rivalry, and "Ru-Mo" became a set phrase. Both were activist movements intent on fixing the problems of the world, and both were moralistic, believing that the foundation for restoring order lay in the promotion of a new (or old) ethical sensibility. The most fundamental commonality between the Ru and the Mohists is their humanism or anthropocentrism. It is not just that they follow an ethics focused on human beings but that they show little interest in anything beyond the human community. The early Ru were concerned more with history and tradition than with the objective patterns of nature. The Mohists base their humanism on heaven, which requires a concern with how nature functions, but even so, the Mohist position seems more like a projection of human beings into the divine rather than a recontextualization of the human into the natural world, a point perhaps best shown in their belief that heaven arranged the rest of nature in order to benefit human beings (27.6: 202–204).

The commonalities between the Ru and Mo starkly appear when contrasted with the *Dàodéjīng*. In fact, the *Dàodéjīng* seems so different—in both style and content—that scholars cannot agree on its proper context. Some have thought the ideas in the text express concerns that preceded Kǒngzǐ and Mòzǐ, whereas others have thought they reflect philosophical debates at the end of the Warring States period, three centuries later. Recent archeological evidence sheds some light on these issues, but it also reveals the heart of the problem—the *Dàodéjīng* defies the very concept of dating a text. There is a general consensus that the materials in the *Dàodéjīng* originated from wise sayings, prescriptions, and poems developed over time. These reflect a range of concerns, from body cultivation practices to guidelines for ruling a state to cosmological speculations. Such sayings were transmitted orally and ultimately were edited and interwoven into what Michael LaFargue calls "chapter-collages" by the "composers" of the text (1992, 198).[1] The resulting text is remarkably coherent in its ideas, style, and images, suggesting that these composers left a strong mark. Even so, excavated texts suggest that this composition itself took place over an extended period of time.

Since the text was modified continually, it makes little sense to assign a date to it. Based on the Mǎwángduī materials, we know that something close to the received version was in existence before 195 BCE.[2] The basic system of thought in the composed text, however, took form earlier, as we find about one-third of the received text in the Guōdiàn materials, buried around 300 BCE. While the wording and arrangement of passages differ, almost all of the significant themes in the received text also appear in the Guōdiàn materials.[3] The Guōdiàn materials include two different versions of chapter 64. Projecting sufficient time for multiple versions to have appeared and been buried, it seems that the basic system of thought of the Dàodéjīng arose at least by the mid- to late fourth century, if not earlier. If we follow the consensus that the written text was composed at the end of a process of oral transmission, many of the ideas or individual strands of the text would go back much further. My concern here will not be directly with those individual strands but rather with the system as seen in the composed text, which formed before that of Mèngzǐ but probably (although not certainly) after that of Mòzǐ.[4]

The Efficacy of Human Action

While the Dàodéjīng differs remarkably from the Mòzǐ and the Lúnyǔ, we can still situate it within shared concerns around fate and the efficacy of human action. In that context, what stands out in the Dàodéjīng is its strong confidence that the appropriate actions will bring beneficial consequences. The most dramatic statement of this efficacy is in chapter 62: "For what reason did the ancients honor this way (dào)? Isn't it said that, with it those that seek attain, and those having crimes avoid retribution? Thus it is honored by the world." These lines employ terms commonly associated with fatalism and the power of human actions. For example, Mèngzǐ tells us that if it is the case that by seeking one attains it, then what is sought can only be internal. Regarding the external, one may seek it with the way (dào), but attaining it depends on fate. The Dàodéjīng aligns more with the Mòzǐ in attacking fatalism. Many passages emphasize the power or efficacy of human action at the political level. Chapter 3 says that if rulers do not elevate worthies or set up desirable goods, the people will not contend, cause disruptions, or become bandits. As a result, everything will be well ordered. Chapter 19 has a similar structure, but says that the people will benefit, be filial and nurturing, and again that there will be no thieves. Chapter 57 says that the people of their own will become correct, prosperous, and simple like uncarved wood (pǔ 樸). Chapter 59 says that such a ruler will have nothing he cannot overcome. Together, these passages claim that it is within a ruler's power to create peace and order and to have people who are filial, kind, just, and prosperous. In the *Dàodéjīng*, it is the ruler who determines whether or not the way is enacted in the world, not fate.

The contrast with the Ru around the power of human actions to bring success is even clearer on the personal level. For example, chapter 44 says,

> Name or body—which is more cherished? Body or stuff—which is greater? Attaining or losing—which is more distressing?
> Caring [*ài* 愛] deeply must have great expense. Storing richly must have much destruction.
> Thus one who knows what is enough is not shamed; one who knows to stop is not harmed and can last a long time.[5]

The use of *bì* 必, "must" or "necessarily," emphasizes the certainty of the causal connections. Many passages express the power of human action without qualification. We can consider one more example, chapter 7, which says,

> Heaven lasts long and earth endures.
> That by which heaven and earth can last long and endure is their not living for themselves; thus they can live long.
> Therefore sagely people withdraw themselves but are first, set themselves aside but are preserved.
> Isn't this by their not having partial concerns? Thus their partial concerns are completed.

The final lines are paradoxical and at face value deeply pessimistic—we can only get the things we want when we no longer want them. The paradox is eased, though, through a contrast between means and ends. One can live long, be first, and be preserved—but only by not directly pursuing these goals. Thus commentator Wáng Bì explains not having partial concerns as "not striving deliberately [*wúwéi* 無爲] for one's self" (Lóu 1999, 19). The term *sī* 私 (partial concerns) is generally negative, and refers to desires or actions that are biased toward one's own interests, in contrast to what is *gōng* 公, impartial or oriented toward the common good. Although quite different on the surface, the logic of this passage echoes the *Mòzǐ*, according to which we get personally rewarded *by* being impartial.

The *Dàodéjīng* contains numerous passages that together show that one who follows the way will meet no harm, have no losses, receive no blame, last long, benefit, be first among the people, complete great works, and leave nothing undone. These passages show no trace of the Ru attention to the ways in which success and failure lie outside of our control, depending on timing, fate, or heaven.

The terse style of the Dàodéjīng makes it difficult to know how strongly to take these passages, but some passages make extreme claims. For example, chapter 50 says, "It is said that those good at holding onto life, walking on land do not evade rhinoceroses or tigers, and entering battle do not bear weapons and armor. The rhinoceros has no place to use its horn, the tiger has no place to use its claws, and a soldier has no place to use his knife." Similarly, chapter 55 describes one with abundant virtuosity (dé 德) as like an infant, not harmed by poisonous insects, wild beasts, or carnivorous birds. Taken literally, such people attain a kind of magical efficacy that makes them invulnerable, but even if we take these passages metaphorically, they strongly emphasize that one who harmonizes with the way will avoid all harm.

The two main words used by the Ru to label the limits of human action—timing (shí 時) and fate (mìng 命)—are almost entirely absent in the Dàodéjīng. Timing appears only in one passage, where it refers to acting in a timely way, not to opportunities that come only at certain times (8). Fate, mìng, appears in the Wáng Bì version of the text in two passages. One says that the honor things have for the way is not commanded (mìng) (51).[6] The other use of mìng is more difficult. Chapter 16 says, "The way of heaven goes round and round, each returns to its root. This is called stillness. Stillness is called returning to mìng. Returning to mìng is constancy. Knowing constancy is insight [míng 明]."[7] It is difficult to know with certainty what fùmìng 復命 means, but its connection to constancy, stillness, and the root all suggest it entails restoring a connection to the constant generative forces of life, probably appealing to the sense of mìng as one's allotment of life.[8] In any case, nothing suggests the kind of unpredictable and irresistible events that the Ru label as mìng.

While excluding concepts of fate and timing, the Dàodéjīng brings another area of unpredictability into human control—luck or good fortune. The Dàodéjīng employs a number of terms associated with divination, fortune, and auspiciousness, but in each case, these are reduced to the effects of human actions. For example, jiù 咎, a common outcome for divination in the Zhōu yì (Book of Changes) meaning blame, fault, or harm, appears twice—one passage says that arrogant people bring jiù on themselves (9), while another says that no jiù is greater than the desire for gain (46). In both cases, jiù has nothing to do with divination or the configuration of the moment but with the natural consequences of our own actions. Misfortune or the unpropitious (xiōng 凶), another common Zhōu yì outcome, follows from military actions (30, 31) or from the reckless actions that result from not understanding constancy (16). Military action is said to be inauspicious (bùxiáng 不祥), whereas avoiding force is propitious, (jí 吉) (31). Huò 禍, misfortune, comes from not knowing what it is to be satisfied (46), and from taking one's enemies lightly (69). We have seen some of these terms already in the Mòzǐ, where they are stripped of their contingency and made dependent on doing what heaven wants. The *Dàodéjīng* goes a step further, removing their connection to anthropomorphic spirits.

The exclusion of fate and luck aligns with one of the central concerns of the *Dàodéjīng*—constancy. The terms *cháng* 常 or *héng* 恆 appear in twenty-one chapters.⁹ In some cases, they describe what sagely people do, such as constantly have no heart of their own (49), or constantly making the people lack desires and knowledge (3). Others describe the way, which is said to constantly have no desires (37) and no name (32), and to be constantly without action (37). Although the first chapter famously tells us that any formulation of the way will not be constant, many chapters make claims about the constancy or regularity of natural patterns: heaven is constantly with the good (79), the feminine constantly uses stillness to overcome the masculine (61), and it is constantly so that opposites always follow each other (2).¹⁰ Because of these constant patterns, sagely people can consistently bring about results: it is constantly so that one can take the world through non-work (48), or that if one understands the dangers of knowledge, one will know (or become) the great pattern (*jīshì* 稽式), and have dark or profound virtuosity (*dé* 德) (65). One passage describes following or practicing constancy thus:

> Seeing the small is called discernment, preserving weakness is called strength. Use its glow but return to its clarity, do not bring disaster on your person.
> This is called following constancy. (52)

Although cultivated constancy sometimes refers to internal imperturbability, as in knowing constant satisfaction (46), here it relates to efficacy—to seeing things when they are small and managing things so as to avoid harm.

This emphasis on the constancy or regularity of natural patterns aligns with Mohist concerns but also points forward to Xúnzǐ, who makes the same points more explicitly and polemically. In fact, a concern with the constancy or regularity of the world appears across a variety of texts buried at the end of fourth century BCE. Some, like the *Dàodéjīng*, describe a steady order for the natural world. Although it does not use the terms *cháng* or *héng*, the *Tàiyī shēng shuǐ* 太一生水 (Great unity generates water), a text found attached to part of the Guōdiàn *Dàodéjīng*, describes the progression of the seasons and the alternation of waxing and waning and then comments, "This is what heaven cannot kill, what earth cannot bury, and what *yīn* and *yáng* cannot finish [*chéng* 成]" (Liú Zhāo 2003, strips 7–8). Other texts bring this constancy to bear on human relationships. *Chéngzhī wènzhī* (Completing it, hearing it) claims,

> Heaven sends down great constancy to pattern [*lǐ* 理] human relations, arranging rightness between sovereign and minister, illuminating familial affection between father and son, and dividing the distinction between husband and wife. Therefore, petty people disrupt heaven's constancy to go against the

great way [*dào*], while gentlemen order human relations to follow along with the virtue of heaven. (Liú Zhāo 2003, strips 31–33)

Other excavated texts, like the *Sān dé* 三德 (Three virtues) or *Péng Zǔ* (彭祖) speak of the constancy of heaven or the Dì's rules, but seem to conceive that regularity in more anthropomorphic terms.[11]

Constancy, as *héng*, was even used to name a kind of ontological state. One recently excavated text, *Héng xiān* (Constancy first) uses *héng* to label the most primordial condition of the universe, the time before any beings had begun to stir (Jì 2005, strips 1–3). The *Zhōu yì* also has a *héng* hexagram. The hexagram judgment is explained thus:

> "Success, without fault, beneficial outcome": that is because of lasting long in its way. The way of heaven and earth is constant and long lasting, never ceasing. "There is benefit in going somewhere": that is because when there is an end there is another beginning. The sun and moon attain heaven and can last long in shining, the four seasons change and transform and can last long in taking form. Sagely people last long in their way and the world transforms and completes. Look at what is constant in them, and then the genuine characteristics of heaven, earth, and the myriad things can be seen. (Gāo Hēng 1998, 224)[12]

In chapter 1, we noted that the breakdown of trust in the Mandate of Heaven left open the possibility not only that the world is not good but that it has no regular order, leaving human beings at the mercy of chance and fortune. The world, after all, appears to be chaotic, unpredictable, and uncontrollable, and such a view would make sense in the tumultuous period in which the *Dàodéjīng* was coming together. The concern with constancy in the *Dàodéjīng* and other fourth-century texts can be seen as a response to such views, not necessarily arguing for a *moral order* but for *some order* that would allow human beings to control their own lives. In early modern Europe, the fact that bad things happen to good people became a problem for theology and ethics, but was less of a threat to the belief in a natural order responsive to human action. Thus, the position of the *Dàodéjīng* is not so easy to place in categories familiar from the problem of evil.

Before considering the problems that arise from the fact that bad things do seem to happen to good (or prudent) people, we should consider the few passages that appear to limit or contradict this focus on efficacy. This first passage might suggest a natural limit on the length of our lives:

> Exit into life, enter into death.
> The disciples of life are three of ten.
> The disciples of death are three of ten.
> People who overly live life, all moving to a place of death, are three of ten. (50)

These line can be read in two different ways, depending on whether one takes the numerical phrase (*shíyǒusān* 十有三) to mean "thirteen" or "three out of ten."[13]

Most now take the latter reading, in which case the passage distinguishes three kinds of people. The disciples of life naturally live out long lives; the disciples of death naturally die young. We might say that the latter, like Yán Huí, have a short *mìng*.[14] Thus far the length of life appears to be fated, but the third group has some agency, bringing an early death on themselves through living excessively or obsessively, a phrase which simply doubles the word for "life" or "to live," *shēngshēng* 生生, meaning something like overly living life, or perhaps living life too deliberately. The concluding half of the chapter describes those who are "good at holding life." They are the ones we have already seen, who cannot be harmed by the horns of rhinos, the claws of tigers, or the weapons of soldiers. Those good at holding onto life appear to be a fourth group, the inverse of the third. Chén Gǔyìng takes them as the remaining one in ten (1988, 260). Through their cultivated efficacy, they are able to live a long life, which suggests, in contrast to the Ru, that even a short *mìng* can be overcome. Just as one meant for a long life can cut it short through reckless actions, one meant for a short life can live long by following the way.

Two other chapters have been read as claiming that success and failure are uncertain and unpredictable. Chapter 73 says,

> Those brave in daring die; those brave in not daring live. Of these two, some benefit and some are harmed.
> What heaven hates—who knows its reason?
> The way of heaven is to not contend but be good at winning, to not speak but be good at responding, to not call but have things come of themselves, to be calm but good at plotting.
> Heaven's net casts far and wide, loose meshed but missing nothing.

Overall, this appears to be another chapter emphasizing the link between actions and their consequences, and both Wáng Bì and Héshànggōng take the main point of the passage as claiming that the good are rewarded and the bad punished.[15] The first line is a strong, direct claim about efficacy—one way of acting leads to death, and one leads to life. The final line on heaven's net emphasizes that nothing escapes these consequences. The difficulty is the line that questions what heaven hates. In addition, the referent of the "some" who benefit and are harmed is unclear. Liú Xiàogǎn 劉笑敢 takes it as allowing for exceptions to the first principle, quoting the Sòng dynasty scholar Sū Zhé 蘇轍: "Those brave in daring die; those brave in not daring live—this is the constancy of the principles of things. But some of the daring attain life and some of the not daring attain death. People hope to get lucky in this indeterminacy and neglect the constant principle" (2006, 692).[16] This reading is possible but unlikely, given that the first line is a strong statement of efficacy and that the last line emphasizes that there are no exceptions. As for the question about what heaven hates, the emphasis may be that no one knows the *reason* (*gù* 故) for it. In any case, many passages do tell us what heaven hates. As Héshànggōng says, "It hates deliberate actions [*yǒuwéi* 有爲]" (Wáng Kǎ 1997, 282).[17]

Chapter 58 might also suggest some uncertainty:

> Misfortune is what fortune leans on; fortune is where misfortune lurks. Who knows their ultimate limit? They are without correctness.
> Correct turns back to be strange, good turns back to be monstrous.
> Human beings have certainly been lost for a long time.
> Therefore, be square without cutting, pointed without jabbing, upright without encroaching, bright without dazzling. (58)

The *Dàodéjīng* contains several claims for the natural alternation between opposites, here between good and bad fortune and from what is correct and good to what is strange and monstrous, terms that suggest aberrations that would have been interpreted as ill omens. We might take this passage as advocating detachment and equilibrium based on the inevitability of misfortune and monstrosity.[18] The final lines, though, suggest the opposite. Sagely people avoid these harms by embodying qualities with balance and flexibility, being "square without cutting" and so on.[19] The difficulty lies in the line, "Who knows their ultimate limit? They are without correctness." "Ultimate limit" (*jí* 極) could refer to the cycle itself, which is endless, or to the point at which good fortune starts to turn bad, which would be difficult to determine. As in the previous passage, one could take the question as implying no one knows or just that it is very difficult to know.[20] The term *zhèng* 正, translated here as "correctness," can be read in two ways. It could refer to regularity or stability, in which case it would state that there is no way to predict for certain when things will reverse.[21] *Zhèng*, however, is usually a normative term meaning "correct" or "rectify," and here it is parallel to "good" or "excellent" (*shàn* 善). The claim that these cycles are without *zhèng* echoes the title of the ode discussed earlier, "Rain without Regularity" ("Yǔ wú zhèng") (194), which also uses the same term. To say that the rains are without *zhèng* implies that heaven's action are not *regular* but also that they are not *right*. In particular, the innocent suffer. In this sense, the *Dàodéjīng* chapter may be claiming that the alternation between good and bad fortune has nothing to do with what it is right or what is deserved in a moral sense. But that does not mean that we must resign ourselves to misfortune. On the contrary, it means that we must shift our focus from morality to what works according to the patterns of nature.

Regardless of how we interpret these few passages, the *Dàodéjīng* clearly grants human actions much greater power than they have in *Qióng dá yǐ shí* (Failure and success are by timing) or in the *Mèngzǐ*. If these claims to efficacy are exaggerated, that only suggests that, like the *Mòzǐ*, they are written in a specific polemical context. In fact, some passages, particularly in the last fifteen chapters, echo the common Mohist claim that good people are rewarded by heaven:

The way of heaven has no favorites; it is constantly with good people. (79)

Now with nurturing care, one wins in war and is secure in defense.
Heaven will establish them, using care to fortify them. (67)

If one found these lines on bamboo strips without further context, one would likely conclude that they were Mohist, and they may in fact come from a source distinct from the Guōdiàn materials.²² The claim in the first passage that heaven lacks favorites or familial attachments (*qīn* 親) means that heaven has no biases, a point we have seen raised in the *Mòzǐ* in relation to elevating worthies. The use of *héng* (regularly or constantly) emphasizes heaven's consistency in supporting good people. We have seen these lines that deny the problem of evil in chapter 1—when Sīmǎ Qiān ends the story of Bó Yí and Shū Qí by doubting that good people are rewarded, he does not appeal to the *Mòzǐ* but rather quotes this line from the *Dàodéjīng* (*Shǐ jì* 61.2124). The second passage holds up *cí* 慈 (nurturing care), as a virtue and claims that heaven intervenes to reward those with it. The term *cí* commonly described the way parents should feel about their children, and was particularly associated with motherly nurturing. Moss Roberts thus translates it here as "a mother's heart" (2001, 165–66), and the *Hánfēizǐ* illustrates *cí* in this passage with the example of a mother's care for her child (using the Mohist term *ài*) (20: 421). The terms *ài* and *cí* were frequently paired in Warring States texts, and the *Shuōwén jiězì* defines *cí* as *ài* (*Shuōwén* 10b.28a; Duàn 1988, 504). In any case, the underlying view is the same—if you care for other people, then heaven will care for you.

Decentering the Human

In spite of the Mohist tone of the last few chapters of the *Dàodéjīng*, the two texts articulate opposed positions, centering on their attitudes toward the human. We can begin with the passage from which the title of this book is taken:

Heaven and earth are not humane,
They take the myriad things as straw dogs.
Sagely people are not humane,
They take the people as straw dogs. (5)

A passage in the *Zhuāngzǐ* explains that straw dogs were honored in rituals, but later thrown aside, trampled under, and used to light fires (14: 511–12; Mair 1994, 136–37). The term translated here as "humane" is *rén* 仁, one of the most central ethical terms in classical Chinese philosophy. In the *Lúnyǔ*, *rén* appears as the highest virtue; thus Slingerland and Waley translate it as "Goodness" or "Good," and Rosemont and Ames as "authoritative conduct." Kǒngzǐ resists giving *rén* any fixed definition, responding differently in different contexts:

Fán Chí asked about humaneness. The master said, "Care for [*ài*] other people." He asked about wisdom. The master said, "Know other people." (12.22)

Now the humane, in wanting to establish themselves establish others, and in wanting themselves to succeed [*dá*] make others succeed. To be able to take analogy from what is near may be called the method of humaneness. (6.30)

By overcoming oneself and returning to ritual one becomes humane. If for one day you can overcome the self and return to ritual, the world will come home to humaneness. Being humane is from oneself—how could it be from other people? (12.1)

Rén is also a key term in the *Mòzǐ*, where it describes dedication to benefitting the world in the same way that a filial son dedicates himself to benefiting his parents (25: 169; Johnston 2010, 25.1). As Ru thought developed in the fourth century, *rén* was paired with, but distinguished from, *yì* 義 (rightness), in which case *rén* is often translated as "benevolence." While *yì* emphasizes appropriate actions, *rén* was associated with natural feelings of care, particularly within the family. This connection to the family was taken to show that the roots of humaneness were in our natural and spontaneous feelings, as opposed to rightness, which had to be learned, leading to the motto "Humaneness is internal, rightness is external."

Given the broad sense of *rén*, the claim that heaven and earth are not humane could have several targets.[23] Some passages in the *Dàodéjīng* criticize moralizing terms, including *rén* and *yì*, because they involve imposed standards that must be worked toward deliberately. The point would not be that heaven and earth are bad (as Lau translates *bùrén* as "cruel") but that they generate a natural harmony that arises spontaneously through non-action, without striving to meet any moral standards.[24] Another possibility, given the Ru association between humaneness and family, is that this line targets partiality, as in the claim we have seen that "heaven has no favorites."[25] The claim that heaven and earth treat human beings as straw dogs, though, suggests another aspect of *rén*. The word *rén* 仁 is closely connected to the term for human beings, *rén* 人, and it is frequently defined in terms of being human. The earliest known example is in the *Yǔ cóng* I (Collected sayings I) Guōdiàn text: "Humaneness is generated from being human; rightness is generated from the way. Some are generated from the inside; some are generated from the outside" (Liú Zhāo 2003, strips 22–23). Similarly, the "Doctrine of the Mean" ("Zhōng yōng" 中庸) chapter of the *Lǐ jì* 禮記 (*Record of Rituals*) quotes Kǒngzǐ as saying, "Humaneness is being human, with cherishing family [*qīnqīn* 親親] as the greatest; rightness [*yì* 義] is appropriateness [*yí* 宜], with honoring the worthy as the greatest" (Zhū 2003, 28). The *Mèngzǐ* says, "Humaneness is the human heart; rightness is the human road" (6A11). The connection between humaneness and being human follows on at least two levels. On one level, humaneness is the proper virtue among human beings dwelling together. The character itself shows a human being (亻) next to the number two (èr 二). This leads Boodberg to translate rén as "co-humanity" (Boodberg 1952/53, 327–330), and Behuniak as "associated humanity" (Behuniak 2004, xxv–xxvi). On another level, humaneness is an expression of natural human feelings, growing from care within the family. An alternate form of the character used in the Guōdiàn texts shows the human body (shēn 身) over the heart (xīn 心), emphasizing the roots of humaneness as embodied in the human heart.[26] In this context, the denial that heaven and earth are rén suggests that heaven and earth are not humanlike and that human beings have no special status, treated only like straw dogs. Thus Hans-Georg Moeller calls this "one of the most outspoken nonhumanist chapters" of the Dàodéjīng (2007, 12), and Wing-tsit Chan says, "In one stroke he removes Heaven and man as the standards of things and replaces them with nature" (1963b, 10).

The significance of the Dàodéjīng's break from anthropocentrism has been widely recognized. Hú Shì, in one of the first histories of Chinese philosophy (published in 1919), praises the Dàodéjīng for fracturing "the absurd view" that heaven is of the same kind as human beings, thus laying the foundation for naturalistic philosophy (2003, 38). Chén Gǔyìng builds on this point:

> Ancient peoples always took the sun, moon, and stars, the mountains, rivers, and earth, as each having a ruler steering from above. Moreover, they took all the natural phenomena that they encountered as animate things. In this infancy, human beings often use their own image to recognize and serve nature, and take their own wishes to personify nature. They then think that the natural world has some special concern or love for human beings. Lǎozǐ opposed this anthropomorphism (nǐrénlùn 擬人論). He considered that all things between heaven and earth move and develop according to natural laws (the way). Among them there is absolutely none of the feelings or purposeful intentions that belong to human beings. In this, Lǎozǐ struck a blow against theism. (1988, 83)

One of the great early explications of this rejection of anthropocentrism in English is Herrlee Creel's essay "The Great Clod" (1970, 25–36). More recently Hans-Georg Moeller has taken up the Dàodéjīng as a "prehumanist" text aligning with contemporary "posthumanism."[27]

The Dàodéjīng decenters human beings on several levels. Classical Chinese philosophers were commonly concerned with origins, but primarily with the origins of human history. Thus the Mèngzǐ starts with a condition in which a chaotic nature dominated fragile human beings, and then recounts how the sages brought order to the world and established human culture (6B9). The Mòzǐ contains similar stories focused more on material culture and on the emergence of political order.[28] In contrast, the *Dàodéjīng* begins with the spontaneous emergence of things and forms. Human history is never mentioned. Another decentering of human beings comes through the elevation of the phrase *wànwù* 萬物 (the myriad things, or more literally, "the tens of thousands of things"). Human beings are approached as just one of the many things generated by nature. When it comes to human beings themselves, the *Dàodéjīng* emphasizes the mother and the pre-social infant rather than the family as a source of socialization. The frequent emphasis on the limits of language and the impossibility of expressing the ultimate in human terms serves as a reminder that nature itself is not commensurable with human capacities. Even the text itself can be taken as dehumanized. There is no "the master says," no dialogues between disciples—only a vague "I" in a few passages (Moeller 2006, 137–38).

We can enter more deeply into this break from anthropocentrism by considering how the *Dàodéjīng* takes up the two terms that were later used to give it an honorific title as a classic: *dào* 道 and *dé* 德. The term *dào* is one of the few Chinese philosophical terms known in English, but ironically, the connotations that have grown around it make "Dao" or "Tao" largely misleading as a translation of *dào*, which I will translate as "way." The primary meaning of *dào* in the context of classical Chinese philosophy is the way that a group of people follow, advocate, or teach. Thus one can speak of the *dào* of the Mohists or the *dào* of the Ru. *Dào* also has a sense of discourse, as the way someone tells or teaches, a sense Hansen nicely captures in taking *dào* as "guiding discourse" (1992). A *dào* is not so much a theory as a way of living. Hansen explains, "Dao's are not so much theories that guide us as they are *conceptual perspectives* that guide us. . . . The mechanism is not like that of rules, evoking a descriptive state of affairs for us to bring about. It affects us more by shaping our taste, our discriminating attitudes" (1992, 213). These uses of *dào* extend from its more concrete meaning of "path." The character itself shows a head (*shǒu* 首) over a foot (辶), the latter representing moving or going. The sense of path is even clearer in an alternate form of the character used in excavated texts from the late fourth century, which shows a person (*rén* 人) between two sides of a path: 行. As Roger Ames and David Hall point out, *dào* frequently has a verbal sense, particularly in its early use, in which it means to make or follow a path, or to lead someone on a way (2003, 57–59). Thus, they translate *dào* verbally as "way-making."

Although the *Dàodéjīng* uses *dào* to refer to the way it recommends, it also introduces a new and striking use for the term. Wing-tsit Chan states the common view: "Hitherto the connotations had been social and moral, but in Lao Tzu it connotes for the first time the metaphysical" (1963b, 6). The claim for such a radical break in meaning naturally arouses suspicion, and several scholars have tried to evade it. For example, Hansen attempts to take *dào* consistently as "a guiding way," taking the more metaphysical passages as strategic claims made to undermine conventional values (1992, 196–230). LaFargue takes *dào* to refer to a state of mind that is then metaphorically portrayed as the origin of everything (1992, 230, 207–13). Nonetheless, some passages clearly present *dào* as an aspect of nature itself:

> *Dào* generates one, one generates two, two generates three, three generates the ten thousand things (42).
>
> There is a form that becomes in indifferentiation, generated before heaven and earth.
> Soundless, shapeless, standing alone but unaltered, it can be considered the mother of heaven and earth.
> Its name is unknown, but it is styled "*dào*"; if I am forced, I name it "great." (25)[29]

Taken at face value, these passages describe how things in the natural world arise, in which case *dào* labels the dynamic and originary aspect of nature that generates and supports all particular things.

Two factors from recently excavated texts further support this reading. First, recent archeological finds now reveal that there was a broad concern with such cosmogonies by the late fourth century, and that the *Dàodéjīng* should be read in that context.[30] Second, some excavated Ru texts show an explicit concern for distinguishing their *dào* as *human*. The *Xìng zì mìng chū* says, "Of what can be a *dào*, there are four. Only the human *dào* can be *dào*-ed [*wéi réndào kě wéi dào yě* 唯人道為可道也]" (Liú Zhāo 2003, strips 41–42). The line is difficult, but I suspect it means that while other things have ways by which they function (and which human beings can thus follow and use), it is only human beings whose way is cultivated and learned. Whatever the other three *dào* in this passage might be, they are not *human* ways.[31] A similar line begins by noting that the various *dào* take the methods of the heart—the locus for learning and human variation—as their center (Liú Zhāo 2003, strips 14–15). Such comments suggest that by the late fourth century, a naturalistic sense of *dào* had become prominent enough that the Ru felt the need to distinguish their *dào* as *human*.[32] The commonality between the above line and the first line of chapter 1 of the *Dàodéjīng* suggests at least an indirect link. The *Dàodéjīng* passage may be meant to distinguish the constant *dào* that generates the natural world from the human *dào*s that can be *dào*-ed.

Dào as the generative force in nature and *dào* as the recommended way are intimately linked. The idea of a path already encompasses both senses—a path forms along the contours of the land itself. Thus "the path" refers both to how to go and something in the world itself, as we could "make" a path or "find" a path.[33] In the *Dàodéjīng*, *dào* should be read with this same ambiguity, as simultaneously the way nature works and the way sages follow.[34] It is important to remember that the text itself expresses dissatisfaction with the label "*dào*," as we saw in chapter 25, above. We can read that passage quite naturally as saying we cannot speak of the ultimate origin in itself, but as it relates to us, we can call it "the guide," or "what leads," or "way-making."³⁵ Furthermore, while the way generates patterns that can be known and followed, "*dào*" itself does not refer to a concrete path or set of rules but rather to a mode of happening—*zìrán* 自然. The term combines the reflexive pronoun *zì*, "self," with *rán*, a term meaning "to be so" or "in a certain manner." Thus *zìrán* most literally means "self-so" or "so-of-itself," bearing a sense of spontaneity and freedom from external coercion. *Zìrán* characterizes the way in both senses—both nature and the sage follow *zìrán*. It is not that the spontaneity of the sage *resembles* the spontaneity at the root of the universe; it *is* that same spontaneity as it works through singular events and situations. *Zìrán* provides a ground shared by heaven, earth, human beings, and all the myriad things. Girardot thus calls the actions of a sage "cosmogonic behavior" (1985, 75), and Schwartz says that the sage imitates the way in "cosmomorphic fashion" (1985, 202).

Although *tiān*, heaven, became more and more naturalistic over the course of the Warring States period, it retained anthropomorphic connotations, as we see in the language of the *Mèngzǐ* and even in some passages of the *Dàodéjīng*. The *Zhuāngzǐ* later uses *tiān* stripped of this humanism, but the *Dàodéjīng* takes a different strategy, displacing *tiān* as a term for the ultimate. It does this partly by pairing *tiān* with *dì* 地 (the earth), which occurs in eight chapters.³⁶ While heaven is still given some priority, only heaven-and-earth (sky-and-land) together constitute nature as a whole. Moreover, *dào* is given explicit priority over heaven-and-earth. The way is said to precede heaven-and-earth (25) and to be their root (6). Other cosmogonic texts from the time more explicitly explain heaven and earth as derivative. *Tàiyī shēng shuǐ* begins with the "great unity" (*tàiyī* 太一) that generates water, which then assists the great unity to form heaven, which then assists them to form earth (Liú Zhāo 2003, strip 1). *Tàiyī shēng shuǐ* says that "heaven" is just the word we use to refer to the *qì* (vital energy) above us, as "earth" is the word we use to label the soil below us (Liú Zhāo 2003, strip 10). In *Héng xiān*, turbid *qì* is said to generate earth while clear *qì* generates heaven, a claim found in later texts as well.³⁷ *Qì*, which I will translate as "vital energy" or "vital energies," was a naturalistic concept used to explain all kinds of dynamic processes, from the formation of heaven and earth to weather patterns to the processes of the body and the human emotions.³⁸

The most important line in the *Dàodéjīng* regarding this displacement of heaven says, "People model earth, earth models heaven, heaven models the way, the way models self-so spontaneity" (25). The term *fǎ* 法, which we encountered in the last chapter as the word for "model," is here used as a verb meaning to "model themselves after" but including a sense of spontaneously following along with patterns, and perhaps even a sense of embodying those patterns. The passage addresses the most obvious difficulty with any cosmogony, the problem of infinite regress. The regress is avoided because at the most fundamental level nature is just so-of-itself. A *dào* that follows spontaneity contrasts a *tiān* that would act deliberately to enforce certain values. Other passages say that the way does not act as a master (*zhǔ* 主) and that it has no desires (34). Several passages say that *dào* births or generates things but does not "possess" or "have" (*yǒu*) them, inverting the Mohist claim that heaven cares for all things because it "inclusively possesses them" (26: 196; Johnston 2010, 26.6). These passages suggest that the shift from *tiān* to *dào* is meant to replace a moralistic and anthropomorphic conception of the ultimate with a conception of the way as a spontaneous process, neither human nor humane.[39]

The difficulty of the other key term, *dé* 德, is reflected by the variety of ways it has been translated even within the *Dàodéjīng*: virtue, virtuosity, integrity, efficacy, potency, power.[40] As this list suggests, *dé* unites several senses that are impossible to capture with any one English term. We can distinguish four dimensions of its meaning, each of which appears across a range of Warring States period texts:

1. *Dé* is associated with character. While it sometimes refers to ethical *actions*, it primarily refers to something a good person *has*.[41] For example, the "Doctrine of the Mean" distinguishes the five realms of proper action (sovereign and minister, father and son, husband and wife, younger and older brother, and interaction between friends) from the three *dé* by which one acts in these realms: wisdom, humaneness, and courage (Zhū 2003, 28–29).[42] In that context, *dé* could easily be translated as "virtue." *Dé* was associated with a range of values in different texts: filial piety, correctness, firmness, softness, harmony, and balance.[43]

2. *Dé* is connected with the heart and the internal. The original form of the character places *zhí* 直, which means "straight" or "vertical" but is a virtue connected to being direct and upright, over the heart, *xīn* 心, a form used in the Guōdiàn texts. This connection between *dé* and the internal is most clearly expressed in the *Wǔ xíng* (Five actions) text from Guōdiàn, which distinguishes good actions (*xíng* 行) from good actions of *dé* (*dézhīxíng* 德之行), because the latter take form from the inside (Liú Zhāo 2003, strips 1–6). As internal, *dé* connects to genuineness, naturalness, and spontaneity, in contrast to correct actions which we might force ourselves to do.

3. *Dé* is connected to divine forces. The *Wǔ xíng* says that *dé* is the way of heaven, while correct actions are the way of human beings (Liú Zhāo 2003, strips 4–7). The *Zhuāngzǐ* links the same concepts: "Heaven is internal, the human is external. *Dé* comes from heaven" (17: 588; Mair 1994, 158). This connection to heaven can be external, as we have seen in the *Shàng shū* (*Book of Documents*), according to which *dé* gains the conscious support of heaven, or internal, where it connects to following one's own spontaneity.

4. *Dé* brings power or efficacy, a sense reflected in its connection to a closely related term which means to attain, *dé* 得. The "Yuè jì" 樂記 (Record of Music) of the Lǐ Jì says simply, "*dé* [virtuosity] is *dé* [attaining]" (Sūn Xīdàn 1988, 982). This power is non-coercive and originally connects to the obligation felt toward one who gives benefits (Nivison 1978–79, 53). In the *Shàng shū* this power is mediated by heaven, but the Ru emphasize the natural way that people respond to the extraordinary charisma exerted by good role models. For the *Dàodéjīng* and the *Zhuāngzǐ*, *dé* is a matter of channeling the generative power of nature itself.

The importance of the concept of *dé* arose in the context of early Zhōu views of the Mandate of Heaven, and its coherence depends on an evasion of the problem of evil. To acknowledge that bad things happen to good people is to drive a wedge between *dé* as ethical actions and *dé* as power or efficacy. In fact, the problem of evil in Warring States thought could be written through the developments and changes of the conception of *dé*, grounded in the split between its meaning as "virtue" and as "power." In general, the Ru maintain the connection between *dé* and humanistic virtues, but they must compromise its efficacy. In contrast, in the *Dàodéjīng* and the *Zhuāngzǐ*, the main emphasis is on the efficacy or power of *dé*, which comes through integration with natural processes but has little connection to virtue in a humanistic sense. In the *Dàodéjīng*, the accumulation of *dé* is explained in nonmoral and nonhuman terms:

> Know the masculine but preserve the feminine to be the ravine of the world. As the ravine of the world, constant *dé* will not leave. Constant *dé* not leaving, one returns home to infancy.
> Know the white but preserve the sullied to be the valley of the world. As the valley of the world, constant *dé* will then suffice. Constant *dé* sufficient, one returns home to the simplicity of uncarved wood.
> Know the white but preserve the dark to be a pattern for the world. As the model of the world, constant *dé* will not err. Constant *dé* not erring, one returns home to the limitless. (28)

One develops *dé* by holding onto the lowly and weak, which draws in the world and returns one to a state of natural potency and simplicity, like uncarved wood or an infant. While human beings gain potency by accumulating *dé*, *dé* itself is not fundamentally human but rather a force of nature, the power or efficacy of the way itself. In this role, *dé* is the power of growth, generating and nurturing things (10, 51). *Dé* is among the most difficult terms to translate consistently, and I will frequently repeat the Chinese term, but will use "virtue" or "virtuosity" as the least problematic stand-in for it.

The ambiguity in the terms *dào* and *dé*—that they refer to forces in nature and the way of sagely people—already indicates that if there is something we could call an "ethics" in the *Dàodéjīng*, it will not be humanistic. Like heaven and earth, sagely people are not humane (4). Thus, when it comes to the problem of evil and the efficacy of human action, the *Dàodéjīng* fundamentally shifts the terrain. Rather than focusing on whether or not *good* actions are rewarded, the *Dàodéjīng* focuses on the power of human action in general, asking, What makes human actions effective? With this orientation, the *Dàodéjīng* opens a broad examination of the way nature operates, placing questions of reward and punishment into the context of efficacious action in general. We can take this example:

> That by which rivers and oceans can be kings of the hundreds of streams is that they can be below the hundreds of streams. Thus they can be kings of the hundreds of streams.
> Sagely people in being before the people place themselves behind them; in being above the people, use words to be below them.
> They are above the people, but the people do not feel burdened; they are before the people but the people do not feel harmed. The world delights in supporting them and does not tire of them.
> Because they do not contend, none in the world can contend with them. (66)[44]

The passage makes a strong claim for the efficacy of human action—sagely people reach a point at which everyone delights in supporting them and no one contends. This efficacy, however, has no connection to whether or not moral actions are rewarded. Its concern is with success in general—how to get ahead, be on top, and have no one resist. Regardless of the original intent, there is little to stop one from using it as advice for how to get ahead in politics or rise to the top of a corporation. This broad applicability follows because the foundation is not a theory about a godlike figure doling out rewards and punishes but rather general observations about nature itself.

In taking the patterns of nature as guide, the *Dàodéjīng* again aligns with the *Mòzǐ* and contrasts with the Ru. The Mohists, though, remain limited by their anthropocentric conception of nature under the guidance of an anthropomorphic heaven. The *Dàodéjīng* approaches nature as a guide while recognizing that it is *bùrén*, neither human nor humane. Hú Shì attributes this shift to an encounter with the problem of evil:

> Lǎozǐ lived in a time of such conflict and great chaos. His eyes having seen people killed, families broken, states destroyed, and other misfortunes, he thought that if there were a willful and knowing heaven or Dì, the world certainly would not have reached these misfortunes. The myriad things struggle against and kill each other, human beings struggle against and kill each other—this is the proof that that way of heaven is without awareness. Thus Lǎozǐ said, "Heaven and earth are not humane, they take the myriad things as straw dogs." (2003, 38)

This reading of the *Dàodéjīng* suggests parallels to European reactions to the problem of evil and the rejection of an anthropomorphic God or universe. In Europe, the growing disbelief that good actions would be rewarded by God meant that human beings could no longer rely on God to ensure peace and justice. It thus initiated a shift toward a scientific approach to ordering human society. Although differences in both methodology and attitude make it problematic to call it even proto-scientific, the *Dàodéjīng* does take a similar orientation toward nature and human action. With the will of heaven gone, human thriving depends on finding and working with the patterns of nature itself.

The Way and the Human Good

The *Dàodéjīng* breaks from anthropocentrism in both its basic conception of the world and in its view of how to act effectively in it. The text, though, is still a guide for human beings; thus, it must bridge nature and *human* concerns. There is a surprising level of disagreement on what would seem like the most basic question of the text: Why should we follow the way? Herlee Creel helpfully distinguished two strands of Daoism, one that is "purposive" and one that is "contemplative" (1970, 37–47). The contemplative strain aimed toward a mystical experience valued for its own sake. The purposive focused on using this experience as a means toward "the furtherment of personal ambitions and political purposes" (Creel 1970, 44–45). We can refine this by distinguishing three kinds of goods. The first would be worldly human goods—including things such as security, health, long life, and peace, basically falling under Creel's category of the "purposive." The second would be internal or subjective goods, primarily contentment or peace of mind but also some kind of mystical experience, all of which would fall into Creel's category of the "contemplative."[45] These goods closely connect to the first, both because having basic needs filled leads to contentment and because calmness or mystical insight might generate power to bring about worldly goods. The third would take some qualities of nature as intrinsically valuable. Thus LaFargue names "organic harmony" as the highest good in the *Dàodéjīng*, and Liú Xiàogǎn takes *zìrán*, "naturalness" or "spontaneity," as its highest value.[46] In this category, we might also put readings that assume union with "the Dao" is an intrinsic good.

The *Dàodéjīng* most often recommends actions by describing what kinds of consequences they generate. The most direct way to investigate the basic values of the *Dàodéjīng*, then, is to examine what consequences are used to recommend actions. What are the goals? Often the consequence is success in general: leaving nothing undone, completing one's tasks successfully, winning. Other passages take avoiding harm or misfortune as the goal. The most common specific goal is lasting long or avoiding an early death, which appears in sixteen chapters. A few passages hold up maintaining or achieving a position, which seems to be what making oneself first refers to (7, 66). Other passages mention being king of the realm (48, 57, 78) or having a state (59). A few passages refer to avoiding shame or blame and several refer to being a model for the world. One passage mentions a continuous line of sons and grandsons (54). This list covers the vast majority of consequences listed in the *Dàodéjīng,* and almost all can be read in terms of self-interest—succeeding in one's endeavors, having a long life, avoiding shame, and holding a position as a leader and model. In this sense, the *Dàodéjīng* is a guide for *effective* rather than *ethical* action.

To read the *Dàodéjīng* as an amoral guide to success not only seems to violate the spirit of the text but also contradicts specific passages, particularly those concerned with governing, in which actions are recommended because they lead to the good of the people. For example, chapter 38 says that the elevation of ritual is bad because it will weaken loyalty and filial piety and lead to chaos. War is rejected as a means because it leads to barren fields and bad harvests (30). Chapter 80 takes good government to be one that allows the people to enjoy simple lives. In such passages, methods of governing are recommended *because* they result in the people being prosperous, peaceful, orderly, and good (that is, filial, kind, loyal, and correct). Passages that recommend actions by describing what a sagely person does also suggest that the well-being of the people is assumed as a good. For example, chapter 49 says,

> Sagely people constantly are without heart, taking the hearts of the common people as their heart.
> Good to the good and also good to the not good. This attains goodness.
> Trusting the trustworthy and also trusting the untrustworthy. This attains trust.
> Sagely people in residing in the world merge into it; for the world, they muddle hearts. The common people all attend to their ears and eyes. Sagely people treat them as children. (49)

Insofar as these passages appeal to no further consequences or ends, they appear to take care for the people as an intrinsic value.[47]

In sum, the *Dàodéjīng* presents a multiplicity of values, from long life to avoiding shame to having the people live in peace. The goals themselves are given no explicit justification, which should not be surprising. The goals assumed by the Mohists are almost identical, and, in spite of the immense cultural gap between them and us, these values—long life, moderate success, peace and prosperity for the people—still seem pretty good. Taking the text as a whole, we can say that the motivation for following the way is that it allows human beings to live decent lives, "to find sweetness in their food, beauty in their clothes, joy in their customs, and peace in their homes" (80). What is most striking in these lists of goods is that all express *human* concerns. The *Dàodéjīng* gives little evidence that union with the way is an intrinsic goal. While passages speak of the way with awe and reverence, chapter 62 says explicitly that the way is honored because it enables those who seek to attain their goals and those who have done wrong to avoid trouble. Although natural harmony (as "organic harmony" or "naturalness") appears necessary for human flourishing, no passages unambiguously express a direct concern for the well-being of nature, either as a system or as concern for specific things like plants or animals.[48] Because of this focus on a good *human* life, we can still speak of the *Dàodéjīng* as a humanistic text. Its fundamental challenge is in showing how human goods can be attained through harmony with a world that is neither human nor humane.[49]

This focus on the ability to attain basic human goods weighs against three common interpretations of the *Dàodéjīng*. First, the *Dàodéjīng* cannot be taken primarily as a skeptical text.[50] Although passages emphasize the impossibility of speaking of the ultimate origin of things, tentatively labeled as "the way," we can know and speak of the regular patterns of nature, even if we must do so through systems of interlocking images rather than in precise, abstract reasoning.[51] Second, the *Dàodéjīng* does not equalize all values, taking success and failure or life and death as equal.[52] The vast majority of passages are structured around attaining a small set of goods assumed as obvious. Third, accepting whatever happens calmly and with peace of mind is not the primary emphasis of the text as a whole.[53] Such a view is undoubtedly present in the *Dàodéjīng*: when chapter 33 says that "one who knows sufficiency is rich," it probably does not mean they become *literally* rich but rather that they *feel* rich. But when chapter 46 says "no disaster is greater than not knowing sufficiency," disaster likely refers to real things such as wars rather than internal dissatisfaction. While contentment and satisfaction are valued intrinsically and as a means to success, the large majority of passages cannot be plausibly read as speaking only of subjective or internal goods, as if avoiding harm or attaining a long life meant only that one is able to accept harm and early death.[54] While all three of these views (skepticism, value equality, and peace of mind) appear centrally in the *Zhuāngzǐ*, we must keep the perspective of the *Dàodéjīng* distinct.

According to the *Dàodéjīng*, those who act carefully will live long lives, maintain their positions, and be fairly successful. Human beings as a group will live in peace and contentment, with secure families and no bandits. While the nonmoralistic system of the *Dàodéjīng* does not exactly confront the problem of "evil," many of the actions it says ensure success look suspiciously like actions others would label as "good." Extreme wealth—inextricably linked with the poverty and exploitation of the people—naturally brings about failure and harm (9). Violence cannot be sustained and brings disaster on one who uses it (30, 31). Any ruler who makes his people poor or who fosters inequality or war will be overthrown. We should avoid doing these kinds of actions or else we will be harmed. The Mohists would say just the same thing, while calling that harm a "punishment." Consider a *Dàodéjīng* passage that appears to describe three virtues:

> I constantly have three treasures, which I preserve and treasure. The first is called nurturing care, the second is called frugality, the third is called not daring to be first.

> Now with nurturing care, one can be brave. With frugality, one can be broad. Not daring to be first, one can become the leader of things.
> Now to abandon nurturing care but be brave, to abandon frugality but be broad, to abandon being last and be first—that is death!
> Now with nurturing care, one wins in war and is secure in defense.
> Heaven will establish them, using nurturing care to fortify them. (67)

All three of these "treasures" could be explicated in naturalistic terms of harmonizing with natural patterns, but they are close to being "virtues," and all are justified by their consequences, as allowing bravery, broadness, and leadership. If those benefits are pursued without these treasures, the result is simple and clear—death. The most difficult to justify as a means to success is nurturing care or kindness, which may be why this passage singles it out, saying that nurturing care leads to victory in war and security in what one protects, even gaining the support of heaven.

Although these passages come close to claiming that good people always succeed, such actions are not conceptualized as moral, human, or humane. They guarantee rewards because they effectively operate in relation to the way the world itself works. Wealth, violence, and exploitation all lead to harm, not because they are *immoral* but because they violate the patterns of nature. Chapter 23 helps clarify this approach:

> A gusting wind does not last a morning; a violent rain does not last a day. Who does these? Heaven and earth, but they cannot make them last—how much less what is done by humanity?
> Those who deal with affairs with the way unite with way; those of gain unite with gain; those of loss, unite with loss.
> Those united with gain, the way also gains them; those united with loss, the way also loses them. (23)[55]

The basic meaning of this passage is that one's path determines whether one gains or loses, whether one lasts or does not. Thus, Wáng Bì comments that the way "unites and responds to them according to what they do" (Lóu 1999, 58). This could be taken as another statement that good actions are rewarded, but the initial example of violent thunderstorms shows that it exceeds the realm of human ethics. What makes one a follower of loss is not having bad purposes but using actions that are not effective. This marks a subtle but critical difference from similar Mohist claims, because it means that even a good person like Mòzǐ would be a follower of loss—not because he was *bad* but because he did not act according to nature. This context helps explain the critique of moralizing in the *Dàodéjīng*. Filial piety (*xiào* 孝), benefit (*lì* 利), and correctness (*zhèng* 正) are criticized in some passages but valued in others. Even the most strongly criticized Ru virtue, ritual propriety (*lǐ* 禮), is not fully rejected, as mourning rituals after war and the maintenance of ancestral sacrifices are both affirmed (54, 31).

The best explanation for this double use of terms is that these virtues are good if they arise naturally, but that if one focuses directly on promoting them—going against the spontaneity of things—then one in fact causes harm.[56] The critique of moralizing is an attack based on efficacy.

The Dàodéjīng makes the claim that good actions are rewarded more plausible by limiting its scope and meaning. That is, we would normally take a good person as someone trying to do good things, someone like Bó Yí or Bǐ Gān or Mòzǐ. We feel that in a good world, such people would be rewarded, and when they instead suffer, we encounter "the problem of evil." The Dàodéjīng would admit that such people often meet harm and defeat, but this fact does not mean the connection between actions and results is uncertain or uncontrollable, with outcomes determined by an inexplicable *mìng* or capricious divinity. Good actions succeed only when accompanied by an understanding of how to act effectively with nature. Furthermore, goodness is not the only goal. Preserving one's own life and even one's position are also valid goals. The Dàodéjīng even says that only one who values his own life above all is sufficient to be king (13). Death is more likely for a Ru or Mohist precisely because avoiding death is not one of their primary concerns. Taking all of these together, the Dàodéjīng is able to give a reasonable account of how "heaven is constantly with good people"—a person who pursues some kinds of goodness through the most effective actions and also seeks to preserve their own life and position in the most effective ways will not achieve fame or great wealth (both of which are dangerous) but will live a long life and be moderately successful in their pursuits.

The plausibility of this view still depends on seeing the forces of nature as generally aligning with a sustainable and satisfying human life, particularly since the most effective action is non-action—that is, not forcing or coercing things but letting them develop of themselves. The goodness of nature centers on *dào* as a force of growth, generation, and life:

> *Dào* generates them, *dé* raises them, things form them, instruments complete them.
> Therefore the ten thousand things respect *dào* and honor *dé*. Respect for *dào* and honor for *dé*—none force it but it is constantly so-of-itself.
> *Dào* generates them, raises them, grows them, supports them, shapes them, matures them, nurtures them, covers them.
> Generating but not possessing them, acting but not relying on them, growing but not controlling them—this is called profound *dé*. (51)

The term translated as "generates" is *shēng* 生, which we have already seen as referring to the generative forces of life—meaning to grow, to live, or to be born. The original character depicts a plant growing up from the soil (*Shuōwén* 6b.4a; Duàn 1988, 274). The term translated as "raises," *xù* 畜, literally refers to raising or bringing up livestock. Both aspects of the way—birthing and raising—are implicit in descriptions of *dào* as a mother.[57] Because of this generative function, things spontaneously respect and honor *dào* and *dé* without being commanded to do so. It is noteworthy that *things* do this, not just human beings; human beings are not special in this process of generation. Another passage links the way to water and benefit, *lì*, one of the key Mohist terms: "The highest good is like water. Water is good at benefiting the myriad things but it does not struggle, residing in what the masses of people despise. Thus it is close to the way" (8).[58] Water benefits by nurturing things and allowing them to grow, and it does so without struggle or contention. Labeling this nurturing power as benefit, *lì*, links the metaphor to the final lines of the received text, which say that the way of heaven is to benefit and not harm, whereas the human way is to act without struggle (81).

This optimistic view of nature rests primarily on generation and growth, but nature has other tendencies supportive of sustainable human life. Nature is impartial, having no familial biases (79). This impartiality includes encompassing those who are good and those who are not, a generosity imitated by sagely people (49, 62). The way naturally seeks moderation and balance, which connects to its sustainability and constancy. This tendency toward balance promotes leveling or equality. One passage thus contrasts the way of heaven with the usual human way:

> The way of heaven is like pulling a bow. What is high it restrains, what is low it lifts up, what has extra it reduces, what lacks it aids.
> Thus the way of heaven is to reduce what has extra and increase what lacks.
> The way of people is to reduce what lacks and add to what has extra.
> Now who can have extra and have something to offer to heaven? Isn't it only one with the way?
> Thus sagely people act but do not possess, complete their work but do not dwell on it.
> In this way, they do not desire to be seen as worthies. (77)

Other passages say that what things (*wù* 物) hate is excess and waste (24), and that for some to have luxuries while the common people lack necessities is not the way (*dào* 道) but is "banditry" (*dào* 盜), playing on two terms with the same pronunciation (53).

The alignment between sagely people and the way explains both the efficacy of sagely government and the sage's reliance on non-action. Sagely government is attainable because it aligns with the tendencies of nature itself. Sagely people do not have to strive to benefit and nurture things because nature itself does this. We see this in the various phrases using the reflexive *zì* 自: if a ruler maintains the way, then the people will transform themselves (*zìhuà* 自化), correct themselves (*zìzhèng* 自正), prosper themselves (*zìfù* 自富), and simplify themselves (*zìpǔ* 樸), and the realm will stabilize itself (*zìdìng* 自定) (37, 57). Another passage says that if the ruler can maintain "the one," then "Heaven and earth will combine together to bring down sweet dew, and the people, without being commanded, will distribute it evenly of themselves [zìjūn 自均]" (32). This passage nicely brings together the generative forces of nature and the impartiality with which they are naturally distributed.

We see here the continuity and the break between the Dàodéjīng and the Mohists. The tendency for the way to bring bad consequences on those who promote war and inequality is practically identical with Mohist views. The aspect of the way as generating life echoes Mohist claims that heaven cares for and benefits the world and that it loves shēng, life/generation/growth (Mòzǐ 26: 193; Johnston 2010, 26.2). The Dàodéjīng even uses the key Mohist term in talking about this generative power, benefit, lì. The Dàodéjīng's claim that the way has no familial bias follows the other main Mohist claim about heaven—that it is impartial or inclusive. One difference, of course, is that in the Dàodéjīng these tendencies are freed of their anthropomorphic foundation. They not only happen without any conscious will or feelings behind them, but they extend to all things, not just human beings. But the most radical break from the Mohists comes through the elevation of non-action. The Dàodéjīng is deeply anti-activist; the Mohists are at the opposite extreme. Because the way itself tends toward benefit, equality, balance, and sustainability, a good—albeit simple—human society naturally tends to emerge. The primary role of sagely people is to keep others from messing it up. This orientation explains why, in the Dàodéjīng, while nature is said to benefit (lì) things, benefit is also *criticized* as a goal (19). Benefit is good, but striving for benefit gets in the way of natural processes and ultimately causes harm. On this point, the Dàodéjīng has the more consistent position and seems to follow from the Mohists' own premises. If heaven is good, why do we need to act at all? The activism of the Mohists suggests that they do not trust that heaven will take care of things on its own. The Dàodéjīng reflects a much deeper trust in natural processes.

Disrupting the Way, Diverging from Nature

There remains a cluster of problems around the reality of harm in the world. The first problem is that the Dàodéjīng's claims for the efficacy of human action go too far. Surely some laid back, healthy living, kind people still get cancer and die young, and some reckless, pushy gluttons live happily into old age. The most plausible response is that, like the Lúnyǔ and Mòzǐ, the Dàodéjīng is concerned primarily with motivating people to follow the way. To that end, it may exaggerate its efficacy and reliability. Along these lines, Liú Xiàogǎn addresses the problem of evil by arguing that héng 恆 and cháng 常 should not be taken to mean "always" or "constantly" but something less strict, such as "regularly." He uses this approach to explain why a good person like Bó Yí might end up having a bad life (2006, 745). Even so, we should not ignore the possibility that the Dàodéjīng attributes something akin to magical powers to one who has the way, and the later development of Daoism into a concern with immortality might support taking the *Dàodéjīng*'s claims to efficacy at face value. Sages with magical powers appear in several chapters of the *Zhuāngzǐ*, and according to legend, the commentator Héshànggōng established his authority with Emperor Wén of the Hàn dynasty by floating a hundred feet into the air and then sitting there (Wáng Kǎ 1997, 4).

The more profound problem concerns nature itself. If we take the way as encompassing nature as a whole, then the claim that the way benefits and does not harm must be false. The entire discussion of efficacy depends on the view that different kinds of action achieve different kinds of results. If harm were not a real possibility, the whole ends/means structure would be pointless. More fundamentally, nature produces everything, but—unlike most mothers—it also destroys them. The *Dàodéjīng*'s descriptions of the way are very selective if taken as descriptions of nature: even natural death by old age is ignored, let alone things like cancer, hurricanes, and lightning strikes. Texts from later in the Warring States period expand to incorporate this destructive aspect of nature explicitly. For example, the *Lǚshì chūnqiū* says,

> People and things are from the transformations of *yīn* and *yáng*. *Yīn* and *yáng* are made from heaven and then are completed. Heaven surely has decline, deprivation, decrease, and submission, and also has flourishing, fullness, increase, and proliferation. People also have difficulty, failure, insufficiency, and exhaustion, and have fulfillment, fullness, success, and achievement. These are all encompassed by heaven, are the integral patterns of things, and are enumerations of what must be so. Thus, sagely people do not let personal feelings harm their spirits, but calmly await what will happen. (20/3: 1355)

The *Hánfēizǐ* reads such a view into the *Dàodéjīng* itself, commenting on chapter 67 thus:

> Heaven and earth cannot be always extravagant or always stingy, how much less human beings? Therefore, the myriad things must have waxing and waning, the myriad affairs must have their contractions and extensions, the state must have cultured patterns [*wén*] and military force [*wǔ*], and government must have rewards and punishments. (20: 421)

Both passages use the destructive side of nature to draw conclusions the *Dàodéjīng* would oppose—in the first passage life and death are equalized, leading to fatalistic resignation; in the second passage, the destructive aspect of nature justifies the use of systematic violence, a conclusion also drawn in the *Lǚshì chūnqiū* (20/4: 1369). Thus the marginalization of the destructive aspects of nature plays a crucial role in the *Dàodéjīng* and must be carefully considered.

At first glance, the *Dàodéjīng*'s emphasis on generation seems hard to justify—given that nothing lives forever, the creative and destructive aspects of nature appear equally balanced. Giving priority to life and generation, however, has some basis. If life and death were equally balanced, we would expect periods of life like ours but also long periods of absolute death in which nothing at all lived. In fact, life is always present, going on and on. Thus, the "Xìcí" ("Attached Verbalizations") commentary takes the foundation of the *Zhōu yì* as *shēngshēng* (生生), "generating and generating," "growing and growing," or "living and living," something we might translate literally as *natura naturans* (Gāo Hēng 1998, 388). This phrase is taken up into the famous description of nature as *shēngshēng bùxī* 生生不息: generating, generating, never ceasing! Given the ceaseless vitality of nature, death is not equal to life but rather a moment within life. In fact, we might see death as just the process of new life displacing old life. While differing in obvious ways, the logic that would give priority to life and generation is analogous to the logic in European philosophy that would give priority to being, particularly if we take being in Spinoza's sense of *conatus*, striving, or Leibniz's sense of being as the dynamic maximization of order and diversity. For both Spinoza and Leibniz, the fact that anything exists at all shows that being has an absolute priority over nothingness and thus that destruction can only be understood as transformation within the generation of more being. Although these conceptions of being remain more abstract than the Chinese conception of *shēng*, this line of thought in Europe eventually develops in a more Chinese direction, passing through Nietzsche's conception of life as "will to power," and then into the vitalism of Bergson or Deleuze.[59]

The priority of generativity and vitality, though, does not fully solve the problem, because from the human perspective, death and harm are still real. Do these come from the way, or are they divergences from the way? If the former, then how can the way be said to benefit and not harm? If the latter, then where do harms come from? We can best approach these difficult questions through the most significant locus of destruction—human beings themselves. As we saw in chapter 1, human beings are explicitly singled out as disruptive in another cosmogonic text buried around 300 BCE, *Héng xiān* (Jì 2005, strip 8).[60] The most straightforward statement of diverging from the way in the *Dàodéjīng* is chapter 53:

> If I had a little knowledge, in walking along the great way, I would only fear going astray. The great way is very smooth, but people love mountainous trails. The court is very clean swept, the fields are very weedy, the granaries are very empty. The clothing is patterned and colorful, with a sharp sword on the belt. Full of food, there are more than enough goods and wealth. This is called great banditry [*dào* 盜]. It is not the way [*dào* 道]. (53)

Human beings can and do deviate from the way. The speaker fears straying from it, most people love to follow narrow trails instead of it, and the banditry of rulers is said to be "not the way." Similarly, chapter 41 contrasts those who can carefully follow or walk along the way with those who hear it and lose it and those who simply laugh at it. As we have seen, chapter 77 distinguishes the way of heaven from the way of humans, saying that heaven balances things by reducing the excessive to assist what is insufficient, whereas human beings do the opposite. Another passage speaks in even broader terms, saying that when the world has the way, horses are used in the fields, but when the world lacks the way, horses are raised for war (46).

This possibility of diverging from the way raises problems on several levels. On a psychological level, the question is this: If the great way is so level and easy, why would anyone choose not to follow it? An appeal to original sin or Kant's "radical perversity of the human heart [*radicale Verkehrtheit im menschlichen Herzen*]" would solve the problem (Kant 1900, 6: 37), but the *Dàodéjīng* has nothing like that ready to hand.[61] The immediate explanation must be human choice in some sense, but this is explained not in terms of free will but through a blend of desire and knowledge. A particularly powerful passage in the Primitivist chapters of the *Zhuāngzǐ* describes how human beings disrupt the environments of each kind of living creature. It then attributes this to the love of knowing (*hàozhī* 好知):

> Thus, they [human beings] rebel against the illuminating brightness of the sun and moon above, scorch the refined essence of the mountains and rivers below, and overturn the orderly progression of the four seasons in between. From little wriggling insects and the tiniest flying creatures, there are none that do not lose their natural characteristics [*xìng* 性]. Deep, indeed, is the disorder brought to the world by the love of knowing! (10: 359; cf. Mair 1994, 89)[62]

In the *Dàodéjīng*, the intersection of knowing and desire is clearest in chapter 3, which gives the following progression:

> Not elevating the worthy makes the people not contend. Not valuing goods that are difficult to obtain makes the people not become robbers. Not showing what is desirable makes the people not disruptive.
> Thus sagely people, in governing, empty their hearts and fill their stomachs, weaken their commitments and strengthen their bones, constantly making the people without knowledge and without desire, and making those with knowledge not daring.
> They simply do not act on it, and thus nothing is not well managed.

Desires are shaped by how things are recognized and labeled. Thus knowledge can generate artificial desires that lead into discontentment and struggle. Through its connection to language and convention, the rise of harmful forms of knowledge is inseparable from the development of civilization and culture. This intersection of desire, knowledge, and socialization is precisely what explains human diversity, a view shared by all early Chinese philosophers. Taking desire and knowledge together, we might say the immediate explanation for our deviations from the way is that we do not act spontaneously or self-so, *zìrán,* but rather by deliberate or purposive action.⁶³

The move to the rise of civilization and artificial desires, though, does not address the more fundamental problem, which is ontological: How can anything generated from the way act contrary to it? That human beings do indeed deviate from the way is supported by the passages quoted above, and it is required if the *Dàodéjīng* is to give any guidance: What is the use of recommending the way if it is impossible to not follow it? From the perspective of European philosophy, it seems there are two ways to address these deviations from the way. One would be a distinction between the causality of nature and the causality of human actions, the latter supplied by free will. The other would be an alternate force counter to the way, something that would play a role analogous to real evil (for Manicheans) or real nothingness (for Augustine or Descartes). The *Dàodéjīng* articulates nothing like either alternative. Furthermore, both of those approaches are dualistic, positing two radically distinct orders, whereas the difference between acting spontaneously and acting deliberately is more a matter of degree.

The *Dàodéjīng* does not acknowledge a problem here. This may be a gap in its account, perhaps even a necessary gap. Benjamin Schwartz points out the problem, but he simply refers to "the unaccountable rise of a new notion of good and evil among those called the sages" (1985, 210). Isabelle Robinet also raises the problem without attempting to resolve it: "However, in an inexplicable way, it happens that people 'separate' themselves from the Dao. . . . This possibility of being lost is paradoxical since the Dao is everywhere and one cannot separate oneself from it; however the Chinese do not attempt to explain this. They only, following Laozi, make this observation" (1999, 149–50). It may be, as Robinet suggests, that the *Dàodéjīng* ignores the problem as irrelevant to its practical concerns—we know that all things are generated out of the way, and we know that human beings go against the way and disrupt things. Why or how does not matter. Before concluding that the text is theoretically incoherent, though, we should consider that it may be working with a conception of generation differing from the strict causality of *creatio ex nihilo,* a conception of generation such that deviations from the way are expected or normal, requiring no explanation.⁶⁴

If human beings can deviate from the way, then things (at least human ones) must have some independence. Contrary to our expectations about "the Dao," the *Dàodéjīng* never identifies *dào* with nature as a whole. Some passages may be taken to suggest that the way is everywhere, but even if the way is *in* everything, it does not follow that the way *is* everything.⁶⁵ The way is not presented as taking on different forms or becoming things but rather as producing or giving birth to them. The metaphor of mother and children makes this relationship clear: the mother gives birth to and guides the child, but this does not mean the child is the mother. Although written later, the *Lǚshì chūnqiū* brings out the connection between life/birth and separation: "Things unite to take form but separate to live" (13/1: 662). The fact that things are said to return to the way also implies some (temporary) independence—one would not need to return if it were impossible ever to leave. The statements that the way generates things but does not control or lord it over them further suggests some independence for things themselves. The way allows things to take their own course.

This independence from the way is taken up on a theoretical level in a passage we have seen on the generation of things: "*Dào* generates them, *dé* raises them, things form them, instruments complete them" (51). The way generates things and *dé* raises them up, but the process does not end there. Things take form (*xíng* 形) because of other things, *wù* 物, a term which would encompass events and processes, "things" in the broad sense that one might say they have "things" to do. They are completed (*chéng* 成) by *qì* 器, a term associated with the particular functionality of things, literally meaning tools, instruments, or vessels.[66] *Qì* seems to have become a technical term—the "Xìcí" draws a distinction between the *dào*, which is above forms (*xíngérshàng* 形而上); and the *qì*, concrete things, which are under forms (*xíngérxià* 形而下) (Gāo Hēng 1998, 407). *Qì* can also have a sense of limitation, as Kǒngzǐ famously says, "Gentlemen do not act as tools," using *qì* as a verb (*Lúnyǔ* 2.12).[67]

The precise distinction between things forming them and tools completing them is unclear but it should be a process of progressive specification. In this process, the work of *dào* and *dé* is good and beneficial, but the work of tools and other things is not necessarily so—the passage only mentions spontaneous honor for *dào* and *dé*. Everything needs a form to exist, but the forms bring limits and vulnerability. As the *Dàodéjīng* puts it, it is only because we have our own bodies (*shēn* 身) that we are vulnerable to trouble (*huàn* 患) (13). We see this in a passage from the *Zhuāngzǐ* that puts together taking form and being completed: "Once they receive their completed form [*chéngxíng* 成形], they never forget it but await its exhaustion. With other things, cutting and grinding against each other, they race toward exhaustion as if at a gallop, and none can stop—isn't it sad?" (2: 56; cf. Mair 1994, 14). *Chéng* 成 (to become, to ripen or mature, or to be completed) usually has a positive sense, but it sometimes has a sense of closure and loss of potentiality, as in the *Zhuāngzǐ*'s famous criticism of a "completed heart [*chéngxīn* 成心]" (2: 56; Mair 1994, 14). The *Dàodéjīng* takes up this sense of closure when it says that because sagely people do not desire to be full, they can "keep hidden and not be completed [*bì ér bùchéng* 敝而不成]" (15).[68] Sagely people remain like uncarved wood, neither completed nor made into specific tools or vessels.[69]

Sagely people thus remain close to the way and its potency, whereas most people become fixed into a form, leading them to exhaust themselves in a struggle with other things. This would explain how human beings leave the way, but if human beings are just one of the myriad things, then we would expect them to differ from other things only in degree. We would expect disruptions to appear elsewhere in nature. A passage we have already discussed supports this position. It begins, "Few words, self-so. A gusting wind does not last a morning; a violent rain does not last a day. Who does these? Heaven and earth, but they cannot make them last—how much less what is done by humanity?" (23). The passage then goes into the lines quoted earlier, that those who manage things with the way unite with the way, those of gain unite with gain, and those of loss unite with loss. The first line links saying little to what is spontaneous and so-of-itself, zìrán. Most likely, saying much involves labeling things, thus increasing artificial desires and striving.[70] The gusting wind and violent rain would be analogous to speaking too much. None of these can last long. That leads into the second half of the chapter—to speak too much is to follow a path of loss and thus to lose and be lost. The gusting wind and violent rain face the same problem, which suggests that they, too, are not zìrán, and that heaven and earth sometimes deviate from the way just as human beings do.[71] Although they are not common, similar claims do appear in other texts, as in the recently excavated *Zhòng Gōng* (仲弓), which says: "Mountains sometimes collapse, streams sometimes dry up, the sun, moon, and stars have irregularities, and of the people there are none who do not err" (Jì 2005, strip 19). This appears as an explanation for why one should be tolerant toward the errors of others—they are natural.

The example of gusting wind and violent rain suggests that not all "natural" things are zìrán. This claim is supported by a key passage that begins with mundane advice about acting before problems become big, and then concludes:

> Sagely people desire not desiring and do not honor things that are difficult to obtain. They teach without teaching, turning the masses back from where they err. Thus sagely people can assist the self-so spontaneity [zìrán] of the ten thousand things but they cannot act on them. (64)[72]

While not acting forcefully or coercively, sagely people draw the masses back from excess or error [*guò* 過], guiding them so that they remain natural and content.[73] The final line presents this as one instance of a broader role, which is to assist (*fǔ* 輔) the spontaneity of the myriad things.[74] In commenting on this passage, the *Hánfēizǐ* illustrates this "assistance" with the way farmers assist the patterns of nature in order to produce abundant grain (20: 451).[75] This term for "assist" may have had cosmological implications at the time. The *Tàiyī shēng shuǐ* uses the same term to explain how what is generated "turns back and assists" (*fǎnfǔ* 反輔) in the next stage of generation (Liú Zhāo 2003, strip 1). In a usage close to the *Dàodéjīng*, the "image" for the *tài* 泰 (peace) hexagram in the *Zhōu yì* reads, "Heaven and earth interacting is '*tài*.' The ruler arranges and completes the way of heaven and earth and assists [*fǔ*] the appropriateness of heaven and earth, in order to help the people" (Gāo Hēng 1998, 113). Wáng Bì explains that when things have great communion (*dàtōng* 大通) they tend to lose their moderation or order (*jié* 節), and so sagely people must assist these natural processes (Lóu 1999, 276).

If sagely people must *assist* the spontaneity of things, then the myriad things include some tendency away from *zìrán*, and thus from the way. The disruptiveness of human beings would be an extreme case of tendencies inherent in the myriad things. This conclusion is what we would expect given the *Dàodéjīng*'s non-humanist approach to action. Deviation from the way follows at least two tendencies. One is toward excess and violence, like the gusting wind or speaking too much. This would include tendencies toward extremes—the movement of the way is reversal, but how far things go in one direction depends on things themselves. The other tendency is toward rigidity, taking form and being completed. This rigidity is closely connected to death, as described in chapter 76:

> People in living are soft and weak; in dying are laid out, hard and strong. The myriad things, grasses and trees in living are soft and weak, but when dying are withered and brittle. Thus it is said: the hard and strong are followers of death, the soft and weak are followers of life. Therefore, if a weapon is strong then it does not conquer, if a tree is strong then it will snap. The strong and big dwell below; the soft and weak dwell above. (76)

This passage is prescriptive, advocating softness and weakness, but in so far as dying is normal for both human beings and plants, it implies a natural tendency toward rigidity. It may be tempting to think of these two ways of deviating as opposites—violence comes from an excess of generative force, whereas rigidity comes from a deficit. This is not quite the case, however. Excessive force is dangerous only insofar as it has hard edges. In itself, generative force has a flexible power like flowing water: "In the world, nothing is softer and weaker than water, but for attacking the hard and strong, nothing can beat it, because there is nothing by which to alter it" (78). Water cannot be altered precisely because, like the way itself, it has no particular form, no hard edges or corners.

We can now return to the relationship between the way and harm. Insofar as the way produces and nourishes things like a mother, it is good: "The way of heaven is to benefit and not harm." Conflict, suffering, and death come not from the way itself but rather the inevitable grinding of one thing against another. Things bring good or bad results on themselves, depending on their actions. This helps explain the perplexing end of chapter 23, which says, "Those united with loss, the way also loses them." Those who pursue loss are literally lost by the way, losing their vital root and becoming entangled in the interplay of things and instruments. Separating the *dào* from rigidity, excess, and death, though, forces us to make a distinction between what we would normally call "natural" and what is the way, or what is so-of-itself. Liú Xiàogǎn makes this point in arguing against the translation of *zìrán* as "nature": "Although under certain conditions these two can be aligned, their content and meaning absolutely are not the same. For example, earthquakes and erupting volcanoes are all part of the natural world, but they are absolutely not Lǎozǐ's *zìrán*" (2006, 274). Liú's point is that if we consider things like gusting winds as natural, then we must distinguish between the natural and the self-so, and thus between nature and the way. Aside from things like violent weather, the progression from life toward death surely is natural, but one line, repeated twice, says that the process of decline is not the way: "Things are vigorous and then old. This is called not following the way" (55, 30). "Vigorous" (*zhuàng* 壯), refers to things in their youthful prime; from that, old age follows. In context, the point of the line is about the danger of hastening death by becoming too vigorous, but the illustration is an observation about the way things naturally develop.[76] This movement toward death, though, is "not following the way," more literally, "not *dào*-ing [*búdào*]." The same point appears in holding up the child as an ideal—children naturally grow old, but the sage remains childlike.

We can now see the complexity of the relationship between sagely people, nature, and the way. We have so far emphasized the alignment between nature and the human good. Since the way itself tends toward life, balance, and sustainability, the primary role of the sage is to not interfere with these natural tendencies, generating and nurturing without controlling or possessing, letting things transform and develop of themselves. Yet if things naturally tend toward excess and rigidity, then sages must keep the natural processes of birth, growth, and death in balance, avoiding extremes in order to achieve stability and constancy. This is "assisting the *zìrán* of things." As applied to the people, sagely rulers "empty their hearts and fill their stomachs, weaken their commitments and strengthen their bones" (3). It is because the way naturally generates enough that—if desires for luxuries and extremes can be prevented—the people will be full, healthy, and content. For this state of natural plenty to arise and continue, though, sagely people must check the tendencies of human beings to deviate from the way through artificial desires and labels. They must ensure that regulations, controls, and incentives are kept to a minimum, and they must be there to step in when clever people wish to act (3, 37). Sometimes they may even be forced into war (31). The activity of the sage is most evident in resistance to the natural trajectory toward rigidity and death. Holding on to youthfulness, spontaneity and life is in some sense "unnatural" but is to accord with *dào* and with *zìrán*.[77] We might say that while anything alive is also dying, one can become either a follower of that tendency toward rigidity and death, or one who is "good at holding life." This resistance to natural patterns in the service of long life appears explicitly in later developments of Daoism, as one sees in the well-known saying, "One who follows along [*shùn* 順] becomes human; one who goes against [*nì* 逆] becomes immortal."

We can conclude by considering again how the *Dàodéjīng* might be taken as in some sense humanistic. Sages do not just let nature go. They carefully guide and assist natural processes in order to realize a specifically human good. The ideal of non-action, *wúwéi*, does not literally mean doing nothing.[78] Sagely people must act without being coercive or willful, the difficulty of which is a frequent theme. A number of strategies are suggested. A few passages state that one can bring about the wanted results by doing the opposite, for example, by strengthening what one wants to weaken (36). Liú Xiàogǎn argues the patterns of rising and falling can be avoided partly by incorporating negative aspects into the positive, for example, by adopting attitudes of those in weak positions (like softness and yielding) while actually being in a strong position (as ruler) (2006, 462–64). The need to counteract natural tendencies toward excess and rigidity helps to explain the *Dàodéjīng*'s one-sided emphasis on the weak, soft, feminine, dark, and so on, what would later be taken up as "*yīn*" forces. One common explanation is that one needs a balance between hard and soft, but since we tend to focus on the hard "*yáng*" side, the text counters that by emphasizing the soft "*yīn*" side.[79] We can see now a more fundamental reason. Things naturally tend toward the *yáng*, leaving their youthful softness and flexibility. A sagely person focuses on maintaining the *yīn* in order to counterbalance this natural tendency.[80]

The work of the sage requires constant vigilance, both in the ability to see the minute beginnings of problems and in carrying this carefulness through to the end (64). In spite of the emphasis on non-action, this vigilance continues and transforms the sense of caution we saw in the *Shàng shū*, the same care that the Ru take up as *yōuhuàn yìshí*, a sense of anxious concern and responsibility. The ability for human beings to succeed in this effort—the confidence in the efficacy of human action—also echoes the "humanistic" turn that derived originally from the Mandate of Heaven. Again we can see analogies between the position of the *Dàodéjīng* and that of the Mohists. The position of the *Dàodéjīng*, though, is considerably more complex. The Mohists take the will of heaven and the human good as perfectly aligned, but in the *Dàodéjīng*, the purpose of the sage and the patterns of nature diverge. This is not to say that sagely people *defy* nature, which would surely lead to destruction, but that sagely people carefully use and maintain—we might go so far as to say manipulate—the patterns of nature to achieve their own ends. The fact that the way itself tends toward most of a sagely person's goals explains why they can be effectively attained without great effort, and why the sage's relationship to the way, in contrast to traditional European attitudes toward nature, is not seen in agonistic terms of struggle and control but rather in terms of harmony and even reverence. Nonetheless, the human good cannot be identified with either nature or the *dào*. As long as we reject an anthropocentric conception of the *dào*, the goodness of the *dào* cannot fully align with what is specifically good for us. From the perspective of the way itself, balance is always ultimately maintained, and there is no way to label any events "bad," let alone "evil." The *Zhuāngzǐ* will draw out the consequences of such a view, as we will see. If we recall our earlier analogy between the generativity of *dào* and the priority of being in European thought, then the problem here is analogous to the difficulty of deriving a recognizably human good from any univocal conception of being, a problem with which, for example, Leibniz struggles valiantly (Perkins 2007, 45–53). The *Dàodéjīng*, however, does not try to derive the goal of life from the way. The goals of sagely people follow from *human* concerns.

4 Reproaching Heaven and Serving Heaven in the *Mèngzǐ*

The *Mòzǐ* and *Dàodéjīng* both claim that we share common goals and that following the regular patterns of nature allows us to effectively reach them. In this sense, both can be seen as opposing the fatalism that developed near the end of the Spring and Autumn Period, restoring a model analogous to the early Zhōu doctrine of the Mandate of Heaven. The disorder and suffering of the times, however, suggested that the fit between heaven and human was not so neat. Given the condition of the world, good people might not want to follow its patterns—they might even feel the need to oppose it. Although the *Mòzǐ* and *Dàodéjīng* at least aim toward the harmony or unity of heaven and human (*tiānrén héyī*), the conditions of the time pointed more toward recognizing their division (*tiānrén zhīfēn*). We have already seen the outlines of such a position in the fatalistic tendency among some of the early Ru. Mèngzǐ's philosophy can be seen as a more complex and developed account of this position, primarily adding two dimensions. One is a detailed account of human motivation in terms of an analysis of *xìng* 性, our natural or characteristic tendencies and dispositions. The other is an attempt to shift the locus of our relationship with heaven away from the external patterns of nature and toward these natural dispositions that heaven gives us. Together, these two points allow *Mèngzǐ* to take the problem of evil more seriously than any other prominent Warring States philosopher, leaving him closest to something like a tragic worldview.

Heaven and the Efficacy of Virtue

It is remarkably difficult to determine the nature of heaven in the *Mèngzǐ*. Unlike the *Mòzǐ* or *Xúnzǐ*, the *Mèngzǐ* does not argue for any particular vision of heaven. The text follows the common Ru approach of emphasizing different points in different contexts, particularly when discussing fate and the efficacy of human action. Mèngzǐ says explicitly that gentlemen label things as "fate" (*mìng*) or as human "nature" (*xìng*) according what will be most helpful for purposes of self-cultivation (7B24). The text itself likely incorporates viewpoints from his disciples as well as quotations from more ancient texts, which may or may not be fully endorsed.[1] It is also possible that Mèngzǐ's own views became more pessimistic and fatalistic later in life, as he gave up hope of finding a ruler to enact his plans.

We can begin with a vexing question: Does Mèngzǐ take heaven to be conscious and intentional? Several passages juxtapose heaven and humans as if they were analogous. One passage says, "Do not reproach *tiān* [heaven], do not blame *rén* [human beings]" (2B13); another says not to "feel shame before *tiān* or blush before *rén*" (7A20). These passages suggest that heaven is an agent that could be blamed or provoke feelings of shame. Others use anthropomorphic language, as one says that heaven does not want or desire (*yù* 欲) peace and order (2B13). Other passages suggest the deliberate planning of heaven, for example, saying that when heaven is about to give someone great responsibility, it first gives them hardships (6B15). Direct evidence against an anthropomorphic view is difficult to find, but Mèngzǐ emphasizes that heaven acts through natural processes, so that we know it only indirectly, by observing events (5A5) and developing our own natural tendencies (7A1).[2] A deeper reason against a more anthropomorphic reading, though, is that if Mèngzǐ believed heaven had intentions, it would be odd that he never analyzes or argues about what heaven's intentions are, particularly since such issues were discussed explicitly by the Mohists.[3]

Whether we take claims about heaven's intentions literally or figuratively makes little difference for the key point here, which is the relationship between heaven and Ru ethics: Is heaven humane? Does heaven reward those who are humane? Can humaneness be justified as a way of following heaven? These questions are difficult to answer because of a tension that appears between two of heaven's roles. Some passages posit a connection between the Ru virtues and heaven through *xìng*, the "characteristic tendencies" or "nature" of human beings. Our nature is to be good, and we should follow our nature because it is given by heaven. These passages seem to require that heaven itself be good. Other passages, however, make heaven responsible for bad things, ranging from the failure of individual projects to the general disorder and suffering of the times. These passages suggest that heaven is bad, or at least morally indifferent. The tension between these two sides is another manifestation of the tension generally between *tiān* and *mìng* in the *Lúnyǔ*, or between heaven's normative and descriptive functions. At the heart of the conflict is the problem of evil: How can we maintain that heaven is humane in the face of all the bad things that heaven generates?

The result is a puzzling view of heaven and a tragic situation for human beings. Several commentators point out this tragic element. Ivanhoe writes, "Heaven encourages human beings to be good, it provides them with a good nature, and on occasion it acts in the world to help the cause of good people. However, it also imposes a cycle of moral light and darkness upon the world. . . . If this too is a matter of 'fate' (mìng 命), then fate can indeed be cruel" (2002a, 72). Michael Puett claims that while heaven is the source of moral norms, heaven itself violates these norms: "The central tension for Mèngzǐ, then, is that although *tiān* is the ultimate source of moral patterns, it can and does arbitrarily act in opposition to those patterns. And yet we must accept what *tiān* commands" (2002, 144). Chén Dàqí writes, "Heaven uses its right hand to create it and uses its left hand to destroy it, so that the will of heaven cannot be unified" (1980, 104).

If we take this tension as a version of the problem of evil, then two coherent solutions appear.[4] First, we might rely on the way the world appears and give up claims that heaven is good. This might lead to taking heaven as a capricious anthropomorphic deity, sometimes benevolent and sometimes not, as Puett suggests.[5] Alternately, one might naturalize heaven into a morally indifferent force. Either view requires explaining the link between heaven and the goodness of our natural tendencies in a way that does not require heaven itself to be good. The other approach to the problem would deny that heaven's actions are ever truly bad, assuming that apparently bad events actually unfold according to some higher plan. This is a common view among Western interpreters, but Mèngzǐ never says anything like it. Its support comes only from the difficulty of making sense of other parts of the text without such an assumption.

We can approach Mèngzǐ's position first by considering his views of the problem of evil and the efficacy of virtue. For the most part, Mèngzǐ falls within the tradition of "Chinese humanism" that attributes power to human virtue and makes us ultimately responsible for order and disorder. One passage lays this out in general terms that could easily be Mohist:

> The three dynasties attained the world by humaneness; their losing the world was by being inhumane. That by which states rise or fall, are preserved or destroyed is also like this. If the son of heaven is not humane, he will not protect all within the four seas. If the various lords are not humane, they will not protect the altars to the land and grain. If the ministers and high officials are not humane, they will not protect their ancestral temples. If scholars and commoners are not humane, they will not protect their four limbs. Now to hate death and destruction but enjoy being inhumane is like hating being drunk but insisting on drinking. (4A3)

Inhumanity causes harm in just the same way that wine causes drunkenness. The subsequent passage draws out the implications, saying that if other people do not respond to our actions, then we should assume it is due to our own lack of humaneness (4A4). The first part of the *Mèngzǐ* consists almost entirely of dialogues with political leaders praising the power of humaneness and rightness to bring success. A few passages make extreme claims that one with full humaneness will surely become a true king (e.g. 1A7, 1A6, 2A6) More often, Mèngzǐ makes one of two more limited claims: that humaneness is the surest way for a ruler to succeed, and that in the long run inhumanity never succeeds.

Although this link between virtue and political success fits early views of the Mandate of Heaven, what is more striking is how the *Mèngzǐ* qualifies it. The limits of virtue appear in a series of progressively more pessimistic dialogues between Mèngzǐ and Duke Wén of Téng. Duke Wén met with Mèngzǐ twice while passing through the state of Sòng (3A1), and he later sent a messenger to ask Mèngzǐ how to best conduct his father's funeral (3A2). Eventually, Mèngzǐ moved to Téng, and perhaps resided there until the end of his life; Brooks and Brooks suggest that a group of Mèngzǐ's disciples may have settled in Téng (2002a, 255). The duke is the only living political leader that the *Mèngzǐ* portrays positively, and he seems to have had a broad reputation for virtue, drawing scholars from other states (3A4). The state of Téng, though, was small and lay in a dangerous position between the great powers of Qí and Chǔ. In the first passage of the series, the duke asks Mèngzǐ with which state he should ally his own. Mèngzǐ responds, "This plan is not something I can reach, but if forced, there is one thing: dig out these moats, build up these walls, and protect them together with the people. If the people will not leave you even when facing death, then it can be done" (1B13). Although Mèngzǐ does not explicitly mention virtue, the only way a ruler could convince his people to remain with him while in great danger would be through his virtue.

The next passage continues on the same topic, as Qí has begun to fortify a nearby city and the duke fears an imminent attack. Mèngzǐ advises,

> Formerly, when King Tài resided in Bīn, the Dí people invaded it and he left to reside at the base of Mount Qí. This was not by his choice but because he had no alternative. If you do good, future generations of sons and grandsons will surely have a king. Gentlemen start an enterprise and dangle a thread that can be continued. As for success, that is with heaven. What can you do about that? Just strive to do good and that is all. (1B14)

Mèngzǐ's response contrasts with his claims elsewhere that the humane have no enemies, or that one with humane government cannot be stopped from ruling the world. None of those would be particularly realistic. Mèngzǐ acknowledges that the duke cannot control the outcome and so should try to free himself from concern. This is the role of heaven—firmly placing success outside human control also places it outside our concerns, allowing for peace of mind and resolve. The uncertainty of the outcome does not diminish the need for the king to be good, nor does it make his efforts insignificant. Goodness must be maintained in dark times so that it can emerge again and flourish in the future.[6]

The last passage in the series informs the duke that he has only two choices—he can follow the example of King Tài and flee with the hope that some of his people will follow, or he can die defending his kingdom (1B15). The duke is caught in a double bind: to flee would save the lives of the people but betray his ancestors; to stay would fulfill ancestral duty, but cost countless lives. Neither alternative is good.⁷ This is one of the bleakest and most tragic passages in the text. Mèngzǐ himself seems unsure which alternative to recommend.

This dialogue with Duke Wén of Téng contrasts with Mèngzǐ's response to an almost identical question regarding the state of Sòng, which was also small and situated between the states of Qí and Chǔ. When asked how Sòng can survive, Mèngzǐ begins by describing how the sage king Tāng started with a small territory but used humaneness to eventually rule the world. He concludes, "If he enacts kingly government, within the four seas, all will raise their heads and look to him, desiring to have him as sovereign. Although Qí and Chǔ are large, how can he fear them?" (3B5). The difference between Mèngzǐ's responses regarding Sòng and Téng recalls Kǒngzǐ's contradictory responses to identical questions from different students (Lúnyǔ 11.22). Here, the difference may follow from differences in the power of the two states, but a more likely reason is that the two rulers needed to hear different things. Mèngzǐ was probably living in Sòng early in the reign of King Yǎn 偃 (also known as King Kāng 康), at a time when the king's character was not yet clear.⁸ In that context, Mèngzǐ's first advice is to recommend the power of virtue, perhaps even to exaggerate it. The situation of Téng is different, since Duke Wén seems already committed to virtue. Mèngzǐ's advice to him is focused not so much on the power that comes from virtue but rather with how to deal with its limits. Ultimately, the king of Sòng rejected Mèngzǐ's advice and gained a reputation for great evil.⁹ Aside from the usual flaws of excess in drinking and women, his most famous action was his open defiance of heaven: he filled a leather sack with blood, suspended it high in the sky, and then shot arrows at it until blood dripped down to the earth. His attendants praised him for "conquering heaven [shèngtiān 勝天]" (Lǚshì chūnqiū 23/4: 1569). Ironically, when the state of Téng was indeed destroyed (around 297 BCE), the destroyer was not the powerful states of Qí and Chǔ but Mèngzǐ's former patron, King Yǎn of Sòng. The fact that the state of the ruler most receptive to Mèngzǐ's teachings was destroyed by an evil king who rejected his advice would not have been lost on the compilers of the Mèngzǐ.

The problem of evil appears even more clearly if we turn from rulers to the opposite end of the power structure—the common people. Descriptions of the suffering and misery of the people appear in many passages, and are probably meant to evoke feelings of compassion and concern. This suffering appears even in those passages that emphasize the fair treatment of rulers. For example, in a dialogue with King Huì of Liáng, Mèngzǐ gives his typical argument that the king's population decreases because he is not humane enough: if he were truly virtuous he would be rewarded with a greater population. Where do the king's actions leave the people? Dying of starvation on the roads (1A3). These passages express the problem we have already seen with the Mandate of Heaven, that heaven works through the people by pushing them to a level of suffering that is literally unbearable. In the Mèngzǐ, the dependence of the people on rulers goes even deeper, though, because rulers largely determine the moral character of the people. One famous passage in a dialogue with King Xuān of Qí says,

> Only a scholar [*shì* 士] can have a constant heart without having a constant livelihood. For the people, if they lack a constant livelihood, then they lack a constant heart. Without a constant heart, they will become dissolute, crooked, evil, and excessive. There will be nothing they do not do. To sink them into crime and then to follow it up by punishing them—this is to ensnare the people. When there is a humane person in a position of power, how can he ensnare the people! (1A7)

If a ruler does not provide a stable base of material goods for the people, he in effect makes them inhumane. To then punish them for it is to doubly wrong them.

The educated elite aspiring for positions of responsibility, the *shì* 士, hold a position between that of rulers (who usually get what they deserve) and the people (whose suffering or flourishing follows from the actions of others).[10] If the main message to rulers is that humaneness triumphs, the message for individuals is to learn to enjoy poverty and obscurity. In a good world (like that portrayed by the Mohists), no one would have to choose between their well-being and their virtue. Ours is not such a world: "A resolute scholar never forgets the possibility of ending up in a ditch or gully; a brave scholar never forgets the possibility of losing his head" (3B1; 5B7).[11] If individual scholars are unlikely to get what they deserve, they still remain less vulnerable than the common people, as they develop a kind of autonomy that frees them from utter dependence on external conditions. This ability to maintain one's resolve (*zhì* 志) in the face of success or failure, wealth or poverty, safety or danger, is one of the central themes of the *Mèngzǐ* and the early Ru tradition. It is inseparable from one of the main Ru responses to the problem of evil, which shifts the meaning of success onto the internal satisfaction that comes from virtue. Mèngzǐ brings together this sense of satisfaction and the commitment to virtue in advice he gives to another scholar, using the same terms (*qióng* and *dá*) as *Qióng dá yǐ shí* (Failure and success are by timing):

> Honor virtue and delight in rightness, and then you can be content. Hence a scholar in failure [*qióng* 窮] does not lose rightness, and in success [*dá* 達] does not leave the way. Failing but not losing rightness: thus the scholar attains from himself. Successful but not leaving the way: thus the people do not lose hope in him. When the ancients attained what they resolved, their saturating kindness was extended to the people. When they did not attain what they resolved, the cultivation of their person was manifest throughout that generation. Failing, they made their own selves good on their own; successful, they inclusively made the world good. (7A9)

This passage assumes that a scholar will not necessarily be rewarded for virtue or effort. Acceptance and the continuation of virtue while poor and obscure may be the best one can hope for, and the only thing one can control.

Heaven's Role in the World

Considering all strata of society, Mèngzǐ sees success as dependent on both virtue and power. The king of a major state like Qí may get exactly what he deserves, but even the ruler of a small state like Téng is insecure. The fate of other individuals depends almost entirely on external factors, most of all the virtue of their rulers. Mèngzǐ ends up with a middle position between that of Mòzǐ, who seems to say virtue succeeds no matter what, and Hánfēizǐ, who sees success as coming entirely from political power. Mèngzǐ's position is probably close to that of the early Zhōu Mandate of Heaven, which, in spite of interpretations of it as a humanistic principle, was really about the fate of rulers. What is most striking in that context, though, is that Mèngzǐ's explicit appeals to heaven function in exactly the opposite way. Heaven explains the *failure* of virtue, not its success. When King Wén is forced either to flee his kingdom or to die defending it, that is heaven (1B14). The passage which follows the series of dialogues with King Wén of Téng uses heaven in a similar way. Mèngzǐ's disciple Yuèzhèngzǐ explains that Duke Píng of Lǔ was going to visit Mèngzǐ, but one of the duke's court favorites, Zāng Cāng, persuaded him against it. Mèngzǐ responds,

> Acting has something that sends it forth and stopping has something that restrains it. Acting and stopping are not something human beings are able to do. My not meeting (*yù* 遇) the Marquis of Lǔ is heaven. How could this fellow of the Zāng family make me not meet him? (1B16)

The duke should have come—the people are in desperate need and Mèngzǐ has the virtue to help them. The appeal to heaven explains why things did *not* work out the way they should.

In contrast, when virtue leads to success, appeals to heaven are absent. For example, the success of good rulers is explained through the psychological tendencies natural to human beings. This position develops the claim in the *Shàng shū* (*Book of Documents*) that heaven sees and hears as the people do, but eliminates heaven as the middleman. One passage removes heaven's influence explicitly. Around 318 BCE, King Kuài of Yān was convinced to turn the throne over to his minister Zǐzhī, in emulation of the early sage kings who passed the throne to the most worthy. A disastrous civil war broke out, led by the king's son. The state of Qí intervened and Mèngzǐ, a minister in Qí at that time, was seen as having condoned Qí's attack.[12] The invasion succeeded quickly and King Xuān, the ruler of Qí, asked Mèngzǐ what he should do next:

> King Xuān asked, "Some tell me not to take Yān while others tell me to take it. For a state of ten thousand chariots to attack a state of ten thousand chariots and in fifty days to attain it—human power does not reach this. If I do not take Yān, there will certainly be disasters from heaven. What if I take it?" Mèngzǐ replied: "If by taking it you please the people of Yān, then take it. Of ancient

people there was one who enacted this, namely King Wǔ. If by taking it you do not please the people of Yān, then do not take it. Of ancient people there was one who enacted this, namely King Wén. For a state of ten thousand chariots to attack a state of ten thousand chariots and have its army welcomed with baskets of food and pots of porridge—what else can it be but that the people are fleeing from water and fire? If the water gets deeper and the fire hotter, they will simply turn again." (1B10)

King Xuān invokes the traditional Mandate of Heaven: heaven gave him aid beyond human power and thus must want him to control Yān. To refuse heaven's command would bring retribution.[13] Mèngzǐ explains that the king's success follows from the natural responses of an oppressed people seeking relief, removing any direct intervention or intentionality from heaven, either in aiding the king's success or in sanctioning the king's control. The king, perhaps trusting his supposed mandate, did try to keep Yān by force (2B11). Qí was driven out shortly after, and the state of Yān later took brutal revenge, nearly eliminating the state of Qí.

In showing a natural causal connection between virtue and success, Mèngzǐ aligns with the Mohists but without any role for heaven. Heaven is invoked only when bad things happen. To take heaven as good thus requires reading these passages as meaning the opposite of what they say. If one wants to take heaven to be a willful anthropomorphic deity, the textual evidence suggests it is malevolent or at least capricious, inexplicably disrupting the natural order we rely on in managing our lives. What seems more likely is that Mèngzǐ has come to equate heaven with fate, *ming*. Heaven simply represents those forces or events in the world that are inexplicable and irresistible. Mèngzǐ explains heaven in just this way: "What no one does but is done—that is heaven. What no one sends but arrives—that is fate" (5A6). Here, heaven and fate are roughly equivalent: Zhū Xī says that in terms of natural patterns (*lǐ* 理) it is called *tiān* and in terms of human affairs it is called *ming*, but what they refer to is the same (Zhū 2003, 309). The functional identification of heaven with fate would explain why one would tend to appeal to it only in bad circumstances. This reduction of heaven to blind fate is exactly what the Mohists opposed.

The potentially agonistic relationship between heaven and human beings appears in a dialogue that comes as Mèngzǐ is leaving the state of Qí after his involvement with the invasion of Yān:

When Mèngzǐ left Qí, on the road Chōng Yú asked, "Master, you look displeased. I heard from you the other day that gentlemen do not reproach heaven and do not blame other people." Mèngzǐ responded: "That was one time; this is another time. Every five hundred years a true king must arise, and in between there must be one famous in that generation. From the Zhōu on it has been over seven hundred years. According to the count, it has passed; examining it by the time, it can be done. It is just that heaven does not yet desire peace and order in the world. If it desired peace and order in the world, in today's age, who is there other than I? How could I be displeased?" (2B13)

This passage is difficult to interpret and can be read as either justifying or rejecting being upset. That depends primarily on how one reads the line translated above as "that was one time and this is another time [彼一時[也], 此一時也]," which might instead be taken as, "that one time is this one time."[14] Time (shí 時) is the word we have seen for timeliness or the seasons, so it implies not an abstract moment but rather a concrete temporal configuration or context. The most natural way to read the passage is that Mèngzǐ is upset and his disciple calls him on it. Perhaps Mèngzǐ starts out to justify his discontent, but as he talks through it, his feelings become more ambivalent. The final line implies that, after all, he should not be unhappy.[15] The problem with reading the passage as an argument for being satisfied, though, is that Mèngzǐ describes only how wrong things are. Some have claimed that Mèngzǐ here appeals to trust in the goodness of heaven, but it is difficult to see how not wanting peace could actually be good, and if that were the key to the passage, Mèngzǐ surely would have told his inquiring disciple.[16] The most plausible explanation is that once Mèngzǐ reminds himself that he has done all he can, he resigns himself to the situation and accepts it.[17] This response would fit other passages that advocate taking comfort in one's own goodness while accepting things that are beyond one's control. It also makes sense of the initial parallel between heaven and human beings: the reason we should not blame other people is not that we trust their goodness but because blaming them distracts from our primary task of self-cultivation. Mèngzǐ's attitude toward heaven is the same.

We still should not entirely dismiss the possibility that Mèngzǐ *is* complaining. If a complaint is justified here, it is only because Mèngzǐ laments not his own suffering but that of the people.[18] His complaint would express the concern that comes naturally for a properly cultivated human being. As Jiāo Xún puts it, "Thus when one's resolve involves worried concern for the world and compassion for the people, this must take form in one's appearance" (1987, 309). Chén Dàqí draws a comparison with parents—normally one should not reproach them, but if a parent's mistake is truly great, criticizing them is one's filial duty. He concludes, "Heaven not yet wishing peace and order in the world—this is a big mistake, not a small mistake" (1980, 107).

The question of resenting heaven appears in a similar story about the sage king Shùn, whose parents were notoriously evil (5A1). Shùn is said to have gone into the fields and tearfully called out to heaven. When a student questions the appropriateness of Shùn's discontent, Mèngzǐ explains that this expressed "angry longing [yuànmù 怨慕]," using yuàn 怨 (to resent, reproach, or be frustrated with).[19] Mèngzǐ goes on to explain that Shùn had everything people want—admiration, beautiful women, wealth, nobility—but he was not happy because he did not have the approval of his parents. Shùn's anguish is taken as demonstrating the seriousness of a filial heart—to simply accept his parent's displeasure would be unfilial. We can see a tragic element in both of these passages. The passage on Shùn says that he felt like a person having no home to return to (*wúsuǒguī* 無所歸), a phrase we could translate literally as *unheimlich*. The ambiguity and differences between these two passages reflect the tension at the root of Ru discussions of fate, between anxious concern and acceptance of what is outside our control. In leaving Qí in trouble and Yān nearly destroyed, should Mèngzǐ be filled with anxious concern for the people—or should he be untroubled, knowing he did his best? I suspect the Ru would avoid a theoretical answer—sometimes one needs to be upset and prompted into action, but at other times one needs comfort. Mèngzǐ initially responds to Chōng Yú's comment by saying now is not the moment for resignation, but as he reflects he realizes that it is, in fact, time to get beyond anger and move toward acceptance.

The description of Mèngzǐ leaving the state of Qí clarifies his views of heaven. Once again heaven is invoked when things turn out worse than they should. Heaven has violated the usual pattern by leaving the people in misery for too long. What is striking, though, is that even the usual pattern cannot be considered *good*. While a true king arises every five hundred years, the implication is that every five hundred years life becomes unbearably miserable. Nature brings periods of order *and* periods of disorder, in a somewhat regular cycle, showing no preference between them. Other passages repeat this cyclical view of history: "The world has been living for a long time, sometimes in order and sometimes in chaos" (3B9). Another passage contrasts times when the world has or lacks the way:

> When the world has the way, little virtue serves great virtue and little worthiness serves great worthiness. When the world lacks the way, the small serve the large and the weak serve the strong. These two are both from heaven. One who follows along with [*shùn* 順] heaven is preserved. One who goes against [*nì* 逆] heaven is destroyed. (4A7)

In good times virtue prevails and in bad times power prevails. Heaven determines *both* courses, indifferent to whether or not the world has the way.

It is important to see how radically this cyclical view of history alters the earlier doctrine of *tiānmìng*, the Mandate of Heaven, taken as either a principle of rightness (in which rulers get what they deserve) or of humaneness (in which suffering people are helped). History had made such a view almost impossible to maintain.[20] For Mèngzǐ, heaven remains responsible for the success and failure of rulers, but keeping the mandate no longer depends simply on deserving it but also on falling in the right place in the cycles of history. This position develops the view of *Qióng dá yǐ shí*, in which success depends on having the right time (*shí*) and being born in the right age (*shì*). The fatalism that might follow from such a position is mitigated by the fact that Mèngzǐ took the chaos and suffering of his age as signs that it was the right time for a sage to arise (2A1).[21] This belief underlies Mèngzǐ's confidence in the efficacy of humaneness on the political level; he might have been less optimistic in a different era. In fact, it is commonly thought that Mèngzǐ eventually gave up on political success and resigned himself to teaching—his failure in the state of Qí may have been a crucial turning point.[22]

A full account of Mèngzǐ's view of the Mandate of Heaven must address a pair of problematic passages on the transmission of power among the early sage kings Yáo, Shùn, and Yǔ. According to legend, the three were unrelated, and Shùn and Yǔ were given the kingship because of their worthiness. The custom of passing the throne to one's son began only with Yǔ, founding the Xià dynasty. The legend of Yáo's transmission of power to the worthy Shùn was obviously problematic for Warring States rulers following heredity, and we now know from excavated texts that transmitting the throne to the worthy was openly advocated by people closely associated with Ru ideas.[23] The debate was complicated by Yān's civil war, which, as mentioned above, was sparked when King Kuài yielded the throne to his supposedly worthy minister.[24] Given his involvement with Qí's intervention, Mèngzǐ obviously had a personal stake in the debate, but he enters it by denying that human beings have any power to decide the issue:

> Wàn Zhāng said, "Was it so that Yáo gave the world [i.e., all-under-heaven, *tiānxià*] to Shùn?" Mèngzǐ said, "No. The son of heaven cannot give the world to a person." "If so, then in Shùn's having the world, who gave it to him?" Mèngzǐ said, "Heaven gave it to him." "In heaven's giving it to him, was it with an explicit mandate [*mìng*]?" Mèngzǐ said, "No. Heaven does not speak. It expresses itself in actions and affairs and that is all." (5A5)

The next passage continues the discussion, with Wàn Zhāng repeating a criticism that virtue declined with Yǔ because he transmitted the throne to his son rather than to the worthiest. Mèngzǐ again shifts the responsibility to heaven, building on his claim that a person cannot give the world: "When heaven gives it to the worthy, it is given to the worthy. When heaven gives it to the son, it is given to the son" (5A6). In these passages, Mèngzǐ sides with the principle of heredity, and the reason he gives is that this is what heaven has set. Nonetheless, Mèngzǐ's argument against transmission of power to the worthy seems not to be that it is wrong, but rather that it is just not how things work. Heaven functions descriptively to indicate the way the transmission of power in fact works.[25]

These passages illuminate the difficulty in determining the agency of heaven. Heaven's "giving" the world appears on at least three levels. On a ritual level, a new ruler must be formally offered to heaven and heaven must show its acceptance by receiving the person's sacrifices. On another level, heaven acts through the people, so that when Yáo died, those among the people who needed decisions made went to Shùn instead of to Yáo's son. In contrast, after Yǔ died, the people went to his son rather than his ministers. These two levels were traditional aspects of the doctrine of *tiānmìng*, but Mèngzǐ adds a third, in which heaven encompasses all conditions. The concrete reasons that the people followed the most worthy in the first two cases and the son in the third lies in two factors: how long each minister served and how worthy the sons happened to be. These conditions are attributed to heaven. Thus heaven is responsible for how long each person served, how well they worked, how worthy their children were, and how the people responded to them. The fact that the son of Yáo was not as worthy as the son of Yǔ would seem to be the fault of Yáo's son, but here it is attributed to heaven. The attribution of human actions to heaven appears in other passages as well. In fact, Chén Dàqí points out that almost every appeal to heaven in the *Mèngzǐ* explains human events (1980, 101). Páng Pǔ goes further to identify heaven with the social world, writing that heaven "is not really a power different from human beings but is only a transformation of human power, expressing the human as heaven. More precisely, it is the power of the human collective, which we might also call social power" (2005, 87).[26]

If we take heaven as a conscious being with purposes, then we have a disturbing view in which heaven manipulates human beings by determining their character and choices. A more likely view is that heaven is identified with the forces of the world, so that attributing human actions to heaven just says that those actions follow from some combination of contingent events (like length of life) and natural psychological laws (the people's tendency to shift their affection from a sage king to his son). On a metaphysical level, all events would be attributed to heaven, and Mèngzǐ indeed says elsewhere that there is nothing which is not fated or mandated [*mìng*], but heaven is *used* more narrowly, to label what we cannot control and must simply accept. That includes natural events such as floods, but sometimes also the actions of other people.[27] Moreover, what is attributed to heaven would be relative to what a particular agent can control. Thus, for example, the first passage claims that if Shùn had taken over by trying to occupy the throne rather than by retiring and waiting when Yáo died, that would be "usurpation, not heaven giving it" (5A1). How to behave when the emperor died was within Shùn's control, and he can be praised or blamed for his choices. At the same time, one suspects that from the perspective of the people being ruled, Shùn's actions would still have been attributed to heaven, as something outside of their control.[28] This functional use of heaven explains why it is invoked primarily to explain bad things. It is when we meet unexpected or undeserved disaster that we must remind ourselves that not everything is within our control.

From Heaven to Human

Mèngzǐ's idea of the world as following cycles that have no particular regard for human well-being is close to views of heaven in the *Zhuāngzǐ* and the *Xúnzǐ*, but it also aligns with the *Dàodéjīng*'s claim that "heaven and earth are not humane, they take the myriad things as straw dogs" (5). What makes Mèngzǐ's position difficult, interesting, and tragic is that he would agree with the premise while opposing the conclusion: "Sagely people are not humane, they take the people as straw dogs." The *Mèngzǐ* admits a fundamental conflict between an ethics aimed at the human good and a world that moves indifferently between good and bad. Numerous passages address the challenges of living within this divergence, proposing strategies like learning to appreciate simple pleasures, or developing a sense of timeliness, *shí*. One passage contrasts the sage king Yǔ, who lived in an age of peace and was able to rule the world, with Yán Huí, who lived in an age of chaos in poverty and obscurity (4B29). The point is that at the right time in the historical cycle, a good person will succeed. At other times, they will not. The sage remains consistent—Yǔ and Yán Huí followed the same way, the same *dào*. The inconsistency comes from heaven, which promoted Yǔ but hindered Yán Huí, and gave Yǔ what he deserved but repaid Yán Huí's identical commitment with poverty and death.

If heaven splits its effort between order and chaos, then Mèngzǐ cannot advocate directly imitating heaven. Being a resolute scholar requires something close to defiance. If heaven does not want peace, then it would seem hubristic and foolish to dedicate one's life to peace anyway—comparable to the *Zhuāngzǐ*'s praying mantis who waved his arms to fend off the oncoming chariot (4: 167; Mair 1994, 36). And as the *Zhuāngzǐ* says, "It has long been the case that things do not conquer heaven!" (6: 260; cf. Mair 1994, 58). Yet this is what Mèngzǐ attempts in promoting peace and order. This strange, almost tragic, relationship to nature can be traced back to the description of Kǒngzǐ as one who knows it cannot be done but does it anyway (*Lúnyǔ* 14.38). Mèngzǐ's stance raises two problems. First, how can human beings be motivated to do actions that will not be rewarded and may even result in death? Second, why would—or should—we do actions that appear to go against the patterns of nature itself? Mèngzǐ's answers lie in a turn away from heaven itself and toward heaven as it is in us—toward human *xìng* 性.

Mèngzǐ is best known for his claim that "human nature is good [*xìngshàn* 性善]." The term *xìng*, usually translated as human "nature," is complex and frequently ambiguous.[29] It commonly refers to the tendencies or dispositions a thing has by being born that kind of thing, but many texts allow that the *xìng* of a thing can be changed, particularly through cultivation or neglect.[30] *Xìng* is often used as a species concept, as Mèngzǐ contrasts the *xìng* of human beings with the *xìng* of dogs (6A3), but some texts refer to different people as having different *xìng*, and some lines of thought associated with the *Zhuāngzǐ* took each individual as having its own unique *xìng*.[31] *Xìng* functions as a unit of individuation, a process-oriented replacement for the concept of substance, but this individuation is provisional and relational, and one can discuss *xìng* within *xìng*, as Mèngzǐ will speak of the *xìng* of a mountain ecosystem (6A8) but also the *xìng* of a tree (6A1). *Xìng* is closely connected to and derived from *shēng* 生, the term we have seen meaning to live, grow, give birth, or generate, and Mèngzǐ's rival Gàozǐ argues human *xìng* is in eating and sex (6A4). Since our dispositions involve inherent tendencies toward action, growth, and change, we can also speak of *xìng* as a tendency to grow or develop in certain ways. Thus, Mèngzǐ thinks our *xìng* naturally develops toward virtue when given a sufficiently nourishing environment. Xúnzǐ similarly sees *xìng* as naturally expanding, but he identifies *xìng* primarily with sensory desires, so that this expansion leads into chaos and strife. Since *xìng* refers to dispositions toward spontaneous reactions, translating it as "nature" is misleading—our ability to reflect and act deliberately is surely part of our nature, but it is not part of our *xìng*. I will generally translate *xìng* as "natural dispositions" or "characteristic tendencies" but sometimes for convenience simply as "nature."

Xìng is Mèngzǐ's most important concept, filling two gaps in the positions we have seen so far. First, the *Mòzǐ* and *Dàodéjīng* both take for granted certain human motivations and desires, but give little specific analysis of them. *Xìng* (along with *qíng*, its affective responses to stimulation) became the main concept for the analysis of human motivation. This more specific and technical account of motivation allows Mèngzǐ to argue that human beings have natural motivations directly toward virtue, so that virtue need not be justified as a means to benefit or a long life. Second, the introduction of *xìng* shifts focus away from the generic processes of nature toward the specific nature of a given thing. It allows Mèngzǐ to discuss what might be unique about human beings (like the *Mòzǐ* and *Lúnyǔ*) while remaining within a broader context of what is natural (like the *Dàodéjīng*). With this emphasis on human *xìng*, Mèngzǐ attempts to maintain a humanism compatible with the fact that in nature, human beings are just one of the myriad things.

Our understanding of the context for Mèngzǐ's discussions of *xìng* has been greatly expanded by recently discovered texts written around the time that Mèngzǐ lived.[32] The most important of those has been called the *Xìng zì mìng chū*, which might be translated as "Dispositions come out from what is allotted."[33] We can draw a few points from that text to help set the context for Mèngzǐ and Xúnzǐ. It begins thus:

> Although all human beings have *xìng*, the heart lacks a stable resolve [*zhì* 志]. It awaits things and then stirs, awaits being pleased and then acts, awaits practice and then stabilizes. The vital energies [*qì*] of pleasure, anger, grief, and sadness are *xìng*. Their appearing on the outside is because things stimulate them. *Xìng* comes out from *mìng* and *mìng* comes down from *tiān*. The way begins from genuine feelings [*qíng* 情] and feelings are generated from *xìng*. The beginning is close to genuine feeling; the ending is close to rightness. Those who know genuine feelings can express them; those who know right-

ness can internalize it. Loving and hating are *xìng*. What is loved and what is hated are things. Affirming as good or not good is *xìng*. What is affirmed as good or not good are circumstances. (Liú Zhāo 2003, strips 1–5)

The first few lines present a basic model of human psychology. Human beings share a nature, or *xìng*, which consists of tendencies to react in certain ways. When stimulated by external things, *xìng* stirs and specific reactions occur, labeled as *qíng*. Concrete psychological states thus arise from the interaction between ourselves and events, and the basic model involves three elements—our nature or characteristic tendencies, external things or events, and concrete reactions (emotions, desires, and so on). These reactions include emotions such as anger and grief but also desires (*hàowù* 好惡) and judgments (*shàn búshàn* 善不善).³⁴

These dispositions and reactions are related through *qì*, a kind of vital force or energy which can flow and is directed—literally, flows to the outside—upon encounter with external things. This movement of *qì* constitutes particular desires and emotions (pleasure, anger, grief, sorrow, and so on).³⁵ *Xìng* and *qíng* thus appear to be two sides or states of the same thing, what the "Zhōng yōng" ("Doctrine of the Mean") distinguishes as the emotions before and after they have issued forth (Zhū 2003, 18), and the "Yuè jì" (Record of Music) contrasts as the stillness (*jìng* 靜) of *xing* and its movement (*dòng* 動) when stimulated (*gǎn* 感) by things (Sūn Xīdàn 1988, 984).³⁶ By the time of Xúnzǐ, the two terms merge into the phrase *xìngqíng*, "dispositions-and-affects." The distinction between *xìng* and *qíng* addresses the status of dispositions or tendencies, allowing for the existence of characteristics or qualities which are not actively expressed at a given moment. Coming from the direction of Western philosophy, it is difficult not to see the relationship between *xìng* and *qíng* as one between potentiality and actuality, but precisely because of this similarity, these terms can be misleading. On an ontological level, this movement does not shift something from potential being into actual being but rather channels an actually existing force into various directions. Moreover, there is no teleology involved, and a discourse of "actualization," "realization," or "fulfillment," would be out of place. Some of the reactions of our *xìng* are good and some are bad; there is no sense that good reactions actualize our *xìng* in ways that bad reactions do not and thus no sense that actions are justified because they actualize our *xìng*. Mèngzǐ diverges from the *Xìng zì mìng chū* in claiming that *xìng* is good, but there is little evidence that he introduces a different ontology based on potentiality.³⁷

The opening lines set up the main concern of the text: how to move from our natural state of reacting to whatever happens to come along to a state in which we have a stable resolve. We have already seen this term, *zhì* 志, which refers to the direction of the heart, sometimes translated as "will" (as in the Mohist phrase "the will of heaven"), but here it means resolve or commitment. Self-cultivation requires steadying and shaping our nature so that we consistently respond to the world in a way that is appropriate or right. We see this in a passage on the ways in which *xìng* is affected:

> Regarding *xìng*, some things move it, some entice it, some restrain it, some hone it, some draw it out, some nourish it, and some grow it. What moves *xìng* are things. What entices *xìng* is being pleased. What restrains [*jié* 節] *xìng* are deliberate reasons [*gù* 故]. What hones *xìng* is rightness. What draws out *xìng* are circumstances [*shì* 勢]. What nourishes *xìng* is practice. What grows *xìng* is the way. (Liú Zhāo 2003, strips 9–12)

While there is disagreement over how to read many of its terms, this passage describes a general progression that starts with the way things provoke immediate reactions, moves to restraining or honing our *xìng*, and then culminates in nurturing and growing.

The *Xìng zì mìng chū* is oriented toward theorizing problems involved in this process of self-cultivation, coming from the tension between two commitments: that virtuous actions must be genuinely grounded in our *xìng*, and that correct behavior involves conformity to rules developed by sages with regard to the needs and structures of the world around us. The fact that our *xìng* must be transformed shows that cultivation must be guided by something beyond our natural reactions, by something external. The progression from our natural reactions to rightness is said to depend on the way, which is not the cosmic *dào* of nature but rather the human *dào* of the Ru: the classics, rituals, and music. The association of rightness with the way is set against the association of humaneness with natural feelings. As one line says, "There are seven kinds of care; only care from *xìng* approaches humaneness" (Liú Zhāo 2003, strip 40). The others kinds of care (*ài* 愛) are not specified, but the care from our *xìng* most likely refers to what emerges spontaneously within family relations. The distinction between humaneness and rightness leads to this well-known motto: humaneness is internal and rightness is external.[38] At least in the *Xìng zì mìng chū*, however, the contrast between humaneness and rightness refers to the *origins* of those virtues. Rightness must be internalized. This relationship fits that given in another Guōdiàn text, the *Yǔ cóng* I (Collected sayings I): "For the human way, some go from the inside out and some from the outside enter in. Those that come from the inside and go out are humaneness, loyalty, and trustworthiness. [Those that] come from [the outside and enter in are rightness, ritual, and (?)]" (Liú Zhāo 2003, strips 18–21).[39] Although rightness is grounded in the external and humaneness in the internal, the ultimate goal is for all of the virtues to be internally motivated.

In this context, we can see that Mèngzǐ's claim that human *xìng* is good really is a claim that our *qíng*—the spontaneous responses of our *xìng* when stimulated—are good, or at least that they tend to lead us toward becoming good. This is just how Mèngzǐ explains his main claim: "By their natural affects (*qíng*), they can become good" (6A6).⁴⁰ The *Mèngzǐ* gives several examples of such reactions. The most famous regards seeing a child in danger:

> This is the reason I say all people have a heart of not bearing [harm to] people: now if people suddenly see a small child about to go into a well, all will have a heart of alarm and compassion, not to get in good with the child's father and mother, not to seek a reputation among their neighbors and friends, and not because of hating the sound of it. (2A6)

Mèngzǐ specifies that one sees the child suddenly and that the feeling of concern precedes all calculation of benefit. This concern is a spontaneous response to an event in the world, not done for any particular reason. The claim is descriptive; it is not a prescriptive claim about how we should feel, and thus Mèngzǐ gives no justification for it.

Another famous illustration comes in a dialogue with King Huì of Liáng. In the course of arguing that the king has the ability to become a humane ruler, Mèngzǐ repeats this story that he heard from one of the king's ministers:

> The king sat aloft in his hall when someone led an ox past below it. The king saw it and said, "Where is the ox going?" The man responded, "'It will be used to consecrate a bell." The king said, "Let it go! I cannot bear its terrified appearance, like an innocent going to the place of death." The man responded, "Then should we abandon the consecration of the bell?" The king said, "How can it be abandoned? Use a sheep in its place." (1A7)

The king's actions obviously make little sense—the sheep will surely be just as frightened as the ox—and the king admits that he himself did not understand why he did it. The actions of the king are probably even incorrect, since he disrupted the proper execution of the ritual. In terms of the *Xìng zì mìng chū*, we could say that the king lacks a fixed resolve, leaving him subject to whatever he happens to come across. In this case, the sight of the ox stimulates the king's *xìng* and the result is a feeling of concern.

A story on the origins of funerals gives a similar example of a different type of feeling:

> In the ancient past some did not bury their parents. When their parents died, they lifted them up and discarded them into a gully. On another day, they passed by and saw foxes eating them and insects sucking on them. Their foreheads began to sweat. They glanced but did not look. Now this sweat was not sweat for the sake of other people. Their innermost heart reached through to their face and eyes. They went home and came back with baskets and shovels and covered them. If covering them thus was genuinely right, then the filial son and humane person, in burying their parents, must also have *dào*. (3A5)

As with the king and the ox, the burial follows from the contingent fact that the people happened to come across the bodies being eaten. Once again, the reaction is spontaneous and done for no particular reason. Although the people's reactions here lead to a very simple burial, another passage suggests a gradual evolution of funeral practices based on the prompting of such spontaneous feelings, leading to a thick dual-layered coffin justified as a way to fully express the human heart (2B7). Once again Mèngzǐ makes only descriptive claims about how human beings naturally feel, without giving any argument that not having funerals would be somehow *wrong*. In fact, in terms of benefit, funerals clearly are a waste of time and resources, a point brought out by the Mohists who took "Restraining Funerals" as one of their main planks. Mèngzǐ's story, which occurs in an argument against a Mohist, shows that we sometimes want to do things even though they bring about no concrete benefit.

These various spontaneous reactions are brought together as the four "beginnings" or "sprouts" (duān 端), of the virtues. These are explained following the story of the child at the well:

> Looking at it from this, to lack a heart of compassion and pain is not human; to lack a heart of shame and aversion is not human; to lack a heart of declining and yielding is not human; to lack a heart of affirming and negating is not human. The heart of compassion and pain is the sprout of humaneness. The heart of shame and aversion is the sprout of rightness. The heart of declining and yielding is the sprout of ritual propriety. The heart of affirming and negating is the sprout of wisdom. People have these four sprouts like they have four limbs. To have these four sprouts and say that you are incapable is to rob yourself. To say that one's sovereign is incapable is to rob one's sovereign. All have these four sprouts within themselves. Know how to broaden and fulfill them and they will be like a fire beginning to ignite or a spring beginning to break through. If one can fulfill them, they suffice to protect all within the four seas. If one cannot fulfill them, they do not suffice even to serve one's father and mother (2A6).

A detailed discussion of these four "sprouts" would go beyond the scope of this chapter.[41] All seem to be examples of *qíng* that spontaneously emerge from our *xìng* when stimulated by events in the world.[42] These feelings include compassion and concern, shame and aversion, feelings of reverence and deference, and the affirming or negating of things as being right or wrong, "so" or "not-so" (*shì* 是 or *fēi* 非). Such feelings do not make one good or virtuous, as one must develop a stable resolve and "broaden and fill out" these reactions. Moreover, these feelings would not lead an individual to all the complex details required for proper actions in a society (such as knowledge of rituals or economic policies). Nonetheless, these four sprouts would naturally lead any group of human beings to develop bonds of care (*rén* 仁), moral rules (*yì* 義), rituals (*lǐ* 禮), and some body of wisdom (*zhì* 智). Moreover, these sprouts are what would drive a person to cultivate the Ru forms of these virtues.[43]

In this context, we can see that Mèngzǐ is not so much concerned with showing that human beings are *good* as with showing that all of the virtues follow from our natural tendencies, that all are grounded *internally*. Another list of the feelings that lead to the virtues thus concludes, "Humaneness, rightness, ritual propriety, and wisdom are not fused into us from outside. We certainly have them, only we do not think of them" (6A6). Mèngzǐ here applies his theory of the goodness of *xìng* to reject the position quoted above from the *Yǔ cóng* I, that some virtues come in from the outside.

Mèngzǐ's four sprouts introduce two significant changes in relation to the views seen in the Guōdiàn texts. One is positing an internal basis even for more conventional and rule-oriented virtues such as rightness and ritual propriety. Two difficult passages recount a debate between the view that rightness and ritual are external (represented by Gàozǐ) and Mèngzǐ's claim that all the virtues are internal. The arguments are impossible to reconstruct with certainty, and there is no consensus even on what exactly is at issue.[44] Using the context of the Guōdiàn texts, though, the most plausible way to read Mèngzǐ's claim that rightness and ritual propriety are internal is as saying that while these virtues require learned behavior, they are motivated by feelings that are natural to us—the heart of shame and aversion and the heart of reverence and respect.[45] The second of Mèngzǐ's innovations is in explaining the internal basis for humaneness. Although earlier Ru also took humaneness as growing from natural feelings of care, these feelings originated only in the family. The *Mèngzǐ* adds a direct spontaneous concern for the child of a stranger, and even for animals.[46] This natural care for a stranger helps explain how our spontaneous reactions themselves make it possible to move from cherishing our family toward being humane toward all people. In both cases, the main implications of Mèngzǐ's innovations are for methods of self-cultivation, which focus on extending, nourishing, and growing our natural feelings rather than restraining or honing them. On a deeper level, making all the virtues flow from our spontaneous reactions connects them to heaven, to vital energies, and to the generative processes of nature itself. The significance of this connection will be taken up in the next section.

We can now see how far the *Mèngzǐ* departs from the *Mòzǐ* and *Dàodéjīng*, both of which focus on motivations for the basic goods needed for survival and a long life. The *Mèngzǐ* displays ambivalence toward sensory desires. One passage emphasizes the importance of making our desires few (7B35), but others encourage a king's desires as long as he shares his pleasures with the people (1B1, 1B4). Some passages criticize benefit, using the Mohist term *lì* 利, while others point out the benefits that come from humane government. These contradictions follow from the strategic way desire is addressed according to the particular context. One passage makes this strategic way of talking explicit:

> The mouth toward flavors, the eyes toward good looks, the ears toward sounds, the nose toward scents, the four limbs toward peaceful ease: these are *xìng* but they have *mìng* in them and gentlemen do not refer to them as *xìng*. Humaneness between father and son, rightness between sovereign and minister, ritual

propriety between guest and host, knowledge for the worthy, sageliness in the way of heaven: these are *mìng* but have *xìng* in them and gentlemen do not refer to them as *mìng*. (7B24)

Strictly speaking, the desires of the senses toward pleasure and the feelings leading to the virtues have the same status. They are all spontaneous reactions of our *xìng*, yet whether or not we succeed in acting on these reactions depends on fate, *mìng*. The difference comes in how one should *speak* of the two kinds of motivation. Saying they are *xìng* emphasizes that they are natural and inescapable. Saying they involve *mìng* decreases our motivation and leads to acceptance, as we have seen. Zhū Xī puts the point nicely, quoting his teacher, Lǐ Yánpíng Chin:

> These two series are all what belong to *xìng* and are fated by heaven. But vulgar people take the first five as *xìng*, and even if they cannot be attained, they surely desire to seek them. They take the latter five as fated, and if once they cannot reach them, then they do not again exert their strength. Thus Mèngzǐ speaks according to the emphasis of each, to extend the one and restrain the other. (2003, 370)

As this passage would lead us to expect, Mèngzǐ generally speaks of our *xìng* simply as good, referring only to the dispositions of the heart. Other passages, though, present sensory desires as part of our natural motivations. The most explicit discussion begins by saying that we inclusively (*jiān*) care (*ài*) for our whole bodies and so we nourish every inch, but then it shifts toward what we might call "graded care," saying, "The parts of the body have noble and lowly and lesser and greater. Do not use the lesser to harm the greater; do not use the lowly to harm the noble. One who nourishes the lesser becomes a lesser person; one who nourishes the greater becomes a greater person" (6A14). The lesser part of the body refers to the desires of the senses, while the greater refers to the reactions of the heart. The desires of the lesser part are not opposed—as Mèngzǐ says, we all inclusively care for our whole body—but they must not be allowed to harm the heart. The next passage explains how the two relate:

> The eyes and ears as officers do not think and are blinded [*bì* 蔽] by things. Things intersect with things and just pull them along. The office of the heart is to think; if it thinks then it attains it and if it does not think then it does not attain it. This is what heaven gives us. First take a stand in the greater and then what is lesser will not be able to coerce it. Thus one becomes a greater person and that is all. (6A15)

Things "pulling" (*yǐn* 引) the senses is close to what the *Xìng zì mìng chū* refers to as things "taking" (*qǔ* 取) or "moving" (*dòng* 動) our *xìng*. The heart's ability to resist this by "thinking" or "attending" (*sī* 思) corresponds to the establishment of a stable resolve that allows for consistency and self-control. If the heart is nourished, the other desires will naturally take up their proper relation to it.

The Division between Heaven and Human

In an ideal world, those who cultivated their hearts and became virtuous would be rewarded, fulfilling the desires of all parts of their bodies. The Mohists claim that is how the world works. The danger of pursuing benefit, however, is that the two do not *always* coincide; for individuals in a chaotic age, they rarely do. This divergence explains one aspect of Mèngzǐ's opposition to the Mohists, which is his harsh criticism of benefit, *lì* 利:

> One who rises when the roosters crow and works diligently for goodness is a follower of [the sage king] Shùn. One who rises when the roosters crow and works diligently for benefit is a follower of Robber Zhí. If you desire to know the division between Shùn and Zhí—it is nothing other than the space between benefit and goodness. (7A25)

Mèngzǐ may play on an ambiguity in the term *lì*, which could have a sense of selfish benefit, in which case this would be unfair as a criticism of the Mohists, who only promoted inclusive benefit.[47] We can take this as a substantive criticism of the Mohist position, though, if we see that the division between benefit and goodness (*shàn* 善) corresponds to the division between the lesser and greater parts of the body. Mèngzǐ does not oppose benefit or the lesser parts of the body, but if one lives by calculating benefit, there will inevitably be times when one is justified in doing the wrong thing (and many more times at which one thinks one is so justified). While the Mohists were famous for sacrificing their own interests for the sake of inclusive care, their denial of the problem of evil amounts to a refusal to admit the possibility of a choice between what is right and what benefits us. That refusal leaves them with no explanation for how such sacrifices are psychologically possible and no guidance on how to cultivate oneself so as to make them.

In contrast, the need to choose between the feelings of the heart and desires of the other senses runs throughout the *Mèngzǐ*. One passage takes up this choice explicitly:

> Mèngzǐ said, "Fish is what I desire. Bear paw is also what I desire. If these two cannot both be attained together, I give up the fish and take the bear paw. Life is what I desire. Rightness also is what I desire. If these two cannot be attained together, I give up life and take rightness. Life is what I desire, but what I desire has something deeper than life. Thus I will not do crooked things to attain life. Death is what I hate, but what I hate has something deeper than death. Thus there are troubles I will not avoid. If in what people desire there was nothing deeper than life, then of any way to attain life, what would they not use! If in what people hate there were nothing deeper than death, then of any way to avoid trouble, what would they not do! Yet there are things one will not use to live and things one will not do to avoid harm. Therefore, in what one desires there is something deeper than life and in what one hates there is something deeper than death. It is not just worthies that have this heart: all people have it. Worthies are just able to not lose it." (6A10)

The love of fish, of delicacies like bear paw, of life, and of rightness are all natural ways human beings respond to the world, and all are good. Yet the tragic condition of being human is that we must make choices between good things. In such conflicts, we should follow the heart rather than the lesser parts of the body, giving priority to rightness even over the desire for life itself.

This requires sacrifice, but it is still what we *want* to do. A cultivated person follows his or her desires, because the feelings of the heart consistently dominate. Even ordinary people recognize that the concerns of the heart are sometimes more important than life itself. If our deepest desire were to stay alive, then we would expect people to do absolutely anything to stay alive. Most people, though, have limits. Mèngzǐ's example in this passage (that a starving beggar will refuse food given in an insulting way) is rather weak, but another passage gives a stronger example, in which someone tries to convince Mèngzǐ's disciple, Wūlúzǐ, that ritual is less important than food or reproduction. The challenger asks this: If the only way to avoid starvation involves being impolite about eating, should one starve? If the only way to marry and have children requires leaving out the formal reception of the bride, should one not marry? Wūlúzǐ cannot answer, because our intuitions are that in these cases, the ritual should be sacrificed. When Wūlúzǐ asks about it, Mèngzǐ explains that one cannot compare the most significant issues of living with minor issues of ritual. That would be like concluding that gold is lighter than feathers because a gold clasp weighs less than a cartload of feathers. Mèngzǐ then gives his own example:

> If you can attain food by twisting your older brother's arm and seizing his food, but cannot attain food if you do not twist his arm—will you twist it? If you can attain a wife by leaping over a family's eastern wall and dragging off their virgin daughter, but cannot attain a wife if you do not drag one off—will you then drag one off? (6B1)

Life and descendants are important and they can legitimately be weighed against the demands of ritual propriety. Yet there are things more important to us than life and reproduction, and so there are things we would not do to attain them—things like causing our own brother to starve or taking a wife by force. Mèngzǐ thinks this is so even for ordinary people, which illustrates his claim that our natural dispositions are good. Although these passages make only descriptive claims, they establish the possibility of taking virtue as our highest goal and greatest joy, showing that this follows rather than contradicts our natural motivations.

Fatalism and appeals to heaven arise as a way of dealing with the loss involved when we must choose between what our heart wants and what the other senses desire. In this context, we can approach Mèngzǐ's difficult concept of "correct fate" (*zhèng mìng* 正命) (7A2), "taking one's stand toward" (*lì* 立) (7A1) fate, or "awaiting" (*sì* 俟) (7B33), fate. Mèngzǐ says this of correct fate: "There is nothing that is not fated; compliantly accept what is correct in it. Thus, one who knows fate does not stand below a precipitous wall. Fully implementing one's way but then dying is correct fate. Dying in fetters and chains is not correct fate" (7A2). This passage is one of the most difficult in the *Mèngzǐ*. It seems to say that everything is fated but also that we control what happens to us—in particular, that we can avoid dying under a collapsing wall or as a criminal.[48] This element of control threatens the very function of *mìng*, which is to help us accept certain outcomes as beyond our control. The bigger problem is that all three examples—dying under a collapsing wall, dying while following the way, and dying as a criminal—seem to have exactly the same status. In each case, the results follow from circumstances and from choices. If the point of the first and last examples is that the results cannot be considered fated because they could have been avoided, that should apply just as well to the middle case. Surely the one who dies while enacting the way could have avoided death by giving up, becoming a recluse, or compromising his or her principles.[49]

We have already seen that Ru appeals to fate must be taken rhetorically and contextually, and this is the most plausible way to make sense of Mèngzǐ's idea of "correct fate." Strictly speaking, events involve some element of our own agency along with many factors outside of our control. All of these can be subsumed under *mìng*, since our actions and character also follow from circumstances. Thus, the first line says this: nothing is not fated. What is actually attributed to heaven or fate depends on the context, though, and the remainder of the passage distinguishes when it is or is not correct *to appeal to fate*. The first example says that we should not act carelessly based on the belief that since everything is fated, it does not matter what we do. In fact, if while lost in thought we foolishly wandered under a collapsing wall, we could say that this was fate, but it is a mistake to appeal to fate to excuse the need for work or attentiveness. Such reasoning has been called the "lazy fallacy" in European thought and has given rise to sophisticated analyses of the relationship between determinism and human agency.[50] For Mèngzǐ the problem is more practical than theoretical—it is just a foolish way to talk about fate.

The distinction between the last two cases is more complex and interesting. Dying in fetters and chains must refer to having done wrong actions, in other words, deservedly dying in fetters and chains.[51] In both cases, the results follow from choices and from factors we cannot control. In a strict sense, either both are fated or neither are. We can begin by considering Mèngzǐ's example of stealing our brother's food in order to stay alive. Someone who has limits on what they will do could legitimately say that in these conditions it is their *mìng* to die, but of course it is not *necessary* that they die. They could wrestle away the food and live. They then might instead say that it was their brother's *mìng* to die. Their *mìng* was to steal his food. That would be like a criminal saying it was his *mìng* to die in fetters, because the only way to fulfill his desires was by stealing. In a sense, all of these claims are true—"nothing is not fated." What is the basis, then, for saying one is correct fate and the other is not? On a superficial level, we could say that what results after good actions can be called fate but what results from bad actions cannot, but *mìng* is not a normative term and does not correspond to "what is right." Labeling events as *mìng* evokes a certain stance, an acceptance of events as unavoidable. But to see certain events as unavoidable requires excluding other actions as impossible. It requires having that which one will not do. Because I see taking my brother's food as impossible, I see my death by starvation as unavoidable, as *mìng*. Correct fate distinguishes the fate that is met by someone who cannot but be correct. Ironically, correct fate is probably more avoidable that incorrect fate. A criminal likely tries every available means to avoid dying in fetters, but the gentleman who dies while enacting the way leaves many options unused. Since these are not even visible as options, the results also appear inevitable.

What is properly labeled as *mìng* thus can only be disclosed from within the limits of the way. We see this explicitly in a saying from *Yǔ cóng* I: "Know what heaven does and what human beings do, and then one knows the way. Know the way and then one knows fate [*mìng*]" (Liú Zhāo 2003, strips 29–30). Knowing the division between what heaven does and what we do is already to recognize that some things are outside of our control, but that is not the locus for *mìng*. Knowledge of the division between heaven and human leads us to pursue the human way, which for Mèngzǐ would mean developing the natural tendencies that make us human. Only once we are set on that path can the obstacles that arise be properly labeled as *mìng*. *Dào* as the condition for the appearance of (correct) *mìng* occurs in other passages, as in a passage we have seen that says, "If seeking it has the way but attaining it has fate, then this seeking is of no benefit to attaining" (7A3). In a strict sense, everything that is outside the power of our seeking can be attributed to fate, but Mèngzǐ specifies that *mìng* refers those events that cannot be controlled *within the limits of the way*. A similar use of *mìng* appears in a passage describing Kǒngzǐ's travels: "Kǒngzǐ entered according to ritual and withdrew according to rightness. Attaining and not attaining—he would say 'there is *mìng*'" (5A8). Kǒngzǐ applied the label "*mìng*" to what could not be avoided or controlled within the confines of ritual propriety and rightness.[52] The passage addresses a time when a corrupt minister in the state of Wèi claimed he could make Kǒngzǐ a powerful minister. Kǒngzǐ declined and left Wèi, leading to the attempt on his life in the state of Sòng. Ending up in danger and suffering was not determined or necessary. Kǒngzǐ *could* have stayed and perhaps ended up rich, powerful, and secure. Nonetheless, he says that his troubles were fated (*yǒumìng* 有命) and that if he had stayed with an improper person, that would have been "without rightness and without fate." On a theoretical level, this makes no sense—both outcomes would involve Kǒngzǐ's choices and circumstances beyond his control.

The point, though, is about how Kǒngzǐ envisioned his possibilities. Some things that in a sense could be chosen, such as serving a corrupt official, are outside the realm of possibility, not even appearing as choices. Bad events that then occur appear to be unavoidable, fated. This account of correct fate explains why some commentators take *mìng* as having a normative sense of what should be done.[53] While *mìng* simply describes what cannot be avoided, it appears within a normative context. In saying that leaving Wèi was fated, Kǒngzǐ is not saying it was *right,* just that it was unavoidable without doing something *wrong.*

Mèngzǐ's account of *xìng* explains the psychological possibility of defying heaven by showing that rewards and punishments are not of ultimate importance to gentlemen, who have something they love more than life and something they hate more than death. The spontaneous responses of the heart drive us to act in the world regardless of the consequences. Thus Kǒngzǐ can know what he is doing is impossible and still do it anyway. This freedom from concerns for reward and punishment leads to a kind of autonomy through a shift from what is subject to fate to what is internal and entirely in our own control—in this realm, if you seek it then you attain it and if you abandon it then you lose it. This orientation allows for the formation of a "steady resolve" in which events in the world do not "pull" or "take" one off course:

> Residing in the broad home of the world, standing in the correct place of the world, enacting the great way of the world—if he attains what he has resolved, the people follow it together with him; if he does not attain his resolve, then he enacts his way alone. Prosperity and honor cannot make him lascivious; poverty and dishonor cannot make him change; awesome military might cannot make him bend. This is what is called a great man! (3B2)

In discussing Ru responses to the problem of evil, Homer Dubs compares the Ru to the Stoics: "This is the enjoyment of the virtuous soul which is contented in virtue without the aid of advantageous circumstances—a truly noble ideal. Virtue is its own reward" (1927, 289). For Mèngzǐ, though, self-control extends from the spontaneous responsiveness to the world that comes from the greater part of our bodies, the heart. Thus it is not a complete autonomy. On the contrary, becoming more humane means making oneself *more sensitive* to suffering in the world.

Reconciling with Heaven

We have seen the opposition, or at least divergence, between gentlemen and heaven, as Mèngzǐ seeks peace even though he believes that heaven does not want it, or gentlemen maintain a constant commitment to human flourishing while heaven dictates cycles of order and disorder. Mèngzǐ's account of *xìng* explains how this opposition is possible psychologically, but it also supplies the ground for such opposition. Rather than emulating natural patterns, our actions follow from the natural tendencies specific to human beings. Such a shift was crucial for grounding the Ru position, since the patterns of nature at best would support something like Mohist inclusive caring, and at worst would require an alternation between promoting order and chaos. By shifting toward human nature, Mèngzǐ can concede that there are no objective reasons in nature why dead bodies must be buried or children saved from wells. Whatever their status in nature, these things matter *to us*. This shift toward human nature as the basis of ethics is a familiar response to the problem of evil. In spite of their differences, both Spinoza and Hume make analogous moves. In fact, it is difficult to see any other basis for ethics once one concedes that the universe itself (or its creator) is not ethical.

The division between heaven and human in the *Mèngzǐ*, however, cannot be drawn so starkly. Mèngzǐ places particular emphasis on the connection between our natural tendencies and heaven, calling our natural capacities "abilities sent down by heaven" (6A7), "what heaven has given us" (6A15), and our "heavenly *xìng*" (7A38). If the reactions and tendencies of our *xìng* come from heaven, then the ethical resolve that leads us to oppose heaven in the world (seeking peace when heaven does not want it), is itself an expression of heaven, a kind of turning of heaven against itself. Thus, what first appears as a division between human and heaven is really a division between two ways of relating to heaven—as it manifests itself in the indifferent cycles of the natural world and as it is expressed in the spontaneous reactions of our nature. This reconciliation with heaven through *xìng* appears most strongly in the following passage:

> Those who have exhausted their hearts know their natures [*xìng*]. Knowing their nature, they know heaven. To preserve the heart and nourish one's nature is the way to serve heaven. Not to think twice about long or short life but to cultivate one's self to await it—this is that by which one takes one's stand toward fate [*mìng*]. (7A1)

The character translated here as "exhaust," *jìn* 盡, means to push or use or extend fully, or, as Behuniak puts it, "to get the most out of" (2004, 113–14). By fully extending or developing the spontaneous reactions of the heart, we come to know our *xìng* and thereby come to know heaven. By preserving these reactions, we nourish our *xìng* and serve heaven. This promotes continuity with heaven, but the passage ends by reminding us of the division. As much as we seek to know and serve heaven, our success and future are uncertain. Mèngzǐ offers no comfort that our service will be rewarded. He just tells us not be confused by the possibility of failure.

Deriving our spontaneous reactions from heaven at a minimum establishes that they are natural and unavoidable. The *Xìng zì mìng chū* (Liú Zhāo 2003, strips 2–3) and the *Xúnzǐ* (22: 428; Knoblock 1988 22.5b) both connect *xìng* to *tiān* for just this reason.[54] Mèngzǐ, however, relies more on this connection than either of those texts, through his main disagreement with them—his insistence that all of the virtues follow from the spontaneous tendencies of our *xìng,* which means that they all trace back to heaven. Why is this connection to heaven so important? From a Western (Christian) perspective, the connection appears obvious—heaven is good and we should do whatever heaven wants. If heaven gives us this nature, then it is imperative on us to follow or develop it. Ivanhoe states this position thus:

> For Mèngzǐ, Confucianism was the unique solution; there could be no substantial variation on the classic themes. Other ways of life were something less. They could not accommodate the full development of our nature; they stunted or warped its natural growth. This violated Heaven's will and prevented the world from being as it should be. (2002a, 17)[55]

This view would provide a strong (if now implausible) justification for the Ru way—we should follow it because that is what heaven wants us to do. The basic structure of Mèngzǐ's position would be the same as that of the Mohists, differing only on what heaven wants us to do (prefer family rather than care inclusively, have large rather than simple funerals) and on how we know this (from our natural impulses rather than observing patterns of nature). As we have already seen, the problem is that Mèngzǐ never says anything like this; on the contrary, there is ample evidence that Mèngzǐ does not take heaven as promoting humaneness in the world. In fact, while other early Ru texts consistently derive *xìng* from *tiān,* none link *xìng* to the will of heaven or justify the importance of *xìng* with reference to heaven's intention. Of course it is possible that Mèngzǐ's position was an unusual attempt to reconcile the Mohist will of heaven with Ru discussions of *xìng,* but while both Gàozǐ and Xúnzǐ criticize Mèngzǐ's view of *xìng,* neither connects this debate to Mèngzǐ's view of heaven.

These problems prompt us to seek another explanation for the link between heaven and our natural dispositions and reactions. One way to approach the problem is to consider the place of human beings in nature. Taking the link between *tiān* and *xìng* as a link between the humaneness of heaven and the imperative to follow the Ru way requires an anthropomorphic conception of heaven and an anthropocentric conception of nature. To claim that heaven is humane is to claim heaven shares *our* tendencies and purposes, but not those of other natural things. It thus requires a *dis*analogy between human beings and the rest of the natural world. Mèngzǐ does emphasize the importance of the differences between human beings and other animals: we should care for (*ài*) animals, be humane toward the people, and cherish (*qīn*) our families (7A45). Maintaining the difference between animals and human beings is the mark of gentlemen: "That by which human beings differ from animals is slight. The masses of people abandon it; gentlemen preserve it" (4B19). If our animal needs correspond to the desires of the lesser parts of our bodies, then preserving our difference from animals means keeping the priority of the heart. Thus one who lacks the sprouts of the virtues is said to be not human (2A6). As the use of "care," *ài*, in the above passage suggests, one of the fundamental problems with the Mohists is that they address only our animal needs, the lesser part of the body.

Mèngzǐ's insistence on the difference between human beings and animals follows, though, precisely because that difference is slight. The analogy or continuity between human beings and other living things is much more fundamental to Mèngzǐ's arguments. For example, Mèngzǐ tells us that when barley is planted, it all grows the same, and if some grow more than others, that is due to differences in their environment. He concludes, "Thus, all things of the same kind are similar to each other—how could this be doubted only when it comes to human beings!" (6A7). Such arguments by analogy rely on the assumption that we are all part of nature—that there is, as Bryan Van Norden puts it, "an underlying ontological correspondence between the natures of things" (2007, 322). Even passages arguing for human uniqueness do so through analogy, as in a passage that argues that human beings must have a distinct *xìng* because the *xìng* of every animal is unique (6A3). The uniqueness of human beings is not in the link between *xìng* and heaven but in the way that *xìng* individuates any species, in the specificity of our sensory pleasures and the reactions of our hearts. Mèngzǐ's arguments suggest that all things "serve heaven" by expressing their *xìng*.

Mèngzǐ's elevation of *xìng* addresses a gap in the naturalistic view appearing in the *Dàodéjīng*. We have seen that the *Dàodéjīng*, in contrast to Kǒngzǐ or Mòzǐ, approaches human action within the context of general causal patterns that apply to all things: weather, water, plants, human beings, states, and so on. This move toward general accounts of nature marks a stage of development in early Chinese philosophy, and all the other philosophers considered here approach human beings from the context of nature as a whole. What is missing in the *Dàodéjīng*, however, is any account of how kinds of things naturally *differ*. This is precisely what the *Mèngzǐ* adds, and it allows Mèngzǐ to maintain the humanistic focus of Kǒngzǐ or Mòzǐ while accepting that we are just one of the myriad things. Filling this conceptual gap may have been a general concern at the time. Although the *Mèngzǐ* comes to *xìng* as a way of placing an analysis of human motivation into a natural context, *Héng xiān* (Constancy first) comes to the same connection from the opposite direction. The text gives a cosmogony roughly analogous to the *Dàodéjīng*, but then turns toward the specificity of things:

> Difference generates difference, returning generates returning, divergence generates opposition, opposition generates divergence, and dependence generates dependence. Seeking and desiring reproduce [*fù* 復] themselves; reproducing generates the course of living [*shēng zhī shēngxíng* 生之生行]. Turbid vital energy generates earth and clear vital energy generates heaven. Vital energy truly is spiritlike. [Things] proliferate, generating each other, extending to fill heaven and earth. Things are the same in their emergence but different in their living, so generating what they desire. (Jì 2005, strips 3–4)[56]

There are many difficulties in reconstructing this passage, but the main concern is to account for how differences in the way things live still come from the same source, all coming from the generativity of vital energy, *qì*. We have already encountered the term *shēng*, "living" or "growing." In being contrasted with emerging in the same way (*tóngchū* 同出), living differently must refer to the specificities in how different kinds of things live. In fact, most scholars take *shēng* here as *xìng*, "natural dispositions."⁵⁷ A similar linkage appears in another passage more specifically concerning human life: "Beings emerge from a vague something [*huò* 或].⁵⁸ Living emerges from beings. Intentions emerge from living. Speaking emerges from intentions. Naming emerges from speaking. Endeavors emerge from naming" (Jì 2005, strips 5–6). With the appearance of beings (*yǒu* 有), one has particular forms of living or the characteristic tendencies of things.⁵⁹ These natural reactions and tendencies generate intentions or desires, which lead to communication, naming, and the organization of society into distinct tasks and duties.

A view that things emerge in the same way but differ in their specific modes of living is crucial for Mèngzǐ, who uses *xìng* to give an account of a specifically human life that still expresses the shared generative power of nature. By advocating conceptions of self-cultivation in terms of nourishing, growing, and extending (rather than carving, grinding, or restraining), Mèngzǐ places the development of humaneness and rightness firmly within the generative forces of nature itself. This connection was made explicit by later interpreters of the *Mèngzǐ*; for example, Zhū Xī takes Mèngzǐ's "heart of compassion" as a continuation of the generation of things by heaven and earth (2003, 237).

The link between *xìng*, self-cultivation, and the generative forces of nature runs through Mèngzǐ's metaphors and analogies, particularly metaphors of flowing water and growing plants.⁶⁰ When asked about Kǒngzǐ's praise for water, Mèngzǐ explains, "The original spring flows immensely, not ceasing day or night, filling all crevices and then moving forward, reaching to the four seas. That which has a root [*běn* 本] is like this. It was just this that he [Kǒngzǐ] emphasized" (4B18; cf. 7A24).⁶¹ The root that allows this ceaseless power is our *xìng*, which is why if one knows to extend the four sprouts of the virtues, it will "be like a spring beginning to break through" (2A6). This image of flowing water is explicitly connected to our natural tendencies in the debate with Gàozǐ, in which Mèngzǐ compares our tendency to goodness with the way water always strives to flow downward (6A2).

Metaphors of natural plant growth are even more central. When Gàozǐ compares human *xìng* to a willow, and rightness to the utensils carved from its wood, Mèngzǐ simply responds that if rightness requires mutilating and robbing ourselves, then this will be a disaster for virtue (6A1). His alternative is to take our natural feelings as "sprouts," *duān* 端, a character which contains the image of a plant sprouting above the ground while sending down roots (duān 端).⁶² These sprouts naturally grow into virtue just as plants naturally grow in the right environment: "If it attains its nourishment, there is no thing that will not grow. If it loses its nourishment, there is no thing that will not die out" (6A8). Mèngzǐ explains to one ruler that the people respond to a good king as dry grass responds to timely rain, concluding that "the people will return to him like water flowing downward, gushing; who can stop it?" (1A6). This passage gives a version of the Mandate of Heaven not in anthropomorphic or teleological terms but through the immanent spontaneous processes of nature. When natural forces are stimulated and harmonized, nothing can stop them.

Metaphors of water and roots function in a similar way in the Dàodéjīng, but Mèngzǐ lays greater stress on the degree of care and protection that must be shown these natural forces, which probably explains Mèngzǐ's greater emphasis on plant metaphors.⁶³ We have seen that the Dàodéjīng does not advocate simply letting nature go—sagely people must "assist the spontaneity of things." This assistance and turning toward human purposes is more central in the Mèngzǐ. A prime example is Yǔ's skill in dealing with floods. While shaping nature to support the human good, Yǔ did so by using "the way of water" (6B11), and "enacting what was without work [wúshì 無事]" (4B26), a phrase that also appears in the Dàodéjīng (48, 57). As with water, we must neither let plants go without cultivation nor force them to grow (2A2), but rather nourish and guide their natural tendencies. The best description of the generative forces of nature and the way those forces can be disrupted is in the famous description of Ox Mountain. Originally the mountain was heavily wooded, but since it was near a large state, people came and cut down the trees. Even so, the rain and dew caused sprouts to grow, until the people brought cattle and sheep to graze on it. Eventually, the mountain was bare, but as Mèngzǐ says, that was not the nature (xìng) of the mountain. Mèngzǐ then turns to human beings:

> As for what is preserved in people, how can they be without a heart of humaneness and rightness? That by which they lose their good heart is like the axes and hatchets in relation to the trees. Daily chopping at them, could they remain fine? With their growth day and night and the calming vital energies of the morning, their loves and hates still are not far from those of other people. But then what they do in the light of day shackles and destroys this. Shackling it again and again, the vital energies of the night are not sufficient to preserve it. When the vital energies of the night are not sufficient to preserve it, then they become close to animals. People see their being like animals and consider that they never had any ability: but how are these the natural feelings [qíng] of human beings! (6A8)

The cyclical processes of nature drive continual growth, but this generative power can be resisted and thwarted, and if such damage persists long enough, anything will die. Mèngzǐ's concern is with the social forces that would destroy our naturally good responses to the world, but the attempt to become good by denying or thwarting our natural tendencies would also lead toward feebleness and death—this is why Gàozǐ's view of rightness as external would be disastrous, like attempting to avoid floods by opposing the natural movement of water.

The most technical discussion of this generative force is in a difficult passage discussing an "unmoved heart" (*búdòngxīn* 不動心), which seems to be what the *Xìng zì mìng chū* refers to as a "stable resolve."[64] We can follow a few steps of the dialogue, beginning with Mèngzǐ's explanation of the relationship between vital energy, *qì* 氣, and the heart's resolve, *zhì*: "Now the heart's resolve is the leader of vital energy and vital energy is what fills out the body. Where one's resolve is set, the vital energy follows next. Thus it is said: 'Maintain your resolve and do not oppress your vital energy'" (2A2). We have seen that vital energy was used to explain all kinds of dynamic processes, and it frequently represents the generative powers of nature, as in the above passage describing Ox Mountain. Here, vital energy is said to fill out the body, the same term, *chōng* 充, used for "filling out" the four sprouts (2A6, 7B31). Like the generative powers of water and growing plants, this force must be guided by our resolve but not coerced or oppressed. Without cultivation, the power of vital energy can overwhelm us. Mèngzǐ explains, "When the heart's resolve is unified then it moves vital energy, and when vital energy is unified, it moves one's resolve. Now stumbling and running are vital energy, but it turns back to move the heart" (2A2). The *Xìng zì mìng chū*, which explicitly takes the emotions and desires as movements of vital energy, gives a different example: "The eyes' love of beauty and the ears' love of sound both involve vigorous *qì*. People do not consider it difficult to die for them" (Liú Zhāo 2003, strips 43–44). When such movement is focused and intense, *qì* dominates and moves the heart. Being swept along by things can only be avoided through the cultivation of a unified resolve and an unmoved heart.

When next asked in what ways he is superior to Gàozǐ, Mèngzǐ replies that he knows words and is good at nourishing his vast "flood-like vital energies," *hàorán zhī qì* 浩然之氣. Mèngzǐ explains,

> As for this vital energy, it is the greatest and the firmest. Use uprightness [*zhí* 直] to nourish it and do not harm it—then it will fill the space between heaven and earth. As for this vital energy, it pairs with rightness and the way. Without these, it starves. It is what collecting rightness generates and not what rightness can take in a sneak attack. If one acts but there is something unsatisfying to the heart, then it starves. Thus I say, Gàozǐ never knew rightness, because he made it external.

For our resolve to be strong, it must have the support of these vital energies through the reactions of our nature. What makes the passage confusing, though, is that it does not say rightness will be starved without *qì* but rather that *qì* will be starved without rightness. This means that *qì* is not an indifferent force guided by our resolve (as Gàozǐ describes whirling water) but rather itself has some need for rightness. This follows if we consider that the emotional responses of our nature are conceived as the movement of *qì*. The heart of shame and aversion that fills out into rightness is a configuration of *qì*, which, when stimulated, moves to be the actual feelings of shame and aversion. If these dispositions are thwarted rather than made to flow—if the heart is left unsatisfied—then the vital energy itself will decline.⁶⁵

The account of *qì* (vital energy) in this passage is not integrated into the rest of the *Mèngzǐ*, although it likely provides an implicit foundation for Mèngzǐ's thought. That basis becomes explicit in a text closely associated with the thought of Mèngzǐ, a commentary on the *Wǔ xíng* (Five actions).⁶⁶ We have already encountered the *Wǔ xíng* text, which is structured around a division between the internal and external, claiming that good actions that take form from the inside and are harmonized with sageliness are the actions of virtue (*dé*), and are the way of heaven (Liú Zhāo 2003, strips 4–5, 19–20). The ideal is one in which our actions follow our emotions and the unified focus of the heart, which generates virtue, proceeds spontaneously, and connects with heaven. The position of the *Mèngzǐ* differs from the *Wǔ xíng*, but the two bear many similarities. The *Xúnzǐ* criticizes Zǐsī and Mèngzǐ for advocating this theory of *Wǔ xíng* (6: 94; Knoblock 1988, 6.7). The closer connection to the *Mèngzǐ* comes through a commentary attached to a version of the text found at Mǎwángduī. Although we cannot know when the commentary was written, it uses several terms specific to the *Mèngzǐ*, such as filling out sprouts, or not letting the lesser parts of the body harm the greater parts (Páng 1999; *Shuō* 21, 22).⁶⁷

The commentary goes beyond the *Mèngzǐ* in its explicit integration of *qì*. The *Wǔ xíng* lists progressions of feelings or attitudes illustrating the extension of the internal toward the virtues. We can consider one example, "If one is not upright, one is not unconstrained. If not unconstrained, then one is not decisive. If not decisive, then one cannot weigh and balance. Not balancing, then one cannot act. Without action, there is no rightness" (Liú Zhāo 2003, slips 21–22; Páng 1999; *Jīng* 11).⁶⁸ Rightness is explained primarily in terms of public actions such as punishing or criticizing those who commit great crimes and honoring those who are truly worthy, all of which require decisiveness and courage. Rightness must be rooted in uprightness, which is internal and is explained as acting correctly from the center of the heart (Liú Zhāo 2003, strips 33–34).

The use of uprightness in this passage connects to Mèngzǐ's claim that the way to cultivate our floodlike *qì* is to nourish it with uprightness, and the commentary gives as an example being unwilling to accept food given in an insulting way (Páng 1999; *Shuō* 15), the same example Mèngzǐ gives for the heart that leads to rightness (6A10). In the commentary, this uprightness is called "the vital energy of rightness [*yìqì* 義氣]" (Páng 1999; *Shuō* 11). Uprightness nourishes this specific *qì*, which leads to decisiveness, bravery, and the ability to make clear decisions. The other virtues are described in similar ways and are summarized in a series of glosses:

> "To see and know it is wisdom": Seeing it is [discernment]. Wisdom means moving from what is seen to knowing what is unseen.
> "To know and be at home in it is humaneness": Knowing what gentlemen follow as the way and gently being at home in it is the *qì* of humaneness.
> "To be at home and enact it is rightness": Once one is at home in it, then enacting it decisively is the *qì* of rightness.
> "To enact and respect it is ritual": Enacting it and respectfully revering it is the *qì* of ritual.
> What one is at home in, enacts, and reveres, is the human way. (Páng 1999; *Shuō* 19)[69]

Humaneness, rightness, and ritual propriety, in so far as they are internal and genuine, are forms of *qì*, vital energies. When cultivated, they lead to a virtuous power able to affect and transform others. This is the utmost of *dé* and has the power to promote humaneness and rightness throughout the world, transforming others in a way that is magical or spiritlike (*shén*) (Páng 1999; *Shuō* 18, 21).

In this commentary, we see a theory in which our genuine reactions are forms of *qì* that develop or fill out into the virtues. The force of this *qì*—which is the generative force of nature—becomes a power to shape the world around us. The *Mèngzǐ* describes the fully cultivated person in similar terms:

> The people of a true king are expansive and content. They can be killed without being resentful and can be benefited without being grateful. The people move daily toward goodness but do not know what makes them so. Where gentlemen pass is transformed and where gentlemen reside is magical. Above and below, flowing the same as heaven and earth—how can one say it is small assistance [*bǔ* 補]! (7A13)

The phrase "expansive and content" (*hàohào* 皥皥), echoes Mèngzǐ's *hàorán* 浩然 (floodlike) vital energy, as the phrase "flowing above and below the same as heaven and earth" echoes the way his vital energy "fills the space between heaven and earth." The terms *huà* 化 (transform), and *shén* 神 (magical), which means "like a spirit," were both commonly associated with spontaneity and the generative processes of nature. This passage has close parallels to the *Dàodéjīng*. The people coming to be good without knowing the cause resembles the people in the *Dàodéjīng* who depend on their ruler but believe the harmonious social order is from their own spontaneity (17). The great assistance (*bǔ* 補) of gentlemen who align with heaven and earth is the *Dàodéjīng*'s assisting (*fǔ* 輔) the spontaneity of things (64).[70]

These passages suggest that Mèngzǐ's reconciliation of human virtues with heaven is not along Mohist lines of a will of heaven but more like the *Dàodéjīng*'s reconciliation of human concerns with a beneficial but morally indifferent world.[71] It is not about obeying a divine force that sets goals but harnessing natural or divine forces immanent in us. In contrast to the *Dàodéjīng*, though, Mèngzǐ stresses the fact that each kind of thing—from mountains to dogs to human beings—has its own specific needs, reactions, desires, and ways of developing. We have these natural tendencies and desires regardless of heaven's own purposes. Heaven makes barley strive to grow, mountains to be wooded, and human beings to be humane and right. Such a claim in no way requires that heaven ensure—or even prefer—tall barley and humane people. In fact, heaven cannot do so—surely a humane person cuts down barley and has oxen carved up to be eaten (even if the gentleman himself stays away from the kitchen). The heaven-derived *xìng* of human beings leads us to humaneness even though heaven itself is not humane, just as the *xìng* of Ox Mountain leads it to grow trees even though heaven itself is not wooded. In shifting the relevant ground for human action from heaven to our own nature, Mèngzǐ makes the purposes of heaven irrelevant.

The move from generic patterns of nature to the specific tendencies of kinds of things leaves Mèngzǐ with a view that necessitates conflict. Barley naturally strives to grow, even though other things naturally strive against it. Human beings strive to bring peace and order to the world, even though other things and even the cycles of history strive against them. This striving against heaven's own cycles does not entail a rejection of heaven, because heaven itself generates these strivings. This kind of struggle is the very nature of life. As Nietzsche puts it in *Beyond Good and Evil*: "'Exploitation' does not belong to a corrupted or imperfect, primitive society: it belongs to the essence of being alive as a fundamental organic function; it is a result of genuine will to power, which is just the will of life."[72] Nietzsche is almost as far as possible from Mèngzǐ in orientation and disposition, but for a view closer to Mèngzǐ's own context, we can consider the *Lǚshì chūnqiū*:

> Heaven is lofty but the sun, moon, stars, clouds and vapors [*qì*], rain and dew are never once at rest. The earth is mighty but the water and springs, grass and trees, the furry and the feathered, the bare and the scaled are never once at ease. For what resides in the space between heaven and earth and inside the six harmonies, do they work toward mutual safety and benefit? Those that harm and endanger each other are more than can be counted. Human affairs all are like this, too. (20/8: 1421–22)[73]

This vision of nature would make the human condition in some ways tragic, but that is hardly surprising. Heaven makes the grass to grow but also makes the weather to dry it up and the oxen and rabbits to eat it. As the arguments by analogy would lead us to suspect, the situation of human beings is no less difficult. A cultivated person sometimes has to grumble, or at least cry. Through our *xìng*, heaven directs us toward humaneness, and a humane person cares if the people suffer; yet heaven determines that the people suffer, for centuries. Not to care would violate our heavenly nature, *tiānxìng;* to care would be to struggle against heaven itself. Mèngzǐ keeps harmony with heaven as a fundamental imperative by showing that we harmonize with heaven not by directly imitating its patterns but by developing the particular tendencies it has given us. In this way, developing our *xìng* is conceptualized within a concern for our role in the whole of nature and with a reverence for the principle of that whole, heaven.

5   Beyond the Human in the *Zhuāngzǐ*

THE CLUSTER OF issues around the problem of evil are more central to the *Zhuāngzǐ* than to any text considered so far. In it, we find one of the most poignant statements of the problem:

> Master Chariot and Master Mulberry were friends. It rained steadily for ten days, and Master Chariot said, "Master Mulberry must be in distress!" He wrapped some rice and brought some food to him. Arriving at Master Mulberry's gate, he heard something between singing and crying, with the strumming of a zither, saying, "Father? Mother? Heaven? Human?" It was like the voice could not bear it and the song was rushed. Master Chariot entered and said, "Your singing this song—why is it like this?" He said, "I was thinking about what made me reach such extremity, but I could not get it. How could my father and mother want me to be poor? Heaven covers all impartially and earth bears all impartially—how could heaven and earth be partial toward impoverishing me? I seek what does it but I cannot get it. So then my reaching to such extremity—it must be fate [*mìng*]! (6: 285; cf. Mair 1994, 64–65)

The text as a whole includes more than a dozen discussions of bad things happening to apparently good people, dragging out the whole sorry cast of characters: Wǔ Zǐxū killed and thrown into a river in a sack; Bǐ Gān having his heart cut out while alive; Bó Yí and Shú Qí starving; Kǒngzǐ in danger between Chén and Cài, dodging a tree in Sòng, and surrounded by troops in Wèi. The responses to these incidents represent almost every option available in the Warring States period. Some evade the problem by arguing that the supposedly good person is in fact bad or concerned only with reputation, while others claim that bad events are fated and a good person must simply maintain their goodness and endure.[1] Some claim that by keeping a low profile and going along with things one will surely attain a long life, but others say that there are no guarantees, that "external things can never be certain."[2] Some passages take danger and suffering as obviously bad, others separate happiness from material circumstances, and others throw into question our very ability to label any event as good or bad—denying the problem of evil by denying a standpoint from which we might label anything as bad.[3]

This range of viewpoints makes the *Zhuāngzǐ* difficult to interpret. Everyone agrees that the received text incorporates multiple viewpoints and passed through several editors, at least one of whom put together a lost fifty-two-chapter version, which was then edited down to the current thirty-three-chapter version by Guō Xiàng in the third century CE. The overwhelming diversity and richness of the text is usually tamed by dividing the chapters of the book among four or five distinct perspectives or "schools," each representing a coherent viewpoint. The two most influential analyses are by A. C. Graham and Liú Xiàogǎn.[4] The perspective of Zhuāngzǐ himself is taken as appearing in the so-called Inner Chapters. Another set of chapters is taken as developing this line of thought, attributed to Zhuāngzǐ's disciples. Graham divides the remaining chapters into three groups: those of a "Primitivist" whose thought is connected to the *Dàodéjīng*, those of the "Yangist" followers of Yáng Zhū, and those of the "Syncretists" who edited the original version of the text. Liú Xiàogǎn groups the Primitivist and Yangist chapters together as representing the thought of an "Anarchist" school, and identifies the Syncretists with what is now known as "Huáng-Lǎo" thought.

While this approach is useful for orientation, it obscures the continuities and intersections *between* the various viewpoints in the text while exaggerating the unity *within* each of those viewpoints. As an approach to the text as whole, it is almost certainly wrong, since several chapters are organized by theme rather than school or perspective.[5] The status of the Inner Chapters is more difficult to address. The repetitions, contradictions, and loose connections in the chapters suggest they are an anthology, and there is no compelling reason to doubt this appearance.[6] My interpretation here attempts to develop a position out of the Inner Chapters, centering on the second chapter, the "Discourse on Evening Things Out" ("Qí wù lùn" 齊物論)," while not insisting that there is *one* coherent position in those chapters. I then show how elements of that position are expressed, developed, and varied in other chapters.[7]

Before moving into an examination of the *Zhuāngzǐ*, we should revisit the context established so far. In spite of their differences, the *Mòzǐ* and the *Dàodéjīng* establish structurally similar positions. We could say that both establish a hypothetical imperative—if you want certain things like a long life, peace, and sustainable prosperity, then you should harmonize with *tiān* or *dào*. The imperative is made less hypothetical by their shared assumption that all people do indeed desire those things. If we map this onto the problem of evil, though, we see the differences between the two positions. The Mohists deny the problem, claiming that good people are always rewarded. According to the *Dàodéjīng*, nature is not structured directly according to our values. This gives a more fragile foundation for our normal, anthropocentric ethical concerns, as it admits that goodness alone is not sufficient for success or self-preservation. Nonetheless, the patterns of nature are such that people who do things we usually consider bad, such as using violence or accumulating too much, end up being harmed. The reason for the congruence of ethics and self-interest is that nature itself is impartial and beneficial, even if these tendencies must still be assisted and tweaked to best provide what human beings want.

From Mèngzǐ's perspective, the Mohist view of heaven is far too optimistic: good people are not always rewarded, a fact proven by the misery of the time and the lives of Yán Huí and even Kǒngzǐ. Mèngzǐ's view of nature is closer to that of the *Dàodéjīng*, but that conception of nature is not robust enough to justify the activism and humanism of the Ru way. From a Ru perspective, the *Dàodéjīng*—with its trust that a decent social order will naturally emerge with minimal human effort—would also appear overly optimistic. Facing the problem of evil, Mèngzǐ is compelled to break with the basic structure of the *Dàodéjīng* and *Mòzǐ*. This break occurs along two lines. The first is to turn toward a detailed account of human desires, arguing that certain social or ethical desires are shared by all human beings. The second break is in the role of nature (as *tiān*), which no longer serves directly as a norm. As a result, Mèngzǐ justifies things like striving for peace when heaven itself does not want it, or following one's values even when facing certain death. This distrust of the patterns of nature, joined with a reliance on the internal, tends toward a disinterest in the patterns of nature as a whole. This indifference is at the heart of Mohist criticisms of the Ru use of fate (*mìng* 命).

The *Zhuāngzǐ* rejects some aspects of these positions and inherits others. Like the *Dàodéjīng* and the *Mèngzǐ*, it takes nature as indifferent to human concerns and values. Unlike the *Dàodéjīng*, though, the *Zhuāngzǐ* shows little concern for distilling natural patterns that would guide our action, showing an orientation toward acceptance and the internal that is closer to the views of Mèngzǐ. But unlike the *Mèngzǐ*, the *Zhuāngzǐ* maintains alignment with heaven as a goal. This alignment with a fully non-anthropomorphic conception of nature/heaven leads to a radical rejection of humanism.

Heaven or Human

The *Zhuāngzǐ* is one of the earliest and most thorough attempts to think through human beings as just another of the myriad things—to take humans and, as Nietzsche puts it, translate them back (*zurückübersetzen*) into nature.[8] Much of the text can be read as an attempt to deflate our sense of self-importance, to show that in spite of how seriously we talk and debate, our sounds are not so different from the chirping of birds. The *Zhuāngzǐ* often puts human beings in their place by grouping them with other animals. One of the most effective passages is a dialogue between "Gaptooth" and Wáng Ní.[9] The dialogue begins with a series of skeptical claims in which Wáng Ní denies knowing what all things affirm in common, denies knowing that he does not know, and denies knowing that nothing can be known. He then enters into a description of disagreements between different animals, beginning with what counts as a suitable home and good food, and then saying,

> Monkeys take gibbons as partners, bucks exchange with does, loaches play with fish. Máo Qiáng and Lady Lì are what people consider beautiful, but if fish saw them they would enter the depths, if birds saw them they would fly high, and if deer saw them they would dash away. Of these four, which knows the world's correct beauty? (2: 93; cf. Mair 1994, 21)

Gaptooth phrases the initial question in a particular way, oriented toward consensus: "Do you know what things agree on as being right [*wù zhī suǒtóngshì* 物之所同是]?"[10] Wáng Ní's response turns toward objective conditions: "Which knows the world's correct [*zhèng* 正] beauty?" The passage thus works on two levels, showing that we cannot know our values are correct in terms of nature itself, nor can we appeal to consensus among all things.

Wáng Ní's point seems obviously true when applied to standards for homes and food, and one finds similar arguments appearing in other cultures.[11] The application to standards of beauty also is persuasive—particularly if we consider erotic beauty, which is the implication of *sè* 色 here. The conclusion, however, goes further. Wáng Ní first says, "From where I see it, the sprouts of humaneness and rightness and the trails of right and wrong are all inextricably confused and chaotic. How could I know their distinctions?" (2: 93; cf. Mair 1994, 21). Wáng Ní then continues his point using the key Mohist terms, "benefit" (*lì* 利) and "harm" (*hài* 害), saying that even they cannot be known, since the ultimate harm—death—may not be a bad thing. The use of *duān* 端 (sprout, beginning) here echoes the terms of *Mèngzǐ* 2A6, suggesting at least an indirect link. The terms translated as "right and wrong" (*shì* 是 and *fēi* 非), also link back to Mèngzǐ, who says that one with a "heart of affirming and negating," literally, a heart that *shì*s and *fēi*s, is not human. *Shì* and *fēi* were the standard labels for affirmation and negation in a broad sense of categorizing things as being so or not so, this or not this, encompassing but not limited to moral judgments of right and wrong. Much of the "Discourse on Evening Things Out" is directed toward undermining the objectivity of *shì*-*fēi* distinctions by showing that they are always relative to a limited perspective.

While this argument undermines any view of the world itself as centering on human values, it does not necessarily displace the importance of the human *for us*. We see the limited implications of this view by the fact that Mèngzǐ shares it. In a remarkably similar passage, Mèngzǐ begins by explaining that people become good or bad based on their environment, in the same way that barley will grow differently in different conditions. Mèngzǐ then uses barley to make a broader point about kinds of things:

Thus all things of the same kind are similar to each other. How could this be doubted only when it comes to human beings? Sagely people and myself are of the same kind. Thus Lóngzǐ said, "In making shoes for unknown feet, I know I will not make baskets!" The similarity of shoes is from the world's feet being the same. Mouths in relating to flavors all have the same taste. Yì Yá first attained that which my mouth relishes. If the natural dispositions [*xìng*] of the mouth in relating to flavors differed from other human beings in the same way that dogs and horses are not the same kind as me, then how could it be that the world's mouths all follow Yì Yá in taste? When it comes to taste, the world looks to Yì Yá. Thus the world's mouths are similar.

He goes through each of the senses and then concludes,

Coming to the heart, is it alone without commonalities like this? What is it that hearts have in common? It is coherent patterns and rightness. Sagely people first attain what is common to my heart. Thus, my heart delighting in coherent patterns and rightness is like my mouth delighting in the meat of domesticated animals. (6A7)

Like Wáng Ní, Mèngzǐ points out that what counts as good food varies according to species, so that dogs and horses have fundamentally different tastes. From the perspective of nature itself, nothing could be labeled as tasting good or bad. Also like Wáng Ní, Mèngzǐ extends an analysis of taste to ethical categories—our taste for rightness and coherent patterns [*lǐ* 理] emerges from the structure of the human heart. Rightness and coherent patterns would have no bearing on fish or horses and, by implication, they have no objective standing in nature itself. Mèngzǐ agrees with Wáng Ní in denying that the world itself centers on human values, but this does not disrupt Mèngzǐ's humanism. Because human beings differ by nature from other animals, certain things are—and should be—important to us, regardless of their standing in nature as a whole. Simply put, the fact that there are no cross-species standards of taste or beauty in no way entails that we humans should begin eating mice or falling in love with deer.

Both speeches, from Wáng Ní and Mèngzǐ, point to a divergence between nature as a whole and the human perspective, a version of *tiānrén zhīfēn*, the division between heaven and human. In the words of Michael Puett, both texts "reveal the tremendous tension emerging at this time between Heaven and man" (2002, 27). A simple way to characterize the conflict between the texts is to say the *Mèngzǐ* holds to the species perspective of human beings, whereas the *Zhuāngzǐ* sides with heaven. This would fit Xúnzǐ's criticism of Zhuāngzǐ—that he only saw heaven but did not know the human, which caused him to only emphasize going along with things (*yīn* 因) (21: 393; Knoblock 1988, 21.4).

The difference is not so simple, though. As we have seen, Mèngzǐ does not reject harmony with heaven but rather inscribes heaven into the human, claiming that the way to "serve heaven" is to preserve the heart and to nourish one's natural dispositions (7A1). Although the *Zhuāngzǐ* sometimes juxtaposes heaven and human in a way that privileges heaven, some passages advocate maintaining both sides, while others undermine the possibility of distinguishing them at all. For example, one passage begins by echoing lines we have seen from *Qióng dá yǐ shí* (Failure and success are by timing) (Liú Zhāo 2003, strip 1) and the *Yǔ cóng* I (Collected sayings I) (Liú Zhāo 2003, strips 29–30), claiming that the utmost lies in knowing what is done by heaven and what is done by humans. It ends, though, by questioning itself: "But how do I know that what I call heaven is not human, or what I call human is not heaven?" (6: 225; cf. Mair 1994, 51–52).

As one would expect given the ambiguous textual evidence, much of the disagreement in interpreting the *Zhuāngzǐ* centers on how to understand the relationship between the heavenly and the human. A cursory look at the secondary literature, though, suggests more disagreement than there really is.[12] There is a general consensus that *tiān* refers to nature itself rather than some distinct divine force. This reading is close to that of Guō Xiàng, who identifies *tiān* with the self-so spontaneity of the myriad things:

> It is so from itself and so this is called so by heaven. What is so by heaven is not *done*, so one uses heaven to speak of it. One uses heaven to speak of it in order to illuminate its self-so spontaneity [*zìrán*]—how could it refer to some blueness up above? But some say that the piping of heaven compels things to follow it and serve it. Now heaven cannot even possess itself [*zìyǒu* 自有], how could it possess other things? Thus heaven is a general name for the ten thousand things; no specific thing fits being heaven, so what could be the master that compels things? Thus things each generate themselves and have no place they come out from. This is the way of heaven. (Guō Qìngfān 1978, 50)[13]

On this reading, harmonizing or uniting with heaven entails a skillful and harmonious attunement to things as they are in their singularity. This skillful attunement is best exemplified by Cook Dīng, whose following the cohering patterns of heaven (*tiānlǐ* 天理) *is* his butchering an ox with perfect attunement to its inherent structures (3: 119; Mair 1994, 26). Harmonizing with heaven allows for a more peaceful, skillful, and harmonious life. Even though heaven does not set moral imperatives, it still serves as a guide.

There is more disagreement on the relationship between the heavenly and the human. The neutrality or impartiality of heaven to some degree undermines our attachment to the human, but the question is this: To what degree is the human given up? The answer largely determines how much of a skeptic (or relativist) one takes Zhuāngzǐ to be. The more one rejects the human, the more one becomes skeptical of human categories and morality. Two examples of scholars who interpret the *Zhuāngzǐ* with more emphasis on the human are P. J. Ivanhoe and Steve Coutinho. Ivanhoe argues that the perspective of *tiān* serves only a therapeutic value, claiming, "We each have particular roles to fulfill in the great scheme of Heaven, according to our differing natures and circumstances. We are not to abandon our individual roles but we must play them in light of an understanding of the greater natural patterns" (1996, 201). Coutinho holds the same basic position, saying, "Zhuangzi's insight into the continuity of things that emerges as we leave behind the human should remain at the level of theoretical appreciation" (2004, 165). Not surprisingly, both Ivanhoe and Coutinho oppose the claim that Zhuāngzǐ is a skeptic.

The best representatives of readings that place Zhuāngzǐ as siding more with heaven are Robert Eno and Lee Yearley. Eno argues that skill mastery allows one access "to *the* Dao, or to Nature," and that Zhuāngzǐ's position is thus fundamentally amoral, compatible with even "skills" like torture. Eno explicitly contrasts this with a Confucian view that emphasizes species constraints (1996, 141–43). Yearley argues against reading Zhuāngzǐ as recommending a "pragmatic approach" that would have us live fairly normal lives but with a bit more tolerance and skepticism.[14] While not appealing to the perspective of heaven, he describes Zhuāngzǐ's ideal state:

> When dissolved, the mind will not organize its perceptions, seeing this as good, that as bad, this as desirable, that as odious. Rather it will simply reflect what appears before it. For example, faced with a murder, you would view the action and your emotions, but you would filter none of these perceptions through ideas about the act's value, about what you ought to do, about why the murderer acted as he did, or about what led the victim to this situation. (1983, 133)

The shocking consequences illustrated by Eno and Yearley show why commentators wish to avoid the more radical Zhuāngzǐ. Nonetheless, we should be suspicious of a Zhuāngzǐ who appears to hold roughly the same position as a tolerant left-leaning American intellectual.[15] At the same time, even if there is what I will follow Yearley in calling a "radical Zhuāngzǐ," we should expect many other, more moderate, perspectives to be mixed into the text, even in the Inner Chapters. In this chapter, I will primarily follow the more radical strands of the *Zhuāngzǐ*, which push a response to the problem of evil to one extreme.

Rather than directly consider the relationship between the human and heaven, we can more easily approach the radicality of the *Zhuāngzǐ* by concentrating on its problematization of the human. This argument will have two branches. One emphasizes the variety among human beings, undermining Mèngzǐ's claim that we share certain desires or perspectives as a species. The other emphasizes the flexibility of human desires, ultimately allowing for human beings to keep human form (*xíng* 形) while lacking essential human feelings (*qíng* 情). With the status of human values and categories clarified, we can then see how the *Zhuāngzǐ* overcomes the problem of evil.

The Problem of Normalizing the Human

It is striking that the term *xìng* 性, the characteristic dispositions or nature of a thing, never appears in the Inner Chapters of the *Zhuāngzǐ*, although there is an explicit rejection of the closely related concept of *qíng*, genuine or natural feelings (5: 217–222; Mair 1994, 48–50). The prevalence of the term *xìng* in the philosophical discussions of the Ru, not only in the *Mèngzǐ* and *Xúnzǐ* but also in recently excavated texts such as the *Xìng zì mìng chū*, suggests we take its absence in the Inner Chapters as deliberate.

The clearest attack on a normative conception of human nature comes through the appearance of various people with abnormal bodies—missing feet, twisted forms, swollen necks, terrifying ugliness. These stories make several related but distinct points.[16] On the surface, they invert the priority of social conformity by praising people perceived as outcasts. Since the amputation of a foot was a common punishment, some of these characters represent people punished as criminals. On another level, these stories emphasize the difficulty of judging someone's virtuosity, their *dé*, based on physical form (*xíng* 形). The most relevant point here is the way these stories challenge the very concept of a normal human being. To bring out this aspect, we can begin with a discussion among Kǒngzǐ (here called Zhòng Ní or Kǒng Qiū), Shūshān No-Toes, and Lǎozǐ (Lǎo Dān):

> In Lǔ there was a footless amputee, Shūshān No-Toes, who went on his heels to see Zhòng Ní. Zhòng Ní said, "You were not careful before, so you offended and were harmed like this. You come now, but what will that attain!" No-Toes said, "It was just that I did not know to be concerned and so I used my body carelessly. Because of this, I have no feet. I come now with something more honorable than feet, and I am concerned to preserve it. There is nothing heaven does not cover and nothing the earth does not bear. Master, I took you to be like heaven and earth—how could I know you would be like this!" (5: 202; cf. Mair 1994, 45)

Kǒngzǐ apologizes, but when No-Toes leaves, Kǒngzǐ damns him with faint praise, telling his disciples that if a person like No-Toes can be this dedicated, how much more one who has kept his virtue whole. No-Toes then discusses the incident with Lǎozǐ:

> No-Toes said to Lǎo Dān, "As far as being a perfected person, Kǒng Qiū hasn't reached it yet, has he? How is it that he kept coming to study with you? Moreover, he seeks to attain a name and reputation with strange and novel things. Does he not know that the utmost people would consider these as manacling and fettering themselves?" Lǎo Dān said, "Why didn't you just have him take life and death as a single line and take acceptable and unacceptable as a single string, releasing his manacles and fetters? Could that be done?" No-Toes said, "Heaven has punished him—how could he be released!" (5: 204–205; cf. Mair 1994, 46)

There are several important points to draw from these dialogues. The first is Kǒngzǐ's discrimination against No-Toes for his physical deformity, which itself symbolizes his having been punished for violating societal norms. The connection between feet and normality here and in the above passage from Mèngzǐ 6A7 (on Lóngzǐ making shoes) seems too close for coincidence. Mèngzǐ's argument that normal human hearts share a certain taste depends on the fact that we can obviously recognize what constitutes a "normal" human body. Shūshān No-Toes and the whole cast of characters with abnormal bodies question the obviousness of recognizing a normal body, and by implication, a normal heart.

The second point to note is the diagnosis of Kǒngzǐ as being "manacled and fettered." Although Shūshān says Kǒngzǐ is shackled by his desire for reputation, Lǎozǐ draws a broader point—Kǒngzǐ is shackled by his categories of "acceptable" and "unacceptable" (kě 可 and bùkě 不可). His problem is not just that he misjudges character based on appearances but that he insists on judging at all. To take a phrase from elsewhere in the Inner Chapters, Kǒngzǐ is shackled by judgments and categories so that he cannot "see singularity [jiàn dú 見獨]" (6: 252; Mair 1994, 57). The passage contains an ironic inversion in that it praises the person who has been punished by having a foot chopped off at the same time that it presents the person enforcing social norms as the one truly shackled and punished. Although Shūshān has been shackled by society, Kǒngzǐ has been shackled by heaven. A similar inversion appears in another passage, contrasting heaven and the human: "Odd people are odd to humanity but match with heaven. Thus it is said, 'The petty person of heaven is the gentleman of humanity; the gentleman of humanity is the petty person of heaven'" (6: 273; cf. Mair 1994, 61).

This claim brings us to the third point from the passage, the link between heaven and the acceptance of things as they are: "There is nothing heaven does not cover and nothing the earth does not bear." The impartiality of heaven continues themes from the Dàodéjīng and the Mòzǐ. Here, heaven covers each thing as it is, without distinction between normal and abnormal. The linking of heaven, impartiality, and singularity appears in another similar episode:

> Gōngwén Xuān saw the Officer of the Right and said with surprise, "What kind of person is this? Why is he unique? Was it given by heaven? Was it given by humans?" The Officer of the Right said, "It was heaven, not human. Heaven generates any 'this' so as to be singular. The appearances of humans have what is given. By this I know it was heaven, not human." (3: 124; cf. Mair 1994, 27)

The meaning of the passage is difficult to determine. The two characters that here mean singular, unique, or different (jiè 介 and dú 獨) could refer simply to the officer's having a single foot, but the regular use of dú to refer to the uniqueness or singularity of things suggests the passage makes a broader point, affirming the connection between heaven and singularity both by saying that heaven makes things unique (rather than in conformity to kinds) and by implying that heaven accepts people as they are.¹⁷ The line on human appearances is obscure and can only be guessed. Most take it as saying that the appearances of human beings are given by heaven, which could have two senses: that he was born strange or that even though he was made strange or punished by human beings, this still ultimately traces back to heaven.¹⁸ Graham interprets the line differently, to emphasize the contrast between heaven's embrace of singularity and the human attraction to conformity, and translates it as "When Heaven engenders something it causes it to be unique; the guise which is from man assimilates us to each other" (2001, 64).¹⁹ In any case, the passage contrasts heaven's generation of singularity with the narrowness of Gōngwén Xuān's perspective. The tendency of human beings toward conformity is explicit in a later passage: "Worldly and vulgar people are all pleased when other people are the same as themselves, and they hate it when other people differ from themselves" (11: 392; cf. Mair 1994, 100). If we consider this tendency toward conformity, then we can see the irony in the initial passage—it is precisely the human tendency to force everyone to conform to a single norm that would lead them to chop off the foot of someone like the Officer of the Right, making him visibly unique or single-footed.

A different line of approach appears in a series of characters odd in their uselessness.²⁰ Several of these involve trees, as in one where a great carpenter passes a humongous tree. When his disciples marvel at it, Carpenter Shí explains that the tree is extraordinarily worthless—boats made from it would sink, coffins would rot, vessels would leak, and buildings would decay. That night, the tree appears to the carpenter in a dream and offers this defense:

> What will you compare me to? Will you compare me to those refined trees? Now the hawthorn, pear, tangerine, or pomelo, those kinds that have fruits or melons, when the fruit is ripe then they are pulled off. When they are pulled off, the tree is abused. Large branches are broken and small branches are bent down. Thus, by their abilities they make their own lives bitter. They do not finish their heavenly years and die in the midst of the way, themselves bringing on the assaults of the worldly and vulgar. Things all are like this. Moreover, I have sought for a long time to have no use, almost dying, but now I have attained it, and this is of great use to me. Suppose I had a use, could I have attained this great size? Moreover, you and I, we are each things. How can things compare themselves to each other? As a worthless human near death, what would you know about a worthless tree? (4: 172; cf. Mair 1994, 37–38)

The giant tree is an oddity and the next iteration of the story begins by noting that the tree "has something different [yǒu yì 有異]" (4: 176; cf. Mair 1994, 38). The story parallels the story of "Shū the Discombobulated" (Zhīlí Shū 支離疏), who is given grain and exempted from military service and hard labor, because his "disabilities" make him useless (4: 180; Mair 1994, 39–40).²¹ The tree challenges the carpenter for judging it based on comparisons to other things. In pointing out that they are both just things among things, the tree appeals to the sense of impartiality we have seen, both that all things are equal, and so cannot be ranked, and that as equal, one thing (the normal human) has no standpoint from which to judge other things (the tree or Shū the Discombobulated).

What is the basis for the judgment of Carpenter Shí? One could say he compares the tree to healthy and flourishing trees, echoing Mèngzǐ's use of plant metaphors to establish a concept of species norms. But is it so clear what counts as healthy or flourishing? Those healthy trees bring destruction on themselves. The story of Shū the Discombobulated makes the same point—his abnormal body could be taken as a sign of dis-ability, but it is precisely what allows him to lead a comfortable peaceful life. In these stories, corporeal nonconformity expresses moral or psychological nonconformity. The next version of the useless tree story concludes that the spiritlike person (shénrén 神人) makes himself useless like the tree (4: 177; Mair 1994, 39), and the story of Shū the Discombobulated ends with praise for one whose virtuosity (dé) would be discombobulated (4: 180; Mair 1994, 40). All of these passages subvert the idea of a species norm or paradigm, but they go further in revealing one bias in how we normalize singular things— the norms skew toward what is useful. A tree which offers us no benefit appears defective or abnormal.

What does this mean for the status of the human? The fact of human diversity does not necessarily eliminate a concept of the human, if we take "human" as a provisional label based on family resemblances. That concept of the human, though, cannot ground an imperative to be a certain way, which requires defining people like Shūshān No-Toes or Shū the Discombobulated as falling short of a norm of what it is to be human. Such a norm must designate some people, such as Yáo and Shùn, as more fully or perfectly human than others, so that all other humans could be exhorted to become like them. There is a kind of circularity in such a view—we induce a concept of the human from the actual variety of human beings but then use that concept to exclude those who do not fit in.[22] The basis of the criticism in the Zhuāngzǐ is that from the perspective of nature itself, things just are what they are—there is nothing heaven does not cover, nothing the earth does not bear. Because there is no objective norm from the perspective of heaven itself, the norms *we* formulate are inevitably skewed toward our own perspective. Another story in the series of misfits illustrates this point nicely. After Duke Líng of Wèi spent time listening to the counsels of a character with a long name that would be translated as "Lipless Crooked-Sixth-Toe the Discombobulated," so-called normal people appeared to him to have scrawny legs. When King Xuān of Qí was with a character named Full-Jar Giant-Goiter, normal people were seen to have tiny necks (5: 216–17; Mair 1994, 48).[23]

Appeals to human normality are not only groundless, but dangerous. One episode describes a man who excelled at emaciating himself during mourning— others in the village emulated him in fasting and died (26: 943–44; Mair 1994, 276). The dangers of such comparisons are explained in a story that begins with

Kǒngzǐ worrying about the survival of his favorite disciple Yán Huí, who is going to the state of Qí to persuade its ruler to reform. Kǒngzǐ explains,

> I fear that Huí will tell the Marquis of Qí about the way of Yáo, Shùn, and Huángdì, and then follow it with the doctrines of Suì Rén and Shén Nóng. The marquis will seek this inside himself but will not find it. In not finding it, he will become confused and when people are confused, there is death. (18: 620; cf. Mair 1994, 171)

This point is illustrated with two metaphors of species distinctions—between human beings and seabirds and between human beings and fish. These differences *between* species are meant to illustrate differences *within* species, in this case, between the Marquis of Qí and the great sages Yáo and Shùn. Kǒngzǐ concludes, "Fish in water live but human beings in water die. Those which differ from each other have loves and hates that are different. Thus the first sages did not take abilities as one and did not make all duties the same" (18: 621; cf. Mair 1994, 172). Táng dynasty commentator Chéng Xuányīng explains, "These fish and human beings are endowed with different natures [*xìng*], so their loves and hates are not the same, and their living and dying differs like this. But how could it only be these two kinds? Each of the myriad things is like this" (Guō Qìngfān 1978, 623).

The main harm caused by emulating exemplars is the anxiety (*yōu* 憂) and sadness (*bēi* 悲) produced by striving to be like them. This emphasis on sadness and anxiety appears in the story of the seabird:

> Formerly, a seabird stopped in the area around Lǔ. The Marquis of Lǔ welcomed it and treated it with a banquet in the court, orchestrating the Nine Sháo to make music and preparing sacrificial meats to make food. Thereupon, the bird's eyes were dazed and it was anxious and sad. It did not dare eat one slice, did not dare drink one cup. In three days it died. This was using what nourished himself to nourish a bird, not using what nourishes birds to nourish a bird. (18: 621; cf. Mair 1994, 171)

Such passages have a close target in Mèngzǐ, who once summarized his whole doctrine as explaining the goodness of human nature and always mentioning Yáo and Shùn (3A1). Mèngzǐ explains,

> Therefore gentlemen have anxiety [*yōu* 憂] until the end of their lives but are without one morning of trouble [*huàn* 患]. What they are anxious about is this: Shùn was a person, I am also a person; Shùn was a model which the world could transmit to later generations, but I still cannot avoid being a mere commoner. This can be an anxiety. What kind of anxiety? To be like Shùn, that is all. (4B28)

Mèngzǐ's argument is explicitly based on the commonality of human nature: because Shùn and I are both human, I can be like Shùn. Thus the fact that I am not like him should be a constant source of concern or anxiety, *yōu*, a key Ru term that we have already seen. This life of constant anxiety has little appeal for someone wandering freely and easily through the world, taking each thing as it is in its singularity. In fact, some passages make fun of the Ru for being so anxious, as in one which compares Kǒngzǐ to a father wandering the world, beating a drum in search of a long lost son (14: 522; Mair 1994, 140). Striving for Ru goals, though, is not the only target of the *Zhuāngzǐ*. A passage in the first chapter begins by listing the varying experiences of time had by creatures with different life spans, and then mentions Péng Zǔ, who was famous for living an extremely long life. His name was associated with the pursuit of longevity, and the passage concludes, "The masses of people want to match him—isn't that sad [*bēi*]!" (1: 11; cf. Mair 1994, 4).[24] Holding ourselves to the standard set by Péng Zǔ is no more relevant than comparing ourselves to a cicada or ancient tortoise. Each thing is different.

The final problem with norms is that society enforces them. The *Zhuāngzǐ* describes this normalization with metaphors of violence. When a disciple of Yáo tells Xǔ Yóu that he was taught to submit to humaneness and rightness and illuminate things with the labels of right and wrong, Xǔ Yóu replies: "What did you come here for? Now Yáo has already tattooed your face with humaneness and rightness and cut off your nose with right and wrong. How will you wander on a path of unbounded ease and transformation?" (6: 279; cf. Mair 1994, 62–63). The terms *qíng* 黥 and *yì* 劓 are technical terms for punishments, the first for tattoos on the face and the second for cutting off the nose (vividly captured in the character itself, which combines the image of a nose (*bí* 鼻) on the left and a knife (刂) on the right). Imitating Yáo and submitting to a moral code is presented as a form of mutilation. As with the earlier claim that Kǒngzǐ had been "punished" (another character with the image of a knife, *xíng* 刑), there is an irony that the one who accepts social morality has been *metaphorically* mutilated, at the same time as they would *literally* mutilate others in order to enforce those conventions. As this suggests, the violence associated with conformity was not just metaphorical:

> In the present age, the executed and dead lie pillowed on each other, those bearing cangues push against each other, and those with mutilated bodies gaze at each other, but the Ru and Mohists now begin to gesticulate and swagger about among the manacles and fetters. Ai! It's too much! Their being unabashed and not knowing shame, it is too much! Don't we know that sageliness and wisdom are the bars of the cangues, that humaneness and rightness are the pins of the manacles and fetters? (11: 377; cf. Mair 1994, 94)

For all of their figurative meaning, the cast of one-legged sages serves as a reminder of the brutality exerted by the good against those labeled as bad. These punishments were not rare—those who had lost a foot were common enough in the state of Qí that there was special footwear sold for them.[25] One of the few passages in the *Zhuāngzǐ* to display anything like righteous indignation begins when a disciple of Lǎozǐ comes across the corpse of an executed criminal. He turns it over, covers it with his robes, and then cries out to heaven, condemning his era and its rulers for accumulating wealth and property and establishing the distinction between glory and shame (25: 901; Mair 1994, 260–61).

We may seem to have drifted away from the problem of evil, but recall that Mèngzǐ's attempt to reconcile human values with a heaven that appears indifferent to them depended on articulating certain values as *human*. The *Zhuāngzǐ* questions the very possibility of making claims about *the* human. This criticism of the *Mèngzǐ* appears more precisely in the appropriation of the term *xìng* in the so-called Primitivist chapters of the *Zhuāngzǐ*, a shift followed by classical *Zhuāngzǐ* commentators like Guō Xiàng.[26] One point that distinguishes the Primitivist chapters from the Inner Chapters is their confident assertion of what is good (*zāng* 臧) or correct (*zhèng* 正) based on an appeal to the natures of things: what is right is what follows our nature. While such statements resemble the use of *xìng* in the *Mèngzǐ*, they subvert it by putting *xìng* on the level of individuals rather than species or kinds. Instead of encouraging conformity around what it means to be human, they attack conformity by appeal to the singularity of any individual.

We can consider the "Fused Toes" ("Piánmǔ" 駢拇) chapter, which begins, "Fused toes and branching fingers come out from our nature [*xìng*] but are superfluous to virtue [*dé*]. Attached cysts and dangling tumors come out from our form [*xíng*] but are superfluous to our nature" (8: 311; cf. Mair 1994, 75). Our fingers and toes grow naturally and spontaneously, following from our *xìng*. Most human beings end up with ten of each, but not everyone. Thus, from the beginning, the chapter denies that there would be *a* human *xìng*. Moreover, such differences have no relevance to one's degree of virtuosity, *dé*, because *dé* comes from following whatever *xìng* one happens to have. The rhetorical use of "fused" and "branching" is complex in the chapter, as it plays on two senses: a purely descriptive sense of how many toes or fingers one has and a normative sense of that number being unnatural or improper. We see this distinction in the contrast between "united" (*hé* 合) and "fused" (*pián* 駢), and between "branching" (*zhī* 枝) and "polydactyl" (*qí* 跂). In each pair, the first term is a neutral description and the second a normative one:

> That which is correctly correct is not losing the genuine affects [*qíng* 情] of its nature and allotment [*xìngmìng* 性命]. Thus what is united is not considered "fused" and what branches is not considered "polydactyl."[27] The long is not considered excessive and the short is not considered insufficient. Thus, although the legs of a duck are short, if you extend them it will be anxious; although the legs of the crane are long, if you cut them off it will be sad. So if what is by nature long is not cut off and what is by nature short is not extended, then there will be no anxieties to get away from. It seems that humaneness and rightness are not natural human affects. Otherwise, why would those humane people have so many anxieties? Moreover, one with fused toes will cry if you

cut them apart, and one with an extra finger branching from their hand will scream if you bite it off. Of these two, one has extra in number and one is insufficient in number, but in their anxiety, they are the same. (8: 317; cf. Mair 1994, 76)

The passage presents a conception of correctness based the nature of each thing, in contrast to a correctness based on conformity to a generalized norm.

This same contrast is central to Guō Xiàng's interpretation of Zhuāngzǐ's whole philosophy, and he applies it in a comment on the "Discourse on Evening Things Out":

> If each relies on the allotment of its *xìng* and things subtly merge into their limits, then even if the form is large it cannot be considered as having extra, and even if the form is small it cannot be considered as inadequate. If each is adequate to its *xìng*, then the smallness of an autumn hair is not alone considered small and the largeness of a large mountain is not alone considered large.[28] If you take being adequate to its *xìng* as being large, then of what is adequate in the world, nothing surpasses an autumn hair. If you take being adequate to its *xìng* as not being large, then even a large mountain can be called small. (Guō Qìngfān 1978, 81)

For Guō Xiàng, normative claims of being too much or too few can be made, but only by appeal to the nature of the particular thing concerned. Thus for one whose *xìng* is to have twelve fingers, it would be too few to have only ten. As the *Zhuāngzǐ* says, biting one off would cause pain, and the desire to conform would cause anxiety and sadness.[29] While the Inner Chapters undermine any norms, the "Fused Toes" chapter is willing to say that coercion against the natural tendencies of a thing is *wrong*. Since the natures of things vary, though, there is no way to know beforehand what is natural for any particular thing. The command to follow a thing's nature dictates only non-interference, letting each thing develop through its own self-so spontaneity, *zìrán*. In effect, "Fused Toes" establishes a norm against the enforcement of norms.

The Flexibility of Human Beings

We have seen so far a line of thinking in the *Zhuāngzǐ* that weakens anthropocentrism by attacking the unity of *anthropos*. What we have instead are individuals with degrees of commonalities and differences, each generated by heaven in their singularity. A second line of attack is through the ability of human beings to alter their perspectives and thus transcend the limits of whatever nature they happen to have. This emphasis on flexibility may explain why the Inner Chapters do not use *xìng* even as the Primitivists do—human beings are a kind of thing for whom having a nature is just not that relevant. The most explicit passage on overcoming the limits of being human comes at the end of the series of misfit stories in chapter 5:

> So sagely people have that in which they wander. They take knowledge as disaster, pledges as glue, virtue as making connections, and craft as commerce. Sagely people do not scheme, so what use is knowledge? They do not carve, so what use is glue? They have no loss, so what use is virtue? They do not sell, so what use is commerce? These four are heaven's nourishment; heaven's nourishment is heaven's food. Since they receive food from heaven, what use are humans! They have human form but do not have human *qíng*. Having human form, they flock with humans. Not having human *qíng*, right and wrong [*shì-fēi*] do not reach to their person. They are fine in their smallness, and by this they are grouped with humans. They are great in their bigness, and by this they are singular in completing the heavenly! (5: 216; cf. Mair 1994, 49)

Sagely people are both human and not human. They do not become spirits or gods; they remain in human form and they gather with other people. Yet they lack essential human feelings or characteristics (*qíng*). The humanity that they overcome is articulated on two levels. It is first associated with wisdom, glue, virtue, and commerce, all of which take their value from striving to force things to be a certain way—scheming, carving, avoiding loss, and selling. These four may represent the main Ru virtues, with wisdom as a means for scheming, the bonds of ritual as glue, the kindness of humaneness as a means of benefiting from social interactions, and the rule following of rightness as a method for ordering commerce.[30] The "Fused Toes" chapter takes up several of the same terms but emphasizes their violence—the compass and square "slice off" (*xiāo* 削, again with the knife radical) the natures of things and glue "invades" (*qīn* 侵) virtue (8: 321; Mair 1994, 77). Sagely people do not need the wisdom, virtue, or glue that usually occupy human life. They are fed by heaven, going along with things as they are. The use of *shí* 食, "to feed" or "to be fed," may echo the *Mòzǐ*'s claim that heaven inclusively feeds (or is fed) by all people.

On a more technical level, the human is articulated in terms of *qíng* 情. We have seen the term *qíng* as the genuine affects coming from the stimulation of our natural dispositions, *xìng*. *Qíng*, though, also has a broader sense of what is genuine, natural, or essential. This passage plays on both aspects. It makes the shocking claim that sagely people no longer have the genuine or essential characteristics of human beings, something that baffles Zhuāngzǐ's friend Huìzǐ in the passage that follows it. At the same time, the essential human quality they lack is fixed affective responses. This freedom from *qíng* involves a distancing from the labels "so" and "not-so," "right" and "wrong," *shì* 是 and *fēi* 非, not letting them reach us, more literally, not letting them get into the body (*bùdé yú shēn* 不得於身). The precise connection between *qíng* and *shì-fēi* in the passage is difficult to determine, and is further obscured by the subsequent passage that seems intended to explain it:

> Huìzǐ said, "Since you call them human, how can they not have *qíng*?" Zhuāngzǐ said, "*Shì* and *fēi* are what I call *qíng*. What I call having no *qíng*

refers to people's not letting loves and hates inside to harm their persons. They constantly rely on spontaneous self-so-ing, not adding to life." (5: 221; cf. Mair 1994, 49)

The main difficulty is in how to punctuate the first line of Zhuāngzǐ's response, which could be translated either as "affirming [shì] and negating [fēi] are what I mean by qíng," or as "this [shì] is not [fēi] what I mean by qíng." On the latter punctuation (followed by Wáng Xiānqiān, Chén Gǔyìng, Mair, and Watson), the passage connects emotions and desires (loves and hates) but gives no significant role to the labels of "so" and "not-so." The other reading (followed by Guō Xiàng, Chéng Xuányīng, Graham, and Ziporyn) takes the passage as showing the mutual implication of emotions (qíng), desires (haò-wù), and categorizing labels (shì-fēi). This connection could follow from placing them all in the same category as discriminating reactions to things in the world, as Mèngzǐ places the shì-fēi reactions of the heart in the same category as feelings of compassion and shame (Mèngzǐ 2A6, 6A6). At the same time, it may express the way that emotions are embedded in implicit evaluations, as we must first see an event as degrading or unjust in order to react with shame or anger. On this reading, being free of shì-fēi labels would entail being free of qíng, and vice versa. Chéng Xuányīng explains it thus: "What I call qíng are shì and fēi, I and other, like and dislike, hatred, and so on. If there is no shì and no fēi, even if one has form and thus is human, where could there be qíng?" (Guō Qìngfán 1978, 222). This reading seems more likely, given the analogy between the phrase "shì and fēi do not get to their bodies" in the first passage and "not letting loves and hates inside to harm their bodies" in the second—both of which explain not having human qíng.

The claim that sages lack human qíng stands in direct opposition to Mèngzǐ's claim that what is essential to human beings are tendencies to feel compassion when seeing a child in danger, to feel shame and aversion, to desire to defer and show respect, and to label things as right and wrong (2A6, 6A6). Zhuāngzǐ would take these as just what sagely people avoid: likes and dislikes that come in to harm us, because they make us anxious (at not being Shùn) and sad (as when a parent dies), and because they lead us to risk our lives and freedom (as when taking political positions). These human qíng compel us to change the world, requiring knowledge, pledges, virtue, and craft. Giving up qíng results in taking nourishment from heaven and having no need to "add to life."

The flexibility and variability of human perspectives ties closely to the Zhuāngzǐ's skeptical arguments, particularly in the "Discourse on Evening Things Out." Rather than give a comprehensive account of those arguments, we can follow one thread, centering on the conception of the heart or heart/mind, xīn 心. This requires linking two key passages, the discussion of a formed or completed heart (chéngxīn 成心) and the discussion of the fasting of the heart (xīnzhāi 心齋). We can begin with the "completed" heart:

> If we follow a completed heart and make it our authority, who alone is without an authority? How would it be only those who know the alternations and whose hearts affirm themselves that have them? The foolish would also have them! Not yet completed in the heart but having judgments of right and wrong—this is like leaving for Yuè today and arriving there yesterday. (2: 56; cf. Mair 1994, 14)

We have already discussed the term *chéng* 成 in chapter 3, seeing that it has a positive sense of successful completion but also a sense of taking form in a way that limits potentiality. This meaning of *chéng* is well illustrated in a famous line in the *Zhuāngzǐ* about the way (or ways) (*dào*):

> A way is walked and then completed, things are called and then are so [*rán* 然]. How are they so? So-ing them makes them so. How are they not so? Not so-ing them makes them not so. Things certainly have what is so, things certainly have what is acceptable [*kě* 可]. No things are not so; no things are not acceptable. (2: 69; cf. Mair 1994, 16)

Imagine an open field that can be crossed in infinitely varied ways. If a few people cross together, the grass bends and breaks, leaving a mark. The next person sees it as the start of a trail, and before long a regular path forms. When people later come along, they no longer see the possibilities that were once there. In just the same way, the heart's possible responses to the world vary infinitely, but through convention a particular perspective forms, restricting our ability to wander freely.

Since *chéng* implies taking form over time, the perspective of a *chéngxīn* is not innate but is formed through experience, language, and the absorption of social norms. We need not push the *Zhuāngzǐ* to the extreme position of claiming that perspectives are entirely arbitrary. The perspective we have emerges from our particular nature and the concrete circumstances in which we live. The point is that there is no universal, innate, or natural human perspective from which all things could be judged. There is no view from nowhere—one can only have judgments of right and wrong *after* a particular perspective has formed. This is why disputes cannot be settled by a supposedly unbiased person—anyone who could settle a dispute would have to do it from a particular perspective, a particular *chéngxīn* (2: 107; Mair 1994, 23). The actual diversity of human perspectives shows that human beings differ widely in how they label the same things, and the *Zhuāngzǐ* provides us with various odd characters that suggest human beings can take almost any perspective. This again problematizes the category of the human by emphasizing diversity, and it can be taken as directly opposing some of Mèngzǐ's claims about our common nature as human beings.[31]

Since these divergent perspectives form through temporal processes of development or completion, it would seem possible to alter or reverse the process, to unform or reform our perspectives. Much of the Inner Chapters of the *Zhuāngzǐ* are directed toward doing just that. We can concentrate on another key passage discussing the heart. Kǒngzǐ's disciple Yán Huí is going to reform the young sovereign of the state of Wèi, and presents Kǒngzǐ with various plans for doing so. Kǒngzǐ dismisses each one, in the end saying that Yán Huí has too many plans and that he is "still following the heart as an authority [shīxīn 師心]" (4: 145; cf. Mair 1994, 32), using the same term for authority as in the passage on a completed heart.[32] When Yán Huí asks what to do, the dialogue continues:

> Zhòng Ní said, "I will tell you about fasting. To do something while having a heart, is this easy? If you think it is easy, this does not fit vast heaven." Yán Huí said, "My family is poor, I have not drunk liquor or eaten meat for several months. Can this be considered fasting?" "This is fasting for a sacrifice, not fasting of the heart." Huí said, "May I ask about fasting of the heart?" Zhòng Ní said, "Make your resolve [zhì 志] one. Do not listen with your ears but listen with your heart. Do not listen with your heart but listen with vital energy. Hearing stops at the ears, the heart stops at symbols. Vital energy is empty and awaits things. Only the way collects emptiness. Emptiness is the fasting of the heart!" (4: 146–47; cf. Mair 1994, 32)

Kǒngzǐ first warns that it is difficult to act appropriately while "having a heart [yǒuxīn 有心]."[33] He then explains the root of the problem, that the heart is limited to symbols or tallies [fú 符]. The origin of the character fú is in a system for guaranteeing the authenticity of commands. It refers to a piece of bamboo that was split into two and then given to two parties; the authenticity of the command could be recognized if the two pieces fit together (in this, it is quite close to the original Greek meaning of the word *sumbolon* [symbol]). Just as one half of the fú fits with only one other, the heart recognizes only what congrues with its categories. All of these criticisms reflect the problems of using a fixed, completed heart. The alternative is the fasting of the heart, making it empty. This emptiness allows for attuned responsiveness to things as they are. The character here translated as "await," dài 待, is an important term in the *Zhuāngzǐ*, having a sense of open responsiveness. In the *Xìng zì mìng chū*, dài is used in relation to our nature (xìng), which awaits/depends on/responds to external things and then gives rise to emotions, desires, and judgments (Liú Zhāo 2003, strip 1). Saying that qì, "vital energy," is empty and awaits things implies a pure responsiveness in which the response follows entirely from the thing encountered, much like a mirror, a common metaphor for empty responsiveness. Giving priority to vital energy rather than the heart can be seen as a rejection of Mèngzǐ's argument in 2A2 that vital energy must follow the heart's resolve, but even in the *Zhuāngzǐ*'s account, the heart remains central—the resolve must be concentrated and the heart must remain empty.

This passage points to a radical result, in which the heart's only role is to keep out of the way. With an empty, unformed heart, one would simply experience things in their singularity, free from judgments, language, and perspective.

Some of the sages in the *Zhuāngzǐ* may have reached such a level, like the "true men of old":

> For ancient people, their knowledge had what reached the utmost. Where did it reach? There were those who considered that things had never begun to exist. The utmost! All the way! Nothing more to be added! Those next considered there were things but they had not begun to have borders. Those next considered there were borders among them but they had not yet begun to have right and wrong. The showing of right and wrong is that by which the way is harmed. That by which the way is harmed is that by which care [*ài*] is completed [*chéng*]. (2: 74; cf. Mair 1994, 17)

This passage describes the process of losing the original potentiality, interconnection, and singularity of things through the formation of a completed perspective. *Chéng* is connected to harm, divisions, and the labels of right and wrong (*shì-fēi*). The kind of care that would be completed—or we might better translate *chéng* here as "fixated"—would stand opposed to a radicalized inclusivity that accepted everything and everyone just as they are.

With the "true people of old," the *Zhuāngzǐ* points toward a radical transcendence of being human and a total alignment with heaven and the myriad things. Transcending the human would also be transcending the ethical, which may be the ultimate outcome of alignment with a natural world that is itself in no way anthropocentric. Any ethics requires labeling things with differing values, most of all, valuing benefit over harm and life over death. This is where one finds the most radical side of the *Zhuāngzǐ*, not in questioning rightness and humaneness but in questioning benefit (*lì* 利) and harm (*hài* 害). Consider again the dialogue between Gaptooth and Wáng Ní on animal tastes. When asked about benefit and harm, Wáng Ní replies,

> Utmost people are like spirits! A great swamp burning could not make them hot, the Hé or Hàn rivers freezing could not make them cold, violent lightning splitting mountains or fierce winds shaking the seas could not startle them. In this way, they ride the clouds and vapors [*qì*], mount the sun and moon, and wander outside the four seas. Life and death make no changes in them—how much less the sprouts of benefit and harm! (2: 96; cf. Mair 1994, 21)

While the terms "benefit" and "harm" may be specific references to the Mohists, the message has broader implications, since preserving life was central to many strands of early Chinese thought, from the *Dàodéjīng* to Yáng Zhū to the longevity practices associated with Péng Zǔ. The *Zhuāngzǐ*'s arguments for accepting death in the Inner Chapters are probably directed at groups that took preserving life as the highest good. The foundation for the *Zhuāngzǐ*'s rejection of these positions is that, in nature itself, death and suffering are as natural as life and growth—there is nothing heaven does not cover and nothing the earth does not bear. The more radical point is that, at least sometimes, we human beings can take up this same stance, "evening things out." Ultimately, there seems to be no possibility to label any actions as good or bad, and thus no possibility for morality. The problem of evil dissolves with the categories of good and bad.

Maintaining the Human

The acceptance of life and death, harm and benefit, radically changes the models we have seen in the *Mòzǐ* and the *Dàodéjīng*. Both were based on the view that we live in an ordered world and that if we grasp its patterns and act according to them, we can achieve the basic goods we seek. The *Mèngzǐ* diverges from this model by shifting the basis of our motivations away from rewards and punishments and toward the internal goods associated with virtue. The *Zhuāngzǐ*—at least along the radical strand that we have been following—breaks in a different direction, through an analysis of human desires that shows that they are not fixed or inalterable. We can become free of human *qíng*. The consequences of this shift are profound, because the fundamental question is no longer how we can act effectively to achieve our desires, but how we can alter our desires in order to enjoy the world as it is. In place of a prudential concern for following nature, we have free and easy wandering, *xiāoyáoyóu* 逍遙遊 (carefree wandering, wandering far and unfettered, going rambling without a destination).[34] Sagely people feed from heaven rather than scheming, carving, or selling. They make themselves useless.

The relative lack of concern for acting successfully according to natural patterns goes along with acceptance of the limits of human power and the recognition of fate. Two passages in the Inner Chapters specifically connect virtuosity (*dé*) with accepting fate, as in a line attributed to Kǒngzǐ: "To know what one can do nothing about and peacefully reside in it following fate—this is the utmost of virtuosity" (4: 155; cf. Mair 1994, 34). Going calmly along with what cannot be changed is a common theme, particularly in relation to death, as when Zhuāngzǐ explains that mourning his dead wife would be failing to comprehend or penetrate fate (18: 615; cf. Mair 1994, 169). Another quotation attributed to Kǒngzǐ gives the scope of *mìng* as including "death and life, preservation and annihilation, failure and success, poverty and prosperity, worthy and inadequate, condemnation and praise, hunger and thirst, cold and hot" (5: 212; cf. Mair 1994, 47–48). Based on such passages, Guō Xiàng reads the *Zhuāngzǐ* as advocating thorough fatalism. Guō Xiàng comments on this passage,

> Although heaven and earth are big and the myriad things are many, what I meet in them cannot be violated, even if the spirit insight of heaven and earth and the sagely and worthy of the states and families exert their full strength and wisdom. Thus whatever is not met cannot be met; whatever is met cannot be not met. Whatever is not done cannot be done; whatever is done cannot be not done. So rely on them and they will be correct of themselves. (Guō Qìngfān 1978, 213)[35]

Many of the most fatalistic passages in the *Zhuāngzǐ* come out of discussions of Kǒngzǐ in trouble. While surrounded in Kuāng, Kǒngzǐ explains,

> For a long time I have tried to avert failure [*qióng*], but its not being avoided is due to fate [*mìng*]; for a long time I have been seeking success [*tōng*], but its not being attained is due to timing [*shí*]. At the time of Yáo and Shùn there were no failed people in the world: this was not because wisdom was attained. At the time of Jíe and Zhòu, there were no successful people in the world: this was not because wisdom was lost. Timing and circumstances go along like this. (17: 596; cf. Mair 1994, 160)

This passage closely resembles *Qióng dá yǐ shí* in both wording and content, and it may be a Ru passage incorporated into the *Zhuāngzǐ*. In another, set between Chén and Cài, Kǒngzǐ explains that success and failure succeed each other like the hot and cold of the seasons, but that one who has the way will feel joy in either case (28: 981–83; Mair 1994, 293–94). Similar words are elsewhere put into the mouth of Zhuāngzǐ himself (20: 688; Mair 1994, 194). The commonality between the *Zhuāngzǐ* and the Ru on this point reflects the fact that neither is concerned primarily with acting effectively in the world—the Ru because they are focused on an internal imperative to act regardless of the consequences, and the *Zhuāngzǐ* because the goals and desires for which we would strive are thrown into question. In both cases, fatalism emerges as a way of becoming content in failure and trouble.

It would go too far to say that the *Zhuāngzǐ*—even at its most radical—gives up all concern for effective action. One of the major divides in the text as a whole is around the value of life. We have seen passages questioning the superiority of life over death, but other passages favor living. One equates staying alive with the utmost joy: "What is right and wrong in the world ultimately cannot be set. Even so, non-action can set right and wrong. The utmost joy, keeping the body alive—only non-action comes close to preserving this" (18: 612; cf. Mair 1994, 168). This passage seems to deliberately contradict claims in the "Discourse on Evening Things Out" that right and wrong always depend on perspective. The utmost joy and long life provide a fixed standard. Many passages justify certain ways of acting—keeping a low profile, going along with others, preserving a calm mind, rejecting politics, avoiding luxury and excess, and even being useless—because they will preserve one's life. Just as the focus on accepting any results goes along with the claim that those results exceed our control, the emphasis on life involves supporting the efficacy of human action:

> If you use the way to view words, the world's sovereigns will be corrected. If you use the way to view distinctions, the rightness of sovereigns and ministers will be illuminated. If you use the way to view abilities, the world's officials will be well managed. If you use the way to view everything, the myriad things will respond completely. (12: 404; cf. Mair 1994, 103)

Similar views arise around discussions of Kǒngzǐ's troubles. Although some passages present these as genuine instances of undeserved suffering, they more often blame Kǒngzǐ for his own suffering, for showing off, making himself too useful, or imposing his outdated categories on other people. One of the passages even begins by asking Kǒngzǐ, "Do you loathe death?" Kǒngzǐ concedes that he does (20: 680; Mair 1994, 191). Such passages value life and emphasize human efficacy, with a position quite close to what we have seen in the *Dàodéjīng*.

Contradictory views about the value of life are one of the main criteria used to distinguish different parts of the *Zhuāngzǐ* as belonging to different "schools," but the contradiction has roots in the Inner Chapters. Arguments against the desire for life are explicit and frequent, but there is an undercurrent of concern for living: dialogues around political involvement are based on avoiding harm, and the recurring useless tree is praised for living long. The story that inspires the name of the third chapter, "Nourishing Life" ("Yǎngshēng" 養生), justifies its advice because it allows people to protect their bodies, keep their lives whole, nourish their parents, and fulfill their years (3: 115; Mair 1994, 26). Similarly, the Inner Chapters do not entirely give up a concern for effective action, as we see advice for everything from keeping monkeys to butchering an ox to surviving in political office.

How are we to reconcile this concern for long life and success with the explicit arguments that all results are equally good, that death should be accepted just as much as life?[36] We must return to a point we have considered in other chapters—the distinction between the position advocated and the effect of advocating that position. The position advocated in the Inner Chapters argues that our distinctions and values are impositions that obscure the way things are in their singularity, interconnection, and variability and that these distinctions tend to make us anxious and sad. The true people of old take up this position and align with nature; they do not even see things, let alone rank them. Such people, though, are not the focus of the text, which recognizes that we begin already situated with perspectives, concerns, and commitments. The main focus of the *Zhuāngzǐ* is on the interplay between the perspective we happen to have and the realization that it lacks ultimate validity and stability. In fact, the *Zhuāngzǐ* must allow for multiple levels and approaches. It cannot argue that we *should* achieve a state in which all things are even, or that it would be *bad* for us not to. Although the text recommends certain ways of life, it can do so only by showing us how appealing such a life would be. If someone instead prefers sadness, anxiety, and struggle, the authors have no grounds for objection.[37] The stories and insights in the *Zhuāngzǐ*, then, can function and be taken up on many different levels, depending on where we are and what we want. The text has benefits even for regular people like the monkey-keeper or seller of hand cream, both of whom are driven primarily by a concern for profit and thus remain vulnerable to stress and harm. The focus of the text is on a middle ground between these purely strategic uses of the way and the sages for whom nothing matters. In this middle ground, we have a perspective but render it temporary and flexible so as to retain the potentiality usually lost in completion or fixation.

This ideal is exemplified in many stories in the *Zhuāngzǐ* and is articulated in the "Discourse on Evening Things Out" with two metaphors of pivoting or turning, the pottery wheel and the hinge.[38] One follows as a comment on the story of the monkey keeper. When he proposes that the monkeys get three nuts in the morning and four at night, the monkeys become angry. So then he proposes that they get four in the morning and three at night, and they are content. The monkey keeper is able to shift from his original view in order to harmonize with the views of the monkeys, without altering the basic condition of seven nuts a day. The episode concludes,

> The name [*míng* 名] and actuality [*shí* 實] were not damaged but pleasure and anger were used, still relying on "so" [*yīnshì* 因是]. Therefore, sagely people harmonize them with so and not-so but rest in the pottery wheel of heaven [*tiānjūn* 天鈞]. This is called walking both. (2: 69; cf. Mair 1994, 17)

The passage has several difficult points. The phrase "relying on 'so'" likely refers to using what the monkeys affirm as so (*shì*)—that is, working from their perspective. Graham, however, takes it as a technical term for a use of affirmation in a way that adjusts to context, translating the phrase, as "the 'that's it' that goes by circumstances."[39] However we take it, the passage affirms a certain use of so and not-so, right and wrong. The phrase translated very literally as "walking both [*liǎngxíng* 兩行]" is also difficult, but should refer to recognizing that anything can be so and not-so, allowing one to employ the two together.[40] The passage plays on an analogy we have seen in the *Mòzǐ*. The first "Against Fate" chapter has this warning: "To speak without a standard is like trying to set east and west on the top of a spinning potter's wheel [*jūn* 鈞]—the distinctions between right and wrong [*shì-fēi*], and benefit and harm cannot be attained and clearly known" (35: 265; cf. Johnston 2010, 35.3). If one is to reach consensus through argument, one must first establish a fixed viewpoint from which to evaluate arguments. For the Mohists, this fixed viewpoint is partly taken as obvious (benefit is good), partly modeled on the inclusive care of heaven, and partly based on politically enforced "conforming upward." In the *Zhuāngzǐ*, these amount to nothing more than an attempt to force one contingent limited viewpoint (a particular *chéngxīn*) on everyone else. Instead, the "Discourse on Evening Things Out" embraces the position the Mohists fear—that of the pottery wheel that turns in every situation, leaving no standard fixed or final.

Another passage uses the metaphor of the pivot or hinge (*shū* 樞):

> This is also that, that is also this. That unites so and not-so [*shì-fēi*], this unites so and not-so. So then is there that and this? Or is there no that and this?

When that and this do not attain their partner, this is called the hinge of the way. The hinge begins by attaining the center of its circle in order to respond without limit. "So" is one without limit; "not-so" is one without limit. (2: 66; cf. Mair 1994, 15)

As with the pottery wheel, the movement of the hinge involves a use of labels and judgments, but with complete flexibility. The hinge is directed toward unlimited responsiveness based on the realization that from the right perspective, anything can be affirmed and anything can be opposed. The word here for "limit," *qióng*, is the same word translated as "failure" elsewhere, so "without limit" may also have a sense of avoiding distress, failure, and blockage.[41] In both passages, the awareness that nothing is so or not-so in relation to heaven does not eliminate the use of labels but allows their utter flexibility. Rather than take *no* perspective, sagely people take *any* perspective.

Since we always approach the radical inclusiveness and impartiality of heaven/nature while situated within a particular perspective, the *Zhuāngzǐ* can allow that sagely people go through much of life in a fairly normal way—eating and drinking, avoiding illness, not antagonizing powerful people, and so on. Although sages see life and death as even, they still take steps to stay alive, such as preparing sufficient food for a journey and making themselves useless so as to avoid danger. Sagely flexibility can apply in whatever circumstances or pursuits one happens to have, and some of these might even fall under our conception of the ethical. For example, the *Zhuāngzǐ* generally assumes bonds of friendship and care. If sages take care to stay alive, one would expect them to show the same regard for the lives of other people and help those around them when they can, as Kǒngzǐ counsels Yán Huí so that he can avoid being killed or punished and Master Chariot takes food to his distressed friend Master Mulberry during a long rainstorm. The *Zhuāngzǐ* at least implicitly promotes tolerance and acceptance of others, criticizing discrimination based on appearance, disability, and even past criminal record. This tolerance and impartiality go beyond just rejecting overt force, extending even to an awareness of the dangers of moralizing, as we have seen.[42] On a deeper level, the *Zhuāngzǐ* (like the *Dàodéjīng*) takes heaven as impartial and beneficial, tending spontaneously toward generating sustainable systems. Advocating non-coercion gives free play to the generative function of nature itself.[43]

A concern for life, sustainability, smoothness, and peace of mind places limits on the kinds of pursuits and goals one would take up. Violence and excess are self-defeating, as we have seen in the *Dàodéjīng*. Politics is generally rejected as too dangerous; uselessness is valued instead. One does not impose views on others, nor struggle to change the world. Thus, even with a shared concern for everyday life, sages would differ from ordinary people. The real difference, though, appears when these everyday pursuits break down—when other people contend with us for some good or we meet failure, harm, or death. In those situations, sagely people can turn or pivot, shifting their labels and goals so as to affirm whatever happens—"evening things out." This ability follows because they know that any event can be labeled as "so" or "not-so," good or bad. Even death may actually be a good thing. In this way, while continuing to use labels, sagely people are able to keep them from getting in to harm them. While the Ru also link acceptance and fatalism, their approach remains fundamentally different. Mèngzǐ sees some failures as genuinely bad but unavoidable, leaving something like resignation. In the *Zhuāngzǐ*, nothing is bad or good in itself and thus any event can be affirmed. Rather than resignation, one has the joy of free and easy wandering.

This ability to engage in everyday pursuits while not remaining trapped by them is difficult to imagine, but Michael Crandell gives one of the most helpful analogies, drawing on Hans-Georg Gadamer's conception of play. He quotes Gadamer: "Rather, in play itself lies a unique—indeed, a sacred—seriousness. Only seriousness in playing makes play wholly play. Not to take the game seriously is to be a spoilsport. The game itself is a risk for the player. One can play only with serious possibilities" (1983, 108).[44] What makes play strange is that this seriousness exists alongside awareness that the game itself is arbitrary and meaningless—it is only a game. With this attitude, when the game ends or is disrupted, or even when it is just no longer fun, we move on to something else. For Zhuāngzǐ, we play seriously in whatever game we find ourselves, but if that goes wrong, we pivot into a new one. When facing conflict, harm, or failure, the emphasis is not on the heroic struggle to persevere at all costs, but rather on shifting perspectives so as to find joy in the new condition. The application of the concept of play to the *Zhuāngzǐ* has some textual basis in the term *yóu*, 遊, which I have been translating as "wandering" but extends to a sense of ease and play, as in a passage in which Cloud General comes across a sage named Vast Ignorance, who is slapping his butt and hopping like a bird (11: 385–86; Mair 1994, 97). When Cloud General asks what he is doing, Vast Ignorance replies: *yóu*.

We can conclude with the clearest illustration of the intersection between flexible perspective and overcoming human feelings, the famous story that describes Zhuāngzǐ's reaction to the death of his wife. His friend Huìzǐ comes to pay condolences and finds Zhuāngzǐ singing and banging on a tub. When Huìzǐ criticizes him for not mourning, Zhuāngzǐ responds,

> It is not so! When she first died, how could I alone have no distress? But I looked to her beginning and that originally she was without life. Not only was she without life, originally she had no form. Not only did she have no form, originally she had no vital energies. Intermingling in the indefinite and vague, change happened and there was vital energy; vital energy changed and there was form; form changed and there was life; now there has been another change and she is dead. This is like the progression of the four seasons—spring, fall, winter, summer. There she sleeps, reclining peacefully in a large chamber. If

I wept and wailed in following her tearfully, I myself considered that it would have been not communing [*tōng*, succeeding] with fate. So I stopped. (18: 614-15; cf. Mair 1994, 169)

Zhuāngzǐ draws comfort from several points. Death is inevitable and one should peacefully accept whatever is fated. Death also is natural—to object would be like opposing the change of seasons. Finally, the passage places the death of Zhuāngzǐ's wife in a broader horizon. Although his wife may be meaningful to him, her unforming is just one moment in an infinite natural world of change, formation, and dissolution. From the perspective of heaven, this one instance has no real significance, no different from knocking off a clump of dirt, as Wáng Tái thought of losing his foot (5: 187; Mair 1994, 43). The most significant thing about this passage is its illustration of a deliberate change in perspective, emphasized by Zhuāngzǐ, who says, "I myself considered that [*zìyǐwèi* 自以為]." Zhuāngzǐ's immediate reaction of sorrow is given no explanation, but it suggests that his initial perspective was that of one particular human being in concrete caring relations to other particular people, in this case, the wife who raised his children and grew old together with him. From that perspective, life is labeled as good and death as bad. Thus, he is initially distressed. From the perspective of heaven (or a fish or a praying mantis), though, his wife's death is neither good nor bad; these labels are possible only from a contingent and fixed perspective. Zhuāngzǐ begins with such a perspective and a feeling of distress, but then he considers the processes of nature, relabels the events, and ends up singing—going freely and easily along with things.

This account of death allows us to more precisely see the contrast between Zhuāngzǐ and Mèngzǐ. With the death of his wife, Zhuāngzǐ suggests that his initial reaction is the typical or normal one. We could translate his initial response to Huìzǐ as "How could I be so singular [*dú* 獨] as to not feel distress?" The claim that mourning is a natural reaction of the heart was fundamental for the early Ru. In a passage explaining the elaborate funeral he had for his mother, Mèngzǐ appeals to the common feelings behind mourning and concludes with almost identical language: "How could I be so singular as to not do so?" (2B7) Mèngzǐ argues from such natural feelings that all human beings *should* mourn and have funerals (in a very determinate way, with an inner and outer coffin, three years of mourning, and so on). Zhuāngzǐ rejects this move from an *is* to an *ought*. A passage from one of the miscellaneous chapters of the *Zhuāngzǐ* contrasts with the *Mèngzǐ* so well that one suspects a deliberate connection. On his deathbed, after hearing of the elaborate funeral planned by his disciples, Zhuāngzǐ tells them to simply expose his corpse: he will take heaven and earth as his coffins; the sun, moon, and stars as ornaments; and the myriad things as funerary gifts. When his disciples respond that wild birds will devour his body, Zhuāngzǐ replies, "Above ground I will be eaten by crows and vultures, below ground I will be eaten by mole crickets and ants; to snatch from one to give to the other—how biased that is!" (32: 1063; cf. Mair 1994, 332). Whatever our immediate reactions or preferences, we can see that it doesn't really matter if a corpse is given a sky burial to be eaten by vultures or if it is buried underground to be eaten by worms. That is seeing things in relation to heaven's inclusivity.

The positions of Mèngzǐ and Zhuāngzǐ express the divergence between two plausible perspectives—that of the human and that of nature. Of course we want a funeral for our parents (and ourselves), but we can also see that this is meaningless from the perspective of nature itself. This returns us to the initial contrast between heaven and human, but we are now in a position to see the difficulty in Mèngzǐ's attempt to generate norms from the human perspective. The first problem is that given the actual diverse reactions among human beings, there is no way to select one reaction as being most human. Zhuāngzǐ does not mind having his corpse exposed, and he feels happy shortly after his wife dies. He has human form and associates with human beings—on what basis can one label him as inhuman? The second problem is that, even if there is something natural for us about mourning for three years and spending money for a good coffin, human beings are not so constrained by our nature. We can shift perspectives and come to see death as natural and not bad. We can keep our human form while lacking fixed human reactions. Mèngzǐ must accept this possibility, but would take it as destroying what makes us distinctively human. Zhuāngzǐ would surely respond, So what? If it is possible for us to accept death as natural and this fits more with what death actually is (neither good nor bad in itself), how would one justify the imperative to maintain a human perspective leading to mourning? The reason not to do so is obvious—would we not rather sing than cry, wander freely and easily rather than anxiously roam the world as if beating a drum in searching of a lost son? Of course, if one wants to mourn, Zhuāngzǐ has no way to claim it is wrong to do so. The *Zhuāngzǐ* only undermines the normative move made toward claiming we all *should* want to mourn. That Ru approach is clear in *Lúnyǔ* 17.21, in which Zǎi Wǒ proposes shortening the three-year mourning period to only one year. Kǒngzǐ asks him if he would feel at ease doing so, and Zǎi Wǒ says he would. So Kǒngzǐ tells him to do it. He should act genuinely. The message, though, is not each to his own! Do whatever feels natural for you! Rather, after Zǎi Wǒ walks away, Kǒngzǐ criticizes him, exclaiming that he is not humane.

In the *Zhuāngzǐ*'s position, we may see the ultimate result of a Warring States view that takes the world itself as less and less anthropocentric, a move driven by awareness of the fact that bad things happen to good people. Mòzǐ could justify "human" responses because heaven itself enforced them, but Mèngzǐ lacks these resources. In the end, he can only fall back on a simple bias—that we wish to hold onto our special status. We do not like to be told that we are like a dog or a wolf or an earthworm. Philosophically, it is difficult to know what status should be granted to our attachment to being human, particularly if we consider that

Zhuāngzǐ cannot argue such attachment is *wrong*, just that it is less fun. In any case, the appeal of Mèngzǐ over Zhuāngzǐ might ultimately come from our longing to *really* matter, at least to matter more than fish or deer or monkeys. The *Zhuāngzǐ* shows not only that we do not matter in the scheme of nature itself (a point Mèngzǐ would concede), but that we need not even matter that much to ourselves.

The results could be shocking. Consider an illustration given by Yearley, which pushes free and easy wandering to its extreme:

> I walk through a forest with my wife. The day is particularly fine—the breeze is gentle, the sun is warm, and the air is fresh. My relationship to my wife is particularly harmonious, the joy in our closeness and communication is especially intense. Suddenly a tree falls on her. I may feel a sudden knife-cut of grief, a moment of shock. But I quickly move from that and begin to enjoy an extraordinary new scene. Beautiful reds and browns now mix with the leaves and the dirt; shattered bones now lie at distinctive and pleasing angles. (1983, 135)

As shocking as it appears, such an appreciation would be no less accurate than the horror and sadness we would expect, since the event in itself is neither good nor bad. In some sense, such appreciation would seem preferable to the trauma and nightmares that would likely follow instead. Such a reaction seems nearly impossible and even inhuman—from the story we have seen, Zhuāngzǐ himself did not reach quite this far. Yet we might wonder how Master Chariot would react if the tree had fallen on one of his friends.

A similar view would apply on the ethical level. Even taking the most extreme case of genocide, Zhuāngzǐ might point out that the death of large numbers of human beings is not really more significant that the death of large numbers of cattle or roosters. The elimination of our whole species would not necessarily be a bad thing from the point of view of nature itself, a point nicely expressed by John Gray, in his book drawing its title (*Straw Dogs*) from the *Dàodéjīng*:

> Nearly all philosophies, most religions and much of science testify to a desperate, unwearying concern with the salvation of mankind. If we turn from solipsism, we will be less concerned with the fate of the human animal. ... *Homo rapiens* is only one of very many species, and not obviously worth preserving. Later or sooner, it will become extinct. When it is gone the Earth will recover. Long after the last traces of the human animal have disappeared, many of the species it is bent on destroying will still be around, along with others that have yet to spring up. The Earth will forget mankind. The play of life will go on. (2003, 151)

We might agree on some theoretical level about our status in nature, but respond that human death is significant to us *as fellow humans*. The response of the *Zhuāngzǐ* is simple: it need not be. And of course, such events do not matter to most people, who lose little sleep over wars in faraway places. We must still be careful not to take the *Zhuāngzǐ* too theoretically. As argued, we would still care for people in our everyday lives, and if the positions the text promotes were widely accepted, they would prevent war and genocide. Nonetheless, the *Zhuāngzǐ* is profoundly and undeniably anti-activist. When bad events occur, we are not to struggle bitterly against them but rather pivot our labels and affirm the world the way it is. In this stance, the *Zhuāngzǐ* can be taken as therapeutic while also being startlingly radical.

Beyond Good and Bad

One finds many responses to the fact that bad things happen to good people in the *Zhuāngzǐ* as a whole, but the response based on what we have developed out of the Inner Chapters is clear: the problem of evil is a residue of a "completed heart" locked into an anthropocentric viewpoint. From the perspective of nature itself, of *tiān*, nothing is good or bad. Things just are what they are in their unique singularity. More importantly, we human beings have the flexibility to take up that perspective, perhaps not always or immediately, but we can generally redescribe events so as to go along with whatever happens. This may be the ultimate consequence of thorough reflection on the problem of evil: the fact that the world is bad according to our categories ultimately negates the very category of bad. This kind of skeptical response to the problem of evil is not unique to the *Zhuāngzǐ*. Someone like Sextus Empiricus would say much the same thing.[45] In fact, tensions between skepticism and anthropocentrism run throughout European discussions of the problem of evil. Appeals to the problem of evil serve to break down anthropomorphic conceptions of God, but those very appeals are rooted in a startling confidence in an anthropocentric conception of value. Both sides appear clearly in Philo's arguments in the *Dialogues Concerning Natural Religion*. Although Philo criticizes Cleanthes (the advocate of natural theology) for persevering in his "anthropomorphism," Philo's arrogant suggestions for how God could have made a better world betray a profoundly anthropocentric view (Hume 2007, 73, 81–85). In the same way, attempts at theodicy—aimed at maintaining an anthropomorphic conception of God—frequently fall back on criticisms of anthropocentrism. For example, when Pierre Bayle argues that a good person would not give human beings as much suffering as God has given us, Leibniz responds by accusing him of "toying with God through perpetual anthropomorphisms" (*Theodicy* §122; Gerhardt VI.177). Leibniz's main response to the problem of evil is to argue that human beings are too limited to make empirical judgments about the quality of the world, and that human beings are not the only good considered in determining which world is the best possible.[46] For Leibniz, the human good is derivative of the more primary metaphysical goods of order, diversity, and harmony.

A more interesting context for dialogue with the *Zhuāngzǐ* is that strand of European philosophy that emphasizes the tragic nature of the human condition.[47] We have already set the context for such discussions in chapter 1. We have also seen that Mèngzǐ portrays the human condition as in some sense tragic, appearing most clearly in his never-ceasing drive to bring about peace and order even though heaven itself does not want it (2B13). This realization generates something like a double bind—we are bound to our own nature, which leads us to seek peace, but also bound by nature itself, which resists and opposes our efforts.[48] The tragic appears in the divergence between the human perspective and the status of that perspective in nature as a whole. We do not have to stretch Mèngzǐ too far to say that the tragic lies in the fact that we care what happens to human beings at the same time that we recognize heaven does not.

Like a tragic worldview, the *Zhuangzi* rejects the optimism that takes the world as conforming to human concerns. The text emphasizes the inevitability of death and the failure of our ethical projects, grounded ultimately in the incommensurability between human categories and the complexity and indifference of the world itself. The radically non-anthropocentric perspective of the *Zhuāngzǐ*, though, overcomes the possibility of tragedy just as it overcomes the problem of evil.[49] In modern Chinese terms, by eliminating *bēi* 悲, "sadness," he eliminates *bēijù* 悲劇, "sad drama," the Chinese word used to translate "tragedy." Tragedy requires a collision between unavoidable paths, a double bind, but such conflict is not possible for one who wanders freely and easily without a path or one who has been released from all bonds. The *Zhuāngzǐ* embraces aporia—not a tragic aporia involving incommensurable but equally binding paths, but a more radical aporia that is literally *a-poros, no-path* or *way-less*, in Zhuāngzǐ's terms, "a way that is not way-ed [*búdào zhī dào* 不道之道]" (2: 83; cf. Mair 1994, 20).[50] This aporia, or *waylessness*, allows an utter freedom to wander. If tragedy lies in the divergence between a human perspective and our actual place in nature, the *Zhuāngzǐ* advocates simply giving up the human perspective, at least when conflicts arise.[51] Human beings are flexible enough to accept their own insignificance.

The *Zhuāngzǐ* helps illuminate how the tragic worldview as taken up in European philosophy remains under the sway of a profoundly anthropocentric tradition. Tragedy continues to take human beings *seriously*. As Aristotle says, tragedy imitates "serious subjects [*spoudaiôn*]" (*Poetics* 1449b10). Even Nietzsche seems possessed by the spirit of seriousness when discussing tragedy, lamenting the decline of Greek culture into "New Comedy" as a "womanish flight from seriousness [*Ernst*] and horror."[52] In taking human beings seriously, we see how the pessimism of tragedy remains bound to a vestige of optimism and humanism, which is just what the *Zhuāngzǐ* undercuts. Ultimately, a thorough rejection of humanism leads to a rejection of tragedy as well, resulting in something closer to the comic, or more precisely, to *play*. In fact, Zhuāngzǐ radicalizes one of Hegel's paradigms for comedy, in which a character earnestly pursues something intrinsically "minor and vacuous " but "when he falls short of this, does not experience any real loss because he is conscious that what he strove after was really of no great importance, and is therefore able to rise superior with spontaneous amusement above the failure."[53] For Zhuāngzǐ, *all* human pursuits can be seen as minor and vacuous, which is why the sage can always react with spontaneous amusement or cheerfulness. This thoroughly comic or ludic viewpoint suggests that we turn back once more to Nietzsche, who asks us to "kill the spirit of gravity," just after he expresses his own whimsical fondness for butterflies: "And even to me, as one who is fond of life, it seems that butterflies and soap-bubbles, and whatever is like them among humans, know the most about happiness. To see these light, foolish, delicate, moving little souls fluttering around—that seduces Zarathustra to tears and songs."[54]

Placing the *Zhuāngzǐ* in the context of tragedy helps illuminate one other important point of contrast. As we have seen, for those in the European tradition who emphasize tragedy, the human perspective is rooted in a freedom that allows us to transcend our immediate conditions, and thus become responsible for our own being. While Mèngzǐ has a more tragic viewpoint, it is not based on freedom but on the inescapability of our nature as human beings. For Mèngzǐ, our struggle to bring peace to the world is not different in kind from the way any living thing struggles—not that different from fish on land struggling against the impossible to survive (6: 242; Mair 1994, 53) or the praying mantis waving its arms to ward off the oncoming chariot (4: 167; Mair 1994, 36). In contrast, while the *Zhuāngzǐ* most thoroughly works through what it means for human beings to be just another of the myriad things, human beings end up distinctive in their ability to change perspectives. Consider the dialogue between Gaptooth and Wáng Ní on animal tastes. Wáng Ní assumes that other species, like fish or deer or monkeys, have fixed perspectives: they must see some things as good homes or good food, as beautiful or as terrifying. These reactions follow from basic biological functions that might all reduce to a love of life and an aversion to death. If we take human beings as being like other animals, we would expect us also to have fixed standards based ultimately on survival, but the *Zhuāngzǐ* portrays human beings as able to radically alter their standards, becoming the pivot of the way.[55] Such people are at home anywhere (never *unheimlich*)—even death may be a return to a long forgotten home (2: 103; Mair 1994, 22). Sagely people become invulnerable to loss because they "hide the world in the world" (6: 243; cf. Mair 1994, 55), and "take heaven and earth as their palace and the myriad things as their treasury" (5: 193; cf. Mair 1994, 43–44).

We see in the *Zhuāngzǐ* an inversion of European conceptions of tragedy, in which the tragic hero asserts himself and his will to defy the world or the gods, in spite of certain destruction. For Zhuāngzǐ a defiant commitment to a single goal in spite of fate—Ahab's pursuit of the whale, for instance—is not an assertion of freedom but the opposite, a blind constraint to one fixed perspective, more complex and self-aware than the praying mantis fending off the chariot, but not fundamentally different. In fact, the praying mantis primarily symbolizes such single-minded focus, as we see in a key passage that some take as describing a conversion experience. In that passage, Zhuāngzǐ follows a strange bird into the king's protected forest. As he draws his bow to shoot it, he sees that the bird is still because it is about to gobble up a praying mantis, who is distracted because she is about to snatch a cicada, who has been distracted by enjoying the shade. Zhuāngzǐ exclaims, "Yikes! Things certainly entangle each other, each one inviting in the next!" (20: 695; cf. Mair 1994, 196). He bolts away, the game warden hot on his trail. In this case, Zhuāngzǐ's willful defiance of the king's power is presented as a case of absorption in a single goal while forgetting other possibilities, just like the praying mantis. Although the *Zhuāngzǐ* presents human beings as distinctive in having something like freedom in our ability to change perspectives and alter our reactions and emotions, this freedom is just what makes it possible to overcome tragedy, allowing us to accept the world as it is. Far from bringing us an infinite ethical burden, freedom of perspective allows us to recognize that no such burden exists. This would appear to be a happy consequence, allowing us to wander through life with joy and ease, but at the same time, it requires us to relinquish our own importance in the world. Our reluctance to accept that, to move beyond tragedy to play or free and easy wandering, may just reveal how difficult it is to escape our own anthropocentrism.

6   Xúnzǐ and the Fragility of the Human

Both Mèngzǐ and Zhuāngzǐ accept the fact that virtue is not always rewarded, but they do so by making it less problematic. Mèngzǐ does this by separating the question of how to act from the question of which actions get rewarded. There are some things we want to do, even if they lead to our deaths. For Zhuāngzǐ, we can realize that outcomes are only bad when labeled from some limited perspective, some "completed heart." If we are sagely enough, we can change perspectives and affirm whatever happens. The *Mòzǐ* and *Dàodéjīng,* in contrast, must minimize the problem of evil: the ways they recommend are justified because they reliably lead to goods we want—things like food, peace, and a long life. The *Xúnzǐ* returns us to this earlier model.[1] In fact, the *Xúnzǐ* can be seen as solving a number of problems inherent in the Mohist position, while aiming toward the same goal of placing responsibility on human beings. The most distinctive and interesting aspect of Xúnzǐ's position in relation to the problem of evil is that he maintains Mohist claims that virtue is rewarded while rejecting the claim that heaven rewards the good and punishes the bad. The apparent contradiction between these positions is avoided by a radical displacement of nature as the dominant force in human life, replacing it with the historically constituted human community. Before turning to this position, we can first consider Xúnzǐ's version of a basic claim we have seen in the *Mòzǐ*—virtue is the surest way to realize the goods that all human beings want.

The Regularity of Nature and the Efficacy of Human Action

One of the most central concerns in the *Xúnzǐ* is to justify and explain the power of human beings to determine their own success and failure, a concern that runs through the discussions of ethics, politics, heaven, and human nature. As with the Mohists, this emphasis on human power is oriented toward human responsibility, toward showing that everything depends on us. On a political level, Xúnzǐ guarantees that the Ru way will bring good results: it is constantly or regularly (*cháng* 常) so, the results necessarily (*bì* 必) follow, and it has never been the case that it has happened otherwise. On the level of the individual, Xúnzǐ's account is slightly qualified but still contains many strong statements that virtue leads to success. This is a central theme in the chapter "Honor and Shame" ("Róngrǔ" 榮辱), which says,

> On the great division between honor and shame and the regular embodiment of safety and danger, benefit and harm: To put rightness first and benefit last is honor; to put benefit first and rightness last is shame. Those with honor regularly succeed [tōng]; those with shame regularly fail [qióng]. Those who succeed regularly arrange other people; those who fail regularly are arranged by other people. This is the great division between honor and shame. Those with substance and earnestness regularly are safe and benefited; those who indulge and are vicious regularly are endangered and harmed. Those who are safe and benefited regularly are joyful and at ease; those in danger and harm regularly are anxious and insecure. Those who are joyful and at ease regularly live to a long age. Those worried and endangered regularly are cut short. This is the regular embodiment of safety and danger, benefit and harm. (4: 58–59; cf. Knoblock 1988, 4.6)

The term translated here as "regularly," *cháng* 常, could have a stronger sense, and Knoblock translates it as "invariably." We have already seen the prominence of *cháng* in linking the regularity of the universe with the efficacy of human action. Putting rightness first leads to honor, success, power, safety, benefit, and a long life.

Such statements directly oppose claims that failure and success (*qióng* and *dá*) depend on timing or fate. Rather than appealing to the will of heaven, the *Xúnzǐ* (like the *Dàodéjīng*) places the efficacy of human action within the regularity of general causal principles:

> The arising of any kind of thing necessarily has something from which it begins. The arrival of honor or shame necessarily is an image of one's virtue [*dé*]. Rotten meat gives out maggots, decaying fish give birth to worms. With negligence and forgetting one's person, misfortune and disaster happen. (1: 6–7; cf. Knoblock 1988, 1.5)

The link between shame and bad actions is just one instance of the causal network that links things of the same kind.

Xúnzǐ's emphasis on the efficacy of the way in producing good results goes along with minimizing other forces that would determine success and failure. The most explicit passage reads like a direct criticism of *Qióng dá yǐ shí* (Failure and success are by timing):

> Are order and disorder from the heavens [*tiān*]? I reply: the sun, moon, stars, planets, and their configurations—this was the same for Yǔ and Jié. But Yǔ used it to bring order and Jié used it to bring disorder. Order and disorder are not from the heavens. Are they seasonal [*shí* 時]? I reply: sprouting and grow-

ing in the spring and summer, gathering and storing in fall and winter—this was the same for Yǔ and Jié. But Yǔ used it to bring order and Jié used it to bring disorder. Order and disorder are not seasonal. Are they from the land [dì 地]? I reply: what attains land lives and what loses land dies—this was the same for Yǔ and Jié. But Yǔ used it to bring order and Jié used it to bring disorder. Order and disorder are not from the land. The *Odes* says, "Heaven made the high mountain; King Tài cultivated it. He made it, and King Wén stabilized it." This is what it refers to. (17: 311; cf. Knoblock 1988, 17.4)[2]

Xúnzǐ takes key terms associated with fatalism and gives them a concrete naturalistic sense—*tiān* refers to the movement of the heavenly bodies, *shí* (timing) refers to the procession of the seasons, and *dì* (earth) refers to the soil needed for growth and life.

Xúnzǐ's argument is nearly identical to those used by the Mohists to oppose fate, and they share the same underlying goal, to show that the explanation for order is entirely with human beings. Xúnzǐ's purpose appears in a famous passage written in verse:

> Magnifying heaven and thinking of it longingly—how can this compare with raising things and arranging them?
> Following heaven and singing its praise—how can this compare with arranging what heaven mandates [*tiānmìng*] and using it?
> Looking off toward timing [*shí*] and waiting for it—how can this compare with responding to the time and making it serve?
> Following along relying [*yīn* 因] on things and considering their multiplicity—how can this compare with intensifying their abilities and transforming them?[3]
> To longingly think of things and take them for granted as things—how can this compare with integrally ordering [*lǐ* 理] things and not losing them?
> To yearn for that by which things are generated—how can this compare with having that by which things are completed?
> Thus to discard the human and think longingly of heaven is to lose the genuine characteristics [*qíng*] of the ten thousand things. (17: 317; cf. Knoblock 1988, 17.10)

As usual, heaven, fate, and timing represent what is outside of human control, but for Xúnzǐ, they do not determine the efficacy of human actions. They simply provide the raw materials that we make use of. The criticism of looking and waiting for the right time has a clear target in the more fatalistic elements of the Ru. These passages also could be taken as directed against Mèngzǐ's claim that peace was impossible because heaven did not then want it (*Mèngzǐ* 2B13).

The placement of heaven, *tiān*, on these lists marks a strong break from the Mohists. This point is expanded in the opening lines of chapter 17, "Discussion of Heaven" ("Tiānlùn" 天論), in a passage that would have startled any of the thinkers discussed so far:

The course [*xíng* 行, "actions"] of heaven has regularity: it is not that it exists for a Yáo and does not exist for a Jié. Respond to it with order and it will be propitious [*jí* 吉]. Respond to it with disorder and it will be unpropitious [*xiōng* 凶]. If you strengthen the root and restrain expenses, then heaven cannot make you poor. If you cultivate basic provisions and move with the seasons [*shí*, timing], then heaven cannot make you ill. If you cultivate the way and do not err, then heaven cannot give misfortune. Thus floods and droughts cannot cause starvation, cold and heat cannot cause sickness, and omens and aberrations cannot be unpropitious. If the root is left wild and use is extravagant, then heaven cannot make you prosperous. If basic provisions are few and movements untimely, then heaven cannot keep you whole. If the way is violated and actions are reckless, then heaven cannot make it propitious. Thus even without floods and droughts arriving, there will be starvation, without cold and heat oppressing, there will be sickness, and without omens and aberrations arriving, it will be unpropitious. The timing [*shí*] they receive is the same as that in an orderly age, but the calamities and misfortunes differ from that of an orderly age. One cannot blame heaven: its way is like this. Thus one who understands the division between heaven and human can be called a person who has reached the utmost. (17: 306–308; cf. Knoblock 1988, 17.1)

Xúnzǐ here rejects the Mohist claim that heaven might punish bad people with floods or famines or that heaven would intervene to assist the good. Xúnzǐ inherits Mohist concerns with the efficacy of human action and the scope of human responsibility, but he sees heaven as an amoral force outside our control and concern. While the Mohists argued that human actions have efficacy *because* heaven assists them, Xúnzǐ argues that human actions have efficacy *in spite of* heaven. If we do the right actions, heaven has no power to harm us; if we do the wrong actions, heaven has no power to save us. We have seen that in the late Spring and Autumn period, the moral forces that support virtue were more associated with *tiān* and the blind forces were associated with *mìng*. In this context, we can say that while the Mohists try to save *tiān* by separating it from *mìng*, Xúnzǐ keeps the association and rejects both. While this contradicts one of the key planks of the Mohist platform, it does so in order to better realize the Mohists' own goals. Xúnzǐ provides a more plausible account of nature but also solves one paradox we have seen in the Mohist position: If heaven really cares inclusively for everyone, why do we need do anything? The *Xúnzǐ* makes it clear that no one can save us but ourselves.

As in the *Dàodéjīng*, Xúnzǐ's emphasis on human efficacy leads to a rejection of prognostication and a co-opting of the terms associated with it, something for which he was particularly well known.[4] This position is most prominent in a chapter opposing *xiàng* 相, the practice of using a person's physical features to determine whether they are auspicious. Xúnzǐ writes,

> If the method is correct, the heart follows it. If the heart's method is good, then even if the form is repugnant [*è* 惡, "bad"] it is no obstacle to becoming

a gentlemen. If the heart's method is bad/repugnant, even if the form is good it is no obstacle to becoming a petty person. Gentlemen are called propitious; petty people are called unpropitious. Tall or short, small or big, good or bad in form—this is not propitious or unpropitious. (5: 72–73; cf. Knoblock 1988, 5.1)

The terms used here for propitious and unpropitious, *jí* and *xiōng*, are key terms in the *Zhōu yì* (Book of Changes) and it may be significant that the *Xúnzǐ* does not list the *Zhōu yì* among the classics, referring to it in only three places—one of which says, "those good with the *Zhōu yì* do not prognosticate [*zhān* 占]" (27: 507; cf. Knoblock 1988, 27.81).[5] Ill omens (*yāo* 祅) like eclipses and falling stars are explained as meaningless variations in natural patterns. What are to be feared as "ill omens" are human actions: disordered government, oppression of the people, disrupting the agricultural seasons (17: 313–14; Knoblock 1988, 17.7). One could add Xúnzǐ's opposition to claims that rituals and sacrifices influence heaven or other spirits, as when he argues that rituals for bringing rain have no ability to affect the weather. In fact, he says it is "inauspicious" (*xiōng*) to believe that these are done for the sake of spirits (17: 316; Knoblock 1988, 17.8). Once again Xúnzǐ's divergence from the Mohists better realizes Mohist goals. Although the Mohists argue that only impartial care can draw divine rewards, the image of a world run by anthropomorphic spirits could hardly avoid tempting people into special pleading. Xúnzǐ's opposition to all forms of anthropomorphism eliminates this possibility.

The *Xúnzǐ* tends to reinterpret the more fatalistic Ru tradition rather than reject it explicitly. The term *mìng* (fate), plays a remarkably minimal role in comparison with other Ru texts, and it usually occurs in contexts that emphasize efficacy rather than resignation.[6] For example, two passages use the phrases, "the fate of a person is with heaven; the fate of the state is with ritual" (16: 291, 17: 317; cf. Knoblock 1988, 16.1, 17.9). In both cases, though, only the second phrase is emphasized, cited to show that the order of the state is entirely within human control. Like other Ru texts, the *Xúnzǐ* contains advice for gentlemen in trouble, but such passages differ subtly from analogous ones in the *Mèngzǐ* or *Lúnyǔ*. Their emphasis is not on accepting failure, but on flexibility and adaptability. Similarly, although the distinction in the above passage between what is in us and what is with heaven (*tiānrén zhīfēn*) suggests a familiar Ru shift away from a concern with external results, Xúnzǐ's point is quite different: the only chance to bring about results is to focus on what is within our power. Even in difficulties one can still bring about some results. Kǒngzǐ is given as an example—he lived a difficult life and never attained a stable position or wealth, yet he ended up honored for generations (6.8: 96–97). Kǒngzǐ is thus transformed from a good man who suffered to a model for the inevitability of success.

Xúnzǐ does admit that life is not *always* fair: "That the King of Chǔ is followed by a thousand chariots is not because of his wisdom. That gentlemen just eat beans and drink water is not because of their foolishness. These are irregularities [*jiérán* 節然]" (17: 312; cf. Knoblock 1988, 17.6). Because there are irregularities in the patterns, bad things sometimes happen to good people. These are described as *jiérán*, which Watson and Knoblock both translate as "accidents of circumstance" and Robert Eno as "rhythms of circumstances" (Watson 1967, 83; Eno 1990a, 200). Xúnzǐ similarly defines *mìng* at the end of a list of definitions as *jiéyù* 節遇 (22: 413; Knoblock 1988, 22.1b). We have seen the term *yù*, which means to meet an opportunity. There is no precedent for this use of the term *jié*, making its sense impossible to determine with certainty, but it must mean something like "accidental" or "contingent." Whatever its precise meaning, the shift away from the term *mìng* helps evade two important connotations: that such irregularities come from a command of heaven and that they are something we must passively accept. For Xúnzǐ, *mìng* refers to brute facts that we must deal with, which is probably what he means in saying that we should "arrange *tiānmìng* and use it" (17: 317; cf. Knoblock 1988, 17.10). The recognition that there are exceptions to the general patterns should have little impact on our actions:

> Humaneness, rightness, and actions of virtue are regularly the method of safety but they do not necessarily avoid danger; foulness, recklessness, snatching and robbing are regularly the method of danger, but they are not necessarily unsafe. Thus it is that gentlemen take this regularity as their way while petty people follow the aberrations. (4: 62–63; cf. Knoblock 1988, 4.8)

A similar passage says, "Heaven has a regular way, earth has a regular order, and gentlemen have a regular form. Gentlemen follow its regularity as their way, while petty people calculate results" (17: 311; cf. Knoblock 1988, 17.5). Virtue need not be a certain route to long-term benefit, as long it remains the most reliable one. Gentlemen follow the most consistently productive path; petty people calculate each action and hope to get lucky.

The Way to Get What Everyone Wants

Xúnzǐ's insistence that rewards follow from the way is inseparable from his view that human beings act primarily for the sake of rewards. His divergence from Mèngzǐ on this point is well known from the repeated motto and chapter title: "human nature is bad [*xìng è* 性惡]." In a broad sense, human beings are naturally self-interested. The *Xúnzǐ* frequently mentions loving benefit (*lì*) and hating harm (e.g., 4: 63; Knoblock 1988, 4.9); loving safety and honor and hating danger and shame (e.g. 8: 144; Knoblock 1988, 8.11); and that when hungry we want food, when cold we want warmth, and when tired we want rest (e.g., 5: 78; Knoblock 1988, 5.4). When it comes to specific analyses of natural desires, though, the focus is on the pleasures of the senses:

> Now, the eyes loving good looks, the ears loving sounds, the mouth loving flavors, the heart loving benefit, the bones, limbs, and patterned skin loving pleasure and rest—these all are generated from natural human dispositions

and affects [*qíngxìng*]. They respond spontaneously; they do not wait for us to work on them to then be generated. (23: 438; cf. Knoblock 1988, 23.2a)

The naturalness of sensory desire follows the nature of sensory perception, which already involves preferences such as distinguishing between what is fragrant or stinking (22: 416–17; 4: 63; Knoblock 1988, 22.2d, 4.9). Sensory desires arise spontaneously when stimulated by external factors and they require no learning, practice, or work. They come from heaven and are so of themselves, *zìrán* 自然 (23: 435, 22: 412; Knoblock 1988, 23.1c, 22.1b).

The placement of the heart in Xúnzǐ's list is significant. Mèngzǐ would agree with Xúnzǐ's account of the eyes, ears, and so on, but Mèngzǐ adds desires that belong specifically to the heart—a taste for rightness and coherent patterns (6A7). Mèngzǐ then builds his claims about human nature around the priority of the desires of the heart over those of the other senses. In Xúnzǐ's list, the heart is only said to love benefit, *lì* 利. Benefit, though, ultimately is explicated in terms of the pleasures of the other senses. The heart seems to have no desires of its own, but functions through wanting and calculating the maximization of sensory satisfaction over time. This contrast goes along with another: Mèngzǐ emphasizes the heart's spontaneous emotional responses, whereas Xúnzǐ emphasizes its cognitive capacities.

The basis of human motivation in desires for sensory pleasure leads to the further claim that desires are naturally unlimited, that they have what Aaron Stalnaker nicely calls a "proliferating expansiveness" (2006, 62). Even with all the benefits of the son of heaven, our desires will not be completely satisfied (22: 428; Knoblock 1988, 22.5b). This position must be understood in the context of broader debates in the late Warring States period. Xúnzǐ explicitly takes as his target the claim that desires are naturally few, which was probably based on the view that our natural desires are for life and thus directed to things like food, shelter, and sex. We have seen such a view in the *Dàodéjīng*, and it is implied by the Mohist definition of benefit in terms of basic needs. The *Lǚshì chūnqiū* gives us a version of this position that is closer in time to Xúnzǐ:

> Heaven generates human beings as having appetites and desires, but some desires are natural affects [*qíng*] and natural affects are moderate [*jié* 節]. Sagely people cultivate this moderation to regulate desires and thus they do not exceed their natural affects. Thus that the ears desire the five sounds, the eyes desire the five colors, the mouth desires the five flavors—these are natural reactions. In these three, the desires are the same, whether one is noble or lowly, foolish or wise, worthy or lacking. Even Shén Nóng and Huáng Dì are the same as Jié and Zhòu. That by which sagely people are different is in attaining natural affects. (2/3: 86)

Desires that come from our genuine nature are inherently moderate. This view is probably derived from the fact that hunger, thirst, and sexual desire are inherently limited—once you get what you desire, you are satisfied, at least for a while.⁷ This contrasts with socially constructed desires—as for money or prestige—which are inherently unlimited.

The opposing view claims that our natural desires are for pleasure rather than for life. We glimpse this debate in a dialogue in the "Robber Zhí" ("Dào zhí" 盜跖) chapter of the *Zhuāngzǐ* between "Nothing Sufficient" and "Knowing Harmony," in which the latter character argues for moderation in service of a long life.⁸ Nothing Sufficient responds that all human beings by their nature (*xìng*) want the pleasures of the senses, spontaneously and without being taught. He concludes, "If one must maintain their reputation, embitter their body and cut off all sweetness, restraining and cultivating so as to maintain life, this is just like being one who is sick and troubled for years but doesn't die!" (29: 1012; Mair 1994, 310). A long life without pleasure is not worth having. A similar position appears in the *Lǚshì chūnqiū*, in a passage that ranks a life unpleasant to our senses as lower than death (2/2: 76–77).

In this debate, Xúnzǐ falls on the side of sensory pleasures. He makes his argument in a dialogue with Sòngzǐ 宋子, who seems to have been a prominent philosopher in the state of Qí:

> So then do you also think that it is a natural human feeling [*qíng*] for the eyes not to desire the extreme of colors, the ears not to desire the extreme of sounds, the mouth not to desire the extreme of tastes, the nose not to desire the extreme of scents, the bodily form not to desire the extreme of ease—are these five extremes not what genuine human feelings desire? (18: 344; cf. Knoblock 1988, 18.10)

If the basis of desire is in the stimulation of the senses, then those desires should be as unlimited as the ways in which the senses can be stimulated. For Xúnzǐ, our unlimited desire for sensory pleasure means that human beings cannot be content with a simple life that merely supplies their basic needs, a view that grounds much of his social-political theory and his main divergence from the Mohists.

Although Xúnzǐ's explicit analyses of human nature center on the senses, the text mentions other motives. The most important and integral is the desire for honor, which appears as a motivating factor throughout the text and is crucial to Xúnzǐ's claim that virtue brings rewards. Conceptually, this desire for honor has a problematic status, both because it does not reduce to sensory pleasures and because it resembles Mèngzǐ's claim that all human beings have a heart of shame and aversion (2A6). Unfortunately, Xúnzǐ never situates the love of honor in his analyses of human nature.

A greater complication appears in Xúnzǐ's chapters on music and ritual, which assume a complex range of human emotions that arise spontaneously from our dispositions. For example, the chapter on music says, "Thus, humans cannot lack joy and joy cannot lack form, but if form is not according to the way, then there cannot but be chaos" (20: 379; cf. Knoblock 1988, 20.1). The chapter on ritual focuses more on sorrow—for example, saying that mourning rituals cut off what might otherwise become endless grief (19: 372; Knoblock 1988, 19.9a). This emphasis on music and ritual as expressing complex human feelings is central to Ru views from the late fourth century, as seen for example in the *Xìng zì mìng chū*, but they play no role in the rest of the *Xúnzǐ*, in which rituals are justified as bringing sensory pleasure and marking social hierarchy, an argument more consistent with Xúnzǐ's analyses of human nature. Another passage in the chapter on ritual appeals to a natural love of family common even to animals: "For anything born between heaven and earth, if it is the type of thing that has blood and vital energy, then it must have knowing, and those things that have knowing all love their own kind" (19: 372; cf. Knoblock 1988, 19.9b). Although familial feelings were taken as natural in earlier Ru texts, they play no further role in the *Xúnzǐ*. In fact, Xúnzǐ argues explicitly that natural feelings lead to hostility among family members:

> Now loving benefit and desiring to attain it—these are natural human dispositions and affects. Suppose that one has resources to be divided among younger and older brothers. If they follow along with their natural dispositions and affects, they love benefit and desire to attain it, so then younger and older brothers will seize from each other. If they are transformed by coherent cultured patterns [*wénlǐ* 文理] of ritual and rightness, then they will yield to anyone from their state. (23: 438–39; cf. Knoblock 1988, 23.2a)

Familial regard originates externally—going against, rather than following from, our natural responses to the world. It may be possible to reconcile natural familial concern with Xúnzǐ's discussions of the bad tendencies of human nature, but it would make Xúnzǐ's account of human motivation in other chapters incomplete and misleading.[9] The fact that the complex account of human affects assumed in the chapters on ritual and music is largely absent in other chapters could be explained by a selective emphasis according rhetorical demands, or it might reflect developments in Xúnzǐ's thought over time. But given that the chapters on ritual and music bear more resemblance to Ru discussions from the late fourth century BCE than they do to other chapters of the *Xúnzǐ*, it is possible that these chapters incorporate materials from an earlier source, materials which may have been only partially or selective incorporated into Xúnzǐ's overall philosophy.[10]

We can now see the structure of Xúnzǐ's position—since human beings are motivated primarily by desires for sensory pleasure, following the Ru way must be justified as the best way to fulfill such desires. Again we see the basic similarity with the Mohist position, although the primacy of sensory pleasure rather than basic needs has far-reaching consequences. Xúnzǐ goes further by providing an analysis of the cognitive ability that enables us to act prudently for long-term fulfillment of desires. This ability is discussed on a general level through *lǜ* 慮, "thinking," "considering," or "deliberating." One passage describes how ordinary people deal with their desires. It begins by saying that natural human feelings (*qíng*) are to eat roasted meat, wear patterned clothes, and travel by horse and carriage. Yet although people have the means, they do not do these things. Xúnzǐ explains,

> Why is this? It is not that they do not desire them, but how could they not consider [*lǜ*] the long term and look to later times, fearing they might have nothing by which to continue? Because of this, they restrain expenses and control desires—harvesting, saving, gathering, and storing so as to have something by which to continue on. This is in their considering the long term and thinking of later times—isn't this profoundly good? (4: 67–68; cf. Knoblock 1988, 4.11)

Common people deny themselves what they desire in order to secure their future, which they are able to do because of their ability to deliberate and consider the long term. The passage places these people between reckless fools who consume as much as they can and end up cold and hungry, and the way of the first kings, which contains the world's "greatest deliberations [*dàlǜ* 大慮]," allowing people to "consider the long term and look to later times, preserving myriad generations."

This ability of the heart to consider and deliberate is placed in the context of human nature in a list of definitions in the chapter on "Correcting Names" ("Zhèngmíng" 正名):

> What is so by being born is called *xìng*. What is born from the harmony of *xìng*, its refined essence combining in relations of reaction and response, so of itself [*zìrán*] without any working—this is called *xìng*. The loves, hates, pleasures, angers, griefs, and joys of *xìng* are called *qíng*. *Qíng* being so and the heart choosing for them is called "deliberating." The heart deliberating and our abilities acting for it is "deliberate action." What takes completed form [*chéng*] after deliberations are accumulated and abilities are trained is called "deliberate action." What is done directed toward benefit is called "work." What is done directed toward rightness is called "ethical conduct." (22: 412–414; cf. Knoblock 1988, 22.1b)

The model is the same as that in the *Xìng zì mìng chū*, in which things stimulate our natural dispositions (*xìng*) into specific desires (*hàowù* 好惡) and feelings (*qíng*). Based on those motivations, the heart makes choices and this is called "deliberating," *lǜ*. When we act on these deliberations, we have *wěi* 偽, "deliberate action," and from deliberate action, we develop a concept of work (*shì* 事), based on benefit, and of ethical conduct (*xíng* 行), based on rightness. Another passage from the same chapter gives a slightly different version:

> *Xìng* is accomplished by heaven; *qíng* is the basic quality of *xìng*; desire is the reaction of *qíng*. To take what is desired as able to be attained and then to seek it is a necessity of *qíng* that cannot be avoided, but to take it as able to be attained and to have a way [*dào*] is what must come from knowing. Thus even

if one is a gatekeeper, desires cannot be abandoned, since they belong to *xìng*. Even if one is the son of heaven, desires cannot be completely fulfilled. Although desires cannot be completely fulfilled, they can be almost fulfilled; although desires cannot be abandoned, seeking can be moderated. (22: 428–29; cf. Knoblock 1988, 22.5b)

While "deliberating" (*lǜ*) does not appear in this list, it corresponds to "taking as able to be attained" (*yǐwéi kědé* 以為可得), which is what lets us moderate our seeking. Being able to deliberate well is knowing or wisdom (*zhī* 知), which is what allows us to find a proper way to act.

This passage introduces a key distinction between desiring (*yù* 欲) and seeking (*qiú* 求). Desires arise naturally and spontaneously from our nature. They cannot be eliminated or fully sated, no matter how rich or poor we become. That we *desire* something, though, does not necessarily mean that we *seek* it. What we seek depends on the deliberations of the heart. When in poverty, we cannot rid ourselves of desires for more pleasure, but we can restrain and moderate our pursuit of those desires (22: 429; Knoblock 1988, 22.5b). This split between desire and seeking explains the distinction between good people and bad people, who have the same desires but seek to fulfill them using different ways. Xúnzǐ addresses this difference in a passage criticizing the attempt to eliminate or reduce desires:

> Having desires and not having desires are in different categories—those of the living and the dead, not those of order and disorder. Desires being many or being few are in different categories—in the number of *qíng* and not in those of order and disorder. Desire does not wait on being able to be attained [*kědé* 可得], but seeking follows what can be [*suǒkě* 所可]. Desire not waiting for what can be attained is something received from heaven; that seeking follows what can be is something received from the heart. The desires received from heaven are the same, but the controls received from the heart are many, so that it is surely difficult to categorize what is received from heaven. (22: 426–27; cf. Knoblock 1988, 22.5a)

Order and disorder have nothing to do with the strength of our desires but rather with how we seek to fulfill them, the ways (*dào*) we follow under the guidance of the heart's deliberations.

A second key point in these passages is an explanation of what it is that the heart considers, which is whether or not something "can be attained," *kědé* 可得, or sometimes simply "can be," *kě* 可. The meaning of *kě* is ambiguous in the same way as "can" in English: when we say, "You can't do that," we could mean that it is *impossible* or that it is *impermissible*. This ambiguity has generated one of the main points of disagreement about Xúnzǐ's system.[11] D. C. Lau even charges that Xúnzǐ relies on this ambiguity to slip from the plausible claim that we never attempt what we consider impossible to the implausible claim that we never attempt what we consider wrong (2000, 211, 216n43). Discussions of human action throughout the *Xúnzǐ*, though, make it clear that to *kě* a course of action is to affirm it as most likely to fulfill our desires. This use of *kě* appears in another passage on considering the long term:

> In exchanges, if you exchange one for one, people say there is no gain and also no loss. If you exchange one for two, people say there is no loss but there is gain. If you exchange two for one, people say it is without gain but has loss. One who calculates takes what they consider most; one who plans follows what they *kě*. Exchanging two for one is something no one would do, because they see how to count. Going out by following the way is like taking one and exchanging it for two: How can you lose? Leaving the way and internally choosing for yourself is like taking two and exchanging it for one: How can you gain? To exchange a hundred years of accumulated desires for one moment of pleasure—acting like this is just not seeing how to count. (22: 430–31; cf. Knoblock 1988, 22.6c)

This passage uses the very same phrase as the one quoted earlier, *suǒkě*, but here it clearly refers to calculating long-term benefit—what one who plans or plots (*móu* 謀) follows. For Xúnzǐ, everyone wants more for less. That is our nature. The way of the Ru, containing the world's greatest deliberations, is just the most reliable way to do that.

Drawing these passages together, we can distinguish three approaches to life. The lowest do whatever they desire in the moment, without restraint or regard for the future. The next are those regular people who restrain their immediate desires in order to save for the future, recognizing that restraint and denial are the only ways to sustainably attain what they seek. The highest group is gentlemen who follow ritual and rightness because they trust that this is the most reliable way to fulfill desires over the course of a lifetime. The distinction between different kinds of people is expressed on a general level in another passage using *kě*: "Humankind dwells together. Their seeking is the same but their ways (*dào*) differ; their desires are the same, but their knowing differs. This is our nature.[12] In each having *kě*, the wise and foolish are the same, but in what they *kě* the wise and the foolish differ" (10: 175; cf. Knoblock 1988, 10.1). All human beings have the same motivations, all seek what they desire, and all base that seeking on what they judge to be most effective. The wise differ only in choosing a more effective way. Given the shared motivation of the wise and the foolish, one could say that Xúnzǐ's system is ultimately one of prudent action, not morality. Nonetheless, there is a fundamental difference between gentlemen and petty people. Gentlemen give up calculations of benefit and rely on the patterns that regularly bring success, the way established over millennia and maintained by the Ru. Their *immediate* goal is the way, even if they choose this goal ultimately for the sake of benefit. In contrast, petty people always calculate benefit. As seen earlier, gentlemen stick with what regularly brings success, while petty people hope for exceptions.[13]

We can see why Xúnzǐ must minimize the problem of evil. If the future is uncertain and uncontrollable, fleeting like a galloping horse glimpsed through a crack (as Robber Zhí says), then a wise person would pursue pleasure whenever possible. If the future is controllable but rewards craftiness and power, it makes sense to save for the future and take care of our health, but not to dedicate ourselves to becoming gentlemen. The way of the Ru has appeal only if it most regularly leads to the greatest sensory satisfaction. In itself, this account yields a deeply pessimistic picture of the human condition. If we enjoy ourselves in immediate pleasures, we inevitably end up in suffering and misery. The only way to avoid disaster is to constantly struggle against our desires, forcing ourselves to work hard and save for the future (as do common people) or to follow the demanding path of ritual and rightness (as do worthies and gentlemen).

Although this account of motivation is elegant and simple, it is complicated by suggestions that self-cultivation alters our desires. Consider this description of how gentlemen cultivate themselves:

> They make their eyes without desire to see what is not it [i.e., the way], make their ears without desire to hear what is not it, make their mouths without desire to say what is not it, make their hearts without desire to consider what is not it. This reaches to their most fully loving it, just as the eyes love the five colors, the ears love the five sounds, the mouth loves the five flavors, and the heart considers the whole world as a benefit. Thus weighing benefits cannot tilt them, masses of people cannot alter them, and the whole world cannot move them. In living they follow it and in dying they follow it, so this is called virtue taking hold. When virtue takes hold, one can be steady; when one can be steady, one can respond. When one can be steady and responsive, that is what we call a completed person [*chéngrén* 成人]. (1: 19–20; cf. Knoblock 1988, 1.14)

The passage does not say the eyes do not *seek* to look at what is improper, but that they do not *desire* to look at it. The senses themselves are changed. This cultivation allows one to become steady in purpose, because the usual temptations are no longer even desired. The same theme appears in other passages in the *Xúnzǐ*. One criticizes three exemplars of what we might label as great willpower—a person named Jí, who lived in a cave and blocked his eyes and ears to in order to concentrate; Mèngzǐ, who left his wife when he thought she had done something out of accord with ritual; and Yǒuzǐ, who would burn his palm to stay awake and study. All of these are criticized as examples of forcing oneself (*zìqiáng* 自強) or resisting oneself (*zìrěn* 自忍). In contrast, sagely people "indulge their desires and inclusively accept [*jiān* 兼] their genuine affects," doing what is right without force or resistance (21: 404; cf. Knoblock 1988, 21.7d). Here, Xúnzǐ maintains the Ru ideal exemplified in Kǒngzǐ's final stage of life: "At seventy I could follow what my heart desired without overstepping proper measure" (Lúnyǔ 2.4).

These passages suggest two broad stages of development. At one level, we force ourselves to do the right thing because we know it will lead to more sustained pleasure, but at a higher level, we eliminate destructive desires and genuinely want what is right. One passage explicitly articulates two stages of change: "Practice alters the resolve and residing in it for a long time alters the basic quality" (8: 144; cf. Knoblock 1988, 8.11). The first stage of cultivation moves (*yí* 移) our resolve, *zhì* 志, making it intent on learning. The second stage moves our natural material, *zhì* 質. Some passages say that we transform (*huà* 化) our *xìng* (e.g., 23: 435; Knoblock 1988, 23.2a). Others use weaker terms to describe what we do to our *xìng*: "correct" (*zhèng* 正), "order" (*zhì* 治), "straighten" (*jiǎo* 矯), "adorn" (*shì* 飾), or "rouse" (*rǎo* 擾) (23: 435; Knoblock 1988, 23.1b).

This claim that self-cultivation alters our basic nature is difficult to reconcile with Xúnzǐ's frequent claims that all people have the same *xìng* and the same desires, but the key is an ambiguity in what it means to have the same desires. To say that our mouths have the same desires could mean that we all want the same foods, but it could more minimally mean that we all want what we consider most delicious. In other words, the claim that we all desire maximum sensory pleasure is compatible with finding that pleasure in different things. This distinction appears in the *Lǚshì chūnqiū*, which says that although the Mán and Yí peoples have different customs, ways of life, and preferences in sounds, sights, and flavors, they are the same in acting on their desires—something even the sage kings could not alter (19/6: 1303). For Xúnzǐ, the process of cultivation does not reduce sensory desires but trains the senses to take their pleasure in more constructive and sustainable things. One passage makes this point through an analogy with taste, comparing the way of Jié and Robber Zhí to beans and rough greens and the way of the first kings to fine roast meat (4: 65; Knoblock 1988, 4.10). Someone who knows only coarse food might be content with it, and at first they will find the fine roast meat a little strange. Once they are used to it, though, they will never go back. Once again, Xúnzǐ takes up but modifies common Ru positions. Whereas Kǒngzǐ and Mèngzǐ both advocate finding pleasure in simple things, Xúnzǐ's gentlemen remain motivated toward extremes of sensory pleasure. They just train themselves to find this pleasure in rituals and music that support harmony and social order. One of Xúnzǐ's more interesting insights is that the insatiable desires of the ruling classes should be shifted away from accumulating greater and greater quantities of stuff and instead directed toward more and more refined aesthetic pleasures, pleasures which require less resources and help to reinforce proper social relations.

Appropriating Nature

Xúnzǐ's response to the problem of evil may be more realistic than that of the Mohists, but his emphasis on the power of a humanistic Ru ethics still seems to require a natural world that is far more humane and fair than it appears to actually be. To grasp the power of Xúnzǐ's position, we must see how he sets the problem of evil on an entirely new terrain. So far, our questions have all been questions about nature, taken as *tiān* or *dào*: Are the patterns of nature regular? Do they consistently reward human virtue? The problem is that any view that elevates the efficacy of human categories and values will require an unrealistically anthropomorphic view of nature (or its creator or divine force). The *Zhuāngzǐ* shows how a thorough rejection of the latter overturns the former.

What is most distinctive and interesting about Xúnzǐ's position is that, like the *Zhuāngzǐ*, he firmly rejects any kind of anthropomorphism, yet he still holds on to the strongest humanism. As with other Ru, Xúnzǐ shifts from the alignment of human beings and heaven and toward their division: "Thus one who understands the division between heaven and human [*tiānrén zhīfēn*] can be called a complete person" (17: 308; cf. Knoblock 1988, 17.1). Once again, however, Xúnzǐ gives Ru positions a new sense. When *Qióng dá yǐ shí* says that one who knows the division between heaven and human knows how to act, the point is that we must recognize the impotence of human power over the external world. For Xúnzǐ, in contrast, the phrase is a declaration of human power and independence. If human beings follow ritual and rightness, then even heaven cannot harm them: "If successful [*tōng*], then they unite the world, and if in destitution [*qióng*, "failure"], then they establish an honorable name alone. This is something heaven cannot kill, earth cannot bury, and an age like that of Jié or Robber Zhí cannot pollute" (8: 139; cf. Knoblock 1988, 8.9). The language of this passage closely follows that of the *Tàiyī shēng shuǐ* (Great unity generates water), but there, what "heaven cannot kill and earth cannot bury" is the waxing and waning implicit in the turning of the seasons (Liú Zhāo 2003, strips 7–8). For Xúnzǐ, it is the power of ritual and rightness. To know the difference between heaven and human is to know that the power to control our lives is with us, not heaven. Just as heaven is no longer the dominant force in our lives, heaven no longer is the model for action.[14] The way that matters is not a cosmic "Dao" but the cultural systems developed by the sages of the past: "The way of the first kings is in exulting humaneness. Hold to its center and enact it. What is its center? It is ritual and rightness. The way is not the way of heaven and is not the way of earth but is that by which human beings make their way and that which gentlemen follow as their way" (8: 121–22; cf. Knoblock 1988, 8.3).[15] The last clause uses *dào* as a verb to say that what gentlemen *dào* is not heaven or earth but the human tradition.[16]

For readers steeped in European thought, the deepest challenges and greatest subtleties in Xúnzǐ's position may not be immediately apparent. In a strange way, some of Xúnzǐ's claims may seem more normal to us than they would have to Mèngzǐ, Mòzǐ, or Zhuāngzǐ. We are quite familiar with the rejection of divine influence in favor of human power, which in many ways was at the heart of the Enlightenment. Xúnzǐ's criticism of "superstitions" could easily have been written by David Hume or Benjamin Franklin. In Europe, this shift from the divine to the human, interlinked with awareness of the problem of evil, left a confidence in the power of human reason and science to grasp and control the natural world.

If we paraphrase Xúnzǐ's words above to say that if human beings work together then even nature cannot stop us, we have a motto that could have been accepted in modern Europe. This parallel has been emphasized by thinkers looking to Xúnzǐ as a Chinese source for scientific thinking. Hú Shì equates Xúnzǐ's position with Bacon's "Conquest of Nature" (Hú 2003, 239).[17] Chén Dàqí also connects Xúnzǐ to Bacon, and then explains,

> This passage from Xúnzǐ can be said to be his most splendid statement for the natural sciences and also most worthy of the attention of later generations. Xúnzǐ wants to make things and nature serve and wants to increase human power to increase natural production. This is not unaligned with the direction of Westerners toward conquering nature and is very close to the spirit of modern natural sciences. (1954, 21)

He goes on to say that if Xúnzǐ had not been ignored, science in China would not have lagged so far behind.

Some similarity between Xúnzǐ and the European Enlightenment is undeniable, but it is misleading. The root of the differences lies in how human power is justified. Whatever its logical ground, the historical ground of modern European confidence in human power over nature derives from a Christian view whose extreme anthropocentrism lay in an equally extreme anthropomorphism. Even though this view of human beings as fundamentally supernatural has been given up by most philosophers and scientists in favor of a view of human beings as complexly evolved animals, its legacy remains largely intact. Even to this day most people take it for granted that we are the only things in nature whose movements are not determined by the laws of physics or biology but rather by free will. The faith that the epistemological capabilities of human beings are uniquely commensurate with the complexity of the natural world also remains largely assumed. The most interesting thing about the *Xúnzǐ* in this context is that he gives us a glimpse of what the attempt to justify human efficacy might look like without roots in a view of human beings as *imago dei,* the image of God. The most profound difference that emerges is that his humanism loses its association with the individual, asserting an almost complete dependence of human beings on the historical community. It is a humanism deeply troubled by the fragility of that community, haunted by a sense of caution and anxious concern, the *yōuhuàn yìshí* discussed in chapter 1.

The challenge faced by Xúnzǐ in relating human beings and nature is thus the inverse of the problem in European philosophy. The challenge for Enlightenment and post-Enlightenment thinkers is how to reconcile a conception of human beings as autonomous with our status as just one of the myriad things. For Xúnzǐ, the problem instead is how one of the myriad things could separate itself, shape its own world, and attain any autonomy at all. How can morality emerge and become effective in a fundamentally amoral world? This question lies at the heart of a criticism commonly raised against Xúnzǐ: If human nature is bad and can only become good through submission to rituals and rightness, then how could rituals and rightness arise in the first place?[18] Xúnzǐ's explicit answer is that these practices were created by the early sage kings, but all human beings are said to have the same nature, and whatever talent sages have must itself emerge from nature. Even if (contrary to Xúnzǐ's statements) we take the sages as in some sense super-*human*, there is no possibility for taking them as super-*natural*.

We can approach this problem first by considering Xúnzǐ's view of nature, which must combine his view of the natural world and his account of nature as it is in us, our *xìng*. Xúnzǐ's view of *tiān* is similar to that in the *Zhuāngzǐ* and it could be adequately translated simply as "nature" or the "order of nature."[19] *Tiān* has no awareness and is not an agent in any literal way. Its patterns are amoral and have no particular regard for human beings. Ultimately, heaven is not bad in that it cannot harm us, but not good in that it cannot help us, either.

Xúnzǐ's view of the nature with which heaven endows us is more negative. His well-known motto is that *xìng* is "bad," *è* 惡, a term which we might also translate as "ugly" and some translate as "evil." The character combines a deformed head (*yà* 亞) with an image of the heart (*xīn* 心). As the verb *wù*, the same character means to hate or detest. Thus we could also translate *è* as "revolting" or "detestable." In spite of Xúnzǐ's strong rhetoric, however, *xìng* is not really evil but amoral, and our *xìng* leaves us enough space to become either good or bad, in just the same way that heaven does not stop us from succeeding or failing. There is an important difference, though, between our relationship with *tiān* and our relationship with *xìng*, in that while *xìng* allows us to become good, we must struggle against its natural tendencies. If we do not actively resist our natural impulses toward ever-greater sensory pleasure, we will become dangerous and disruptive, harming and robbing others, even snatching food away from our own brothers. Xúnzǐ's view is thus more pessimistic than that articulated by Gàozǐ in the *Mèngzǐ*, who claims that our nature is neutral and can become good just as easily as it can become bad (6A1, 6A2).

When we combine Xúnzǐ's view of *tiān* and his view of *xìng*, we see how bleak his vision of nature really is. Xúnzǐ does not explicitly discuss a state of nature, but he describes what life would be like without rituals and social structures: alone in a state of nature, we are too weak to fill our needs, ending in desperation and poverty; together in a state of nature, we brutalize each other in a struggle for benefit, ending in misfortune (10: 176–77; Knoblock 1988, 10.1). Our situation is like that of Schopenhauer's hedgehogs huddling together to keep warm, torn between the avoiding the cold and avoiding the pricks of their fellows. Another passage in the same chapter summarizes what life would be like without a political order: labor has no results, groups have no harmony, wealth is not gathered, positions are insecure, people do not live long, fathers and sons are distant, younger and older brothers disobey, the young will not grow and the old will not be nourished. Men and women cannot even get pleasure together (10: 182; Knoblock 1988, 10.6)! The desperation and misery of human beings in a state of nature follows from the conflict between the "proliferating expansiveness" of human desires and the limits of what nature can provide: "Desires and aversions are toward the same things. Desires are many but things are scarce. This scarcity must cause conflict" (10: 176; cf. Knoblock 1988, 10.1).

In a world without ritual and social roles, life is bad for everyone, but worst for the weak. In nature itself (taking *tiān* and *xìng* together), success follows power and failure follows weakness, with some role for luck. The only possibility for human beings to live decent lives, let alone for virtue to be consistently rewarded, is to fundamentally reorder the world we live in. The passages mentioned above that describe life without political order center on what Xúnzǐ calls *fēn* 分, which means "to divide" or "to separate," often with the specific sense of differentiated and hierarchical roles. These *fēn* allow us to cooperate together with minimal conflict (9: 164–65; Knoblock 1988, 9.16a).[20] These roles are instituted through ritual and require the ability to make distinctions (5: 78; Knoblock 1988, 5.4) and have rightness (9: 164; Knoblock 1988, 9.16a). This hierarchical social organization makes us superior to animals in both power and value.[21]

Restructuring the world through social divisions is a process of appropriation, in both the sense of incorporating things for our own use and in the sense of instituting a concept of what is and is not appropriate: "The myriad things share the same world [*yǔ* 宇] but have different forms [*tǐ* 體]. They have no appropriateness but have uses for human beings" (10: 175; cf. Knoblock 1988, 10.1). Lǐ Dísheng explains the line in terms the *Zhuāngzǐ* would support: "Appropriateness and inappropriateness are not in things but with human beings, just as fire and water can benefit people or can harm people" (1979, 196). Appropriateness has no basis and no sense in nature itself. Things just are what they are, as the *Zhuāngzǐ* would say, and they take on meaning and value only within particular perspectives.

The term *yí* 宜 (appropriateness), is closely linked to *yì* 義, (rightness). The two characters are sometimes used interchangeably, and early texts sometimes define rightness as appropriateness.[22] Xúnzǐ thus begins with the recognition that morality and appropriateness are human constructs not inherent in nature itself. In this sense, things resemble names: "Names have no fixed appropriateness, one agrees on it to name them. What is set by agreement and completed [*chéng*] as custom is called appropriate, and what differs from the agreement is called not appropriate" (22: 420; cf. Knoblock 1988, 22.2g). The connection between the system of names and the appropriation of things is even more complex if we consider that Xúnzǐ distinguishes names "added to the myriad things" from names involving social positions and cultural roles.[23] In the latter case, the act of naming simultaneously creates the object named, which is just to say that *fēn* (social roles) are not preexisting objects we name but are created by the very act of naming. The way that things or names become appropriate is of course not arbitrary. Appropriateness emerges from differences in the forms of things, which makes them useable in different ways and for different purposes. Xúnzǐ's view is not far from the *Zhuāngzǐ*'s claim that what we label as right and wrong is skewed toward what we find useful. Although the above passage suggests ordering the myriad things of the natural world, we human beings are the primary object of this appropriation. Ritual and rightness emerge as the mechanisms by which these unruly and originally amoral beings maintain order and cooperation.

As we organize ourselves socially, our ability to use nature increases:

> Water and fire have vital energy but are without life; plants and trees have life but are without knowing; birds and beasts have knowing but are without rightness; human beings have vital energy, have life, have knowing, and moreover also have rightness. Thus they are the most noble in the world. Their power is not like oxen, they cannot travel like horses, but oxen and horses are used by them. How? Because people can gather together and those others cannot gather together. How is it that people can gather together? It is social divisions [*fēn*]. How can social divisions be enacted? Through rightness. Thus when rightness is used to make social divisions there is harmony, with harmony there is unity, with unity there is more power, with more power there is strength, and with strength things can be conquered. (9: 164; cf. Knoblock 1988, 9.16a)

When human beings gather together according to the proper way, they both appropriate and make appropriate the myriad things. In a remarkable passage on trade, Xúnzǐ imagines bringing the whole world into this human order: "Thus in all that heaven covers and all that the earth bears, nothing does not exhaust its fineness and maximize its use, above to adorn the worthy and good and below to nourish the people and make them secure and joyful. Now this is called great divinity [*dàshén* 大神]!" (9: 162; cf. Knoblock 1988, 9.14). The initial phrase had been associated with the impartiality of nature, but while heaven and earth embrace all things evenly, human beings order that world to their own needs. This reordering of the world explains Xúnzǐ's claims that "gentlemen by birth are not different; they are good at borrowing from things" (1: 4; cf. Knoblock 1988, 1.3), or that "gentlemen make things serve; petty people are made to serve by things" (2: 27; cf. Knoblock 1988, 2.5). The result is a shift from immersion in nature to a life in a medium of our own making—including material landscapes, complex social hierarchies, language, rituals, and so on. This world displaces the injustice that permeates a state of nature, so that in a well-ordered society, no one gains power or survives by luck (*xìng* 幸) (9: 159; Knoblock 1988, 9.12). This is the deeper sense of Xúnzǐ's phrase, "the fate of a person is with heaven; the fate of the state is with ritual." Without a state, everyone's fate depends on heaven and luck, but with the creation of ritual and social hierarchy, we control our own destinies. The outcome is a world that consistently rewards virtue. This world is not grounded in the will of heaven but rather built by human effort and artifice.

The status of this human order in relation to heaven is one point of disagreement among interpreters of the *Xúnzǐ*. We have seen Chinese scholars such as Hú Shì and Chén Dàqí take this order as an imposition on nature, making Xúnzǐ look more scientific. Recent English-language sources, though, tend toward the opposite direction, emphasizing continuity with heaven and making Xúnzǐ look more religious.[24] One of the stronger formulations of the latter view comes from Aaron Stalnaker: "Heaven for Xúnzǐ is like the sage ruler, who takes no apparent action yet governs and orders the entire realm. In this aspect of the metaphor, however, it is human beings who must act as the faithful ministers, implementing policies and following their own Way, which is to actively order the cosmos" (2006, 71, 126). Some use language of realization, as Ivanhoe says: "Xúnzǐ believed the rites showed human beings the unique way to cooperate with heaven and earth for the fulfillment of all three, a way that realized a design inherent in the universe itself" (1991, 309–10). Others use terms of teleology, as Puett says that culture is "the teleological (if not immediate) product of Heaven" (2001, 70). Paul Goldin says human beings must play out their part in the "plan" which Heaven has "decreed" (1999, 74).

It is clear that the order created by human beings fills our own purposes and is good relative to our needs. The crux of the issue is whether this order also supplies something needed or intended by nature itself.[25] The only direct evidence for the latter claim is a problematic passage from the "Discussion of Ritual" ("Lǐ lùn" 禮論) chapter, which says of ritual, "Through it, heaven and earth unite, the sun and moon are bright, the four seasons are ordered, the stars and constellations proceed, the rivers flow, the myriad things thrive, loves and hates are moderated, and pleasure and anger are appropriate" (19: 355; cf. Knoblock 1988, 19.2c). If this passage claims that rituals created by human beings bring order to the natural world, it flatly contradicts chapter 17, which says that the constancy of heaven does not change for the most sagely or most evil (17: 306–308; Knoblock 1988, 17.1). The independent regularity of nature includes normal cycles of seasonal growth: "The myriad things each attain their harmony to live, each attain their nourishment to become complete" (17: 308–309; cf. Knoblock 1988, 17.2b). If, instead, the passage claims that ritual is not created by human beings but is in nature itself, it contradicts the many statements claiming that the rituals were created by sages (e.g., 23: 436, 23: 437; Knoblock 1988, 23.1b, 23.2a). Given that this passage is unique in the *Xúnzǐ* and contradicts more integral positions in the text, little can rest on it alone.[26]

Aside from this one passage, the question of the status of human order depends on ambiguities in the terms the *Xúnzǐ* uses for that order. The claim that "things have no appropriateness" shows clearly enough that appropriateness does not pertain to the relationships between things in nature but only their relation to us, which concerns not what is objectively right but what is useful. Another term for this order, *zhì* 治, generally refers to political order rather than the order of nature. This follows from the contrast Xúnzǐ draws between the regularity (*cháng*) of heaven and the categories of order (*zhì*) or disorder (*luàn* 亂), which depend on us. The most problematic term is *lǐ* 理, which I have been translating as "coherent patterns."[27] The *Xúnzǐ* is one of the first texts to give *lǐ* a significant role, but it is probably not yet a technical term.[28] It occurs with a variety of meanings, and—in spite of his attention to definitions and correcting names—Xúnzǐ never explains it. Centuries later, *lǐ* was used to refer to an objective and proper order of nature which encompassed correct human relations. In that context, it is conventionally translated as "principle." There are some cases in the *Xúnzǐ* in which *lǐ* refers to patterns in nature, such as patterns on skin (4: 63, 23: 439; Knoblock 1988, 4.9, 23.2a) or patterns of colors differentiated by the eye (22: 416; Knoblock 1988, 22.2d). Nonetheless, the *Xúnzǐ* generally uses the term in ways hard to reconcile with objectively proper order. When used normatively, *lǐ* is not spoken of as something to which we *conform,* but rather something to which we *contribute.* Right actions are said to accomplish (*chéng* 成) or add to (*yǒu yì yú* 有益於) *lǐ,* whereas bad actions disrupt (*luàn*) *lǐ*.[29]

The key passage says, "Without gentlemen, heaven and earth do not *lǐ* and ritual and rightness are without system [*tǒng* 統]" (9: 163; cf. Knoblock 1988, 9.15). This is preceded by the claim, "Heaven and earth generate gentlemen and gentlemen *lǐ* heaven and earth." These lines seem to state clearly that, like appropriateness, *lǐ* has no grounding in nature but is a human construct. Thus, Chén Dàqí takes this very passage as evidence that heaven itself has no *telos* (1954, 4).[30] These lines use *lǐ* as a verb, which follows its earliest uses—it originally meant to lay out the boundaries of fields according to the contours of the terrain. The character contains the symbol for jade, pointing to another early verbal use: to polish or carve jade according its intrinsic textures. If we follow this early use, then to *lǐ* heaven and earth aligns with making the myriad things appropriate, arranging things into coherent patterns according their varying qualities and our needs. In fact, a similar passage makes the same point but uses more human terms: discriminate (*biàn* 辨), divide (*fēn*), and order (*zhì*) (19: 366; Knoblock 1988, 19.6). In all cases, an order is brought about for the sake of human life by taking into account the intrinsic differences between things and the regular patterns of the natural world. As a noun, *lǐ* would refer to the human order that integrates nature according to our needs, and indeed the most common uses of *lǐ* in the *Xúnzǐ* are in relation to human products: rightness, ritual, social divisions, and cultural patterns.

The claim that human beings arrange nature to serve their own purposes does not necessarily return us to Hú Shì's claim that we "conquer" nature. Xúnzǐ retains a humility and perhaps even reverence for heaven that leads him to focus primarily on going along with natural processes.³¹ His focus on not examining heaven reflects this orientation:

> Completed without being deliberately done, attained without being sought—this is called the work of heaven. For what is like this, even if profound, people do not add their deliberations to it; even if great, they do not add their abilities to it; even if refined, they do add their examinations to it. This is called not contending with the work of heaven. Heaven has its seasons, earth has its resources, people have their order—this is called being able to three [sān 參]. Abandoning that by which one threes and yearning for those with which they three—this is confusion! (17: 308; cf. Knoblock 1988, 17.2a)

Xúnzǐ uses a standard phrase for the three ingredients necessary for successful action: the timing or seasons from heaven, the resources or position from earth, and the order or harmony of human beings.³² Xúnzǐ's point, though, is that we need concern ourselves with only one of those factors—the human, so that we can form a third alongside of the other two. The use of "three" (sān 參) as a verb emphasizes division, in contrast to "one-ing" (yī 一) or forming an organic body (tǐ 體), but it does situate human beings within the broader context of nature.³³ Although the text makes a few remarkable statements about the human ability to overpower heaven, Xúnzǐ's focus is on not interfering with natural cycles—some passages read like prescriptions for sustainable agriculture, with rules for cutting firewood or netting fish only in certain seasons so that things have a chance to grow (9: 165–171; Knoblock 1988, 9.16b–9.17). The result is a human order that appropriates nature to our needs in a sustainable and harmonious way:

> If the way of gathering people is proper, then the myriad things each attain their appropriateness, the six domestic animals attain their growth, and those gathered to live each attain their fate. Thus nourishing and growing are timely, so that the six domestic animals are raised up; reaping and growing are timely, so that the grass and trees proliferate; government orders are timely, so that the common people are united and the worthy and good serve. (9: 164–65; cf. Knoblock 1988, 9.16a)

The order that results is oriented toward our own good, as the appropriateness of things lies in their usefulness for us, but this order must harmonize with the rest of nature. Thus, even if based on human goods, it still results in what Ivanhoe nicely describes as a "grand ecological ethic" (Ivanhoe 1991, 309–10).

Knowing the Difference between Heaven and Human

The emergence of a human world from nature must be in some sense dialectical, given the lack of radical transcendence. This dialectical movement is beautifully captured in a metaphor Xúnzǐ gives for self-cultivation: "Blue is taken from indigo but is bluer than indigo" (1: 1; cf. Knoblock 1988, 1.1). Humanity comes from nature but becomes more and more human. Human beings initially use their natural abilities to create some small space of autonomy within nature. In that small space, social institutions emerge that allow more space, which allows for the refinement and development of those institutions, which allows for more space, and so on, until we live in a morally ordered world of our own creation:

> Heaven and earth are the beginning of life, ritual and rightness are the beginning of order, gentlemen are the beginning of ritual and rightness. They enact it, practice it, accumulate and emphasize it, most fully love it—this is the beginning of gentlemen. Thus heaven and earth generate gentlemen and gentlemen integrally order [lǐ] heaven and earth. (9: 163; cf. Knoblock 1988, 9.15)

This passage describes two dialectical processes. On a broad level, human beings order heaven and earth but are themselves a product of heaven and earth. On another level, ritual and rightness begin with gentlemen, but gentlemen begin by internalizing ritual and rightness. Xúnzǐ explains this process through the activity of sagely people:

> Thus sagely people transform their nature and give rise to deliberate action. Deliberate action rises and generates ritual and rightness. Ritual and rightness are generated and institute models and measures. In this way, ritual, rightness, models, and measures are what are generated by sagely people. (23: 437; cf. Knoblock 1988, 23.2a)

Deliberate action precedes the creation of rituals and rightness, implying the progression from immediate pursuit of desires to prudential planning for the future to the realization that ritual and rightness are the best means to secure long-term benefits (4: 67–69; Knoblock 1988, 4.11).

Since the human is generated from heaven, the real locus of the division between heaven and human must be within the human itself. We can begin by reconsidering the passages discussed earlier regarding motivation. Our *xìng* comes from *tiān*, is common to all people, reacts spontaneously and involves no study or work. Affects (*qíng*) and desires (*yù*) are *xìng* as it is moved in response to things in the world. All of this follows directly from nature. The properly human, then, lies in *wěi* 偽, deliberate action, which is defined by the role of the heart, explained as making selections for feelings based on considering options and as judging what is possible to attain. *Wěi* is a complex term with two overlapping dimensions: action that is consciously chosen or deliberate, and action that resists immediate desires for the sake of long-term fulfillment. A third sense of *wěi* extends to the results of deliberate action, that which arises from study and work, from accumulating (*jī* 積) thoughts and deliberations, and from practicing deliberate action (23: 436–37; Knoblock 1988, 21.1c–23.2a). In this sense, *wěi* also refers to the artificial.[34] The division between *xìng* and *wěi* is the division between heaven and human within the human. *Wǔ xíng* (Five actions) draws the line in a similar way: "What heaven extends into people is heaven; what people extend into people is practice" (Liú Zhāo 2003, strips 48–49).³⁵ To act on *xìng* is to remain within the realm of amoral nature, although it leads to a miserable condition we would all label as bad. Social institutions and morality come only from *wěi*, so much so that the arguments of chapter 23 each conclude with the repeated motto "The *xìng* of human beings is clearly bad; their goodness is from deliberate action."

Our initial separation from nature comes in the natural ability of the heart to deliberate about future action and the dominance of the heart's judgments over immediate sensory desires, all of which allow for *wěi*, deliberate action. Thus, the division between heaven and human appears in the division between the heart and the other organs. Even so, passages throughout the *Xúnzǐ* indicate that all people know (*zhī*), affirm options as possible (*kě*), and are directed by their hearts. The ability to deliberate must itself come from heaven and be natural. One long passage addresses this point:

> Once heaven's work is established and heaven's accomplishments are completed, form is provided and spirit [*shén*] is born. Love and hate, pleasure and anger, grief and joy are contained therein—these are called heavenly feelings [*tiānqíng*]. Ears, eyes, nose, mouth, and bodily form each can have that which they sense but cannot exchange abilities—these are called the heavenly officials. The heart resides in the empty center and manages the five officials—this is called the heavenly sovereign. Using what is not of its kind as a resource to nourish its kind—this is called heavenly nourishment. Those who follow along with their kind are called fortunate and those who go against their kind are called unfortunate—this is called heavenly governance.³⁶ Dimming the heavenly sovereign, disordering the heavenly officials, abandoning heavenly nourishment, running against heavenly governance, going against heavenly feelings, and so losing heaven's accomplishments—this is called greatly unpropitious. Sagely people clarify their heavenly sovereign, correct their heavenly officials, prepare heavenly nourishment, follow along with heavenly governance, and nourish the heavenly feelings, in order to keep whole heaven's accomplishments. In this way, they know what they do and what they do not do. Thus heaven and earth fulfill their offices and the ten thousand things serve. Their actions are everywhere well managed, their nourishing is everywhere fitting, and their living is not harmed. This is called knowing heaven. (17: 309–310; cf. Knoblock 1988, 17.3a)

At first glance, this passage seems to absorb the human entirely into the heavenly or the natural. The heart naturally controls the rest of the body like a sovereign. Human beings naturally sustain themselves by using other things (what is not of our kind) and find order by harmonizing with each other (what is of our kind). The key, though, is that these relationships are by nature empty and indeterminate.³⁷ That the heart judges and controls is natural but the content that determines those judgments is contingent, following from what we happen to accumulate through experience and study. In fact, Xúnzǐ echoes the *Zhuāngzǐ* in describing the heart as empty (*xū* 虛). Similarly, that we survive by appropriating other things to our needs and by following our own kind in forming communities is natural, but the forms those take depends on experience, history, and tradition.

Ultimately, what allows human beings to turn back and shape nature is that the heart accumulates knowledge and human beings as a whole accumulate culture. We can now see this dialectical process more clearly. At first, the natural fact that our heart determines decisions would be guided only by what we happen to come across according to our place in nature. But as that knowledge accumulates, our experience would become more directed and our environment more shaped by our own actions. That would allow for further knowledge and further appropriation of the natural world. If we consider this process not in terms of one individual but a community of people working over millennia, we can see how a human world would emerge.

The division between heaven and human points toward two very different forms of development. One follows from the natural and spontaneous reactions of things, their regular causal interactions, and the overarching cyclical patterns of heaven and earth. The other comes through accumulation. The main term Xúnzǐ uses is *jī* 積, which means "to gather" or "to accumulate," and was probably originally connected to the harvest, since it contains the symbol for grain (*hé* 禾). Accumulation is progressive rather than cyclical. It is where apparent contingency can appear, in that what we accumulate will depend on what we happen to experience in our own particular location. Diversity also emerges with accumulation. Xúnzǐ says, "The sons of the Gān, Yuè, Yí, and Mò peoples are born making the same sounds, but grow up with different customs—it is education that makes them so" (1: 2; cf. Knoblock 1988, 1.2).[38] The *Xúnzǐ* again works from the same foundation as the *Zhuāngzǐ*. The heart by its nature (as given by *tiān*) is empty, and its perspectives form through the accumulation of experience. Whereas the *Zhuāngzǐ* takes this to show that we can remain free from a "completed heart," Xúnzǐ takes it as allowing for accumulation over time, which can eventually overcome our immediate submission to nature and restructure the world according to our needs.

Xúnzǐ's account of the formation of knowledge helps to clarify this process of accumulation. The origin of knowledge is in sensory perception, which always involves awareness of multiplicity and difference. Based on similarities and differences in sensory experience, we categorize things and agree on names (22: 415–16; Knoblock 1988, 22.2c). Higher levels of knowledge depend on the ability to apply and extend across categories, what Antonio Cua calls "analogical projection" (1985, 78–86). This projection allows our knowledge to extend beyond what we immediately perceive and, thus, to predict future consequences:

How is it that sagely people cannot be deceived? Sagely people use themselves as measure. Thus they use other people to measure other people, use genuine characteristics [qíng] to measure genuine characteristics, use categories to measure categories, use words to measure accomplishments, use the way to see fully. The past and the present are one. The categories are not violated; even after a long time they have the same coherent patterns [lǐ]. By using this to measure them, sagely people can reside in deviance and crookedness without being lost and can look into muddled things without being confused. (5: 82; cf. Knoblock 1988, 5.12)

This ability is described as the ability to integrate or systematize categories, tǒnglèi 統類. It is what allows sagely people to adapt what they have learned in order to effectively respond to any situation (8: 140–41; Knoblock 1988, 8.10).

The formation of knowledge is far more difficult than this brief sketch suggests, however. Given the singularity of any event, experience can be categorized in infinitely many ways, most of which will prove not very useful. As the Zhuāngzǐ shows, things all can be considered similar or different, big or small, so or not-so. Developing a system of names and categories that will prove stable and effective in ordering the world according to our needs is a profoundly difficult task. Individuals hoping to attain it through their own observation and reason have as little chance of success as individuals alone in nature hoping to satisfy their desires for sensory pleasure. The incommensurability between nature and human beings bears similarities with ideas found in the Zhuāngzǐ: "Our living has boundaries but knowing has no boundaries. To use what has boundaries to follow what has no boundaries—this is dangerous! To do so while knowing this—that is really dangerous!" (3: 115; cf. Mair 1994, 25). Xúnzǐ makes an almost identical claim: "Will you try to exhaust the inexhaustible [qióng wúqióng 窮無窮] or pursue the unlimited? Even if you break your bones and wear out your joints, to the end of your life you will still not be able to reach it" (2: 31; cf. Knoblock 1988, 2.8).

Xúnzǐ's position is explained further in a passage that begins with the possibility of knowledge but then moves to its limits:

In general, that by which one knows is human nature, and that which can be known is the coherent patterns [lǐ] of things.[39] With a human nature that can know, one seeks the coherent patterns of things that can be known. Yet if you have nothing by which to stop and limit it, then even in exhausting your years and going to the limit of your life, you cannot get through it all. To try in this way to string together the coherent patterns in them, even if you stop only after millions of attempts, it will not suffice to comprehend the changes of the myriad things, and you will be the same as the fool. To study until your body is old and your sons are grown but remain the same as a fool only not knowing to give up—this is called a reckless foolish person. Thus studying certainly must have an end. What ends it? It ends in utmost sufficiency. What is utmost sufficiency? Sageliness. Sageliness fully exhausts relationships; kingliness fully exhausts institutions. Exhausting these two suffices to be the ultimate for the world. Thus study takes sageliness and kingliness as teachers, court decisions takes the institutions of sageliness and kingliness as models. Model yourself on their models to seek its systematicity [*tǒng*] and categories [*lèi*], and work to become an image and example of these people. (21: 406–407; cf. Knoblock 1988, 21.9)

We can know the world because we naturally have an ability to learn and our world has patterns that can be known. The match between the world and our abilities, however, is in fact a mismatch, since our capabilities are limited while the patterns that can be known are limitless. One could study and gain genuine knowledge for an entire lifetime but still remain a fool. Xúnzǐ and Zhuāngzǐ hold the same view and for the same reason. Human beings are simply one of the myriad things, with no privileged status in nature. How could such beings comprehend this infinite and ever-changing world?

The profound awareness of how nature infinitely exceeds the individual shapes many aspects of Xúnzǐ's thought. It explains his insistence that we limit our studies to what is useful for becoming a gentleman, avoiding things like investigating heaven or the subtle debates of people like Huìzǐ. It also requires that we keep a single-minded focus. Given the infinity of the world, we could wander forever without getting anywhere. Xúnzǐ contrasts the crab, which has eight legs and two claws but cannot dig a hole to live in because its heart is restless and distracted, and the worm, which has no limbs at all but can bore holes through the earth because it uses its heart in a unified way (*yòng xīn yī* 用心一) (1: 8–9; Knoblock 1988, 1.6). Similarly, a team of exceptional horses pulling in different directions cannot get as far as a lame turtle that persists in one (2: 30–31; Knoblock 1988, 2.8).

Our greatest limit is in attempting to grasp the multiplicity of any moment. Because any moment holds a multiplicity of perceptions, when we see one thing we miss others: "In general, the myriad things are different, so that they always conceal each other. This is the common trouble for methods of the heart" (21: 388; cf. Knoblock 1988, 21.2). The term translated here as "conceal," *bì* 蔽, is a key term in the *Xúnzǐ* for bias. Although it is sometimes translated as "obsession," this misses the way *bì* works.[40] The character itself contains the symbol for bamboo and originally referred to a bamboo screen, taking on the meaning of "to hide" or "cover." If one has a *bì*—a bias, fixation, or obsession—they see only the thing they are biased toward, which works like a blind or screen, concealing or blocking everything else.[41] Thus, Xúnzǐ criticizes other philosophers for their *bì*, using it as a verb, which I here translate as "could see only":

> Mòzǐ could see only use and did not know cultured refinement [*wén*]. Sòngzǐ could see only desire and did not know attaining satisfaction. Shènzǐ Chīn could see only law and did not know worthies. Shēnzǐ Chīn could see only

techniques and did not know wisdom. Huìzǐ could see only expressions and did not know facts. Zhuāngzǐ could see only heaven and did not know the human. (21: 391-93; cf. Knoblock 1988, 21.4)

These philosophers are not criticized for making poor *judgments* but for their *perception*: in their attention to one idea, they could see nothing else. In the chapter entitled "Dispelling *bì*," ("Jiěbì" 解蔽) Xúnzǐ describes three intellectual virtues, all of which concern not letting things block or conceal each other: one must make the heart empty so that stored knowledge does not conceal the present, make the heart unified so that one aspect of experience does not conceal others, and make the heart still so that its restlessness does not cause delusions (21: 395-97; Knoblock 1988, 21.5d). This reflects Xúnzǐ's recognition that experience does not just objectively mirror reality but also reflects the perceiver, another point that follows the *Zhuāngzǐ*. One passage in the *Xúnzǐ* lists sources that distort experience, including physical conditions such as distance, pressure on the eye, and intoxication, but also psychological disturbances such as fear (21: 405-406; Knoblock 1988, 21.8).

The problem with being blinded toward one thing again lies in the infinity of nature. In the "Against the Twelve" ("Fēi shíèrzǐ" 非十二子) chapter, Xúnzǐ gives a brief summary of rival philosophical positions, repeating the same line in regard to each: "Even so, what they hold has reasons and their speech forms coherent patterns, sufficing to deceive and confuse the foolish masses" (6: 91; cf. Knoblock 1988, 6.2). In a sense, none of the positions are wrong: each theory has reasons (*gù* 故) for it and forms or completes (*chéng*) coherent patterns (*lǐ*). Each philosopher sees things that are genuinely important: use, desire, law, techniques, expressions, and heaven. This is precisely why they are convincing. Yet because they cannot get the whole, their theories lead to harm and confusion. Xúnzǐ gives several general statements of the problem:

> These calculations and methods each are one corner of the way. Now the way embodies constancy but exhausts all changes: one corner is not enough to raise it up. People with skewed knowledge look at one corner of the way but are never able to know, thus they consider it sufficient and ornament it, inside using it to disrupt themselves, outside using it to perplex others, when above blinding [*bì*] those below and when below blinding those above—this is the misfortune of being crude and blocked. (21: 393; cf. Knoblock 1988, 21.4)[42]

For Xúnzǐ, the challenge of philosophy is not in finding truth. Truths are easy, since we have a nature that can know the world and we live in a world with patterns and differentiations that can be known. The problem is in reconciling that knowledge with the infinite complexity of nature itself. Kurtis Hagen makes this point nicely: "Xúnzǐ does not maintain that we simply make up a structure to describe what is itself unstructured. On the contrary, the world is not unstructured; it is overstructured. If we try to cut at its joints, one cut restricts the next" (2007, 28).[43]

Authority and the Fragility of the Human

This incommensurabilty between the individual and nature explains the most obvious contrast between Xúnzǐ and most thinkers of the European Enlightenment—his skepticism of individual judgment. Although Xúnzǐ acts like a philosopher, his philosophy is directed toward an attack on individual thinking. The reason other philosophers end up getting only one corner is because they rely on their own judgment. Xúnzǐ repeatedly criticizes those who innovate on their own, using the term *shàn* 擅, which means to usurp, monopolize, or take on as one's own.[44] A passage quoted earlier contrasts the certain benefits of following the way with those who leave the way and "internally select for themselves [*nèi zì zé* 內自擇]" (22: 430; cf. Knoblock 1988, 22.6b). This "selecting" (*zé* 擇) is the same term applied to what the heart uses its knowledge to do in relation to feelings (22: 412; Knoblock 1988, 22.1b). The likelihood of loss follows from the limits of any individual but is intensified because what leads to success is often counterintuitive—to directly pursue life results in death, to seek only pleasure leads to suffering. Only the way of the first kings suffices to navigate these paradoxes. A lone individual has no chance.

In terms of the individual, Xúnzǐ's position is quite close to that of the *Zhuāngzǐ*.[45] The *Zhuāngzǐ* does not deny that the differences revealed in experience can guide our actions, nor that labels and categories can be used effectively in particular contexts for particular purposes. The problem is in constructing a set of labels that can reliably guide us across different perspectives and contexts. The knowledge an individual builds from the limits of his or her own experience locks him or her into a narrow perspective that is ultimately incommensurable with nature and with the perspectives of others. Xúnzǐ would agree. This agreement follows from their shared rejection of a conception of nature as either humanlike (anthropomorphic) or human-centered (anthropocentric) and thus their awareness of the profound gap between one of the myriad things and the awesome power and complexity of nature itself. Xúnzǐ, however, believes a decent human life is possible only through large-scale human cooperation. Thus, he cannot accept these results. His solution is to shift from the individual to the community. The incommensurability between a single human being and the infinity of nature is reduced if we shift to a large human community working together over thousands of years. If the world has an order that can be grasped and human beings have some ability to grasp it, even if what each person grasps is very small, it could eventually accumulate into a significant body of knowledge. The individual's limited power to understand nature is overcome in exactly the same way as the individual's limited power to survive in nature—through the organization of human beings into complex structured communities.

The way Xúnzǐ strikes a middle ground between the Mòzǐ and the Zhuāngzǐ can be seen through the problem of criteria. The problem was first raised by the Mohists, who point out that we cannot take rulers, parents, teachers, or customs as our standards, because they disagree among themselves (and few are right). The Mohist alternative is to establish objective criteria based in nature as expressing the "Will of Heaven." More concretely, the Mohists base their claims on a mix of the views of the sages, the experiences of the people, and an analysis of what produces benefit. The Zhuāngzǐ also recognizes the problem of disagreement and turns toward heaven, but pushes the inclusivity of nature to a point where it is impartial even to life and death, eliminating it as an ethical model. For the Zhuāngzǐ, once we fall into a dispute, there are no criteria by which to resolve it. The Xúnzǐ draws on both positions. His epistemology develops the Mohist criteria, in which the unbiased evidence of the senses is categorized so as to guide us toward maximizing human benefit. This basis allows for an effective tradition to develop over time. At the same time, Xúnzǐ largely accepts the Zhuāngzǐ's skepticism of individual judgment, as well as the claim that heaven cannot provide an ethical standard. The result is that Xúnzǐ almost never appeals to experience or analogical projection as criteria for settling disagreements.[46] The way of the sagely kings is "the compass and square" (19: 536; cf. Knoblock 1988, 19.2d). Several passages state that ritual and tradition are the *only* criterion:

> Ritual is that by which to correct the body/self; teachers are that by which to correct rituals. Without ritual, what is there to correct the body? Without teachers, how will I know what is correct in the ritual? If one is so when the ritual is so, then genuine feelings [*qíng*] come to rest in ritual; if one says what the teacher says, then knowledge is like that of the teacher. When feelings rest in ritual and knowing is like the teacher, this is a sagely person. Thus to negate the rituals is to be without a model; to negate the teacher is to be without a teacher. Not to affirm teachers and models but love to use oneself [*hào zìyòng* 好自用] instead—this is like having a blind person distinguish colors or a deaf person distinguish sounds. (2: 33–34; cf. Knoblock 1988, 2.11)

Self-cultivation lies in acting exactly as ritual prescribes and saying exactly what our teacher says, until we become at ease in the rituals and think like the teacher. Whatever knowledge we could acquire on our own counts as nothing—we would be like a blind person distinguishing colors.

The objective bases for knowledge that Xúnzǐ describes thus do not suffice for letting an individual make good decisions. In this sense, Xúnzǐ is closer to Zhuāngzǐ than to Mòzǐ. At the same time, the roots of knowledge in experience and judgment suffice for developing an effective way when they are accumulated over millennia. By invoking history, Xúnzǐ hopes to avoid the Zhuāngzǐ's skepticism. Over time, human beings develop a system of names and practices that, while not capturing or representing the infinite complexity of nature, at least provide a reliable way through it. This system of human culture is inseparable from the appropriation of the myriad things into a world structured according to human needs, and social divisions are the core of both. The dominance of heaven that would reign in a state of nature is displaced by the dominance of the historical community, in just the same way as our material relationship to nature is displaced by a complex system of trade and division of labor. Instead of an amoral order in which rewards go to the strong and survival depends on luck, we construct a world in which good people end up in palaces, listening to orchestras while sipping ape soup (5: 78–79; Knoblock 1988, 5.4). The problem of evil is eliminated through cumulative human effort.

The value Xúnzǐ places on the human is striking. We have seen that Xúnzǐ's rejection of the power of heaven in favor of the power of human beings bears at least some analogies with the European Enlightenment. In Europe, this entailed a shift from a concern with natural evils to the moral evils caused by human beings. In a sense, Xúnzǐ would agree—if heaven is no longer the dominant force, then the blame must fall on us human beings. The text minimizes natural disasters and attributes all bad things to human action. What is striking, though, is that this is not conceptualized as a shift from natural to human evil. On the contrary, Xúnzǐ equates evil with the loss of the human. To be bad is to be less cultured and less human. Although such views are not unfamiliar in European thought, they deeply contrast with the idea of "radical evil," in which what distinguishes human beings is free will as the source of both good and evil. Xúnzǐ's view reflects the more naturalistic and less anthropocentric context of early Chinese thought. Since we are generated by heaven, at least some elements of our actions must be attributable to heaven itself. But for Xúnzǐ, it is the *bad* in us that most expresses our connection to heaven and nature.

One of Xúnzǐ's great insights is that any human system adequate to guide us through the infinity of nature must itself become too complex for the individual to grasp. The gap between the finite individual and the immensity of nature shifts to the relationship between the individual and the historical community. This shift appears in the interplay among metaphors of measuring deep water:

> One who crosses water must have markers [*biǎo* 表] for the depth; if the markers are not clear then people will drown. One who manages the people must have markers for the way; if the markers are not clear then there is disorder. Rituals are the markers. Without ritual, it will be a darkened age, and a darkened age is great disorder. (17: 319; cf. Knoblock 1988, 17.11)

Managing the people is compared to plumbing deep water. Through millennia of development, ritual becomes an adequate measure for the depths of nature, but as a result, ritual itself becomes too deep to measure: "Petty people cannot plumb its depths" (19: 356; cf. Knoblock 1988, 19.2c). Those who attack or reject ritual are overwhelmed by its complexity:

> The coherent patterns of ritual are so truly deep, that examinations of "hard and white" and "same and different" enter into them and drown. Its coherent patterns are so truly great that those who take it on themselves to create institutions and systems with perverse and crude doctrines enter into them and are bereft. Its coherent patterns are so truly lofty that those who consider violence, neglect, self-indulgence and contempt for custom as lofty enter into them and collapse. (19: 356; cf. Knoblock 1988, 19.2d)

It is not that ritual responds to arguments tit for tat but that critics drown (nì 溺) in its immensity, as they would drown in nature itself.

Although the human order of culture and tradition exceeds the individual just as much as nature itself, our relationship to it differs crucially. The order of nature is indifferent toward us, and—if we factor in our own natural dispositions—we could say it is hostile. Thus, the individual must resist and control it. The tradition, in contrast, contains a moral order that allows everyone to thrive. It calls for trust and submission rather than defiance. This difference between nature and the human order entails different stances toward our own selves as well. In the face of nature, we assert our own views and desires in spite of its overwhelming force. To go along with nature would lead to destruction and unhappiness even more quickly than our feeble attempts to resist it. In contrast, regarding the tradition, we give up our own views and desires and follow along. Thus, when our teachers appear to us to be wrong, we assume the error lies on our side and we follow them. The passage above, about needing the way as a measure, ends by saying that it is better to follow ritual without understanding than to make even good judgments on one's own (1: 17; Knoblock 1988, 1.11). Even truth can be bad if it is incomplete, and individuals have no chance of getting the complete picture on their own.

The way the tradition exceeds individual grasp explains one side of what is now most disturbing about Xúnzǐ—his reliance on authority. The vast majority of people will never be able to understand the rituals and social structures they depend on to thrive (22: 422; Knoblock 1988, 22.3e). This incomprehension is not due to innate lack of ability—since anyone could become a sage—but rather because of circumstances and the demands of a division of labor. Ultimately, some will follow the system blindly and others will follow it for material rewards, but very few will follow it because they see how it is right. Even those people must submit long before they really understand. Stalnaker puts the point well:

> For Xúnzǐ, only if we become convinced that we need external help to become truly human will we be in a position to acquire what we need. We will only succeed if we are able to find the right teacher and follow him diligently, from ignorance, anxiety, and questioning, through difficulties we only slowly come to grasp, to deeper understanding, commitment, and tranquility. (2006, 159)

The limits of our intellect and the power of our desires leads to a position Stalnaker nicely calls "chastened intellectualism." Such a view undermines self-reliance, seeing "personal formation as a voluntary submission to an authoritative teaching" (2006, 279).⁴⁷

The emphasis on authority in the *Xúnzǐ*, however, is qualified by Xúnzǐ's own practice. As far as we can see from the text, Xúnzǐ submits to no political authorities; on the contrary, he criticizes them all. He does this because—based on his own (cultivated) judgment—the current rulers are bad. While he never doubts the sages, he does argue that some records should be trusted and others should not. Similarly, his embrace of the Ru tradition does not prevent him from opposing and criticizing leading Ru figures, particularly Mèngzǐ and Zǐsī. He clearly trusts his own judgment more than theirs. Although he appeals to historical authority, he also gives arguments based on reason and experience. Recently excavated texts show that Xúnzǐ was closer to the mainstream of the Ru tradition than had been previously thought, but many of his ideas are clearly innovations, as he must have known. Xúnzǐ criticizes those who are blinded by (*bì*) the past just as much as those who are obsessed with the new (21: 388; Knoblock 1988, 21.2). In all of these ways, Xúnzǐ seems to be doing just what he opposes—using his own judgment to oppose independent judgment, using philosophy to reject philosophy.

In part, Xúnzǐ's method exemplifies what one must do when a coherent set of conventions is breaking down. In an infamous passage, he explains that if gentlemen had the power they would punish those with wicked doctrines, but since they lack power, they are forced to debate and persuade (22: 422, 6: 98–99; Knoblock 1988, 22.3e, 6.9). In such debates, one cannot simply appeal to authority, as one passage goes on to explain:

> If the fact is not understood, then name it. If the name is not understood, then come to agreement. If the agreement is not understood, then persuade. If the persuasion is not understood, then debate. Thus agreeing, naming, debating, and persuading are the greatest cultured forms [*wén*] for what is useful and are the beginning of the work of a king. (22: 422–23; cf. Knoblock 1988, 22.3f)

When the relationship between words and things breaks down, one must go back to agreement and discussion. Another passage that addresses specific paradoxes explains in more detail that where names have already been confused or are disputed, one must test the words in experience, clarify distinctions recognized by the senses, or consider the conventions already agreed upon (22: 420–21; Knoblock 1988, 22.3a–c).

The problem is not just with the breakdown of tradition, however. Xúnzǐ must walk a fine line in relation to the power of individual judgment. If he allows too much, he tempts us to figure out the world on our own: If a sage like Yǔ did it, why can't I? If he eliminates the power of individual judgment entirely, though, the whole system falls apart. If the tradition has any validity at all, it is because it accumulates the work of individuals. The tension between these two sides shows the complexity of the dialectical process through which one part of nature emerges and turns back to appropriate nature to its own needs. In one sense, the process of appropriating or humanizing the natural world arises from a dialogue between human beings and the rest of nature—allowing a movement from immediate perceptions, categorizations, and desires toward a system that is better and better able to restructure the world from which we arise. But that dialogue is not between an individual and nature, but between nature and the historically constituted human community. For the individual, the dialogue is primarily with this community rather than nature itself. Yet these two dialectical movements—one between human beings and nature and the other between individuals and the tradition—cannot be entirely separated. The process of embodying and internalizing the tradition cannot occur unless that tradition is made sense of in terms of our lived experience. The more one masters the tradition, the more one is able to apply, adapt, and develop it in relation to novel conditions.

We can now summarize Xúnzǐ's position by considering these two realms. One is the realm of shared convention, developed gradually by sagely people over millennia. It is the human realm that allows for the appropriation of the myriad things and shifts control from heaven to the human. Ideally, people follow the rules of this realm, using a common language, enjoying common rituals and music, following the morality embodied in the exemplars of the tradition, and working diligently on their specific tasks within a diversified economy. Through persistent study, some of these people develop the ability to bring this realm back into dialogue with the world itself—applying, interpreting, and expanding it. These people teach those who want to join them and they engage in critical discussions of the tradition, of political authorities, and of each other. Xúnzǐ probably sees himself as part of this group. Once in a great while, an exceptional person, a sagely person, arises and is able to make more significant changes, primarily through *tǒnglèi*, the integration of categories. Xúnzǐ took the Ru tradition as the culmination of such a process.[48]

Outside of this human system, there remains the infinite amoral natural world and the amoral but destructive tendencies we receive from it. Xúnzǐ's philosophy is marked by a profound sense of the fragility of the human. How could these animals seeking unlimited pleasure in an indifferent world ever achieve a system that allowed them to flourish? No wonder so many cultures attribute this achievement to the gods! Yet without divine support, our unruly natures and limited comprehension always threaten to engulf this precious achievement. Xúnzǐ's authoritarianism is sometimes taken to show his belief that the Ru way is objectively true or perfect, but the opposite is more likely.[49] If the Ru way were perfect and somehow an objective part of the universe, it would be much more secure. It is precisely because social life depends so heavily on convention that those conventions must be protected, by force if necessary.[50] To understand the intensity of Xúnzǐ's worries, it is helpful to recall the *Zhuāngzǐ* on the impossibility of settling disputes: anyone who could settle a disagreement between you and me would either do so from my perspective or your perspective or some other perspective, none of which would actually resolve the dispute. This follows from the lack of fixed standards in nature itself. Disagreements can only be settled when some common conventional perspective is assumed. Xúnzǐ would almost completely agree with Zhuāngzǐ's point, as we can see in his discussion of names:

> Thus, kings, in instituting names, set names so that facts were distinguished, and enacted the way so that intentions were communicated. Thus, they conscientiously led the people to become one in this. Thus, analyzing terms and taking it on oneself to make words so as to disrupt correct names makes the people doubtful and confused and causes people to argue and debate more and more. Thus, this is called great wickedness. Its crime is like the crime of falsifying tallies and measurements. (22: 414; cf. Knoblock 1988, 22.1c)

Weights and measures are arbitrarily set but establish the common standards that make possible communication and the resolution of disputes. If we disagree on the weight of a bag of grain, we can throw it on the scale. But if the scale itself is in question, our conflict can never be resolved, or can be resolved only by force. Culture and tradition similarly provide the common set of standards that allows us to communicate and argue. Without reliance on them, the social order falls apart. Xúnzǐ had good reason to think he was in the midst of the fragmentation and collapse of these shared conventions, and this drove the need to suppress those who would further disrupt it. This authoritarianism is where Xúnzǐ's humanism most radically contrasts with European versions, but it may be the only humanism possible once we take seriously our position as just one of myriad things living within a heaven and earth are not themselves humane.

Conclusion

There is a well-known Chinese verse that one still hears today:

> Good with good is repaid,
> Bad with bad is repaid.
> It is not that they are not repaid,
> Just the timing might be delayed.[1]

One finds a similar sentiment way back in the *Shī jīng*, in lines that were widely quoted during the Warring States period:

> No words are unanswered, no virtue is unpaid;
> Toss me a peach and I'll repay it with a plum.[2]

Such statements are not philosophical claims but expressions of wishful thinking, words we repeat to comfort ourselves or others precisely when things do not work out so nicely. They are similar to our telling someone, "It was meant to be," or "It all works out in the end." The fact that we find such expressions across distant times and disconnected cultures shows how troubled we are by the fact that bad things happen to good people. Chinese philosophers were above all concerned with the concrete, practical ways in which the apparent moral indifference of the world troubles us, and with what we can say and do to deal with it. At the same time, this moral indifference caused fractures and shifts in early Chinese views of heaven, humanity, and the relationship between them, generating a variety of philosophical problems.

My goal has not been to find a "solution" to the "problem" of evil, but rather to illuminate the multiplicity of ways the fact that bad things happen to good people can become problematic, and to explore how some of those problems were addressed by philosophers of China's Warring States period. Some of these positions are familiar from European philosophy and others are not, but all of them take on a different sense in the more naturalistic context of Early Chinese thought. The development of Warring States philosophy and the roughly chronological presentation of thinkers here may suggest that I take Xúnzǐ as most plausible, but that is not the case. The configuration of Warring States philosophy may tend toward a choice between Zhuāngzǐ and Xúnzǐ, but each of the positions presented here contains important and valuable insights, just as each has crucial weaknesses and problems. Any attempt to think adequately about the problem of evil now would require drawing elements from various positions, and supplementing them with other perspectives (including those of European philosophy). That work is best left to the readers. This conclusion will simply draw out some general points about the configuration of the problems in early China.

One of the things that is most striking when one looks for Chinese analogues to the problem of evil is that on the one side, early Chinese philosophers were quick to give up the idea that there is a good, divine being that determines the content of ethics and ensures that good people are rewarded and bad people are punished. We could give many reasons for this willingness, the most obvious being that the divine and the natural world were never clearly separated and that there was no conception of punishments in the afterlife. The resulting this-worldly orientation makes the fact that good people sometimes end up with bad lives almost impossible to interpret away. On the other side, however, Chinese philosophers maintain a generally positive view of nature—keeping a sense of reverence, humility, and gratitude. All agree that nature could provide enough for human beings to lead decent lives. The only disagreement was on how much human beings must also contribute their own effort. This surely reflects the brutality of the political situation of the time: a world with only natural evil would have looked pretty good. It may reflect the values of an agrarian society, a sense of gratitude for the fact that anything grows at all. One must also again consider the lack of radical transcendence—while the divine could not be free of the apparent moral indifference of the natural world, the natural world also could not be free from a lingering sense of reverence toward the divine.

Early Chinese philosophers thus took a middle course between on one side, a denial of the problem of evil that would allow us to maintain that there is a God who designed the world and basically shares our values, and, on the other side, an acceptance of the problem that would lead to a radical disenchantment of nature, leaving nature as an amoral force that we must oppose and control. We might say there was neither "God" nor "death of God." In this middle ground, one central question is how or if the human good can be linked to the tendencies of nature itself. The *Mòzǐ* and the *Zhuāngzǐ* can be placed at two poles—the Mohists take nature itself as anthropocentric, whereas the radical strand of the *Zhuāngzǐ* I have emphasized gives up anthropocentrism entirely. Both views link the human good with nature itself. This link is based not on nature's order or harmony, as we might expect, but rather on the generative force of nature toward never-ending birth and growth, a tendency closely connected to nature's inclusivity. The roots of this position appear in the *Mòzǐ*, where heaven's inclusive caring is manifested in the way nature generates resources for us without any bias. The same tendencies are central in the *Dàodéjīng*, where the way is the spontaneous force of growth in the myriad things, without attachment or bias. This emphasis on life bears some resemblance to the priority of being in European philosophy, and the attempt to link the generative force of nature to the human good is in some ways analogous to Spinoza's attempt to account for human actions through the nature of being as *conatus*, or "striving," Leibniz's attempt to account for the human good through the maximization of being in terms of complexity (the most variety with the most order), and even Nietzsche's attempt to think human motivation through a "will to power" common to all living things.

If life is at the center of the human good, then this good aligns with the priority of life in nature, and in fostering life, sagely people simply continue the processes of nature itself. The attempt to align a human good with the force of life in nature, though, breaks down once one rejects the Mohist anthropocentric conception of heaven. If heaven supports life, it supports the life of all things, without any particular preference for human beings. Some did advocate promoting life as the highest value, as we have seen in Huì Shī's saying that we should care for all the myriad things, forming one body with heaven and earth (*Zhuāngzǐ* 33: 1102; Mair 1994, 344). A similar position appears in the "Rooting in Life" chapter of the *Lüshì chūnqiū*, as in a passage that begins, "That which begins life is heaven; that which nurtures life are human beings. One who can nurture that which heaven gives life to without harming it is called the son of heaven" (2/1: 21). The problems with such views are brought out well enough in the *Zhuāngzǐ*. If we distinguish life from death, then nature is too inclusive a model since it equally encompasses both—everything born eventually dies. If we instead take life and death as moments of transformation within a more inclusive generativity, then death and loss disappear entirely and we have nothing to strive against.

One way to avoid this trajectory toward the *Zhuāngzǐ* would be to maintain a link to heaven's generativity while avoiding its inclusivity. A simple possibility would be to shift toward self-interest. Such a view appears in its most basic form in the position we have seen advocated in the *Zhuāngzǐ* by Robber Zhí: I express the tendencies of nature through my own struggle to survive and thrive. Such a view is associated with Yáng Zhū, who was famed for saying that he would not sacrifice a hair on his head even in order to rescue the world. It appears again most clearly in the *Lüshì chūnqiū*: "The genuine in the way is maintaining one's body. Its fringes and leftovers are for the state and district. Its dirt and weeds are for managing the world" (2/2: 76).[3] An earlier passage supports this self-concern with an argument—although someone else may have hands much more skillful than my own, I value my hands more, because they are mine and I benefit from them (1/3: 34). Spinoza takes a similar approach in reconciling *conatus* with the individual: as a mode of infinite substance, it would be a category mistake to identify my interests with that of life or substance in general. My interest lies in a struggle with and against other modes, all expressing striving or *conatus* in their own ways. Although Spinoza brings this striving into a fairly conventional ethics of enlightened self-interest, Nietzsche brings out how far such an interpretation of life might go toward overturning our usual conceptions of morality. One finds similar variety in late Warring States thought, with prudence and moderation emphasized in many passages in the *Lǚshì chūnqiū*, but then Robber Zhí advocating enjoying life and power while you can (an argument he makes while snacking on human livers).

We can take Mèngzǐ as articulating a middle ground between the radical inclusivity of nature and individual self-interest, through his emphasis on *xìng*, natural dispositions or tendencies. Mèngzǐ's insistence on linking *xìng* to heaven focuses precisely on showing how our natural reactions to the world channel the generative forces of nature. Like the move to self-interest, Mèngzǐ shows that continuing the processes of life does not entail the radical inclusivity of nature itself but rather following the particular configurations of life that make us what we are. For human beings, this entails developing bonds of care (*rén*), moral rules enforced by feelings of shame (*yì*), rituals that express reverence as well as joy and sorrow (*lǐ*), and some body of wisdom (*zhì*). Mèngzǐ's stance is plausible and appealing. The main problem would come from the *Zhuāngzǐ*, which, as we have seen, argues that human beings are not bound by their natural spontaneous reactions but can come to see things from the inclusivity of nature itself.

The *Xúnzǐ* responds to these problems by emphasizing the disjunction between the tendencies of nature and the human good. Although we depend on the resources generated by nature, our primary task is to resist the spontaneous natural tendencies that are within us, the reactions of our *xìng*. The choice between following nature's radical inclusivity with Zhuāngzǐ or breaking from nature to make a human world with Xúnzǐ sets the stage for the emergence of a new attempt to align human beings and nature, this time through an emphasis on harmony and order rather than (or in addition to) generativity. The attempt to think of human ethics as continuous with nature's *order* is the dominant approach in the Hàn dynasty, taking the form of what has come to be known as "correlative cosmology." This shift was furthered by the need to rationalize a unified empire. An emphasis on nature simply as generating life—with its elements of creativity and inclusivity—is probably inherently disruptive to political hierarchy. This shift toward harmony and order, though, should be seen as a consequence of debates in the Warring States period rather than as a default "Chinese" worldview.

We can now turn to the human. If nature provides enough for us to live decent lives, then the responsibility for disorder lies with human beings. Xúnzǐ carries this point the furthest in claiming that if human beings act properly, even heaven cannot harm us. The elevation of the problem of evil in early modern Europe initiated a similar change, prompting a shift in concern away from "natural evil" and toward the "moral evil" done by human beings. Differences in the forms taken by this shift, though, are striking. The root of these differences is that, in the early Chinese context, human beings themselves are seen as part of nature. We might say that in a strict sense, there is no moral evil and the evil done by human beings was seen simply as a particularly destructive kind of natural evil. We should remember that although Mèngzǐ and some other early Ru saw chaos in the world as determined periodically by heaven, they did not see heaven as acting primarily through natural forces such as droughts and floods, but rather through human beings themselves. If we alternate between historical cycles of order and chaos, that is because we human beings naturally bring them on ourselves. One interesting consequence is that the division between good and bad was considered not simply within the realm of human choice but was mapped onto the relationship between human beings and nature. This again is clearest in the *Xúnzǐ*, where moral evil comes from remaining close to our *xìng* and moral good comes with distance from it. Xúnzǐ assumes a remarkably positive view of culture. While he would surely claim that some cultures are better than others, he shows little concern for the evils that come from being taught to do bad things. Even the philosophers he criticizes are rejected not for having wrong ideas but for being partial and fragmented. Mèngzǐ is closer to Xúnzǐ on this point than we might assume. Mèngzǐ's claim that human *xìng* is good is not an argument for staying close to nature. His claim that human nature is good means that human beings tend naturally to develop culture—moral codes, rituals, wisdom, and so on. What is striking is that Mèngzǐ takes a tendency to develop *culture* as a tendency to becoming *good*. For both Xúnzǐ and Mèngzǐ, any culture is better than no culture.

The *Dàodéjīng* and the Primitivist chapters of the *Zhuāngzǐ* invert this position—what is good comes from closeness to nature, whereas badness lies in the artificial desires created by the development of culture. The Inner Chapters of the *Zhuāngzǐ* are more complex. The true men of old transcend all distinction making, becoming free of culture and able to simply align with nature. At the same time, insofar as we remain within language and culture, the ideal is to make these as flexible and adaptable as possible. This ability is something like a hyper-enculturation, in which the conventionality of culture is pushed so far that anything can be seen as good or bad, depending on which conventional perspective one takes. This flexibility appears to be uniquely human, but it allows for alignment with heaven. In any case, aside from the Mohists, good and bad are taken by all of the thinkers considered here as corresponding to closeness and distance from nature, with the question being which is good and which is bad. Warring States thinkers show remarkably little concern with whether or not particular cultures are good. At issue is the status of culture in general, and, ultimately, the status of the human. Thus, while in both Europe and China the problem of evil left a focus on human responsibility, in China this responsibility was not so much a question of how human beings should act but more a question of how human we should become.

The very possibility of distance from nature and becoming more human shows that we cannot simply collapse moral and natural evil. We have seen over the development of this study an increasing specification of the ways that human beings differ from other animals. The *Dàodéjīng* presents human beings as excessively disruptive in our ability to act deliberately, but pays little attention to this uniqueness, taking it as just a more extreme form of natural tendencies toward rigidity and excess. The *Mèngzǐ* places greatest emphasis on the analogy between human beings and other animals, with human beings differing only in the specificity of their spontaneous reactions. Parts of the *Zhuāngzǐ* introduce a more radical division. The human heart fundamentally is empty, which means that we have no natural perspective and instead vary widely by convention and experience. Moreover, by fasting of the heart we can become unbound from any given perspective—even the perspective that life is good and death is bad. Thus, unlike other animals, human beings can go along with any change freely and easily.

Human beings also appear quite exceptional in the *Xúnzǐ*. Aside from human beings, it seems that the rest of nature spontaneously proceeds in an orderly and sustainable pattern of growth and decay, each thing following the reactions of its nature. For human beings to act in the same way, though, would lead to misery, conflict, and chaos. For the *Dàodéjīng*, the challenge is in explaining how and why human beings (unlike other natural things) fail to act naturally. For the *Xúnzǐ*, the challenge is in explaining why human beings (unlike other natural things) must avoid acting naturally. Although the *Dàodéjīng* emphasizes the disruptiveness of human beings, the *Xúnzǐ* emphasizes our advantages. Nature as a whole system is orderly and sustainable, but life for individual things in nature is always fragile and full of strife. A natural life for human beings might be worse than for other animals, but only by degrees. Our unique ability to act deliberately and to accumulate culture does not return us to a harmonious condition like that naturally available to other animals. On the contrary, it allows us to take up a uniquely powerful position by reshaping the world around us, literally making the world itself anthropocentric.

The varying ways in which human beings appear as unique in these texts suggest that even in a fully naturalistic context lacking anything radically supernatural, human beings appear strange. Whether it is our tendency to disrupt nature with artificial values, our unique ability to "hide the world in the world" and embrace death, or our cumulative power to restructure the world according to our needs, human beings appear to be—in the words of the *Antigone*—*deinon*, both wonderful and terrible. The problem of evil, the fact that bad things happen to good people, helps to illuminate this ineradicable strangeness. Of course to believe that we are made in the image of God or that heaven shares our basic values secures our specialness in the world. Such beliefs become difficult to maintain in the face of a world that appears neither human nor humane, and Chinese philosophers gave them up much more quickly than did philosophers in Europe. Our very ability to accept that, though—to accept that we are just one of the myriad things—suggests that we are *not* just one of the myriad things. The clash between ourselves and the world remains an issue and a challenge for us, whether the challenge is to alter the world or to alter ourselves. Awareness of this clash between us and the world, of "the division between heaven and human," may be common for human beings, at least in certain circumstances. Without some commonality, these early Chinese discussions would have been utterly unintelligible and irrelevant. They obviously are not. My hope, though, has been to bring out the specificity of how this division emerged and was theorized in Warring States China, not in its commonality or difference but rather in its own singularity. Bringing out this singularity has the potential both to illuminate new possibilities for thinking and to reveal limits and constraints in European thought that might not be visible without a point of contrast.

Notes

Introduction

1. Rodolphe Gasché provides a good survey and analysis of the idea of Europe as uniquely open in the works of Husserl, Heidegger, Patočka, and Derrida. Gasché himself writes, "Only in Europe does the concept of universality entail the demand for a responsible self-justification and hence a constitutive openness to every other. There is no question that this conception of universality is a philosophical invention that occurred solely in Europe" (2009, 341).

2. Stephen C. Angle best articulates this approach, which he calls "rooted global philosophy." Angle explains: "'Rooted global philosophy' means to work within a particular live philosophical tradition—thus its rootedness—but to do so in a way that is open to stimulus and insights from other philosophical traditions—thus its global nature" (2009, 6-8).

3. Sean D. Kirkland calls this approach a "hermeneutic of estrangement" (2012, xix). Kirkland writes that the most illuminating approach to Socratic paradoxes "involves the recognition of his profound and fundamental estrangement *from us*, such that resolving the paradox requires a radical transformation on our part" (2012, xvii). Of course it takes less work to make early Chinese thought strange, and we must be wary of the common prejudice that Chinese thought is too strange and inscrutable to be worth engaging at all (see Billeter 2006, 49-50, 81-82). This calls for a delicate balancing between "estrangement" and "domestication."

4. My view of comparative philosophy as a process of self-transformation and hybridization is heavily indebted to Jason D. Hill's vision of "radical cosmopolitanism" (1999).

5. I draw this point from Henri Bergson, by way of Gilles Deleuze. Bergson writes, "The truth is that in philosophy and even elsewhere it is a question of *finding* the problem and consequently of *positing* it, even more than of solving it. . . . But stating the problem is not simply uncovering, it is inventing. Discovery, or uncovering, has to do with what already exists actually or virtually; it was therefore certain to happen sooner or later. Invention gives being to what did not exist; it might never have happened" (1946, 58-59). Deleuze comments, "In this sense, the history of man, from the theoretical as much as from the practical point of view is that of the construction of problems. It is here that humanity makes its own history, and the becoming conscious of that activity is like the conquest of freedom" (1988, 16).

6. My approach is deeply influenced by Michael J. Puett's argument that we best carry out comparisons by focusing on debates and questions rather than shared assumptions (2001; 2002). Regarding comparisons between ancient Greece and China, Puett writes, "This is not to say, of course, that the positions taken within the two cultures were identical or that the course of the debates was similar. My argument is, rather, that the debates are comparable in terms of motivating concerns and tensions. The interesting issue from a comparative perspective lies in discovering how and why the debates worked out as they did in the two cultures" (2002, 95).

7. I follow the now common practice of using the Chinese term Ru (*Rú* 儒) rather than "Confucianism." Using "Ru" avoids misleadingly characterizing the Ru as defining themselves as followers of "Confucius," which itself is a Latinization of the original name Kǒngzǐ, which I will use throughout (as I will use Mèngzǐ rather than Mencius). For an excellent discussion of the identity of the Ru and the problems with the term "Confucianism," see Csikszentmihalyi 2004, 15-32.

8. For a discussion of some of the problems that arose from constructing Chinese thought as "Chinese philosophy," see Zheng 2005.

9. This claim would be complicated by the inclusion of the *Zhōu yì*, the *Book of Changes*, which mixes divination and philosophical concerns through levels of commentary added over time. A consideration of the *Zhōu yì* in the context of the problem of evil would be illuminating, but the complexity of that text would require more than can be accommodated in this book.

10. On this point, I am again influenced by the work of Michael Puett, particularly Puett 2002.

11. See Csikszentmihalyi 2004; Defoort 2004; and Brindley 2010, 230–36. For a broader attempt to problematize divisions into "schools" in the Warring States period, see Csikszentmihalyi and Nylan 2003.

12. The most important are the *Dàodéjīng* (found in Guōdiàn, Mǎwángduī 馬王堆, and in several transmitted versions); the *Zī yī* 缁衣 (Dark robes; found in Guōdiàn and the received *Lǐ jì*); the *Xìng zì mìng chū* (found in Guōdiàn and the Shanghai museum, the latter also known as the *Xìng qíng lùn* 性情論); the *Zhōu yì* (found in Shanghai, Mǎwángduī, and transmitted versions), and the *Wǔ xíng* 五行 (Five actions) found in Guōdiàn and, with an added commentary, at Mǎwángduī.

13. I draw these points primarily from Liú Xiàogǎn 2006, 1–42.

1. Formations of the Problem of Evil

1. In some cases, the "we" seems restricted to Europeans and their descendants. For example, Neiman justifies her focus on modern Europe because it is "the period in which we began to be most recognizably who we are" (2002, 10). Other times, though, the "we" seems broader, and Neiman at least once refers to the "human need" to see evil as evil (2002, 316).

2. Yearley 1988, 432–33; Eno 1990a, 27; Chen Ning 1994; Csikszentmihalyi 2004, 43.

3. My formulation echoes Péng Guóxiáng's claim that "Confucianism is not humanism or religion, but it also is humanism and religion" (2007, 11). His subtle discussion of the advantages and disadvantages of applying these terms in a Chinese context is helpful for thinking more broadly about the cross-cultural application of concepts (2007, 1–15).

4. On this point, I am influenced by Bill Martin, who puts it bluntly: "Theodicy can and ought to be rejected on ethical grounds (it glorifies a monstrous, hateful god and absolutely denigrates humanity in a way far beyond a contingent universe's 'disinterest')" (2008, 413).

5. The phrase *tiānrén zhīfēn* appears by the late fourth century BCE, in the Guōdiàn text *Qióng dá yǐ shí* (Failure and success are by timing) (Liú Zhāo 2003, strip 1). For a discussion of this, see Liáng 2008, 447–67. The phrase *tiānrén héyī* arose much later, coming from the eleventh century Sòng dynasty Ru philosopher Zhāng Zǎi 張載 (Zhāng Zǎi 1978, 64). We might say that the systems which the phrase describes arose earlier, but primarily in the Hàn dynasty. For an excellent discussion of the shift from a focus on harmony (*hé* 和) to unity (*hé* 合) in the thought of the Hàn dynasty philosopher Dǒng Zhòngshū, see Robin Wang 2005. For a critique of reading such views of unity back into the Warring States period, see Billeter 2006.

6. My analysis here does not necessarily disagree with that of Puett, who argues that Chinese philosophers generally began with an assumption of discontinuity and then strove toward achieving continuity and harmony, a position that underlies Puett 2001 and Puett 2002. It was the conflicts and tensions between human and heaven that led to and conditioned the various attempts to achieve harmony with heaven (whether in theory or in practice). Ultimate-

ly, though, I do not think any Chinese philosophers considered the possibility of a radically bifurcated ontology or of forces that radically transcend the natural world.

7. *Novissima Sinica* §10; translation from Cook and Rosement 1994. For a discussion of Leibniz's call for Chinese missionaries in relation to the division between theory and practice, see Perkins 2004, 146–57.

8. Táng Jūnyì takes the Mohists as representing "secondary humanism," Zhuāngzǐ as "transcending humanism," Legalism as "anti-humanism," and Zōu Yǎn as "non-humanistic" (1958, 16–19).

9. For a discussion of the significance of both events, see Neiman 2002, 238–58.

10. I am aware of no cases of mass death being raised as a problem in the Warring States period, but Hàn dynasty texts describe the capital of Lìyáng, which suddenly sank and became a lake, killing all the residents at once. The *Huáinánzi* says that the brave and wise died just the same as the cowardly and foolish, which shows that success does not entirely depend on our own effort but also requires being in the right age (*shì* 世) (Hé Níng 1998, 2: 160; Major et al. 2010, 2.14). Wáng Chōng uses the same story to show that external events sometimes overcome individual fates, so that a person fated for a long life might still die young in a great disaster. In the same passage, he mentions the live burial of 400,000 Zháo soldiers who had surrendered to the Qín general Bái Qǐ (6: 44–45).

11. The story of Wǔ Zǐxū appears in several Warring States texts, including the *Zuǒ zhuàn*, *Guó yǔ*, and *Lǚshì chūnqiū*. I primarily follow the version of the story in *Shǐ jì* 67.2171–2184 (Nienhauser 1995, VII, 49–62). A longer (and more entertaining) version of his life appears in the *Wúyuè chūnqiū*, written in the first century CE. For a detailed discussion and comparison of the different versions, see Johnson 1980, 1981; and Shào 2007, 3–12.

12. *Shǐ jì* 64.2180. See also *Zuǒ zhuàn* Duke Āi 11; Yáng Bójūn 1990, 1664–65.

13. According to Sīmǎ Qiān, the whole series of events was orchestrated by Kǒngzǐ, through his disciple Zǐgòng 子貢, as a way of saving his home state of Lǔ from the larger state of Qí. Sīmǎ Qiān summarizes Zǐgòng's accomplishments in this way: "Thus Zǐgòng in one trip preserved Lǔ, disordered Qí, crushed Wú, strengthened Jìn, and made a hegemon out of Yuè. Zǐgòng in one mission had their powers crush each other, so that within ten years time, five states were transformed" (*Shǐ jì* 7.2201; cf. Nienhauser 1995, VII, 71–74).

14. *Lǚshì chūnqiū* 14/5.2: 798. The king appeals to the rightness of not attacking a submissive enemy and the humaneness of helping those in need. The passage ends by noting that within three years, Wú had a famine and when it asked Yuè to help, King Gōu Jiàn instead attacked. The actions described in the *Wúyuè chūnqiū* are even more devious: when Yuè repaid the loan of grain, they did so with grain that had been steamed so as not to grow. The people of Wú planted it, which is what caused their own famine (Johnson 1981, 141).

15. The fact that Wáng Chōng provides a long argument against these supernatural events shows their prominence at the time (16: 180–87). For a discussion of the cult around Wǔ Zǐxū, see Johnson 1980, 465–500.

16. The text was found at Zhāngjiāshān in 1983, in a group of texts buried in the early Hàn dynasty. There is disagreement on when it originated, but Shào Hóng argues for it being no earlier than the end of the middle Warring States period, long after Wǔ Zǐxū's death (2007, 3). For a reconstruction and explanation of the text, see Shào 2007.

17. Epicurus A86; translation from Inwood and Gerson 1988, 64. Epicurus lived 341–271 BCE, but the quotation appears and is attributed to Epicurus only in Lactantius's *On the Anger of God*, written about six centuries later. Sextus Empiricus (probably second century CE) employs the same argument. He concludes, "If they say that the gods provide for everything, they will say that they are a cause of evil; and if they say that they provide for some things or even for none at all, they will be bound to say either that the gods are malign or that they are

weak—and anyone who says this is clearly impious" (*Outlines of Scepticism* III.iii; translation from Annas and Barnes 2000, 146).

18. Wáng Chōng defines three kinds of fate: a correct fate (*zhèngmìng* 正命), which is when a good life comes with little effort; a compliant fate (*suímìng* 隨命), which follows from one's own effort, for better or worse; and an adverse fate (*zāomìng* 遭命), which is a bad result that comes no matter one what does (6: 49–50).

19. This account of Bǐ Gān is based primarily on *Shǐ jì* 3.91–110 (Nienhauser 1995, I, 41–54).

20. This account is based primarily on *Shǐ Jì* 61.2121–2129 (Nienhauser 1995, VII, 1–8).

21. *Shǐ Jì* 61.2124; cf. Nienhauser 1995, VII.4. The quoted line appears in identical form in *Dàodéjīng* 79, but it may have been a common saying. The *Hé Lú* text quoted above is similar, and the *Zuǒ zhuàn* quotes a similar line from the *Shàng shū*: "Majestic heaven has no familial attachments, only virtue [*dé*] is assisted [皇天無親, 惟德是輔]" (*Zuǒ zhuàn* Duke Xī 5; Yáng Bójūn 1990, 309). The line appears now in the "Charge to Zhòng of Cài" chapter of the *Shàng shū*, which is thought to be a later forgery.

22. See Brindley 2010, 234; and Lǐ Ruì 2009.

23. The term *shì* 士 refers to the educated class of people who would be political or military leaders, and it can often be translated as "officers" or "aspiring officers." At the same time, it often refers to those worthy of taking office, even if they have decided to withdraw and not seek office. In that context, it means something more like "worthy people." I have translated it consistently as "scholars," which should not be taken in the academic sense but rather in the sense of educated, cultivated people with potential to be leaders.

24. Mair cuts the passage from chapter 5 and Chén Gǔyìng and others argue that it was transposed from a later chapter (Chén Gǔyìng 1983, 203–204). For an alternative reading of the passage, see Ziporyn 2009, 41. Some claim that Xǔ Yú is Wǔ Zǐxū, but that is uncertain (Guō Qìngfān 1978, 233–34).

25. The passage is from the first chapter of the *Mòzǐ*, which was probably added at a later time. The ideas expressed in this passage are close to the *Dàodéjīng*, particularly *Dàodéjīng* 9.

26. The *Guǐshén zhī míng* juxtaposes Wǔ Zǐxū to Róng Yí Gōng 榮夷公, said to have caused disorder but lived a long life (Mǎ 2005, strips 3–4). The identity of Róng Yí Gōng is uncertain, and there is dispute on whether that is even the correct reconstruction of the characters. Wáng Chōng sometimes mentions a Zhuāng Qiāo 莊蹻 along with Robber Zhí (e.g., 6: 51). For debates on his identity, see Huāng 1990, 51, and Chén Qíyóu 1984, 638–39.

27. Hú Shì lists five stances in relation to the troubled times of the Spring and Autumn period, one of which was that rather than worry about the affairs of the world it was better to enjoy yourself whenever the opportunity arises. Hú cites this ode as evidence, as well as odes 85 and 114 (2003, 30–31).

28. The events around Zǐlù's death provide another illustration of how bad the times were. Duke Líng 靈 of Wèi 衛 appeared overly infatuated with his concubine, Nánzǐ, a woman Kǒngzǐ was criticized for meeting with (*Lúnyǔ* 6.28). In 496 BCE, the crown prince Kuǎi Kuì 蒯聵 failed in an attempt to have her assassinated, after which he was forced to flee. When Duke Líng died, Kuǎi was passed over in favor of his son. Kuǎi then attempted to invade Wèi and depose his own son. The two fought back and forth for more than twenty years. For this episode, see *Zuǒ zhuàn*, Duke Āi 15 (Yáng Bójūn 1990, 1695–96) and *Shǐ jì* 7.2193 (Nienhauser 1995, VII, 68–69). The episode is discussed in Hui-chieh Loy 2008, 225–26; and Allan 2009, 121–23.

29. These events are explained in Chén Gǔyìng 1983, 435–36, and Guō Qìngfān 1978, 513.

30. For discussion of various incarnations of the trouble between Chén and Cài, see Makeham 1998; Chen Ning 2003; and Lǐ Ruì 2004.

31. In a passage from the *Zhuāngzǐ*, Kǒngzǐ says that his disciples and friends have scattered after he encountered so many difficulties (20: 684; Mair 1994, 192–93). Kǒngzǐ's statement in

Lúnyǔ 11.2—that of his disciples who suffered with him between Chén and Cài, none are now at the gate—may be a reference to this.

32. This is the case, for example, in the "Yòu zuò" Chin chapter of the *Xúnzǐ* (28: 326–27; Knoblock 1988, 28.8). For the relationship between *Qióng dá yǐ shí* and the stories of Kǒngzǐ in trouble, see Lǐ Ruì 2004.

33. I here follow convention in using the term "gentlemen" as a stand-in for *jūnzǐ*. *Jūnzǐ* originally referred to the nobility (literally, the sons [*zǐ*] of lords [*jūn*]), but its meaning came to refer to those who are morally cultivated. In this way, it resembles the terms "gentlemen" or "the noble" in English. Neither English term is fully adequate, though, and it should be clear from context that *jūnzǐ* is a much more robust concept than "gentlemen." Ames translates *jūnzǐ* as "exemplary person," which may be closer to its meaning for the Ru but loses its original class connotations.

34. *Zhuāngzǐ* 14: 511–12, 20: 680–85, 31: 1031; Mair 1994, 136–37, 191–93, 321.

35. Although philosophical texts are largely silent on the matter, burial practices and ancestral sacrifices indicate a widespread belief in some kind of afterlife, including a belief that some people become ghosts (as we see in the *Mòzǐ*). Nonetheless, the afterlife was not conceived of as a place where rewards and punishments would be received and the Mohists never appeal to it, even though it would have greatly strengthened their position. The lack of rewards and punishments in an afterlife partly explains why many philosophers so quickly gave up belief in the goodness of heaven (see Xú 1969, 41, and Dubs 1958, 243). For a discussion of views of the afterlife in the Warring States period see Poo 1998, 62–66. Praise and blame after one's death was accepted as a form of punishment and reward. Xú Fùguān says that although most religions offer judgment in heaven, early China turned to judgments by history (Xú 1969, 56). A few passages suggest that rewards and punishments might fall on one's descendants, as in *Mèngzǐ* 1B14 and the *Sān dé* 三德 (Three virtues) excavated text (Mǎ 2005, strips 2–3). This develops into the idea of "inherited burden" (*chéngfù* 承負) in the *Tàipíngjīng* (Hendrischke 1991). Chen Ning labels this as "posterity theodicy" and gives more examples (Chen Ning 1994, 60–61). The Mohists do not make use of this argument, though, which suggests it was not common at that time.

36. There are many disagreements on the details of this passage. See Chén Qíyóu 1984, 1570–74.

37. "Kāng gào"; Gù and Liú 2005, 1299–1300; Karlgren 1950, 39. For the dating of chapters, I rely on Shaughnessy 1993.

38. The outlines of my account of late Shàng and early Zhōu views are widely accepted, but I draw particularly on Chén Lái 2009a, 110–29; and Xú 1969, 15–35. Chen Ning has a particularly good account centering more directly on issues of theodicy (1997c). For views of Shàngdì and its relation to *tiān*, see also Eno 1990b, and Joseph Shih 1969/70.

39. Similarly, Mu-chou Poo writes, "There are no tender feelings expressed in the oracle-bone inscriptions. Everything is businesslike. There is, moreover, no problem of morality. The communication between man and the extra-human powers does not, at least on the surface, entail any moral or ethical qualifications. One does not ask, for example, if a certain disaster was connected with one's moral or political behavior" (1998, 28).

40. For an interesting discussion of the connections between conceptions of heaven and astronomical observation, see Pankenier 1995.

41. "Kāng gào"; Gù and Liú 2005, 1336; Karlgren 1950, 42.

42. "Jiǔ gào"; Gù and Liú 2005, 1381; Karlgren 1950, 43.

43. See Chén Lái 2009a, 199–206.

44. The received version of the "Great Declaration" is thought to be a later forgery, but both lines are quoted in other Warring States texts. The first appears in *Mèngzǐ* 5A5. The second ap-

pears in several places, for example in *Zuǒ zhuàn* Duke Xiāng 31 (Yáng Bójūn 1990, 1184). For a discussion of these passages, see Chén Lái 2009a, 206–208.

45. Joseph Shih argues that because the Zhōu state was larger and more diverse than the Shàng, it could not secure its authority by appeal to a divine being associated with its own ancestry. Zhōu religion instead shifted emphasis onto the sky (heaven) and the soil or earth (1969/1970, 114–15). Pankenier puts the point nicely: "In striving to emulate Heaven, which overarched the world and provided the rhythmic backbeat to the phenomena, the Zhōu reasserted the primacy of universality and inclusiveness, in apparent marked contrast to the former Shàng overindulgence in exclusivist hegemony, itself a logical outgrowth of their preoccupation with the cult of the royal ancestors" (Pankenier 1995, 175–76).

46. "Jūn shì" Chin; Gù and Liú 2005, 1554; Karlgren 1950, 59, 61.

47. This phrase is quoted from the *Shàng shū* in the *Mòzǐ* (27: 206–207; Johnston 2010, 27.9). A version of these lines appear in the "Great Declaration I" chapter of the received text (Legge 1985, 285–86).

48. Gāo Hēng 1998, 435. For the discussion of *yōuhuàn yìshí*, see Xú 1969, 20–24. For a discussion in English and an interesting comparison with the origins of Greek philosophy in wonder, see Wang Huaiyu 2008.

49. *Yuèyáng Lóujì* 岳陽樓記 (Records of Yuèyáng Tower); Fàn 2002, 195.

50. "Jiǔ gào"; Gù and Liú 2005, 1408; Karlgren 1950, 45.

51. "Lǚ xíng"; Gù and Liú 2005, 2055; Karlgren 1950, 78. The point of the passage is clear, but its precise meaning is not. I here follow Gù and Liú. For an alternate interpretation, see Karlgren 1950, 78.

52. "Gù mìng" Chin; Gù and Liú 2005, 1712; Karlgren 1950, 70. Robert Eno, working from bronze inscriptions, suggests that "the doctrine of the 'mandate' probably was only partially elaborated during the early Zhōu, holding prescriptively that the king had to work hard to be worthy of the mandate, and that the mandate could be withdrawn, but not stressing the descriptive implication that if *tiān* withdrew the mandate it meant that the king had not been worthy. If *tiān* were not ethically perfect, this would not be a necessary implication, and these late kings obviously preferred not to draw it, instead suggesting the waywardness of *tiān*" (1990a, 213–14).

53. Dubs writes of the mandate of heaven, "It implies that when the people are misgoverned, Heaven sends upon them civil disorder, in order to change the dynasty. Then Heaven punishes the innocent people for the sins of the guilty ruler, for it is the people who suffer in civil disorder. So Heaven cannot be just" (1958, 243). Chén Lái also points out that the burden of suffering falls on the common people. He concludes that this followed because the god of the Western Zhōu was really a god for the ruling classes (2009a, 240).

54. Puett writes, "The reigning assumption, then, would appear to be that the relations between humans and spirits were, without this ritual action, agonistic and potentially dangerous; the goal was thus to domesticate the spirits and thereby render them controllable" (2002, 54). While Puett here describes the Shàng, he shows that such views continue through the Zhōu as well (2002, 61–68).

55. Eno writes, "There is evidence, however, that during the Western Zhou, the notion of *Tiān* as the benevolent god of state may have existed side by side with popular agricultural traditions, most likely very old, which cast *Tiān* as the unpredictable ruler of the sky, whose whims were as likely to be malevolent as otherwise" (1990a, 26). See also Poo 1998, 30, 38.

56. There are many disagreements on how to read the last lines, but I follow Zhōu Zhènfǔ 2002, 303–307. Gāo Hēng takes this ode as blaming heaven, but takes "does not plan" as referring to the ruler (1980, 286).

57. "Shào gào"; Gù and Liú 2005, 1442; Karlgren 1950, 51. For a list of passages making a similar point, see Chen Ning 1994, 53.

58. Dubs comments on this ode, "Such complaints were inevitable once the Lord on High had been conceived as exhibiting a providential care. Is it surprising that in the end intelligent Chinese should have doubted the existence of any supreme God? The problem of evil comes with an advanced religion" (1958, 243).

59. Pines summarizes the situation in the Spring and Autumn period thus: "For some, Heaven remained a powerful symbol of justice, the last resort of the weak and the oppressed; others conceived of Heaven as an impersonal law, possibly lacking moral features; still others simply argued that the Way of Heaven is distant, and that inscrutable Heaven's will cannot be a reliable guide in everyday affairs" (2002, 207).

60. Pines says that heaven came more to be identified with actual events, so that "acting according to Heaven's will meant merely seizing the proper opportunity" (2002, 64). We have already seen suggestions of this view in the importance of timing, *shí*.

61. Eno uses the terms "prescriptive" and "descriptive" to label the two functions of heaven as giving moral commands and as referring to what happens outside our control (1990a, 102). This goes back to A. C. Graham's distinction between the "factual" and "normative" sides heaven (2002, 44). Kwong-loi Shun takes up this distinction as well (1997, 17–18).

62. For an excellent account of the emergence of a concept of blind fate, see Chen Ning 1997c. See also Xú 1969, 39–40.

63. For example, Xú Fùguān calls his chapter on the Spring and Autumn period "The Emergence of a Humanistic Age that Takes Ritual as its Center, and Religion's Becoming Humanistic" (1969, 36–62). Yuri Pines also emphasizes this point (e.g., 2002, 88).

64. I draw primarily on treatments of the problem in early modern philosophy, particularly those by Gottfried Wilhelm Leibniz and David Hume. For a collection of influential contemporary discussions, see Adams and Adams 1991.

65. For a more refined analysis of the problem and its premises, see Adams and Adams 1991, 1–24.

66. Nussbaum discusses the Greek combination of a duty to respect all gods and the fact that these gods impose different and even conflicting demands (1986, 30). According to Nussbaum, Socrates' refusal to admit truly tragic conflicts prompted him to revise traditional religious beliefs in favor of a unified good (1986, 25–26, 30).

67. See Perkins 2007, 43–54.

68. The comment of Alfonso appears in Leibniz, *Theodicy* §§193, 194 (Gerhardt 1978, VI.231–32). For further discussion of Alfonso and his significance, see Neiman 2002, 14–18.

69. The most influential contemporary advocate for this position as a response to the problem of evil is Alvin Plantinga. For a brief account of his view, see the excerpt from *The Nature of Necessity* in Adams and Adams 1991, 83–109.

70. Kant writes, "The human being must make or have made *himself* into whatever he is or should become in a moral sense, good or evil. These two must be an effect of his free power of choice, for otherwise they could not be imputed to him and, consequently, he could be *neither* morally good nor evil" (Kant 1900, 6:44; translation from Wood and di Giovanni 1998, 65).

71. Kant 1900, 6:23–24; Wood and di Giovanni 1998, 49. Augustine similarly claims that the will can only be enslaved to inordinate desires through its own choice to do so (*On Free Choice of the Will*; Augustine 1993, 17).

72. Kant 1900, 6:41; translation from Wood and Di Giovanni 1998, 62–63.

73. *Ethics*, Part III, preface; translation from Curley 1994, 152–53.

74. For an excellent discussion of this point, see Nussbaum 1986, 4–5.

75. Stanzas 332–34. The translation is slightly modified from the word-for-word translation in Meineck and Woodruff 2003, 62. For an excellent discussion of the meaning of *deinon*, see Nussbaum 1986, 52–53.

76. *Principles of Nature and Grace* §15; Gerhardt 1978, IV.65; translation from Ariew and Garber 1989, 212.
77. *Birth of Tragedy* §17; Nietzsche 1988 1.114.
78. *Poetics* 1453a4–5; translation from Barnes 1984.
79. *Meditations on First Philosophy*, Meditation 3; translation from Cottingham, Stoothoff, and Murdoch 1985, 35.
80. *Birth of Tragedy* §1, Nietzsche 1988, 1.28. For a discussion of the term *das Ungeheure* in relation to tragedy, see Heidegger 1996, 70–71.
81. *Birth of Tragedy* §9, Nietzsche 1988, 1.70.
82. Hegel 1952, 334; Paolucci and Paolucci 1962, 278.
83. *Birth of Tragedy* §9, Nietzsche 1988, 1.68; translation from Guess and Speirs 1999, 49.
84. *Birth of Tragedy* §22, Nietzsche 1988, 1.141.
85. Wáng takes the line out of context, where a dying person says them to explain why he is not upset: "The great clod burdens me with form, labors me with life, rests me with old age, and ends me with death. Thus, affirming my living is that by which I affirm my dying" (*Zhuāngzǐ* 6: 242; cf. Mair 1994, 59).
86. Puett 2002, 68–76. Puett writes that both stories involve "human transgressions and capricious gods" (2002, 75). The ode is "Generating the People" ("Shēng mín" 生民) (245). Puett labels the final chapter of *The Ambivalence of Creation* "The Tragedy of Creation" (2001, 177–212).
87. Hegel 1955, I.422; Paolucci and Paolucci 1962, 165.
88. Wang Huaiyu has a nuanced discussion of this contrast: "In contrast to the Greek ideal of men as heroes, the early Chinese conception of the human self is much more humble. But we must not confuse such humbleness with slavishness, timidity, or self-denial. Early Chinese people held deep veneration for the human self, though not as an egoistic and arrogant master who lorded it over other human and natural beings, but as a vigilant and diligent follower and preserver of the proper enactment of the way, of the vital emergence of life between sky and earth" (2008, 149).

2. The Efficacy of Human Action and the Mohist Opposition to Fate

1. For example, A. C. Graham writes, "That the Mohists came from a lower social stratum than other schools is suggested by their uniqueness in maintaining, side by side with incisive criticism of traditional values, a belief in rewarding and punishing divinities which belongs rather to folk religion." He then adds that the Mohists are "otherwise forward-thinking" (1989, 47). Similarly, Dīng Wèixiáng takes the Mohist view of heaven as reflecting "primitive religion" (2008, 411). Mohist views of heaven are sometimes taken more seriously, with the best example being Augustinus Tseu's reading of the *Mòzǐ* as a work of philosophical theology (1965); see also Lowe 1992. For a summary of the way Mohist discussions of ghosts have been neglected or dismissed, see Wong and Loy 2004.
2. The *Lúnyǔ* has traditionally been taken as the authoritative source for the views of Kǒngzǐ, but that status is questionable. It is almost certain that numerous collections of sayings of Kǒngzǐ circulated throughout the Warring States period and that the *Lúnyǔ* was compiled from them in the early Hàn dynasty (this view is shown convincingly in Makeham 1996 and Csikszentmihalyi 2002; see also Eno 1990a, 239–240n2). For reasons explained in the introduction, I assume that most (but certainly not all) of the things attributed to Kǒngzǐ probably go back to something the master said, but that no parts of the text can be taken to be word-for-word "authentic." The most thorough attempt to distinguish what is authentic and

what is interpolation in the *Lúnyǔ* is Brooks and Brooks 1998. For summaries of other views, see Brooks and Brooks 1998, 201–204; Van Norden 2002, 13–18; and Lau 1979, 220–33. When I speak of particular people such as Kǒngzǐ, I refer to characters in texts rather than historical persons.

3. The phrase derives from the "Xìcí" ("Attached Verbalizations") of the *Zhōu yì* (*Book of Changes*) (Gāo Hēng 1998, 388).

4. After summarizing his account of Confucianism in the *Discourse on the Natural Theology of the Chinese*, Leibniz concludes, "For me I find all this quite excellent and quite in accord with natural theology.... It is pure Christianity, in so far as it renews the natural law inscribed in our hearts—except for what revelation and grace add to it to improve our nature" (*Discourse* §31; translation from Cook and Rosemont 1994). For a discussion of Leibniz's interpretation of Confucian thought as natural theology, see Perkins 2004, 191–94. For a discussion of Wolff's position, see Louden 2002.

5. Creel 1932 has an excellent analysis of these alternations in Chinese interpretations, including trends in the twentieth century. Csikszentmihalyi 2002 has an overview of Hàn interpretations. See also Ivanhoe 2002b.

6. Such comments were likely to have been made after Kǒngzǐ's death, perhaps much later. Passage 5.13 also mentions human nature (*xìng* 性), a term which became philosophically significant only in the mid-fourth century. In that context, "the way of heaven" may be meant to contrast "the way of human beings," as Waley suggests (1989, 110). For a discussion of later Chinese readings of this passage, see Ivanhoe 2002b. Passage 9.1 is notoriously difficult, since it also lists humaneness, *rén*, which Kǒngzǐ did frequently discuss. For a summary of the various attempts to deal with this, see Brooks and Brooks 2002b. For an alternate reading, see Slingerland 2003, 86.

7. Although some modern readers take this passage to illustrate Kǒngzǐ's agnosticism about spirits, classical commentators generally do not. For example, Zhū Xī Chin quotes Chéng Yí 程頤: "If one knows the way of life, then one knows the way of death; if one exhausts the way of serving people, then one exhausts the way of serving ghosts. Life and death, human beings and ghosts—these are one but two, two but one" (2003, 125). Csikszentmihalyi shows that Hàn commentators took Kǒngzǐ as very concerned with spirits (2002). For a selection of more humanistic commentaries on this passage, see Slingerland 2003, 115. A couple of passages imply that spirits do exist (2.24, 6.6), and another passage praises the sage king Yǔ for his piety toward spirits (8.21). In another passage, though, Kǒngzǐ says that one should sacrifice *as if* spirits were present (3.12), which might suggest agnosticism about spirits or at least their attention to sacrifices. For an argument that Kǒngzǐ did believe in spirits, see Creel 1932.

8. Eno brings this point out with particular clarity, in relation to Ru texts in general: "Consequently, we abandon any effort to look for a consistent referential meaning of the term '*tiān*'—any stable image or concept that could provide a dictionary style gloss for the term in each text—and determine instead to look for coherence in the instrumental relation that Ruist statements about *tiān* may have borne to the preservation and growth of the school's practical core" (1990a, 11).

9. The criticism was about Kǒngzǐ having a meeting with Nánzǐ, the disreputable concubine of Duke Líng of Wèi. The attempt by the duke's son to have her killed caused the civil war that led to Zǐlù's death, discussed in chapter 1.

10. *Shuōwén* 1a.12b (Duàn 1988, 6). Hall and Ames translate *zuì* as "guilt," and claim that it always "indicates a transgression against some established standard" (1987, 174).

11. Eno thus claims that these references to heaven show nothing more than "Confucius' skillful ability to employ traditional religious rhetoric in order to say something about matters other than *tiān*" (1990a, 96). I think these passages do reflect Kǒngzǐ's views of heaven, but articulating a view of heaven is not what the passages are about, and this at least leaves open

the possibility that, as Eno concludes, "*tiān* probably performed no significant function in the philosophy of Confucius" (1990a, 96).

12. The Hàn commentator Hé Yàn 何晏 explains that it is "like losing himself" (Liú Bǎonán 1990, 447; Slingerland 2003, 114; see also Zhū 2003, 125). For an excellent discussion of this point, see Olberding 2008, 147.

13. Zhū Xī says this in relation to the death of Bó Niú (2003, 87).

14. Two passages place great importance on the phrase *tiānmìng* (*Lúnyǔ* 2.4, 16.8), but the meaning of the phrase in those passages is impossible to determine with enough certainty to use as evidence. I have refrained from speculating on them.

15. See the excellent discussion in Yearley 1988. Chen Ning makes a good case for a similar view, pointing out that it is common to find cultures that believe in both providential gods and blind fate (1997b, 335, 346–47).

16. Michael Puett take this view: "Thus, the patterns that should guide human behavior can be traced to Heaven—they are patterns observed by the sages and brought from Heaven to humanity. However, the commands of Heaven do not necessarily involve support for those who follow these patterns" (2002, 100; for a similar account in terms of *mìng*, see Puett 2005, 52–53).

17. Lee Yearley (in relation to the *Mèngzǐ*) makes a similar point in distinguishing between a "known" and an "unknown" mandate, the latter of which reflects an indiscernible ethical plan (1988, 438; cf. Yearley 1990, 167).

18. *Discourse on Metaphysics* §3; Gerhardt 1978, IV.429; translation from Ariew and Garber 1989, 37.

19. In the *Lúnyǔ*, there is one possible case in which an apparently bad event is explained as actually good, the gatekeeper's explanation of Kǒngzǐ's political failure (3.24). The *Mèngzǐ* also contains just one example, which says that heaven sometimes sends suffering in order to prepare a person for greatness (6B15). Given all of the bad events mentioned in both texts, these cannot be taken as intimating a thorough denial of the problem of evil. Rather, they make the common sense point that sometimes bad events actually lead to good results, and that this should give us some comfort.

20. Homer Dubs, who emphasizes the theistic element of the *Lúnyǔ*, thus takes Mòzǐ as the real successor to Kǒngzǐ, while the other Ru fell away from the views of their master (1958, 253).

21. Chad Hansen makes this point in different terms: "He [Mòzǐ] accepts nature's will about the constant standard for naming, but not the notion that nature fixes names. Society fixes the names using the standard approved by nature.... Aside from the name pair *lì-hài*[benefit-harm], nature does not lock the name system in place nor are names divinely assigned to people" (1992, 122).

22. *Chéngzhī wènzhī*, *Táng Yú zhī dào* (Way of Táng and Yú), and *Zūn dé yì* 尊德義 (Honoring virtue and rightness) all seem Ru in orientation, but they present positions and use terms closer to the Mohists than other received Ru texts. For a discussion of this point in relation to the *Táng Yú zhī dào* see Defoort 2004. Defoort argues that it is a Ru text that incorporates explicitly Mohist and Yangist positions. I suspect rather that some of the ideas we associate with those schools were not so clearly marked at the time.

23. I follow Liú Zhāo 2003 in reading *dù* 度, translated here as "measure." Others, though, take the graph as *zhái* 宅, which would mean "to rest in" or "to depend on." Dīng Sìxīn takes it as having both senses (2000, 304). For examples and analysis of the phrase "heaven's heart," see Dīng Yuánzhí 2000, 183–84. It should be noted that the phrase is used in relation to a quotation from text no longer extant. Thus Dīng Yuánzhí takes the phrase as originating from "primitive religion" but as used humanistically to mean only the guiding force that coordinates the movement of the myriad things (2000, 184). That may be the case, but begs the question by assuming the Ru would not appeal to heaven's intentions.

24. For a translation and discussion of the *Zǐgāo* 子羔 text and this particular point, see Allan 2009.

25. It is possible that the excavated texts are not representative of mainstream Ru views, but this contrast suggests intriguingly that the received texts may have deliberately omitted the more theistic Ru materials.

26. Sīmǎ Niú is commonly identified as the younger brother of Huán Tuí, a corrupt court favorite said to have been behind the attempt to assassinate Kǒngzǐ in Sòng (*Lúnyǔ* 7.23). Since Zǐxià concludes by saying that Sīmǎ Niú should see all people as his brother, the passage may play on a distinction between the way things are (that he has evil brothers) and the way those circumstances are interpreted (as having no brothers, or as having all as brothers). From this Rosemont and Ames conclude, "This passage, far from justifying fatalism, demonstrates the fluidity of circumstances and the inseparability of fact and value in the description of these same circumstances" (1998, 250n192; see also Hall and Ames 1987, 214–15). The passage makes more sense, though, read in the opposite way, as advocating a distinction between what is fated (the external, which lies with heaven) and what is in our control (the internal, which lies with human beings). This how Slingerland takes it: "[I]f the gentleman focuses on what is in his control (self-cultivation), he has no need to be anxious or worry about things out of his control" (2003, 127). For a persuasive criticism of Hall and Ames on this passage, see Chen Ning 1997b, 329–32. Yáng Bójūn makes a good case that Sīmǎ Niú here is not the brother of Huán Tuí and probably just literally had no brothers (2002, 125).

27. For a detailed discussion of the relationships between various versions of the text, see Lǐ Ruì 2004.

28. *Yù* became a prominent term in discussions of the link between worthiness and success. The first chapter of the *Lùnhéng* is called "Coming Across and Meeting" ("Féngyù" 逢遇), and the first line is this: "Actions may have constant worthiness, but taking office lacks constant meeting. Worthy and unworthy are in ability; meeting and not meeting are in timing [*shí*]" (1: 1). The *Lǚshì chūnqiū* also has a chapter titled "Meeting and Fitting" ("Yùhé" 遇合), which concludes, "Meeting and fitting have no constancy" (14/7.3: 823).

29. Mèngzǐ distinguishes these two senses by introducing a technical distinction between *yōu* and *huàn*, saying that gentlemen have lifelong worry (*yōu*) but are never troubled (*huàn*). They are never troubled because they have confidence in their virtue; they have lifelong worry because they know they still fall short of being a sage (Mèngzǐ 4B28). This terminological distinction, though, is not strictly maintained even in the *Mèngzǐ*, and other texts tend to use both terms with both meanings.

30. *Ethics*, Part V, Proposition 6; translation from Curley 1994, 249.

31. The strips were damaged and are missing three characters. The first should end the first sentence and refer to some negative feeling associated with failure. Lǐ Líng takes it as resentment, *yuàn* 怨 (2002, 86); Liú Zhāo takes it as troubled, *kùn* 困 (2003, 174–75). I follow Liú Zhāo in filling in the second sentence as a parallel to the first.

32. I agree with Dan Robins that we misread the *Mòzǐ* if we take it as written primarily to engage in theoretical debates with other philosophers (Robins 2008, 385). Robins concedes, however, that the Mohist discussions of fate, heaven, and ghosts are directed against other theoretical claims (although motivated by practical concerns) (2008, 397). Robins argues that these concerns emerged later in the Mohist school, but there is little evidence for that, and we have seen that there were people who advocated fate and skepticism of heaven's goodness as early as the Spring and Autumn period. Given that context, it is unlikely that the earliest Mohists would have had no views of heaven and fate.

33. The text of the *Mòzǐ* raises many difficulties, as it divides into several parts that are distinct in style and content. The core of the text consists of ten topics, each appearing in three versions (some of which have been lost). Some have explained these versions as representing

different factions within the Mohist school, while others have explained them as earlier or later versions. Some combination is likely true, but the evidence is insufficient to judge. The chapter called "Against Ru" is usually grouped with these. Another section of the text (chapters 46–49) consists of short dialogues in a style similar to the *Lúnyǔ* or *Mèngzǐ*. These seem intended more for insiders and, since they often respond to challenges, they must be later than the various planks. Even so, the objections they address are fairly obvious and are likely to have arisen in Mòzǐ's own lifetime. In reconstructing early Mohist views, I rely on these dialogue chapters and the various versions of the core chapters. These cannot be taken together as representing one viewpoint, though, and differences or tensions are pointed out when relevant. The first seven chapters mix materials from different sources and I use them only to clarify or develop points established by other parts of the text. I assume the logic chapters (40–45) represent a later period of Mohist thought, and so use them only to project later directions the Mohists may have taken. For discussions of the nature and authenticity of the text, see Fraser 2010; Graham 1989, 35–37; Mei 1934, 52–58; and Hú Shì 2003, 115–16.

34. Tseu puts the point as bluntly as it deserves: "It is obvious to anyone who has read the original text of Mòzǐ that he never undermined the special affection due to one's own father" (1965, 245). For evidence on this point, see Tseu 1965, 250–54; Robins 2008, 386–88; and Fraser 2010.

35. There is at least a tension between valuing familial relations and looking on others as one looks upon oneself, but the Mohists clearly advocated both. One might compare this to the tension in Christianity between the family and Jesus' advice to his followers that they should love their neighbors as themselves (Mark 12:28–31). Although this has raised debates about the family within the church, in practice, few Christians take this to entail the elimination of the family. Even outside a Christian context, it is quite common for people now to believe that all human beings have equal moral worth *and* to believe that we have special duties to our families and friends. The Mohists hold something analogous to this view. I am indebted to discussions with Chris Fraser and Dan Robins on this point.

36. The first appears several times in "Inclusive Caring III" (e.g., 16: 116; Johnston 2010, 16.4). As an example of the second, Mòzǐ tells a former student that "if one has extra resources, distribute them to the poor" (49: 477; cf. Johnston 2010, 49.16). For an example of the third, Mòzǐ says, "That for which the humane work is certainly to elevate the world's benefits and eliminate the world's harms" (15: 101; cf. Johnston 2010, 15.1).

37. The other two disastrous policies are promoting long funerals and extravagant musical performances.

38. This association of the evil kings with reliance on *mìng* precedes the Mohists, as the *Mòzǐ* quotes a passage from the "Great Declaration" chapter of the *Shàng shū*, in which Zhòu is said to have neglected his duties because he was certain that the *mìng* was his (27: 206–207; Johnston 2010, 27.9). Robert Eno quotes several Spring and Autumn period bronze inscriptions in which rulers blame heaven for disasters rather than their own incompetence (1990a, 24–26). That probably captures what the Mohists have in mind.

39. Although claims about timing must precede the Mohist arguments, it is likely that the *Qióng dá yǐ shí* text was composed after this passage from the *Mòzǐ*, perhaps in part as a response. It may deliberately invert the Mohist argument to claim that, without a change in virtue or wisdom, the same person sometimes succeeds and sometimes fails.

40. See Fraser 2008. Chad Hansen may be the first to emphasize the role of emulation, saying that obedience to heaven relies on a combination of threats and a natural tendency to emulate superiors (1992, 121). Owen Flanagan also discusses the role of emulation, which he sees as significant for the Mohists but as playing a more limited role than it does for the Ru (2008).

41. The assumption of care for family appears in several Mohist arguments, as we have seen. In the argument against offensive wars, Mòzǐ says that if someone breaks into a neigh-

bor's orchard and steals their fruit, everyone will condemn it, because the person harms others to benefit himself (17: 128–29; Johnston 2010, 17.1). A passage in the dialogue chapters says that people will sacrifice their lives for rightness (47: 439; Johnston 2010, 47.1). The Mohist portrait of a state of nature at the start of the "Conforming Upward" chapters assumes that each person has their own sense of rightness and that they act on this and wish to hold others to it. For an analysis of those passages in terms of motivation, see Fraser 2008, 441–44. It should be noted that while those passages assume we naturally act on what we consider right, they also imply that we have no common standard for what counts as right.

42. On this point, see Flanagan 2008.

43. This focus on motivation toward what is needed for survival, coupled with a general disregard for sensory pleasure, suggests the Mohists hold a view similar to the *Dàodéjīng*, which takes human beings as naturally desiring what is needed for life, and takes desires for luxuries as either insignificant or artificial. Such views are developed explicitly later, and they will be addressed in more detail in chapter 6. Nonetheless, the Mohist view seems to be a generalization about how most people act rather than a strict claim about human nature. David Nivison has suggested influentially that the Mohists are "voluntarists" who assume human beings can change their motivation on command (1996a, 130–32). This view is developed and defended by Van Norden, who says the Mohists believe "the structure of human motivations and dispositions is highly malleable" (2007, 195). This view has some basis, but we must distinguish basic motivational structures and specific contents or rules. The Mohists undoubtedly assume natural motivational structures, most of all response to rewards and punishments, but these structures are content neutral. That is, emulation and rewards can be used to induce a wide range of behaviors. Similarly, although we naturally enact what we think is right, our moral codes have no natural content.

44. Mòzǐ is presented as not motivated by rewards (49: 474–75; Johnston 2010, 49.14), and he expects this of his disciples (49: 478–79; Johnston 2010, 49.20). The *Zhuāngzǐ* says that the Mohists "used skins and rough fabric for clothing, wore simple sandals, and did not rest day or night, taking their own suffering to the ultimate" (33: 1077; Mair 1994, 337). The *Mèngzǐ* also criticizes the Mohists for excessive self-sacrifice (7A26). The *Lüshì chūnqiū* contains a story of a Mohist leader choosing to die with 180 disciples rather than flee a city he had committed to defend (19/3.4: 1266). But precisely because the early Mohists deny the problem of evil, they also avoid the question of sacrificing one's own benefit for the good. This element of self-sacrifice may have become more prominent for the later Mohists. For example, the "Canon" explains *rèn* 任, "duty or responsibility" (originally referring to bearing something on a shoulder pole) as "a scholar-official [*shì* 士] causing loss to himself in order to benefit what he does." This is further explained as "doing what one dislikes in order to complete what is urgent for other people" (40: 314, 337; cf. Johnston 2010, 40.A19).

45. Wáng Chōng gives the most specific analysis of the contradictions in the *Lúnyǔ* and *Mèngzǐ* when they are taken literally, primarily in his chapters "Questioning Kǒngzǐ" ("Wèn Kǒng" 問孔) and "Taking Jabs at Mèngzǐ" ("Cì Mèng" 刺孟). Many of the contradictions he points out are around fatalism—for example, that when Mèngzǐ leaves the state of Qí he lingers, hoping the king will change his mind (2B12), but when a minister persuades the Marquis of Lǔ not to come and see him, he attributes this to heaven and gives up immediately (1B16) (30: 455–57). Wáng Chōng also points out the tension between Kǒngzǐ's appeal to heaven's punishments (6.28) and his attribution of the death of Yán Huí to *mìng* (6.3) (28: 410–12), and between his claim that Zǐgòng does not accept *mìng* while allowing that Zǐgòng succeeds in increasing his wealth (11.19) (28: 418–19).

46. The Stoic philosopher Epictetus writes, "Some things are up to us and some are not up to us. Our opinions are up to us, and our impulses, desires, aversions—in short, whatever is our own doing. Our bodies are not up to us, nor are our possessions, our reputations, or our

public offices, or, that is, whatever is not our own doing.... If you think that only what is yours is yours, and that what is not your own is, just as it is, not your own, then no one will ever coerce you, no one will hinder you, you will blame no one, you will not accuse anyone, you will not do a single thing unwillingly, you will have no enemies, and no one will harm you, because you will not be harmed at all" (*Encheiridion* §1; Epictetus 1983, 11).

47. Van Norden puts this point well: "[A] virtuous person will not (unlike Western Stoics) strive to be unaffected by the evil and suffering of the world" (2007, 116). Olberding also is excellent on this point: "The capacity to experience intense grief is, in Confucius's view, a laudable trait that stems from our ability to recognize and honor the significance of others in a flourishing life" (2008, 139). Regarding Mèngzǐ, Yearley says that there are two limits on peace of mind: the desire for others to avoid suffering, and a concern about not being as cultivated as possible (1990, 160).

48. Slingerland takes this interpretation in an attempt to find a consistent theory of *mìng* in early Ru texts, writing, "*Mìng* refers to forces that lie in the outer realm—that is, the realm beyond the bounds of human endeavor, or the area of life in which 'seeking does not contribute to one's getting it.' This external world is not the concern of the gentleman, whose efforts are to be concentrated on the self—the inner realm in which 'seeking contributes to one's getting it'" (1996, 568). D. C. Lau also takes a fatalist reading: "Whether or not a man is going to end up with wealth, honour and long life is due to Destiny. No amount of effort on his part will make any difference to the outcome" (1979, 29).

49. The broad meaning for the phrase is shown by the range of translations: "was lost in thought for a moment" (Slingerland 2003); "with some frustration" (Rosemont and Ames 1998); "said ruefully" (Waley 1989).

50. The clearest example of this interpretation is Wú Jìn'ān 2003, 344–47. Csikszentmihalyi says explicitly that the Ru believed that some outcomes were determined by fate while others were not (2004, 39–41). Creel denies that Kǒngzǐ believes in fate but allows that later Ru may have. He takes Kǒngzǐ himself as using *mìng* to label things we have limited rather than no control over (1960, 120–21). Hall and Ames claim that "although *mìng* sets certain limitations on possible futures, none of the given factors are in any sense incontrovertible" (1987, 211).

51. Several passages in the *Lúnyǔ* express strong confidence that rulers can transform the people (e.g., 2.19, 2.20, 9.14, 12.18, 12.19, 13.4). A few passages express Kǒngzǐ's confidence that if he were employed, he could bring order to the world (13.10, 17.5). That he did not get a position, though, would have been due to heaven or fate.

52. Qīng dynasty commentator Liú Bǎonán explains this passage in a very Mohist way, concluding, "If they do not have punishments from superiors, then surely heaven will send disasters. If one can avoid these, it is only by luck" (1990, 335).

53. I follow the Chinese text in Cáo 2006, 173–92 (strips 2–3); cf. Mǎ 2005. Scott Cook takes the last line in a slightly different way: "They will not come to an end with your own self, but will reach to your descendants" (2010, 110).

54. For the connections between *Sān dé* and other texts, see Cook 2010 and Cáo 2006, 241–66.

55. For example, Wáng Chōng defines *fù* and *huò* as coming from luck (*xìng* 幸), explaining, "Its attainment is not from our own effort, so it is called fortune; its coming is not from myself, so it is called misfortune" (2: 10). Wáng Chōng takes *lù* to be a technical term for the prosperity or failure that is fated for us (6: 55). Regarding *suì*, the *Hánfēizǐ* explains it as when ghosts harm people by making them sick (20: 403), and the *Shuōwén* defines it as "misfortune from spirits" (*Shuōwén* 1a.16b; Duàn 1988, 8).

56. How one situates the Mohist *tiān* in relation to the categories of "God" and "nature" seems to be a product of how favorable one is to the Mohists and to theism. For one of the most

theistic readings, see Tseu 1965. For one of the most naturalistic, see Hansen 1992 (Hansen translates *tiān* consistently as "nature").

57. We can rely on Tseu on this point, since he is otherwise dedicated to showing the alignment of Mòzǐ with Christianity: "Any further relation such as revelation, contemplation, ecstasy, or some kind of physical commixture of natures is absolutely alien to him. This kept him strictly in the rank of philosophers without his entering the field of mysticism" (1965, 44).

58. Regarding disruptions of normal patterns, one extreme version lists the following disasters as punishments from heaven: cold and hot without restraint; snow, frost, rain, and dew without timeliness; the six animals not growing up; barren fields and pestilence; violent winds and bitter rains (12: 82; Johnston 2010, 12.7). The "Against Invasions III" chapter includes a long description of divine signs that accompanied the downfall of evil kings like Jié and Zhòu, including ghosts calling out, women becoming men, and heaven raining down flesh (19: 145–53; Johnston 2010, 19.5–7). These descriptions, though, are given to limit arguments for offensive wars in the name of something like "humanitarian intervention." The Mohists claim that such wars can only be justified by an extraordinary and undeniable wealth of divine signs. The point may be that in practice, such wars are not permissible. For a discussion of this argument that takes the role of divine signs more seriously, see Wong and Loy 2004.

59. In the "Gēng Zhù" (耕柱) chapter, Mòzǐ argues that ghosts and spirits are more knowing than sages, and he uses the accuracy of an ancient divination to support it (46: 422–26; Johnston 2010, 46.2). Scott Lowe takes this as showing that the *Mòzǐ* "places great faith in imperial oracles as a method for communing with the ghosts and spirits" (1992, 165). The point of the passage, though, is not about oracles but that spirits have awareness, and there is no other evidence that the Mohists appealed to divination as a valid source of knowledge.

60. Based on an analysis of excavated "Day books" (*rìshū* 日書), Poo writes: "[G]ods, ghosts, and demons in the daybooks did not act as arbiters of morality and ethics. They were not part of the mores, i.e., moral standards and behavior of the people using such handbooks. Their actions were therefore not responses to human behavior but expressions of extra-human intention, for good or for ill" (1998, 82).

61. The claim that sacrifices should be done even if ghosts and spirits do not care (or exist) is argued explicitly in the *Xúnzǐ* (19: 376–77; Knoblock 1988, 19.11). Although some Mohists may have held the same position, a passage in the "Gōng Mèng" chapter argues that if the spirits did not exist, then the sacrifices would not be justified, comparable to making a fishnet when there were no fish (48: 457; Johnston 2010, 48.9).

62. This line is ambiguous and could be read as saying they are very far from humaneness and rightness, which is how Johnston (2010, 243) and Ivanhoe (Ivanhoe and Van Norden 2005, 94) translate it. That is possible, but the passage emphasizes the diversity of opinions rather than the fact that no one is correct. Watson translates it as I have (1967, 83).

63. One passage says that the sagely king Yǔ modeled himself on heaven (*Lúnyǔ* 8.19), and in another Kǒngzǐ compares his wish to give up speaking to heaven, which orders the cosmos without issuing commands (*Lúnyǔ* 19.19). Both refer to the power and subtlety of heaven's influence, not to following concrete patterns of nature.

64. For example, a passage in the "Against Ru" chapter begins with a Ru claim that gentlemen must follow the ancients and then responds that what the ancients did was new when they did it. Thus it seems the ancients themselves were not gentlemen (see Puett 2001, 42–51). Kǒngzǐ's claim to transmit but not make is also explicitly criticized (46: 434–35; Johnston 2010, 46.17).

65. Behuniak emphasizes that every enactment of tradition occurs in a new situation and thus has a kind of singularity or uniqueness (2008). Tan emphasizes the creativity and critical thinking required in applying a tradition (2008). Neither argues that Kǒngzǐ radically al-

ters tradition, but rather that tradition itself requires uniqueness and creativity. Both develop points out of Hall and Ames, who argue that creativity must be understood as ways of adopting and transforming experience and tradition rather than as a kind of creation ex nihilo (see Hall and Ames 1987, 16–17, 78).

66. Loy Hui-chieh writes, "[O]ne important aspect of upholding Heaven's will as a standard for right conduct is that the standard becomes public and impersonal and to that extent objective." This serves the need to "give *publicly assessable* reasons" (2008, 463). Fraser points out that the Mohist state of nature implies that people consider *yì* (rightness), to be "a public, objective standard of conduct to which everyone should conform, not only themselves" (2008, 441). For a negative view of this universalizing tendency, see Dīng Wèixiáng's argument that the Mohists objectify and standardize human beings in a way that tends toward totalitarianism (2008, 411–15).

67. Although the status of this chapter of the *Mòzǐ* is unclear, this passage itself is consistent with positions in the core chapters, at least on this point.

68. Flanagan gives a more specific twist on this passage, as claiming that in the current condition of society, emulation cannot play a fundamental role because the number of positive role models is too limited. Thus, he takes this as a criticism of the Ru reliance on emulation (2008).

69. The Socrates of the early dialogues might not say such things, and the relationship between the divine and the conventional in Plato's works is more nuanced than can be conveyed here. Nonetheless, consider the *Symposium,* in which Diotima begins by telling Socrates, "But how would it be, in our view, if someone got to see the Beautiful itself, absolute, pure, unmixed, not polluted by human flesh or colors or any other great nonsense of mortality, but if he could see the Beauty itself in its one form? . . . [I]n that life alone, when he looks at Beauty in the only way that Beauty can be seen—only then will it become possible for him to give birth not to images of virtue (because he's in touch with no images), but to true virtue (because he is in touch with the true Beauty)" (*Symposium,* 211e–212a; translation from Cooper 1997, 494).

70. Heidegger explains, "*Veritas* as *adaequatio rei ad intellectum* does not imply the later transcendental conception of Kant—possible only on the basis of the subjectivity of man's essence—that 'objects conform to our knowledge.' Rather, it implies the Christian theological belief that, with respect to what it is and whether it is, a matter, as created (*ens creatum*), *is* only insofar as it corresponds to the idea preconceived in the *intellectus divinus*, i.e., in the mind of God, and thus measures up to the idea (is correct) and in this sense is 'true'" ("On the Essence of Truth"; translation from Heidegger 1993, 118).

71. Even Tseu, set on constructing a Christian *Mòzǐ*, says that *tiān* meets all the necessary criteria for God but one: that God is "the reason for the correspondence between things and human thought" (1965, 89–90).

72. *Meditations on First Philosophy*, Meditation 6; translation from Cottingham, Stoothoff, and Murdoch 1985, 57.

73. For a fuller direct discussion of these issues in the context of the conflict between Mèngzǐ and Mòzǐ, see Perkins 2011a.

74. The term *yì* 義 is the term translated so far as "rightness," in which case the Mohist claim is that in a state of nature, each person has their own moral code. The same character, though, is sometimes written in the *Mòzǐ* in place of *yí* 儀 (36: 273), which the *Shuōwén* defines as a standard or measure, *dù* 度 (*Shuōwén* 8a.21a; Duàn 1988, 375). Thus, it is possible that the conflict in a state of nature comes from the lack of a clear standard—which would include, but go beyond, morality. Fraser explains the likely sense of *yì* here as "a norm or code representing what one considers proper" (2008, 441). Johnston translates it as "principles" (2010, 11.1),

Watson as "views" (1967, 34), and Ivanhoe as "norm for deciding what was right and wrong" (Ivanhoe and Van Norden 2005, 65).

75. Fraser points out that in a condition in which norms are not shared, there would be no way to even agree on taking heaven as a norm (Fraser 2008, 453n30).

76. If everyone disagrees, it is difficult to see how a worthy leader could end up in control, and the Mohists themselves seem unsure. The first two versions say that the worthy and able were selected, but do not give the subject that does the selecting (11: 75; 12: 78; Johnston 2010, 11.2, 12.2). The third version expands to say, "The world wanted to unify the world's standards, and thus selected the most worthy and established him as son of heaven" (13: 91; Johnston 2010, 13.3). The "world" is literally tiānxià 天下 (all under heaven), which can refer to all the people, but Sūn Yíràng suggests the subject may originally have simply been heaven, tiān 天 (2001, 91). That is supported by a line in the second version of the chapter, which explains an ancient quote as claiming that Shàngdì and the ghosts and spirits set up states and rulers for the people (12: 86; Johnston 2010, 12.9); a passage on heaven ordering nature for human benefit also says that heaven established rulers for the people (27: 202–204; Johnston 2010, 27.6). For an argument that the people set up the ruler, see Hansen 1992, 131; for an argument that heaven selects the ruler, see Van Norden 2007, 164–66.

77. For a discussion of these terms, see Hui-chieh Loy 2008, 456–57.

78. The meaning of míng 明 here is ambiguous. My translation follows its association with the impartial illumination of the sun and moon. Watson translates it as "enlightens" (1967, 82) and Ivanhoe as "sheds light upon" (Ivanhoe and Van Norden 2005, 93). The same term, however, is used for the discernment of heaven and ghosts in rewarding and punishing, so Johnston translates it as "completely understands them" (2010, 239niii). It is likely both senses are intended.

79. Similar references to spirits accepting sacrifices appear in other texts. In Lúnyǔ 6.6, Kǒngzǐ ties it to impartiality, referring to spirits accepting the sacrifice of a good ox whose parents would not have been suitable. The point is about accepting a good person in spite of an improper family background. The Mèngzǐ explains the legitimacy of Shùn taking the throne from Yáo in part by the fact that spirits accepted his sacrifices (5A5).

80. Johnston translates shízhī as "provides food for them all" (see Johnston 2010, 267ni). That would help my overall interpretation, but makes the transition into the next sentence on sacrificing difficult to understand. Watson and Ivanhoe both take it as referring to accepting sacrifices (Watson 1967, 82; Ivanhoe and Van Norden 2005, 93).

81. Puett interprets the Mohist argument this way, saying of heaven, "[I]f he accepts sacrifices from all, he will send down blessings to all" (2002, 104).

82. I follow Sūn Yíràng in taking dé as xī 息. Another possibility is that dé 德 (virtue) should be dé 得 (to attain), meaning that heaven extends generously without seeking gain. Johnston takes dé as virtue and translates the phrase as "without considering itself virtuous" (2010, 4.3). The passage is not in the core chapters of the Mòzǐ and may reflect Daoist influences.

83. Hansen brings out this point well: "[W]hen Mozi brings tian[nature:heaven] into the justification phase of his argument, it is to exploit nature's associations with constancy, reliability, objectivity, and fairness" (1992, 100).

84. According to Hú Shì, Huì Shī gave the doctrine of inclusive caring "a scientific-philosophical foundation." He explains: "'Care overflowingly for all the myriad things' is the extreme limit of the doctrine of inclusive caring. Mòzǐ's doctrine of inclusive care was based on the 'will of heaven.' Reaching a later time when thought was more developed and religious superstitions weakened, the foundation of Mozi's religious doctrine of inclusive caring had to follow these changes and be reformed" (2003, 179).

85. Although the point of the passage is clear, its details are not. My translation follows the interpretation of Cáo Jǐnyán (Mǎ 2005, 316–20); for an alternate version, see Liào 2006. For an English translation and discussion, see Brindley 2010.

86. Brindley translates *míng* as "perspicuity" and explains, "All three aspects of vision, moral knowledge, and compensatory action are thus linked, as though the very act of seeing something entails them all" (2010, 220).

87. See Brindley 2010 and Lǐ Ruì 2009.

88. While I agree with Brindley 2010 that we must be cautious in placing the text in a particular school, I do not think the text diverges from the dialogue chapters of the *Mòzǐ* as much as Brindley argues (Lǐ Ruì 2009 is even more extreme on this point). Brindley claims that the *Guǐshén zhī míng* differs from the *Mòzǐ* in "showing that humans sometimes neither deserve nor can be blamed for what happens to them" (2010, 227), but the story of Mòzǐ's illness in the "Gōng Mèng" chapter shows exactly that Mòzǐ's illness is not blamed on his own actions.

89. The Mohists see this point, as they use it in an attempt to persuade Prince Wén not to invade the state of Zhèng (49: 468–69; Johnston 2010, 49.4). The prince claims that since the people of Zhèng killed their own sovereign, they are being punished by heaven and thus an invasion would follow heaven's will. Mòzǐ gives an analogy—imagine a neighbor's son misbehaves and is punished by his father. Afterward, you go over yourself and beat the son some more, claiming to be following the father's will. Mòzǐ concludes that the punishment given by heaven is sufficient itself and needs no assistance. This argument could easily come from the *Dàodéjīng*, and it logically would apply to all punishments. The fact that the Mohists do not make such an argument again shows their focus on inducing certain actions rather than building coherent theory.

90. For a discussion of this point, see Chen Ning 1997c, 158–59.

91. The Mohist view has interesting similarities to the interpretation of Robert Eno, who writes, "There is a sense here that the decree [*mìng*] that determines the failure of the Ruist political mission almost frees the Ruist, extricating him from the toils of political responsibilities and allowing him to retire, at least partially, into the pure ritual practice of the Ruist community" (1990a, 92–93).

92. The saying appears also in 39: 296–97 (Johnston 2010, 39.8). The saying is found in several Ru texts, appearing in the "Record on Learning" ("Xué jì" 學記) chapter of the *Lǐ jì* (Sūn Xīdàn 1988, 969) and in the *Xìng zì mìng chū* (Liú Zhāo 2003, 5), although it is used differently in both cases (see Lǐ Tiānhóng 2003, 140). This principle might be implicit in Mèngzǐ's attempt to justify his role in Qí's invasion of Yān (*Mèngzǐ* 2B8). An official of Qí asks Mèngzǐ if Yān can be invaded and Mèngzǐ answers that it can. When later accused of sanctioning Qí's invasion, Mèngzǐ explains that if he had been asked if the state of Qí could invade Yān, he would have said no, that only a worthy king could do so. But this was not the question. Mèngzǐ's explanation seems weak and odd, but it would make more sense if it implicitly invoked an established policy of answering questions according only to what is asked.

93. Although defending the Ru conception of *mìng*, Slingerland acknowledges this point: "This awe [of *mìng*] is, however, rather passive in the sense that it pertains to something beyond the realm of human agency. Just as one should 'show reverence for ghosts and spirits but keep them at a distance,' one should maintain a healthy respect for the power of *mìng* while nonetheless concentrating on the task at hand—self-cultivation" (1996, 573).

94. A. C. Graham puts the point nicely: "But there is little evidence of a spiritual dimension deeper than a guilty fear of ghosts. The Mohists are in a sense *less* religious than some they would denounce as sceptics. The awe and resignation with which thinkers as far apart as Confucius and Zhuāngzǐ accept the decree of Heaven has much more of a sense of the holy than anything in *Mòzǐ*" (1989, 48).

95. The need to read Mohist doctrines functionally was recognized as least as early as Y. P. Mei, who argues that the coherence of Mohist views is on the level of values, so that one must look not only at their claims about what exists but more importantly at how those claims function (Mei 1934, 151–56). Hansen places particular emphasis on this point (1992, 143–48). For the activist context of Mohist arguments, see Robins 2008 and Hui-chieh Loy 2008. In contrast, Van Norden argues that the Mohists see truth as aligning perfectly with their activist goals, so that the *Mòzǐ* can be read as giving arguments about objective truths (2007, 151–61). He admits, however, that such a reading makes the *Mòzǐ* neither convincing nor inspiring (2007, 197).

96. There are some differences in terms and content between the three versions, particularly in the second chapter, which includes the will of heaven as a criterion and does not mention the eyes and ears of the people. For a discussion of these criteria, see Hui-chieh Loy 2008.

97. Van Norden makes an intriguing argument that the divergence between what is true and what is beneficial to believe follows only from naturalistic assumptions about the world, and that since the Mohists believe heaven is good, it makes sense that they would assume heaven has made the world such that whatever is true is beneficial to believe (2007, 160–61, 375). The implausibility of such a view is perhaps clearest if we consider that what is most beneficial to believe varies by context—in one situation it might be most beneficial to believe there is no fate (e.g., before one acts), but in another it might be most beneficial to believe that failure was fated (e.g., after one fails). Of course, one might argue that it is never beneficial to believe something that is false, but this would make the criteria of use redundant.

98. My interpretation follows that of Chris Fraser: "We might say that the Mohists are applying a very basic, primitive conception of correctness, of which truth, obligation, permissibility, and other notions are species. The crucial point is probably that their main theoretical focus is not descriptive truth, but the proper *dào* (way) by which to guide social and personal life. (2010). Hui-chieh Loy similarly says that these criteria are meant to evaluate "a doctrine that *correctly guides human conduct*, rather than, for instance, a claim that *fits the facts*" (2008, 457). See also Hansen 1992, 143–46.

99. My view here is close to that of Hansen 1992, 143–46.

100. LaFargue makes a helpful comparison to our use of aphorisms, where we might make contradictory claims in different circumstances, depending on our purposes (1998, 263–67). One example he gives are the aphorisms "better safe than sorry," and "nothing ventured, nothing gained." LaFargue argues that we should read statements in the *Dàodéjīng* like we would read aphorisms, but his point applies more generally to early Chinese philosophy. For an excellent account of the maintenance of contradictory positions as a general type of "practical" religious view, see Yearley 1988.

101. *Phaedrus* 275e (translation from Cooper 1997, 552). In "Plato's Pharmacy," Derrida brings out many of subtleties and ironies of this criticism of writing (1981, 61–171).

102. A passage from the "Record on Learning" chapter of the *Lǐ jì* captures this point well: "Those who learn have four errors and those who teach must know them. Of people who study, some err in being excessive, some err in being deficient, some err in changing and some err in stopping. In these four, the hearts are not the same. If you know their hearts, then you can rescue them from their errors" (Sūn Xīdàn 1988, 967). Teaching requires knowing the heart of the student, but such knowledge is only possible through close personal contact.

103. For the discussion of Mòzǐ travelling with many books, see 47: 445 (Johnston 2010, 47.13). A note to the *Wén xuǎn* 文選 quotes the *Mòzǐ* as saying Mòzǐ presented books to King Huì of Chǔ and the king praised them, but the line is not in the received version of the *Mòzǐ*. Bì Yuán argues they were cut from a passage in the "Honoring Rightness" ("Guì yì" 貴義) chapter (Sūn Yíràng 2001, 440). Edward Shaughnessy has an excellent discussion of the formation and organization of "books" based on his study of excavated texts. While not saying when the

widespread circulation of texts on bamboos strips began, he does argue that at least the *Shī jīng* had something near its definitive contents "no later than the fourth or even the fifth century BC" (2006, 55).

104. Similar claims are made in many chapters, which usually present writing as the attempt to transmit views to later generations (e.g., 16: 120–21; Johnston 2010, 16.9). Eno points out that while the Ru quote bits of classic texts orally, the *Mòzǐ* includes longer passages suggesting a basis in written sources (1990a, 57).

3. Efficacy and Following Nature in the *Dàodéjīng*

1. Ivanhoe nicely calls these editors "cobblers" (1999, 253).
2. The Mǎwángduī materials were buried in 168 BCE, but since the A manuscript follows no Hàn dynasty taboos on characters, it is assumed to have been copied before 195.
3. Although all the consistent themes in the received text are found at least once in the Guōdiàn materials, some are emphasized more or less. The two most relevant divergences are that the Guōdiàn materials have less explicit criticism of Ru and Mohist terms such as humaneness and rightness, and they have less focus on the "way of heaven." Henricks has a good list of differences in content between the Guōdiàn and received versions of the text (2000, 17–19). See also Allan and Williams 2000, 154–58; and Moeller 2007, 191–93.
4. The Guōdiàn materials tell us nothing conclusive about the remaining two-thirds of the received text. The Guōdiàn strips may represent something like a complete text to which other materials were added, but it is also possible that the Guōdiàn materials are selections from something closer to the full received version. For a discussion of various possibilities, see Allan and Williams 2000, 142–46, and Henricks 2000, 19–22. I generally quote from the earliest version available, which is the Mǎwángduī version, unless otherwise noted. Where differences between the versions are relevant, I will discuss them explicitly.
5. Based on Guōdiàn A, strips 35–37.
6. Thus, the Mǎwángduī manuscripts use *jué* 爵 instead of *mìng*; chapter 32 makes the same point but uses *lìng* 令 instead of *mìng*. The Guōdiàn manuscript has an additional use of *mìng* as "command," which was replaced by *lìng* in later texts (19). These changes suggest that *mìng* was not taken as a technical term.
7. The first line is taken from Guōdiàn A, strip 1. The rest of the passage is missing in Guōdiàn. The first line of the Mǎwángduī text has the strange phrase "heavenly things" (*tiānwù* 天物) rather than "way of heaven."
8. Thus, Moss Roberts translates the phrase as "returning life" (2001, 64). Héshànggōng explains it as returning to one's nature-and-allotment (*xìngmìng* 性命) in order to avoid death (Wáng Kǎ 1997, 63). Many Chinese commentators, from Wáng Bì to Chén Gǔyìng, take *mìng* to refer to the basis of one's nature, either as *xìngmìng* or *běnxìng* 本性, which is then taken either as emptiness or spontaneous generativity. Chén Gǔyìng has a good selection of commentaries on this (1988, 126–27). The phrase *fùmìng* is commonly used for reporting back to a superior after an assignment, but it is difficult to see how it could have that meaning here (see LaFargue 1992, 63). The phrase appears once in the "Zéyáng" chapter of the *Zhuāngzǐ*, where it is associated with one's nature (*xìng*) and with acting spontaneously (25: 880; Mair 1994, 255). For commentaries on the phrase in the *Zhuāngzǐ*, see Guō Qìngfān 1978, 881.
9. *Cháng* appears in nineteen chapters of the Wáng Bì text; the Mǎwángduī text adds *héng* to chapters 2 and 67. In the Guōdiàn materials, *héng* appears in four chapters and *cháng* in one. The Mǎwángduī and Guōdiàn versions use both *héng* and *cháng*. In the received versions of the

text, *héng* was changed to *cháng* to avoid using Emperor Wén of Hàn's name, Liú Héng 劉恆. According to Liú Xiàogǎn, there is no difference in meaning, but *cháng* is used as a noun while *héng* is used as a modifier. Because of this use, Liú takes *cháng* to be a technical concept (2006, 514–15). "*Héng*," however, is used as a noun and a technical term in the *Héng xiān* text discussed below.

10. After listing the interdependence of various opposites in chapter 2, the Mǎwángduī text then comments that, these "are constant" (héngyě 恆也). This comment is missing, however, in other versions, including the Guōdiàn materials.

11. For *Sān dé*, see Mǎ 2005, strips 1–2. The "Péng Zǔ" text refers to the "constancy of the Dì" (Jì 2005, strip 1).

12. The hexagram judgment itself was written down by the late fourth century and is found in the Shanghai Museum bamboo text (Jì 2005, strips 28–29). It is difficult to know when the line commentary was written.

13. The "Jiě Lǎo" chapter of the *Hánfēizǐ*, which is the earliest extant explanation of this passage, takes it as referring to the four limbs and nine orifices, which enable us to live but also make us vulnerable to death (20: 416). Héshànggōng follows the same interpretation (Wáng Kǎ 1997, 192), but Wáng Bì takes it as three out of ten (Lóu 1999, 135). Moeller takes it as thirteen and gives a plausible explanation for this meaning (2007, 118). If the passage is read as saying "thirteen," then its focus on control over the length of our lives is even more apparent.

14. Jiǎng Xíchāng 蔣錫昌 explains the "disciples of death" with the same term Kǒngzǐ used in reference to Yán Huí (*Lúnyǔ* 6.3): "They belong to those with a short *mìng* (Chén Gǔyìng 1988, 258).

15. Wáng Bì writes, "If one follows along [*shùn* 順] then there is good fortune and if one goes against [*nì* 逆] there is misfortune—this is not speaking but being good at responding" (Lóu 1999, 182). Héshànggōng says, "Although the way of heaven is broad and extensive, it is good in planning and considering human affairs, whether cultivating good or enacting bad, each receives his repayment" (Wáng Kǎ 1997, 283).

16. LaFargue takes the lines on not knowing heaven's hates as a "criticism of confidence in predictability," but he takes the final lines as saying that "in the long run no one gets away with anything" (1992, 127).

17. Wáng Bì takes a different approach: "Who can know the intentions of heaven? Only a sagely person" (Lóu 1999, 182). His point is that it is difficult, but not impossible, to know what heaven hates.

18. Moeller reads the passage in this way: "The indifference or equanimity in the face of good and bad luck acknowledges the equal validity of two necessary events or stages. They equally contribute to a cycle of change, and it would be terribly one-sided to attach one's feelings to one stage at the expense of the other" (2006, 100).

19. Both the *Hánfēizǐ* and the *Héshànggōng* commentary give practical causal explanations for this alternation—one who is in trouble strives for self-improvement, leading to eventual success, while one with good fortune becomes lazy and arrogant, leading to future disaster. The *Hánfēizǐ* leaves out the phrase "it is without correctness" (20: 286–390), whereas Héshànggōng takes the phrase as a hypothetical—"if the ruler has no correctness" (Wáng Kǎ 1997, 226).

20. Wáng Bì answers the question, saying that the ultimate is the government that cannot be recognized (Lóu 1999, 152). Liú Xiàogǎn takes the question as emphasizing only the difficulty of knowing the limit (2006, 567).

21. For example, Chén Gǔyìng takes *zhèng* as "fixed standard" (*dìngzhǔn* 定准). For similar readings, see Chén Gǔyìng 1988, 290.

22. Both of these passages, as well as the previous passage that mentions "what heaven hates," are missing in the Guōdiàn materials, which do not include the last fifteen chapters

of the received text. In those chapters, heaven is noticeably more central and more anthropomorphic, and the term *dào* is not used to describe an element of nature. Henricks plausibly suggests the last set of chapters may have a different origin (Henricks 2000, 18). I suspect these chapters represent a different faction of "Laoists," who maintained a more anthropomorphic view of heaven. Even if the original authors of these last chapters intended them to be taken anthropomorphically, it is likely that the *composers* of the text as a whole did not take them that way. At the same time, these passages introduce a basic tension around anthropomorphism in the *Dàodéjīng*, a tension that is reflected in the divergent ways the text is taken up in "philosophical" and "religious" Daoism.

23. It should be noted that these initial lines are missing in the Guōdiàn text, as is another passage which presents *rén* as a stage of decline. In general, explicit criticisms of the Ru are less pronounced in the Guōdiàn materials than in later versions.

24. The earliest extant commentaries follow this interpretation. Wáng Bì says, "Heaven and earth rely on what is so of itself (*zìrán*), without acting and without creating, so the myriad things are ordered of themselves. Thus they are not humane" (Lóu 1999, 13). Héshànggōng says, "Sagely people care for and nourish the myriad people not by using humaneness and kindness but by modeling heaven and earth to enact what is so of itself (*zìrán*)" (Wáng Kǎ 1997, 18). Ames and Hall emphasize this interpretation, translating *bùrén* here as "not partial to institutionalized morality." They add, though, that this passage also is meant to strike a blow against "human exceptionalism" (2003, 84–85).

25. Chén Gǔyìng comments on this passage, "Heaven and earth have nothing toward which they have partial care," Sū Zhé says, "Heaven and earth are without partial concerns [*sī* 私]," and Gāo Hēng says, "Not humane just is without anything toward which it has familial attachment or care" (Chén Gǔyìng 1988, 78–79). Roberts emphasizes this connection by translating *rén* here as "kin-kindness."

26. For a discussion of the significance of the variants for the character *rén*, see Páng 2005, 94–100; and Liáng 2008, 61–68. Liáng argues that the two forms bring out two dimensions of *rén*, one toward human relations and the other toward cultivation of the body/self.

27. Moeller makes this point in several places, but see in particular the chapter "'Without the Impulses of Man': A Daoist Critique of Humanism" (2006, 133–45).

28. The "Restraining Expenses" chapters discuss the origins of food, clothing, weapons, and buildings. Chapter 6 ("Renouncing Excess" ["*Cíguò*" 辭過]) repeats the same points but with more description of the original condition of human beings. Each of the "Conforming Upward" chapters begins with the emergence of political order from a state of nature. For an analysis of the origin stories in the *Mòzǐ* and *Mèngzǐ*, see Puett 2001, 105–12.

29. This passage is translated based on Guōdiàn A, strips 21–22. It is the only chapter in the Guōdiàn materials that clearly describes *dào* as part of nature rather than as a way of living.

30. While differing in structure and details, the *Dàodéjīng*, *Tàiyī shēng shuǐ*, and *Héng xiān*, all share a basic logic of deriving diversity spontaneously from simplicity. The *Yǔ cóng* I shows similar cosmogonic concerns, including a claim that each thing is generated from non-being or lack (*wú* 無), but it gives a simpler account taking heaven as the foundation (Liú Zhāo 2003, strips 104).

31. Another Guōdiàn text, *Zūn dé yì* 尊德義 (Honoring virtue and rightness) mentions the human *dào* in a list with the *dào* of water (guiding flood control), the *dào* of horses (for charioteering), and the *dào* of the earth (for farming) (Liú Zhāo 2003, strips 5–8). It gives priority to the human *dào* as what is closest. Some take the four *dào* in the *Xìng zì mìng chū* as referring to these four (e.g., Chén Lái 2009c, 54). *Zūn dé yì*, however, does not say there are four *dào* and in fact says that there is nothing which does not have a *dào*. The four listed seem to just

be examples. For various interpretations of this passage and the other possible *dàos*, see Lǐ Tiānhóng 2003, 147–49.

32. The *Xúnzǐ* also distinguishes the human way from the way of heaven and way of earth (8: 122; Knoblock 1988, 8.3).

33. My account here draws on the excellent discussion of how to reconcile the two senses of *dào* in Robins 2011a.

34. Hans-Georg Moeller nicely captures this double sense in taking *dào* as "a structure or order of efficacy." Moeller explains, "The Dao of the *Laozi* seems to be the 'way' (this is the literal meaning of the word) that processes (or mechanisms or organisms or things) function when they function well. The images show that this model of efficacy is not limited to any particular realm. It is applicable to nature or the cosmos as well as to social or political issues. It applies to agriculture, government, and also artisanship" (2006, 20).

35. Graham says that although European philosophers, with their focus on truth, naturally think to call the ultimate "Reality," Chinese philosophers, with their focus on practice, just as naturally labeled the ultimate as "the way" (1989, 222).

36. Heaven is paired with earth in eight chapters of the Mǎwángduī manuscript (1, 5, 6, 7, 23, 25, 32, 39), three of which are in the Guōdiàn materials. In contrast, *tiān* does not appear paired with *dì* at all in the *Lúnyǔ*, only twice in the *Mèngzǐ* (2A2, 7A13), and only once in the core chapters of the *Mòzǐ* (19: 141; Johnston 2010, 19.2). Aside from the *Dàodéjīng* and "Great Unity Generates Water," *tiān* and *dì* are paired only three times in the Guōdiàn texts, one of which takes them to refer to spirits (*Táng Yú zhī dào* Liú Zhāo 2003, strip 14), while another seems to subordinate earth to heaven (*Yǔ cóng* I; Liú Zhāo 2003, strip 12). Zhōng xìn zhī dào 忠信之道 (The way of loyalty and sincerity) associates earth with great loyalty and heaven with great sincerity (Liú Zhāo 2003, strips 4–5).

37. Jì 2005, strip 4. The *Huáinánzǐ* says that clear and bright (*yáng*) *qì* spreads and becomes heaven, while heavy and turbid *qì* settles and becomes earth (Hé Níng 1998, 3: 166; Major et. al. 2010, 3.1).

38. For a thorough discussion of *qì* taking into account recently excavated texts, see Csikszentmihalyi 2004, 144–60. For other helpful discussions of *qì*, see Behuniak 2004, 1–21; Wang 2012, 59–62; Shun 1997, 67–68; and Yearley 1990, 152–57.

39. This displacement of *tiān* may shift not only away from *anthropomorphic* conceptions of the divine but also from *masculine* conceptions. Roberts places particular emphasis on this point, writing that "The Dao De Jing presents a universal cosmic mother to replace the dead hand of paternal ancestral direction" (2001, 10). Henricks and Kaltenmark both suggest that the *Dàodéjīng* may be drawing on earlier traditions of feminine divinity (Henricks 2008, 38; Kaltenmark 1969, 59–60).

40. D. C. Lau, Wing-tsit Chan, and Robert Henricks use "virtue," Chad Hansen uses "virtuosity," and Victor Mair uses "integrity." Hans-Georg Moeller uses "efficacy," and Ames and Hall sometimes use "efficacious," but more often use "potency." Waley translates it as "power." For discussions of *dé* in the *Dàodéjīng*, see Ames 1998; Ivanhoe 1999; and Kaltenmark 1969, 27–28. For a broader discussion of *dé*, see Chén Lái 2009a, 316–38.

41. This meaning of character probably preceded the sense of being specifically good. For lists of passages using *dé* as a morally neutral quality of a person's actions, see Chen Ning 1997c, 147–48; and Chén Lái 2009a, 317–18.

42. For a discussion of this point and passage, see Chén Lái 2009a, 333–334. See also the *Liù dé* 六德 (Six virtues) Guōdiàn text.

43. See Chén Lái 2009a, 334–35.

44. Translation based on Guōdiàn A, strips 2–5.

45. Both interpretations are common, but the most consistent and explicit account of contentment as the highest good is LaFargue 1992; for mystical experience, the best account is Roth 1998, 59–96.

46. LaFargue writes, "Among my own attempts to spell out explicitly the single thing that Laoists value most, forming the basis for the Laoist perspective on the world, the concept I have found most satisfactory overall is that of 'organic harmony'" (LaFargue 1992, 239). Liú Xiàogǎn says, "The highest value—that Lǎozǐ both seeks and venerates—is naturalness [zìrán]. Naturalness thus serves as the core value of Lǎozǐ's philosophical system, while wúwéi is the basic method or principle for action he recommends to realize or pursue this value" (1999, 215). This view is developed and defended in Liú Xiàogǎn 2006.

47. It must be admitted that some passages justify this concern for the people as a means rather than an end. For example, in chapter 66, which we have already seen, the *goal* is to be above and in front of the people, to have the people happily promote them and not contend. The *means* is not to burden or harm the people. Wáng Bì frequently emphasizes this connection (see for example, his comments on chapters 66 (Lóu 1999, 179), 29 (Lóu 1999, 71), and 49 (Lóu 1999, 129). It is thus possible to read *all* passages on concern for the people as intended toward securing the power of the ruler.

48. The one possible exception is chapter 64, which says sagely people "assist the self-so-ing of the myriad things." This passage is discussed below.

49. My account here is close to Wing-tsit Chan, who emphasizes the *Dàodéjīng*'s break from anthropomorphism but adds that it is still centered on human concerns (1963b, 10). Schwartz also speaks of its "strong 'humanistic' concern," although he sees this as in contradiction with the bulk of the text (1985, 211, 204). Liú Xiàogǎn articulates "humanistic naturalism" (*rénwén zìrán* 人文自然) as a central concept in the *Dàodéjīng* (2006, 46–61), and Chén Gǔyìng has argued for a "humanistic spirit" (*rénwén jīngshén* 人文精神) in Daoism (2013).

50. The most consistent skeptical reading of the *Dàodéjīng* is Hansen 1992, 196–230. Van Norden also reads it as skeptical of all language and discursive knowledge (but not all values) (1999, 195). Robinet points out that while classical Chinese commentators mention the limits of language, none take the text as making the broad claim that "one must distrust language" (1999, 141).

51. Schwartz makes this distinction: "[T]he Lao-tzu book while not casting doubt on the language which describes the natural order (although it does indeed cast doubt on the received language descriptive of the human order) finds that that which makes the determinate *dào* possible lies beyond all language" (1985, 197). The claim that the *Dàodéjīng* advocates skepticism of language depends largely on ignoring this distinction.

52. Schwartz takes the *Dàodéjīng* as contradictory on this point, claiming that while its mysticism "points to a realm 'beyond good and evil,'" "Lao-tzu had not entirely freed himself from 'value judgement'" (1985, 204, 213). Csikszentmihalyi claims that readings of the text as unifying good and bad only arise with Sòng dynasty commentators (Csikszentmihalyi 1999, 47–48).

53. Schwartz claims that since sages identify with non-being, they are able to accept the troubles of life with complete equanimity (1985, 206). Although Moeller generally emphasizes the *Dàodéjīng* as a manual for successful action, he also claims that sages attain indifference to good and bad fortune (2006, 100, 105–110). The most thorough attempt to read the text as focused on internal contentment rather than external success is LaFargue, who describes claims for efficacy as "exaggerated and utopian imagery" extrapolated from the fact that the way wonderfully solves "the *main* life problem, the problem of meaning" (1992, 221–22). Ames and Hall suggest a similar view in taking the main purpose of the text as teaching "the fullest appreciation of those specific things and events that constitute one's field of experience" (2003, 11). While a concern for meaning and appreciation may fit the more elite perspective of the

Zhuāngzǐ, I think such questions would have been foreign to the *Dàodéjīng* and the vast majority of people from the time, for whom "the *main* life problem" would have been staying alive.

54. For examples of the difficulty of reading the text in this way, see LaFargue's reading of the claim in chapter 7 that sagely people complete their partial concerns (*chéng qí sī* 成其私), as "perfecting one's character through self-cultivation" (7), or his taking the usefulness (*yòng* 用) of the way as referring to "a concrete sense of personal satisfaction in one's own being" (45) (1992, 23 and 13, respectively).

55. The received versions of this chapter vary widely, but I follow the Mǎwángduī version, which is oldest and which I think makes the most sense. These lines are discussed further below.

56. This is a common way to read the criticisms of virtues in the *Dàodéjīng*. See Chén Gǔyìng 1988, 135; and Liú Xiàogǎn 2006, 398–99 for examples.

57. Henricks emphasizes this connection: "But the maternal nature of the Dao is seen not only in the fact that it gives birth to all phenomenal things; that being done, it continues to feed and nourish each of the ten thousand things; it has no favorites. And it does this in a totally selfless way; it claims no credit for what it has done, and it does not try to own or control the things that it helps develop" (1999, 163).

58. I have followed the received text, but the Mǎwángduī version has "has struggle" (*yǒuzhēng* 有爭) instead of "do not struggle" (*bùzhēng* 不爭). Thus, Moeller translates it as "when there is contention, takes on the place that the masses detest." Others take *yǒu* 有 as *yòu* 又, so Ames and Hall translate it thus: "Yet vies to dwell in places loathed by the crowd." Neither alternative seems very plausible, though, since the final line says that it is only by not contending that one has no disasters. For a discussion of other possibilities and an argument for following the received text, see Liú Xiàogǎn 2006, 148.

59. Although they do not discuss *shēng*, Parkes 1983 and Ames 1983 both discuss the possible link between *dé* and Nietzsche's will to power.

60. Jì Xùshēng comments thus on the line: "Disorder was produced because human beings did not follow the laws of nature" (2005, 201).

61. Nonetheless, the link to biblical terms is apparently difficult to resist. Girardot frequently refers to a "fall from paradise" and even says that other texts connect it to something like "original sin" (2008, 55). Schwartz also refers to an artificiality and deliberateness that disrupted "the Eden of the *tao*" (1985, 207).

62. Although the point of the passage is clear, the specific terms are difficult to work out. Compare the translations in Mair 1994, 88–89; Ziporyn 2009, 65–66; and Graham 2001, 209–10.

63. Chad Hansen explains this point particularly well: "*Wei*$^{do:deem}$ is not 'purposeful' in the sense of free, rational, conscious, or voluntary action. On the contrary, for Laozi *wei* signals socially induced, learned, patterns of response—the opposite of autonomous or spontaneous response" (1992, 213–14).

64. While not specifically addressing deviations from the *dào*, the emphasis of Ames and Hall on novelty is helpful here. They write, "The irrepressible presencing of novelty within the context of what already exists guarantees the uniqueness of each emerging event, and preempts notions such as strict, linear causality, absolute predictability, and reversibility. The world is ever new. And the propensity of things—the force of circumstances—inching ahead in its seeming ineluctability, is always underdetermined, attended as it is by the contingency of real novelty" (2003, 16). Liú Xiàogǎn also emphasizes that the *dào* as origin is not fully determining (2006, 415–16, 504–506).

65. Although the all-pervasiveness of the way is taken up in later texts like the *Zhuāngzǐ*, the *Dàodéjīng* gives no conclusive evidence for it, and LaFargue claims that it has no textual basis at all (2008, 179). One passage says, "The way streams along, able to go left and right!"

(34). Another chapter says that the way *zhōuxíng ér búdài* 周行而不殆 which could mean that it extends everywhere but more likely means that it cycles without end (25). For an excellent discussion of the complexities of the relationship between the way and things, as taken up in Chinese commentaries, see Robinet 1999, 134–36.

66. The Wáng Bì, Héshànggōng, and Fù Yì versions of the text all have *shì* 勢 rather than *qì*, which would mean "circumstances." *Shì* was associated with the development of things, as the *Xìng zì mìng chū* says, "what draws our nature out are circumstances" and then explains circumstances as "the circumstances of things [*wùzhīshì* 物之勢]" (11–12).

67. Zhū Xī explains, "Regarding tools, each suits its function and they cannot be exchanged. A scholar with complete virtue embodies all applications and thus their function has nowhere it does not reach. They are not merely for only one talent or one art" (2003, 57).

68. This line is perplexing if one takes *chéng* as positive. My reading is close to that of Ames and Hall, who translate the line as "they are able to remain hidden and unfinished." They explain, "The progressive and synergistic forces at work in way-making render the language of discreteness and closure inappropriate" (2003, 99). This line appears differently in the Héshànggōng and Wáng Bì versions of the text (which add "new" before *chéng*), and is missing in the Guōdiàn version of the chapter.

69. Chapter 28 of the *Dàodéjīng* attributes the creation of tools to the dispersion of simplicity (*pǔ* 樸, literally "uncarved wood"), and then comments that sagely people avoid this result because they do not cut.

70. It is also possible that *xīyán* 希言 means "words that are faint or barely heard," which is how Wáng Bì takes it (Lóu 1999, 57). Moeller follows this interpretation, translating the phrase as "silent speech."

71. I take this point primarily from Liú Xiàogǎn 2006, 274. Moeller comments on this passage, "even nature, it seems, is not always productive and timely" (2007, 56).

72. The Guōdiàn materials have two versions of the last part of this passage. I have followed the A version, strips 10–13, which Liú Xiàogǎn argues is older and more coherent (2006, 621–22).

73. The line on excess or error is difficult and two other readings are possible, either that sagely people avoid the errors the masses make (Lau 1994; LaFargue 1992) or that the sagely people go to the places that the masses pass by or neglect (Moeller 2007; Ames and Hall 2003). That sages correct the errors of the people, though, is supported by the fact that the Guōdiàn A version has "teaching without teaching" rather than "learn without learning," which suggests that the line concerns the sages' positive influence on the people. Héshànggōng explains it as making the people return to the root (Wáng Kǎ 1997, 251). Moss Roberts translates it as "redeem the wrongs many have done" (2001). Chén Gǔyìng also reads the passage in this way (1988, 310).

74. Although this is the most common reading of the final line, some read it in an opposite way by equating assisting (*fǔ* 輔) with acting (*wéi* 為), in which case it means that sagely people *could* assist the spontaneity of the myriad things but do not dare to do so. Thus, Ames and Hall translate it in this way: "Although they are quite capable of helping all things (*wanwu*) follow their own course (*ziran*), they would not think of doing so" (2003, 178; see also Henricks 2000, 42). This reading is compatible with most versions of the text, but is difficult to reconcile with the Guōdiàn A version, which repeats "able" (*néng* 能) to emphasize the difference between assisting and acting on: sagely people can assist (*néng fǔ* 能輔) the spontaneity of things, but they cannot act on them (*fúnéng wéi* 弗能為). Since the latter reading is compatible with all versions of the text, it is more likely. See Liú Xiàogǎn 2006, 617–18, 621–22.

75. The *Hánfēizǐ*, however, quotes the line with *shì* 恃, meaning "rely on" or "support," instead of *fǔ*, "to assist." Wáng Chōng also uses farming as an example of human beings assisting (*fǔ*) heaven's spontaneity (54: 780).

76. Because of this context, Lau (1994) translates the line as "a creature old in its prime," and Ames and Hall (2003) similarly have, "For something to be old while in its prime." While the point is about getting old too soon by becoming too vigorous, the line itself reads most plausibly as describing the natural progression from youth to old age.

77. Puett puts this point most strongly: "In the Laozi the sage does not model himself on nature: he models himself on the Way, which is the ancestor of the natural and human worlds. He thus gains power over both: the natural world, like the human world, submits to him, not the other way around. Moreover, the sage does not act naturally at all. To begin with, he reverses the natural generative process to return to the Way" (2002, 167).

78. This focus on the effort of a sage is most clearly articulated by Liú Xiàogǎn and LaFargue, both of whom emphasize the claim in chapter 64 that sagely people "assist the *zìrán* of things." LaFargue writes, "A natural state of society is not achieved easily. People start being disruptive, things start going in the wrong direction, and soon the organic harmony of the world is gone. Something must be done. And yet 'working ruins'—this solution can be as disruptive as the problem. The answer is this: pay careful attention all the time, as though you were always at the beginning of something" (1992, 157). Liú Xiàogǎn writes, "The ideal of naturalness would not preclude the exertion of external force or acquiescence to the influence of such force, it would just preclude the use of external force in a *coercive* manner" (1999, 217). Liú Xiàogǎn has a useful list of all the things sagely people are said to do (2006, 387–89).

79. Hansen says that the emphasis on the *yīn* side is "a heuristic corrective to our conventional presuppositions of what has positive value" (1992, 225). This takes up a suggestion from A. C. Graham (1989, 230). For critiques of this position, see Van Norden 1999; and LaFargue 1992, 237.

80. For similar arguments, see Lau 1963, 28, Van Norden 1999, 199–202, Graham 1989, 228–30, and LaFargue 1992, 79. LaFargue describes the negative tendencies as tendencies toward "the *yang*/aggressive," basing his argument on chapter 42, which says that things, in most literal terms, "bear *yīn* on their backs and embrace *yáng* in their arms [*fùyīn ér bàoyáng* 負陰而抱陽]." LaFargue takes it as a claim that things "turn their back on the quiet and dark, and embrace the aggressive and bright" (1992, 78). See also the excellent discussion of this line in Wang 2012, 144–49.

4. Reproaching Heaven and Serving Heaven in the *Mèngzǐ*

1. The *Mèngzǐ* is relatively coherent, and given that Ru texts were circulating on bamboo by the time Mèngzǐ was teaching, there is some reason to assume the sayings attributed to Mèngzǐ generally trace back to things he said. Even so, they must be filtered through the varying perspectives of his students and the compilers of the text. For claims for its coherence and "authenticity," see Shun 1997, 235; Van Norden 2007, 211–13; and Eno 1990a, 99. For a more skeptical view, see Brooks and Brooks 2002a. As usual, when I refer to Mèngzǐ, I intend the character in the text rather than the historical person.

2. One possible exception is 5A5, which says that one sign of heaven accepting Shùn as the new emperor was that the hundred spirits accepted the offerings he made to them. As we have seen, the *Mòzǐ* uses the same claim to illustrate heaven's will, claiming that we know heaven accepts all people inclusively because it accepts their sacrifices inclusively (28: 210–11; Johnston 2010, 28.5).

3. Yearley argues that the more anthropomorphic passages "invalidate any simple picture of Mencius's Heaven as a 'pattern' or 'structure' or 'machine'" (1988, 432; 1990, 163). Chén Dàqí also takes heaven in the *Mèngzǐ* as having desires and will (1980, 94). Ivanhoe says, "Mèngzǐ,

like Kǒngzǐ, did not regard Heaven as a personal deity, but he did conceive of it as an agent with a plan for the world and one that on occasion acts in the world to realize its will (see Mèngzǐ 5A6 etc.)" (2007, 217). In contrast, James Behuniak acknowledges a range of uses of heaven in the Mèngzǐ, but says "Mencius disassociates tiān from the more anthropomorphic 'Heaven' of Mòzǐ, which results in a more secular notion of 'forces'" (2004, xxiii; cf. 101–104). Shun (1997, 207–209) has a helpful survey of other views.

4. There are two other possibilities. One is that heaven is good, but weak, so that bad things happen in spite of heaven. I am aware of no one who argues in favor of this interpretation, and it would not fit the textual evidence. Another possibility is that the Mèngzǐ does not present a coherent view. Lee Yearley argues that the Mèngzǐ is a distinct type of "practical" religious text that is guided by a concern for the direct religious usefulness of whatever is thought about and the desire to maintain rather than eliminate certain basic tensions (1988, 433). Yearley takes responses to the problem of evil as an example. Robert Eno also emphasizes the contradictions that come from the practical orientation of the text (Eno 1990a, 101–106; 2002). Both Yearley and Eno, however, ultimately take Mèngzǐ as holding a consistent view that heaven is good.

5. See Puett 2002, 143–44. Chén Dàqí takes a similar view, claiming that not all things that come from heaven are good and that heaven sometimes does things so bad that it is appropriate to be angry at it (1980, 17–18, 106–107).

6. King Tài was the grandfather of King Wén, who founded the Zhōu dynasty. We might take the passage as literally claiming that if one is good, then they will be rewarded by having a descendant become king. This may have been a common view, as noted earlier, but it is implausible as a general rule and it does not come up again in the Mèngzǐ. Most likely, Mèngzǐ invokes a common view to comfort the duke. The general point is that if we are good, people in the future will continue our work.

7. A number of texts hold up King Tài as an exemplar of nourishing and valuing life, as in Zhuāngzǐ 28: 967 (Mair 1994, 285–86) and Lǚshì chūnqiū 21/4.2: 1463–64. Ru commentators, though, tend to side with staying and fighting. Zhū Xī emphasizes that only one with extraordinary virtue like King Tài can flee; others must follow the proper rules and stay (Zhū 2003, 225).

8. Mèngzǐ took travel money from the ruler of Sòng (2B12) and was living in Sòng when Duke Wén of Téng comes to visit him (3A1), which must have been after 326 BCE. Mèngzǐ's connection to Sòng is problematic given how evil the king appears to have been. Zhōu Guǎngyè 周廣業 argues that Mèngzǐ must have been in Sòng early in the reign of King Yǎn, before it was clear how bad he really was (Jiāo 1987, 431). Jiāo Xún questions the veracity of the accounts of the evil of King Yǎn, suggesting they may they may have been rationalizations for the destruction of Sòng by the states of Qí and Chǔ (1987, 431).

9. See Shǐ jì 38.1632; Lǚshì chūnqiū 23/4.4: 1569; and Jiāo 1987, 430–31.

10. Chen Ning makes a similar distinction between the collective level, where virtue usually brings rewards, and the individual level, where we are subject to blind fate (1997a, 506). He develops this point from a comment by Max Weber (1964, 207). It is important to add, though, that the collective level is determined by the ruler rather than the people themselves.

11. Zhū Xī explains, "A resolute scholar is firm to the limit and often thinks of dying without a coffin and being abandoned in a ditch, without anger. A brave scholar treats life lightly and often thinks of dying in battle, losing his head but not looking back" (2003, 264). The use of "resolute scholar" (zhìshì 志士) echoes Kǒngzǐ's words in the Lúnyǔ: "Resolute scholars and humane people do not seek to live by harming humaneness; rather, they will sacrifice their lives to complete humaneness" (15.9).

12. Discussions of Qí's invasion appear in Mèngzǐ 1B10, 1B11, 2B8, and 2B9. Nivison gives more details and historical sources (2002, 297). See also Shǐ jì 34.1555–58.

13. The view that not taking an opportunity provided by heaven might bring punishment seems to have been fairly common. See Jiāo 1987, 150.

14. The grammar in the received text may support the latter view more, but the same line is quoted in the Hàn dynasty *Lùnhéng* with a slightly different grammar that supports the former, adding *yě* 也 after the first clause (30: 457). Jiāo Xún (editing the *Mèngzǐ*) and Huáng Huī (editing the *Lùnhéng*) both argue that the *Lùnhéng* version is correct, and Jiāo argues that it is the version commented on by Zhào Qí (Jiāo 1987, 309–310; Huáng 1990, 457). D. C. Lau, James Legge, and Yáng Bójūn all follow this reading in distinguishing the two times (Lau 1970; Legge 1970; and Yáng 2003). Bryan Van Norden, however, translates it as "the situation has not changed from when I said that" (2008, 61); Ivanhoe interprets it in a similar way. For an excellent discussion of various interpretations of this passage, see Ivanhoe 1988.

15. Legge (1970) translates the final line as "How should I be otherwise than dissatisfied?" and Behuniak has "Of course I am frustrated" (2004, 108), but neither gives a justification for reversing its meaning. One possibility is suggested by Qīng dynasty commentator Zhào Yòu 趙佑, who takes the final line as a counterfactual—*if* heaven used him to bring about peace, *then* he would have no reason to be unhappy (Jiāo 1987, 311).

16. Ivanhoe takes this position, as does Yearley (Ivanhoe 1988; Yearley 1990, 164).

17. This seems to be the view of Zhào Qí, who concludes his comment on the passage in this way: "Thus one who knows fate does not worry and does not fear" (Jiāo 1987, 312). See also Puett 2005, 60.

18. Chen Ning notes this distinction, saying the "that time" refers to individual success, when one should not complain, but "this time" refers to the collective good (1997a, 509).

19. The richness of the phrase is reflected in translations of it. Van Norden translates the two characters as "He was bitter over the fact that he did not receive the affection of his parents" (2008). Lau translates them thus: "He was complaining and yearning at the same time" (1970). Legge has, "He was dissatisfied, and full of earnest desire" (1970).

20. An alternative to Mèngzǐ's cyclical view was to view human history as one of steady decline. Sarah Allan discusses such a view as it appears in the *Róngchéngshì* 容成氏 bamboo text. She explains that this paradigm "reflects conditions in which the idea of dynastic cycle determined by a moral spiritual force (sky/heaven) had become increasingly difficult to defend" (2010, 76).

21. This may have been a common view. The *Lǚshì chūnqiū* (14/3.5: 774) makes the same point, saying that just as hungry animals cannot be stopped when they see food, the people of a disordered age will flock to those who are worthy. The extremity of the disorder makes the time right. Such claims may address the Mohist argument that Tāng succeeded even in a time as bad as that of Jié. Mèngzǐ would reply that the badness of Jié is precisely what made the timing right for Tāng.

22. Brooks and Brooks make this claim, giving an insightful analysis of passage 2B13 (2002a, 56).

23. This point appears throughout the Guōdiàn text *Táng Yú zhī dào* (Way of Táng and Yú), and it also appears prominently in the *Zǐgāo* and *Róngchéngshì* texts. The position was not unknown in extant texts, and Jiāo Xún quotes several texts criticizing Yǔ for passing the throne to his son (Jiāo 1987, 646–47). For an excellent discussion of this theme, see Liáng 2008, 166–77. For a discussion of "The Way of Táng and Yú," see Defoort 2004; for the *Zǐgāo* and *Róngchéngshì* texts, see Allan 2009 and 2010.

24. Liáng Tāo sees this event as the turning point in the debate (2008, 174–76). Nivison also emphasizes the incident in Yān as the background for Mèngzǐ's comments (2002, 294–98).

25. For this view, see Puett 2002, 138. The final line of the passage might seem to contradict this. Mèngzǐ quotes Kǒngzǐ as saying "Táng [Yáo] and Yú [Shùn] yielded to the worthy; the

Xià, Yīn, and Zhōu continued in the family: their rightness is the same." The form of this statement, though, parallels the common claim that what is right depends on the circumstances and so sages can end up acting quite differently from each other. This is how Zhào Qí and Jiāo Xún take the emphasis (Jiāo 1987, 652). The point is not that first transmitting the throne to the worthy was right and then heaven changed its mind and made heredity right, but rather that all these sages were right because they correctly responded to the conditions set by heaven.

26. Behuniak (drawing on the work of Páng Pǔ) has a good discussion of the way heaven encompasses social forces. He takes references to heaven as referring to the conditions of the age (2004, 101–14).

27. Páng Pǔ nicely explains the connection to the social: "The society which is originally formed by human beings themselves in the end becomes a divine entity that transcends humans; what was originally human power then is expressed as a fate that arranges human beings" (2005, 87).

28. Chén Dàqí makes this point well, saying that heaven can be taken in a narrow sense when distinguished from something else, but also in a broad sense as encompassing that something else as well (1980, 103–104). That is, we can distinguish heaven (narrow sense) from human beings, but at the same time, human beings themselves are produced by heaven (broad sense).

29. For an excellent discussion of *xìng*, including a critical summary of other views, see Robins 2001 and 2011b. The classic study of the background for the concept of *xìng* is Graham 2002. For reconsiderations of that background in light of recently excavated texts, see Chen Ning 2002 and Perkins 2010b. The main disputes around *xìng* are on how fixed it is and how normative or teleological it is. For the poles of interpretations, compare Van Norden 2007, 201–203 and Behuniak 2004, 10–14; or Ames 2002 and Bloom 2002. For Chinese views, see Xú 1969.

30. The *Xìng zì mìng chū* lists various ways in which *xìng* is modified through cultivation (Liú Zhāo 2003, strips 9–12), and the *Xúnzǐ* says that repeated practice will "transform" (*huà* 化) *xìng* (e.g., 23: 435; Knoblock 1988, 23.1b).

31. The idea that different people have different *xìng* appears in the *Zuǒ zhuàn*, which describes the *xìng* of a petty person as being brave in aggression and greedy for disaster (Duke Xiāng 26; Yáng Bójūn 1990, 1123). For other examples, see Shun 1997, 38–39. The view that each individual has its own *xìng* is in the so-called Primitivist chapters of the *Zhuāngzǐ* (ch. 8–10), as well as in Guō Xiàng's commentary. These are discussed in chapter 5, below.

32. The precise relationship between the *Mèngzǐ* and the Guōdiàn texts is difficult to determine, but the Guōdiàn texts are almost certainly earlier and the *Mèngzǐ* reacts against some of the positions we find in them. At the same time, the Guōdiàn texts introduce several technical terms that fit the *Mèngzǐ* but appear only peripherally in the text, terms such as *qíng* and *qì*. It is possible that Mèngzǐ took those terms for granted without raising them explicitly. It is also possible that the thought of the *Mèngzǐ* arose in relative independence and then incorporated terms of analysis from the Guōdiàn materials as it encountered them. In either case, the terms from the Guōdiàn texts are helpful in illuminating the *Mèngzǐ*.

33. Behuniak 2004 translates the title as "Dispositions Arise from Conditions"; Erica Brindley translates it as "[Human] Nature Derives from [Heavenly] Decree" (Behuniak 2004; Brindley 2006). I have relied on the Guōdiàn text but have also consulted the version of the text found in the Shanghai Museum materials, known as the *Discussion of* Xìng *and* Qíng (Jì 2004). My translations here have benefited from the assistance of Dìng Sìxīn. There are many disagreements on how to reconstruct the text. For a fuller treatment of the text and disagreements in interpreting it, see Perkins 2009 and 2010b. Lǐ Tiānhóng and Jì Xùshēng both include thorough summaries of the disagreements around each passage (Lǐ Tiānhóng 2003; Jì 2004).

34. I take *shàn* here putatively, so that "good" would mean to "affirm as good" or "judge as good." Puett translates it as "deem as good" (2004, 47). This natural tendency to judge would be close to the "heart of affirming and negating" which Mèngzǐ names as the sprout of wisdom (2A6). Some scholars take *shàn* instead as meaning something like "become good." For discussions of the various positions, see Lǐ Tiānhóng 2003, 138–39, and Shirley Chan 2009, 365–67. For my own argument, see Perkins 2010b.

35. For an excellent discussion of *qì* in relation to the emotions and to *xìng*, see Alan Chan 2002.

36. Zhū Xī explains the line from the "Zhōng yōng" in these terms, saying that pleasure, anger, sorrow, and joy are *qíng* and that the condition of their not having yet issued forth is *xìng* (2003, 18). Similar passages are given in Lǐ Tiānhóng 2003, 135. See also Andreini 2006, 155–56.

37. Robins provides ample evidence from a wide range of received texts showing that *xìng* refers to actual characteristics rather than potentiality or the proper course of development (2011b). Behuniak also argues that *xìng* should be understood in terms of configurations of actual force rather than in terms of potentiality or teleology (2004).

38. The motto has been known from debates with Gàozǐ in the *Mèngzǐ* (6A4, 6A5, 2A2) and it appears in several of the Guōdiàn texts, most explicitly in the *Liù dé* (Six virtues), which says, "Humaneness is internal, rightness is external, ritual and music combine them" (Liú Zhāo 2003, strip 26).

39. The last part of the sentence is missing but is fairly easy to reconstruct based on the previous line. Commentators agree that rightness and ritual are among those that enter from outside, but there is disagreement on the third term.

40. A. C. Graham made an influential argument that the *qíng* never means "passions" in pre-Han literature, but only something like "the facts," or "genuine" (Graham 2002, 49–55). We now know that Graham's claim was incorrect, since the *Xìng zì mìng chū* takes *qíng* as emotions and as the movement or activation of our *xìng*. Given the similarity in contexts, here *qíng* almost certainly refers to emotions, with the list of feelings that lead to the virtues then given as examples of such *qíng*. Jiāo Xún quotes Chéng Yáotián 程瑤田 making just this point (1987, 752–55). Zhū Xī also comes close to the *Xìng zì mìng chū* by saying that "*qíng* are the movements of *xìng*" (2003, 328). Zhào Qí mentions grief as an example of *qíng* (Jiāo 1987, 752).

41. The most thorough discussion of the four sprouts is in Van Norden (2007, 247–77). See also Shun 1997, 49–71.

42. Mèngzǐ does not directly apply the term *qíng* to these reactions, but these clearly fit what the *Xìng zì mìng chū* labels as *qíng*. Zhū Xī explicitly calls them *qíng* (2003, 238), and Zhào Qí labels the reaction of concern for the child in danger as *qíng* (Jiāo 1987, 233).

43. I here follow what Chad Hansen calls the "weak" version of the four tendencies, taking them as basic ways of reacting to the world that could develop in different forms in different contexts (1992, 172). The "strong" version would claim that the specific form of the Confucian way is already implicit in human nature. Lee Yearley analyzes the same tension as between the derivation of virtue from our nature, which should be able to take many forms, and the derivation of one specific set of virtuous practices from the sages (1985; 1990, 46). Ivanhoe expresses something like the strong view: "He [Mèngzǐ] believed that the pattern described by the rites was encoded in the heart and mind of each and every person. If one cultivated one's moral sprouts, one could find the Way within" (2002a, 111). Kwong-loi Shun also seems to take the strong view, saying that "the heart/mind of human beings already contains an ethical direction, so that human beings do not need to seek ethical guidance from outside the heart/mind" (1997, 212). For my own argument for the "weak" version, see Perkins 2011a.

44. Kwong-loi Shun has a thorough discussion of the various positions and possible readings (1997, 94–112). For a variety of arguments on what is at stake in the debate, see Van Norden

2007, 287–301; Liu Xiusheng 2002, 107–14; Chong 2002, 108–11; and Behuniak 2004, 38–46. For a good overview of the debate in light of excavated texts, see Liáng 2008, 378–89.

45. For a fuller argument for this claim, see Perkins 2011b, 26.

46. Liáng Tāo argues that this marks an important development of Ru thought, which had been closely bound to a family system that was becoming less and less relevant (2008, 315–19, 378–79). I suspect this change is a response to the Mohist emphasis on inclusive caring.

47. Lau (1970) and Van Norden (2008) both translate *lì* as "profit" here. Wáng Chōng points out positive uses of *lì* in the *Zhōu yì* (Book of Changes) and claims that *lì* has two different senses: the benefit of wealth and materials and the benefit of peace and good fortune. He accuses Mèngzǐ of unfairly construing the term in the first sense (30: 450).

48. One common explanation of the passage is that we can change our fate, so that in some sense dying in fetters might be fated but still can be avoided. Chen Ning lists some who take this view (1997a, 497–98), and Rosemont and Ames give such a view of fate in the *Lúnyǔ* (Rosemont and Ames 1998, 250n192; cf. Hall and Ames 1987, 214–15).

49. Another common interpretation of the passage is that it distinguishes between what is truly fated (correct fate) and what is not. For example, Zhū Xī takes correct fate as referring to what happens without being sought. Because dying under a falling wall or as a prisoner can be avoided, these are not correct fate (2003, 349–50). Jiāo Xún reads it as distinguishing what can be avoided from what is necessary (1987, 879–82). It is implausible, though, to think that dying while enacting the way is any less avoidable than dying as a criminal.

50. The problem and the term "lazy fallacy" goes back to Hellenistic philosophy and is discussed in Cicero's *On Fate* (Inwood and Gerson 1988, 130). Leibniz frequently discusses the problem, arguing that the claim that effort is not needed because outcomes are fated mistakenly leaves out the contribution of our own (fated) actions (e.g., *Theodicy*, preface; Gerhardt 1978, VI.30).

51. Zhào Qí takes the passage as distinguishing a fate in which you get what you deserve (correct fate) and a fate that is undeserved, which would be dying in fetters and chains (Jiāo 1987, 879). This draws on what seems to have been a common Hàn dynasty distinction between three kinds of fate, mentioned already in chapter 2, above (see *Lùnhéng* 6: 52). The problem with this reading is that the passage is prescriptive, telling us to have a correct fate, but whether we get what we deserve is not within our own control. Wáng Chōng reads the passage this way but points out that it contradicts common sense and other claims in the *Mèngzǐ* (11: 467–68). He mentions specifically that Zǐlù died pickled and hung above a gate, which is worse than dying in fetters.

52. Qīng dynasty scholar Zhāng Ěrqí 張爾岐 nicely explains this and connects it to peace of mind: "Gentlemen use rightness to rest peacefully in fate, so their hearts are constantly at peace; petty people use wisdom and strength to contend with fate, so their hearts have much resentment. Even so, the masses of people do still sometimes rest peacefully with fate. Generally, once they know that nothing can be done, then they rest in it. Sagely people rest in fate, but really they do not take fate as a standard but take rightness as a standard. So even if strength has what it can contend and circumstances have what can be examined, they withdraw and rest in it, saying it is not what rightness can allow. If it is not what rightness can allow, then they call it fate" (Jiāo 1987, 657–58).

53. For a summary of such views, see Shun 1997, 78–81.

54. For a good discussion of the link between *tiān* and *xìng* in light of recently excavated texts, see Liáng 2008, 143–45.

55. For similar views, see also Van Norden 2007, 309, 345; Yearley 1990, 36; and Vincent Shih 1963, 238.

56. There are numerous difficulties in reconstructing this passage: see the discussions in Jì 2005, 198–203; and Cáo 2006, 107–22; as well as the translation by Erica Brindley, Paul Goldin, and Esther Klein (2013). For an elaboration of my own interpretation, see Perkins (2013). My understanding of *Héng xiān* is heavily indebted to discussions at "Reading and Understanding the *Heng Xian* (Bamboo Event II)," held at Pennsylvania State University, November 13–14, 2010, organized by Erica Brindley.

57. Lǐ Líng (Mǎ 2004, 292), Jì (2005, 221), and Cáo (2006, 116), all take *shēng* in this phrase as *xìng*.

58. This is a strange use of *huò* 或, but I follow Cáo Fēng in taking it as referring to something still indefinite (2006, 115). Some scholars take *huò* instead as *yù* 域, meaning space or spatiality (see Brindley, Goldin, and Klein 2013). For a discussion of various views, see Jì 2005, 210.

59. Once again, most Chinese scholars take *shēng* in strip 5 as *xìng*: Lǐ Líng (Mǎ 2004, 292–93), Jì Xùshēng (2005, 202, 226), and Dìng Sìxīn (Jì 2005, 226) all read it this way. Jì Xùshēng paraphrases it as "the internally differentiated *xìng*, which the myriad things possess, emerges from beings" (2005, 226).

60. For an excellent study of plant and water metaphors in early Chinese thought see Allan 1997.

61. For Kǒngzǐ's comments on water, see *Lúnyǔ* 9.17 and 6.23.

62. There has been some debate about whether or not *duān* has the sense of "sprout" or simply means "beginning," which is its proper meaning when joined with the radical 立. Van Norden's argument on this is convincing (2007, 217) and is supported by a similar use of *duān* in *Yǔ cóng* I, which uses the character for sprout, *duān* 耑, without the additional radical, saying, "Mourning is the sprout of humaneness" (Liú Zhāo 2003, strip 98).

63. The metaphors of plant growth are often taken to illustrate teleology, as showing that seeds or sprouts have an inherent purpose that they are meant to realize (e.g., Van Norden 2007, xii–xvii, 37–41). I do not think that is such an obvious interpretation of plant growth that it should be assumed as universal. For an argument that plant growth was not seen teleologically in early China, see Behuniak 2004, xii–xvii, 37–41. A deeper problem is that since water clearly moves according to circumstances and its own immanent force rather than toward realizing some end, a teleological interpretation of the plant imagery would set Mèngzǐ's two main metaphors in opposition to each other. It is more likely that both water and plant growth were conceived through configurations of vital energy, and that slightly greater emphasis is placed on plant imagery because it more clearly shows the complex interaction between natural forces and cultivation.

64. A full explanation of this difficult passage would go beyond the scope of this chapter, but for excellent explanations that take recently excavated texts into account, see Alan Chan 2002 and Csikszentmihalyi 2004, 149–60. See also the discussions in Shun 1997, 66–68, 72–76, 112–23, and 154–63.

65. My interpretation draws heavily on Alan Chan 2002, which also uses *qì* to integrate these various dimensions of Mèngzǐ's thought, as well as Behuniak 2004, 1–22. See also Wong 2002, 193–96; Chen Ning 2002, 20–21; and Yearley 1990, 151–57.

66. The main text is referred to as the *Jīng* (classic), while the commentary is referred to as the *Shuō* (explanation). Unless otherwise noted, I use the reconstruction by Liú Zhāo 2003 of the *Wǔ xíng* Guōdiàn text, and Páng 1999 for the "*Shuō*" commentary found with the text at Mǎwángduī. Citations are by strip numbers in the Guōdiàn text and by paragraph divisions (as *Jīng* or *Shuō*) in Páng 1999. For an excellent English translation and analysis, see Csikszentmihalyi 2004.

67. For thorough discussions of the links between the *Mèngzǐ* and the *Wǔ xíng* commentary, see Chén Lái 2009c, 191–200. See also Liáng 2008, 390–419; and Csikszentmihalyi 2004, 103–112.

68. There is a general consensus on the characters but disagreement on the meaning. I follow Liú Zhāo 2003, except in interpreting *jiǎn* 簡 (weigh and balance), which he takes as firm or hard. *Shuō* 11 explains it is not letting something small harm something great, or something light harm something weighty. *Shuō* 20 says that *jiǎn* is like *héng* 衡, which means to weigh or balance. Guō Yí translates it as "light and heavy not losing balance" (2001, 175). Páng 1999 takes it as making distinctions.

69. There is wide disagreement on the adverbial phrases translated here as "gently" and "decisively." Chén Lái takes them as emphasizing that "actions are realized under the determination of motivating states of the heart" (2008, 161). Csikszentmihalyi 2004 translates them as "warmly" and "directly."

70. The *Dàodéjīng* and the *Mèngzǐ* may in fact use the same term. This line appears in two versions in Guōdiàn, each of which uses the same phonetic (*fǔ* 甫) but with different radicals (fǔ 尃 in Guōdiàn A strip 12, and 木 + 甫 in Guōdiàn C strip 13). While commentators, relying on the received texts, take these as variants of *fǔ* 輔, they could just as well be variants of *bǔ* 補. In explaining this passage, Zhū Xī quotes the Sòng dynasty scholar Fēng Jì 豐稷, who connects it to the *Dàodéjīng*: "Assist [*fǔ* 輔] the spontaneity [*zìrán*] of their *xìng*, making them attain it from themselves, and thus the people daily move in goodness and do not know who makes them so" (2003, 352). It is worth noting that when Wáng Chōng shows that farmers can assist (*fǔ*) heaven's spontaneity but not force things to grow, he gives Mèngzǐ's example of the man from Sòng who tried to make his plants grow faster by pulling on them (54: 780).

71. Hú Shì emphasizes Mèngzǐ's focus on the generative powers of nature through his emphasis on agriculture and providing food for the people, which Hú Shì takes as a maternal dimension. On that point, he takes Mèngzǐ as influenced by both the *Dàodéjīng* and the Mohists (2003, 231–32).

72. *Beyond Good and Evil* 259; Nietzsche 1988, 5.208; translation from Horstmann and Norman 2001, 153.

73. I follow Fàn Gēngyán 范耕研 in taking the phrase on safety and benefit as a rhetorical question (Chén Qíyóu 1984, 1424). It is possible that the meaning instead is that while things try to help each other, they actually harm each other. This is how Knoblock and Riegel 2000 take the passage. For various interpretations, see Chén Qíyóu 1984, 1424.

5. Beyond the Human in the *Zhuāngzǐ*

1. The strongest example of the former is in Robber Zhí's criticism of Kǒngzǐ, discussed above (28: 994–1000; Mair 1994, 301–304). For an example of the latter, see Kǒngzǐ's explanation for his peace of mind while surrounded in Wèi (17: 595–96; Mair 1994, 160).

2. The latter appears in 26: 920; Mair 1994, 268. The former point is made in many places, as when, after explaining Kǒngzǐ's danger between Chén and Cài, an old man offers to tell him of "the way of not dying" (20: 690; Mair 1994, 191).

3. The first view appears in many places but is most extreme in chapter 29. For the second, see Zhuāngzǐ's explanation of his own poverty in 20: 677–78 (Mair 1994, 194). The third runs throughout the Inner Chapters and will be the main focus of this chapter.

4. Graham 2003b; Liú Xiàogǎn 1995; see also Roth 2003b.

5. For example, chapter 28 collects stories about avoiding political office, but offices are avoided for different reasons in different episodes.

6. In fact, there is little evidence for associating the Inner Chapters with Zhuāngzǐ himself, and they are not the chapters associated with Zhuāngzǐ in the Hàn dynasty. For an excellent study of Hàn views of Zhuāngzǐ and an interesting argument that the Inner Chapters are actually relatively late, see Klein 2010.

7. In this approach, I follow Lee Yearley's hope to avoid the problem of composition by talking about "tendencies or motifs or strands in the *Zhuangzi*" (1983, 125).

8. *Beyond Good and Evil* 230; Nietzsche 1988, 5.169. For a brief comparison of Nietzsche and Zhuāngzǐ on opposition to anthropocentrism, see Parkes 1983, 237–39.

9. I follow Graham in translating Niè Quē 齧缺 as "Gaptooth." For the meaning of the names, see Chén Gǔyìng 1983, 90.

10. Most contemporary commentators and translators take the line this way, but Guō Xiàng has an interesting variant, taking it as asking—do you know that what all things agree on is actually so? Guō Xiàng answers that what is agreed on is not necessarily correct and what is singular is not necessarily false (Guō Qìngfān 1978, 91).

11. Sextus Empiricus gives an argument almost identical to that of Wáng Ní, first describing differences in taste between animals, and then concluding that we cannot know which is correct, "For we shall not be able ourselves to decide between our own appearances and those of the other animals, being ourselves a part of the dispute and for that reason more in need of someone to decide than ourselves able to judge" (*Outlines of Scepticism* I.xiv; translation from Annas and Barnes 2000, 17).

12. The English language secondary literature on Zhuāngzǐ not only suffers from a focus on what David Loy nicely calls an inquiry into "which of our boxes he would fit into," (1996, 52) but even more so from disagreement on what the boxes are, with the most contentious boxes being "skepticism," "relativism," and "mysticism."

13. For another translation of the passage and its context, see Ziporyn 2009, 139. Ziporyn nicely expresses a similar view of heaven: "Heaven then is not the secret hidden essence of things, the harmonious creator behind their present conflicting appearances, but rather the surface of obvious conflict itself, once we cease the futile attempt to try to get to the bottom of it or find out what harmony lies behind it" (2003, 49).

14. Yearley makes this argument in Yearley 1996, 152–88 (cf. Yearley 1983, 125–39). It should be noted that Yearley is particularly sensitive to the multiplicity of positions in the *Zhuāngzǐ*, which is why he labels this particular strand "the radical Zhuāngzǐ."

15. Yearley warns, "The danger is that of domestication, of making the foreign, the strange, and the challenging into the homey, the familiar, and the acceptable" (1983, 137–38).

16. Such stories fill chapter 5, which reads most naturally as an anthology organized around the topic of "abnormal" bodies rather than around any one perspective. In particular, there is a tension between stories that suggest a person is good in spite of their abnormalities and those that undermine the very concept of normality. I make no attempt to reconcile those aspects here but simply follow the latter line of argument. One might add the passages illustrating the value of uselessness in chapter 4, discussed below. The description of the death of Master Chariot in chapter 6 also invokes language of deformity, as if the coming of death distorts his body to the edge of what can count as human.

17. Graham gives a brief argument for taking *jiè* as "singular, unique in appearance or character" (2003c, 18–19).

18. Chén Gǔyìng takes the passage as saying that the officer's having one foot was by birth rather than the result of punishment (1983, 122; see also Watson 1968, 52). On that reading, though, the passage seems irrelevant, and it contradicts the characters whose appearance of missing a foot was caused by punishment. Chéng Xuányīng takes it in a more radical direction, as showing that everything—even having your foot chopped off by the government—is ultimately fated and due to heaven (Guō Qìngfān 1978, 125–26).

19. Ziporyn translates it with a similar meaning: "When Heaven generates any 'this,' it always makes it singular, but man groups every appearance with something else" (2009, 23).

20. The second half of chapter 4 has a series of stories on the importance of uselessness, which appears to be a corrective to the first half of the chapter explaining methods of political service. At the end of chapter 1, Huìzǐ compares the words of Zhuāngzǐ to a useless tree, a claim Zhuāngzǐ does not rebut.

21. I follow Ziporyn's translation of the name, which is descriptive of the character. Graham and Watson translate it simply as "Cripple Shu." Zhī refers to the limbs of the body, but the root originally refers to the limbs of a tree and so may echo the other stories in the series.

22. For a nuanced attempt to justify the derivation of the labels "normal" and "abnormal" based on so-called representative samples of human beings in relation to the *Mèngzǐ*, see Van Norden 2007, 221–25. The problem is that if "representative sample" refers to what is true of the vast majority of the type considered, then Yáo and Shùn must be considered abnormal and less human. If "representative sample" instead means "those most human," the question of what counts as most human remains.

23. There seems to be some corruption in the original lines, since the characters have bodies that are unusual in different ways, but both are said to make others appear to have small necks. I follow Graham's emendation of the text (2003c, 25).

24. A comment in chapter 15 describes followers of Péng Zǔ doing various breathing exercises and bodily movements with the goal of longevity and nourishing the physical form (15: 535; Mair 1994, 145). For a discussion of references to Péng Zǔ in various early texts, see Jì 2005, 250–51.

25. Yànzǐ criticizes the Duke Jǐng's excessive punishments by telling him that in the market, this footwear for people missing a foot is more expensive (that is, in greater demand) than regular shoes (*Zuǒ zhuàn* Duke Zhāo 3; Yáng Bójūn 1990, 1238).

26. Graham takes chapter 8–10 and part of chapter 11 as having been written by one person during the breakdown of the Qín dynasty, around 205 BCE (Graham, 2003b, 80–86). Roth dates the chapters earlier, between 243–237 (Roth 2003b, 198–207). Liú Xiàogǎn labels them instead as "Anarchist" and argues that they were written before 240 BCE (1995, 134–43, 165–66).

27. The relationship between the terms can be taken differently. Ziporyn translates it thus: "In this, what is joined is not so because of extra webbing and what is branched is not so because of additions" (2009, 58). Mair translates it as "Therefore, joining is accomplished without a web, branching is accomplished without extraneousness" (1994, 76). That reading fits the following sentence less well, however.

28. This refers to the fine hair that grows on animals in the autumn.

29. The use of physical abnormalities here has direct echoes with Mèngzǐ, who says that a person with a crooked finger will go to great lengths to fix it simply because it is unlike that of other people. While presenting such differences as trivial, Mèngzǐ's point is that if our heart is unlike that of other people, we should be concerned with normalizing it (6A12).

30. At least some of these connections are made by most commentators, but the four are brought together by Wáng Xiàoyú 王孝魚 (Chén Gǔyìng 1983, 192). The connection of rightness to craft is most tenuous, but Wáng Xiàoyú makes it through the original meaning of the word translated as "craft," *gōng* 工, which refers to the carpenter's square and thus to standards.

31. Hansen makes this connection to Mèngzǐ (2003, 49), as does Raphals 1996, 31–32.

32. This passage closely connects with the debate between Mèngzǐ and Gàozǐ in *Mèngzǐ* 2A2, discussed in chapter 4. There Mèngzǐ says that the heart leads and the vital energy follows, uses a term for "leads," *shuài* 帥, that is almost identical to the term Zhuāngzǐ uses for following an authority, *shī* 師.

33. In the received text, "heart" (xīn 心) is missing, but there is evidence that it was in the version of the text commented on by Guō Xiàng and almost all contemporary editions insert it. See Chén Gǔyìng 1983, 140. Another possible emendation would be to eliminate "and" (ér 而), so that it would literally read "have enacting it" (yǒuwéizhī 有爲之). The phrase yǒuwéi is used in the Xìng zì mìng chū to mean acting deliberately (Liú Zhāo 2003, strips 13, 15–16).

34. The phrase is the title of the first chapter, which I follow Watson 1968 in translating as "free and easy wandering." The other translations are from Mair 1994, Ziporyn 2009, and Graham 2001, respectively.

35. For a discussion of the role of fate in the Zhuāngzǐ, see Puett 2003.

36. One might respond that a *natural* death should be accepted, whereas a *premature* death should be avoided, but determining a so-called natural life span would require a species norm, something we have seen undermined in general and criticized specifically in relation to life span through those who wish to emulate Péng Zǔ. Long and short life appear in lists of alternations that must be affirmed either way (12: 407; Mair 1994, 104).

37. This approach is the most plausible response to the main difficulty in interpreting the Zhuāngzǐ, which, as Kjellberg and Ivanhoe put it, is "reconciling Zhuāngzǐ's skepticism with his normative vision" (1996, xiv). A sophisticated account of a similar approach is developed in Fraser 2012, who argues that the basis for Zhuāngzǐ's philosophy is the recognition that values are heterogeneous and multiple, and that any one perspective will recognize some values but exclude others. Flexibility in perspective thus allows for greater appreciation of these values. A more common response to the difficulty is to deny (to some degree) the skepticism; the best survey and criticism of such approaches is Fraser 2012, 440–46. Another approach is to claim that the position recommended is simply what remains when one becomes thoroughly skeptical. The best articulation of this position in relation to the Zhuāngzǐ is Ziporyn 2003, 33–63. Sextus Empiricus articulates a similar vision of skepticism (*Outlines of Scepticism* III.xxviii; translation from Annas and Barnes 2000, 52).

38. One might add the whetstone as a third metaphor, using the phrase tiānní 天倪. Graham follows Zhū Guìyào Chin in taking ní as yán 研, meaning "whetstone" (2003c, 16); the phrase tiānní is identified with the pottery wheel of heaven (tiānjūn) in chapter 27 (27: 949–950; Mair 1994, 279). Coutinho nicely develops the intersection of the two metaphors of the whetstone and the pottery wheel (2004, 169–74). Unfortunately, there is little evidence for taking ní as yán. Mair translates the phrase as "the framework of nature," Watson as "Heavenly Equality," Ziporyn as "Heavenly Transitions," and Chén Gǔyīng as "natural limits." The same character, ní, is in the name of Wáng Ní, the character we have seen in dialogue with Gaptooth.

39. See Graham 2003a, 110–111. Ziporyn translates the phrase as "He just went by the rightness of their present 'this'" (2009, 17).

40. Guō Qìngfān 1978, 74. Graham takes liǎng as a technical phrase referring to the two sides of an argument (2003a, 106).

41. Thus Ziporyn translates "respond without qióng" as "it responds to all the endless things it confronts, thwarted by none" (2009, 12).

42. For an intriguing Zhuangzian argument that morality does more harm than good, see Moeller 2009.

43. Puett particularly emphasizes this function of sagely people, writing "the liberated spirit accords with Heavenly patterns, helps things be as they naturally ought to be, and allows things to fulfill their Heaven-given allotment" (2002, 132).

44. Crandell compiles the passage from sentences throughout "The Concept of Play [*Der Begriff des Spiels*]" section of *Truth and Method* (Gadamer 1994, 101–10). Lee Yearley appeals to the concept of play to describe a similar position, although he attributes that position to Xúnzǐ

rather than Zhuāngzǐ (1980, 479–80). See also Brook Ziporyn's comparison of a Zhuangzian perspective to a "wild card" that remains valuable regardless of the rules of the game (Ziporyn 2012, 178–181).

45. On the connection between tranquility and skepticism of good and bad, see *Outlines of Scepticism* I.xii (Annas and Barnes 2000, 10). For a comparison between Zhuāngzǐ and Sextus Empiricus, see Kjellberg 1996.

46. On this point, see Perkins 2007, 49–57. For an interesting account of the link between the problem of evil and the displacement of the human, see Allen 1991. Allen writes, "Suffering can teach us that we are a very small part of the universe and that we are not to expect as much as we do from its workings. . . . Indeed in our humbled and more realistic condition we can see the glory of the entire world-order and be grateful for our capacity to yield ourselves to it courageously and magnanimously even when we are caught in its workings" (1991, 192–93).

47. For a more detailed discussion of the relationship between the *Zhuāngzǐ* and tragedy, see Perkins 2011b.

48. Puett writes, "Although Confucianism is often portrayed as fundamentally optimistic, Mencius' argument is based on a very different cosmology. Calling it 'tragic' may be going too far, but Mencius clearly conceives a potential for tension between Heaven and man and advises us to side with Heaven" (2002, 140). Mèngzǐ does not simply side with heaven, though, so the tension is heightened by the internal conflict between natural human caring and accepting whatever happens.

49. Van Norden suggests a similar point in saying that the *Zhuāngzǐ* seeks to overcome "the fragility of goodness," drawing on a phrase from Martha Nussbaum (1996, 261).

50. I draw this contrast from discussions with Sean Kirkland. Kirkland takes Greek tragedy as illustrating the transition from *dromoscopic time*, in which one races toward a fixed goal, and *aporetic time*, in which one realizes that "one's very own motivations and aims, were not fixed and clear at all, but complex, obscure, and inscrutable" (forthcoming). This shift induces caution, hesitation, and uncertainty. What the *Zhuāngzǐ* helps reveal is that this way-less-ness is only *tragic* for those still committed to *getting somewhere*. Otherwise, it blends into comedy.

51. Puett writes, "Accordingly, for Mencius, the agon of Heaven and man arises because man makes moral judgments on the world. For Zhuangzi, man should accept whatever Heaven decrees; once men stop using moral norms to criticize Heaven, there will be no agon" (2002, 144).

52. *Birth of Tragedy* 11, Nietzsche 1988, 1.78.

53. Hegel 1955, vol. 2, 553; translation modified from Paolucci and Paolucci 1962, 54.

54. *Thus Spoke Zarathustra*, "On Reading and Writing"; Nietzsche 1988, 4.49; translation from Parkes 2005, 36.

55. For a broader study of the relationship between animals and human beings in the *Zhuāngzǐ*, see Perkins 2010a.

6. Xúnzǐ and the Fragility of the Human

1. The *Xúnzǐ* consists primarily of essays rather than attributed quotations, so evidence for a single author rests only on the fact that later editors grouped these materials together and on their internal coherence. Several chapters are widely accepted to be collected materials from different authors, but setting those aside, the text is remarkably consistent and systematic. For convenience, I will speak of Xúnzǐ as the author of that system, although it probably mixes his ideas with those of his disciples. All of the material in the text, though, is in some doubt and I

try not to rely too heavily on any single passage. For a broad discussion of the compilation and authenticity of the *Xúnzǐ*, see Knoblock 1988, 105–28.

2. The ode is "Heaven Made" ("Tiānzuò" 天作) (270).

3. There are several difficulties with this line, but to follow along with or rely on things (*yīnwù* 因物), refers to going along with the way things spontaneously are of themselves. When Xúnzǐ criticizes Zhuāngzǐ for being biased toward heaven and not knowing the human, he says that as a result, Zhuāngzǐ knows only going along, *yīn* (21.4: 393). If the parallel between lines is maintained, "multiplying them [*duōzhī* 多之]" should refer to an attitude toward things rather than an actual action. I take the term *duō*, then, as putative, something like "consider their multiplicity." Táng dynasty commentator Yáng Liàng 楊倞 takes the phrase as meaning relying on things to multiply of themselves (Wáng Xiānqiān 1988, 317), a reading followed by Lǐ Dísheng, Knoblock, and Watson (Lǐ 1979, 378; Knoblock 1988; Watson 1968, 86). Hutton and Eno instead take it as human action in multiplying things (Hutton 2000, 273; Eno 1990a, 203). Both readings are plausible, but neither fits the parallel with other lines.

4. Xúnzǐ's opposition to shamans and divination is one of the few points specifically mentioned in his biography in the *Shǐjì* (*Shǐjì* 74.2343). Chén Wénhào takes this as one of the most important aspects of the *Xúnzǐ*, and claims that Xúnzǐ took belief in fortune and misfortune "as one of the most serious problems of his time" (2008, 29). Paul Goldin includes a nice selection of passages illustrating some of the views Xúnzǐ was probably arguing against (1999, 38–46).

5. The other two are in 5: 84 and 27: 498 (Knoblock 1988, 5.6 and 27.49). At least some Ru already included the *Yì* in the lists of classics, since it appears in lists in the Guōdiàn texts *Liù dé* (Six virtues) and *Yǔ Cóng* I (Collected sayings I) (Liú Zhāo 2003, strips 24–26, 38–41).

6. *Mìng* occurs with the sense of fate only seven times (excluding quotations from classic texts), and several of those appear in what were probably common phrases (e.g., 16: 291, 4: 58; Knoblock 1988, 16.1, 4.6).

7. I take this observation from Moeller 2006, 96.

8. A similar view is developed in *Lǚshì chūnqiū* 1/2: 21–22 and 2/2: 75.

9. For attempts to reconcile natural familial feelings with Xúnzǐ's view of human nature, see Ivanhoe 1991, 314n7, and Hutton 2000, 230.

10. There have long been suspicions about the authenticity of these two chapters, based on their significant overlap with chapters in the *Lǐjì* and other texts (see Lau 2000, 212; Hú 2003, 235). The most common view takes those as derived from Xúnzǐ (see Cook 1997), but we now know that similar views were expressed earlier in the Guōdiàn texts. We must again be wary, though, of a simple dichotomy between what is authentic and what is interpolation. The incorporation of earlier materials into the *Xúnzǐ* suggests at least some acceptance of their contents, but it does not necessarily require the acceptance of every element.

11. David Wong distinguishes a "weak" sense of *kě* as guiding desires and a "strong" sense in which the ability to *kě* would be an independent source of motivation that can override desires (2000, 140). The clearest statement of the "strong" position is Van Norden 2000. Stalnaker says that Xúnzǐ makes a "rather sharp distinction between two kinds of motivation," and that people follow what they *kě* "even when their existing desires point in another direction" (2006, 283, 137). Wong argues persuasively for the weak view, a view also held by Yearley, who takes the role of the heart to be deciding between long-term and short-term desires (Wong 2000; Yearley 1980, 466).

12. The received text says, "this is life." I follow Wáng Niànsūn's argument that *shēng* should be *xìng*, a reading followed by Wáng Xiānqiān, Lǐ Dísheng, and Knoblock (Wáng 1988, 175; Lǐ 1979, 196; Knoblock 1988).

13. As discussed below, a further difference is that gentlemen cultivate their senses so that they find pleasure in different sources. These points address the main difficulty for this inter-

pretation of *kě*, which is the claim that a cultivated person can *kě* dying for virtue (22: 428; Knoblock 1988, 22.5a). How one motivated by sensory desires might still choose to die can be explained in two ways. First, if our motivations are for pleasure rather than survival, some forms of survival might be worse than death, a position seen in the *Lǚshì chūnqiū* (2/2: 76–77). The second comes from the danger of calculating benefits rather than following regular patterns. While there are surely cases where our pleasure would be better served by violating virtue, one who looks for exceptions more often ends up suffering. For discussions of this problem, see Yearley 2000, 467; and Lau 2000, 211.

14. Janghee Lee takes Xúnzǐ's overriding concern as opposing the "naturalism" of the time, which he explains as "an ancient Chinese philosophical tradition that seeks the source of normativity in the natural realm" (2005, 2). See also Chén Dàqí 1954, 64–70.

15. The last line is difficult to translate, but literally, the phrases are: "that by which the people *dào* [*suǒyǐdào* 所以道]" and "that which gentlemen *dào* [*suǒdào* 所道]." Hutton translates it thus: "It is that whereby humans make their way and that which the gentleman takes as his way" (2000, 267). Knoblock has this: "the Way that guides the actions of mankind and is embodied in the conduct of the gentleman" (1988).

16. The common capitalization of "Dao" in the context of the *Xúnzǐ* is misleading, since it suggests *dào* is a more-than-human principle. Goldin goes so far as to say, "In the term dao 道, or Way, Xúnzǐ postulates a single and universal ontology. The Way is the way of the universe, the 'plan and pattern' of reality, and theories are 'heterodox' if they do not conform to it" (1999, 98). Goldin does not explain how this fits with Xúnzǐ's explicit claim here that the *dào* is *not* the *dào* of heaven or the *dào* of earth.

17. Hú Shì provides the English phrase as a gloss to the Chinese phrase *kāntiān zhǔyì* 戡天主義. Edward Machle has a good discussion of how early-twentieth-century Chinese thinkers were oriented toward reading Xúnzǐ as a scientist, which led them to taking *tiān* as "nature" rather than a divine force (Machle 1993, 3–5).

18. The problem is raised by many people, but for the most precise analyses, see Wong 2000, 135–54; and the response in Kline 2000, 155–75.

19. Knoblock translates *tiān* as "nature." While roughly correct, the phrase *tiāndì* 天地 (heaven-and-earth), is probably closer to our term "nature." For an argument that "nature" is misleading as a translation for *tiān*, see Machle 1993, 1–2.

20. The way in which *fēn* bring order is simply illustrated in a story in the *Lǚshì chūnqiū*, which says that if a rabbit runs by, a hundred people will chase after it, but when rabbits are gathered in the market no one goes after them. That is because in the market, the *fēn* have been firmly set (17/6.5: 1120).

21. It would be misleading to take Xúnzǐ as claiming that what makes us superior is reason or something like innate morality. One passage says that human beings are distinct from (and able to eat) other bipeds because we make distinctions (*biàn* 辨), but it takes social roles as the main kind of *biàn*, suggesting it is social organization rather than reason that distinguishes us (5: 78; Knoblock 1988, 5.4). In another passage, human beings are said to be the most valuable or honorable (*guì* 貴) because we have rightness—but, again, the value of rightness is explained as allowing us to sustain social roles (9: 164; Knoblock 1988, 9.16a). Xúnzǐ certainly does not think human beings naturally have rightness, so what distinguishes us from animals is not something natural but something developed through study.

22. The *Liù dé* and *Xìng zì mìng chū* Guōdiàn texts both use the character for *yí* 宜 with the meaning of *yì* 義. For a discussion of early variants of *yì* 義, see Páng 2005, 42–44. The "Zhōng yōng" (Zhū 2003, 28) and the *Yǔ cóng* III (Collected Sayings III) (Liú Zhāo 2003, strip 35) both define rightness as appropriateness.

23. At the start of the "Correcting Names" chapter, the *Xúnzǐ* lists names added to things as one of four kinds of names, the other three being names for punishments (*xíngmíng* 刑名), names for offices (*juémíng* 爵名), and cultural names (*wénmíng* 文名) (22: 411; Knoblock 1988, 22.1a).

24. For the most thorough attempt to do so, see Machle 1993.

25. Ivanhoe writes, "The Way enables human beings to put not only themselves but the entire universe in 'a state of godlike order'" (1991, 317). Stalnaker writes, "For Xúnzǐ, we reform ourselves and order the larger natural world, for the greater good of human beings and the entire range of myriad things" (2006, 72). Aside from the scant textual support, the fundamental problem with these interpretations is that Xúnzǐ gives no basis for value or motivation other than fulfilling human desires. There seems to be no way in which either order or the well-being of other animals can be taken as goods outside their function in fulfilling human desires. Values like sustainability are part of the way, but they still arise from human needs.

26. The strangeness of this passage is another reason to suspect that the "Discourse on Ritual" incorporates materials that are not fully consistent with the rest of Xúnzǐ's system. For discussions of the passage, see Stalnaker 2006, 169–70; and Hagen 2007, 103–105.

27. For a brief discussion of *lǐ* and its translation as "coherence," see Ziporyn 2012, 9–12.

28. There are intriguing uses of *lǐ* in the Guōdiàn texts, but without enough context to draw conclusions. For example, *Chéngzhī wènzhī* (Completing it, hearing it), says, "Heaven sends down great constancy, to coherently pattern [*lǐ* 理] human relations" (Liú Zhāo 2003, strip 31). See also *Yǔ cóng* III (Liú Zhāo 2003, strips 17–19).

29. For examples see 6: 91, 19: 373, 8: 124, 17: 318; Knoblock 1988, 6.2, 19.9c, 8.4, 17.11.

30. Since the passage says explicitly that *lǐ* is accomplished by human beings, taking *lǐ* as an objectively proper order requires a sophisticated and bizarre metaphysics in which *lǐ* simultaneously exists and does not exist. Although we could find such a metaphysics in Aristotle, there is no evidence for it in early Chinese thought.

31. How reverent the *Xúnzǐ* is toward heaven is a question of tone and depends more how one hears it than on the text. My "ear" is closer to that of Chén Dàqí, who says that one of Xúnzǐ's radical points is his rejection of reverence and awe toward heaven (1954, 15). In at least a few passages, though, Graham seems right in saying that Xúnzǐ retains "a certain residual awe of the sacred in nature" (1989, 239).

32. For example, Mèngzǐ says that the timing of heaven is not as important as the benefits of earth, which are not as important as human harmony (2B2). For an excellent account of the interplay of these three elements, see Wang 2012, 136–42; for more examples, see Sato 2003, 316–23.

33. Scholars seem compelled to read "three" as emphasizing unity. Machle goes furthest in this direction, translating "three" as "to make up a perfectly aligned threesome" (1993, 47). Masayuki Sato and Janghee Lee both invoke Christian language to translate it as "to form a trinity" (Sato 2003, 149; Lee 2005, 70). Knoblock translates it as "form a Triad," putting "triad" in capital letters (Knoblock 1988, 17.2a). The fact that Xúnzǐ uses "three" instead of "one," though, should not be ignored. The term "three" does not imply union and could be just as well translated as "form a third alongside of." For background on the use of *sān*, see Sato 2003, 316–23.

34. Páng Pǔ argues that the *Xúnzǐ* originally distinguished two characters for *wěi*, the first using a heart radical to mean deliberate action and the second using the person radical to indicate the artificial that results from sustained deliberate action (2005, 40). The form of *wěi* using the heart radical appears in several Guōdiàn texts but later disappeared. Páng claims that this replacement obscured a distinction Xúnzǐ was making.

35. I follow Liú Zhāo 2003 and Páng 1999 in taking *xiá* 狎 as *xí* 習 (practice).

36. Knoblock and Eno take this line differently, that we call those thing which go along with our kind "auspicious" and what goes against our kind as "inauspicious" (Knoblock 1988; Eno 1990a, 199). That would nicely align with claims in the *Zhuāngzǐ* that we label good and bad according to what is or is not useful to us. Nonetheless, such a reading seems less likely when paired with the preceding line. Together they account for relationships within a kind and between things of different kinds. Moreover, "heavenly government" more likely describes the good and bad consequences that come from acting according to or against one's kind, rather than describing how we label things.

37. Although not in this context, several people have pointed out that Xúnzǐ allows for natural capacities with no set content. Addressing the sense of rightness, Nivison writes that human beings have "a bare capacity that enables men to form societies with hierarchical social distinctions and to apprehend an obligation as a *moral* obligation; yet a capacity that has no positive *content*" (1996b, 324). Stalnaker comments that the heart has the capacity to make distinctions, but that this can be done according to any set of standards (2006, 67). See also Hutton 2000, 221–24.

38. Similar statements appear in 4: 62 and 8: 144 (Knoblock 1988, 4.8, 8.11). Xúnzǐ's line is remarkably close to the *Xìng zì mìng chū*, which says, "Within the four seas their natures are the same. It is in the use of the heart that each is different. Education is what makes it so" (Liú Zhāo 2003, strip 9).

39. I follow the reading of Lǐ Dísheng (1979, 498) taking this line as a version of the claims that anyone can become a sage because all people have a basic quality (*zhì* 質) capable of knowing, and rightness and ritual have coherent patterns that can be known (23: 443; Knoblock 1988, 23.5a). Knoblock reads the passage this way. Another possibility is to take this line as saying, "by knowing human nature one can know the integral patterns of things," a reading given by Yáng Liàng (Wáng Xiānqiān 1988, 406) and followed by Watson 1967, 135. Although that reading is somewhat more natural grammatically, it fits less well the context of the passage or Xúnzǐ's overall epistemology.

40. Watson translates the chapter title as "Dispelling Obsessions"; although Knoblock translates the title as "Dispelling Blindness," he sometimes translates *bì* as "obsess the mind" (Watson 1967; Knoblock 1988, 21.2). Hutton translates *bì* as "fixation" (2000).

41. For this understanding of *bì*, I am indebted to discussions with Chris Fraser, who has suggested translating *bì* as "blinkered by." See Fraser 2006, 533–35.

42. For another version of the same point, see 17: 319–320 (Knoblock 1988, 17.12).

43. Ziporyn takes a similar view, focusing more on patterns of coherence: "Xunzi sees real coherences existing in nature, real divisions in the world, real similarities and differences. The problem is that these coherences themselves do not cohere. There are too many of them, too many alternate, equally *real* ways in which things group" (2012, 208).

44. For examples, see 19: 356, 22: 414, 22: 422; Knoblock 1988, 19.2d, 22.1c, 22.3d.

45. Lee Yearley is one of few people to bring out this point of connection to Zhuāngzǐ's skepticism (1980, 468).

46. A few passages suggest the reactions of an empty unbiased heart as a criterion (21: 400–401; Knoblock 1988, 21.7b), but passages that push the analysis further say it is not the heart itself but the way (21: 395–96; Knoblock 1988, 21.5d) or methods (5: 72–73; Knoblock 1988, 5.1) followed by the heart.

47. "Chastened intellectualism" is meant to describe a similarity between Augustine and Xúnzǐ. Stalnaker explains, "Such a position affirms the value of intellectual apprehension and reflection, but it questions the neutrality and absolute sovereignty of thinking" (2006, 275).

48. That the tradition developed over time is suggested in a discussion of the origins of names, some of which came from the Shàng, some from the Zhōu, some from ritual texts,

and some from the formation of customs among the people (22: 411–12; Knoblock 1988, 22.1a). Xúnzǐ never lists which sagely person invented which things but rather refers to a vaguely defined group of people spread over two millennia of time. For this interpretation, see Nivison 1996b, 328; Kline 2000; and Chén Wénhào 2008, 74–83. Ivanhoe goes so far as to claim that not even the sages could grasp the whole system (1991, 238). The *Xìng zì mìng chū* explicitly presents the formation of the classics as a cumulative process (Liú Zhāo 2003, strips 15–20).

49. As Homer Dubs puts it, "Since it could not be absolute as inhering in the nature of things, as Confucius held, it was to be absolute as supported by the greatest authority and power in the country, and so could be universally established" (1927, 237).

50. The point is fairly obvious, but an example might help. No one would claim that the current Pinyin system of transliterating Chinese characters into the Roman alphabet is perfect, or even the best available. Yet most scholars would oppose introducing a new system because it would most likely lead to further incommensurability between different systems and texts. Most would even advocate using force (e.g., denying publication) to prevent new systems from coming into use. If Pinyin were perfect, such controls would be unnecessary.

Conclusion

1. I've tried to capture the rhyme, but the final line more literally says, "the moment has not yet arrived."

2. I quote the lines from the *Mòzǐ*, which cites the "Greater Odes" as their source (16.13: 125). They appear with slightly different wording in the *Shī jīng*, but in different stanzas (256). The first line is frequently cited in Warring States texts, as in the "Record on Standards" ("Biǎo jì" 表記) chapter of the *Lǐ jì* (Sūn Xīdàn 1988, 1300), and the "Enriching the State" ("Fù guó" 富國) chapter of the *Xúnzǐ* (10: 183; Knoblock 1988, 10.6).

3. The same lines appear in slightly different form in *Zhuāngzǐ* 28: 971; Mair 1994, 288.

Bibliography

Adams, Marilyn McCord, and Robert Merrihew Adams, eds. 1991. *The Problem of Evil*. Oxford: Oxford University Press.
Allan, Sarah. 1997. *The Way of Water and the Sprouts of Virtue*. Albany: State University of New York Press.
———. 2009. "Not the *Lun yu*: The Chu Script Bamboo Slip Manuscript, *Zigao*, and the Nature of Early Confucianism." *Bulletin of the School of Oriental and African Studies* 72.1: 115–51.
———. 2010. "Abdication and Utopian Vision in the Bamboo Slip Manuscript, *Rongchengshi*." In Cheng and Perkins, *Chinese Philosophy in Excavated Early Texts*, 67–84.
Allan, Sarah, and Crispin Williams. 2000. "An Account of the Discussion." In *The Guodian Laozi: Proceedings of the International Conference, Dartmouth College, May 1998*, ed. Sarah Allan and Crispin Williams, 115–83. Berkeley, Calif.: Society for the Study of Early China.
Allen, Diogenes. 1991. "Natural Evil and the Love of God." In Adams and Adams, *The Problem of Evil*, 189–208.
Ames, Roger T. 1983. "Nietzsche's 'Will to Power' and Chinese 'Virtuality.'" In *Nietzsche and Asian Thought*, ed. Graham Parkes, 130–50. Chicago: University of Chicago Press.
———. 1989. "Putting the Te Back in Taoism." In *Nature in Asian Traditions of Thought*, ed. J. Baird Callicott and Roger T. Ames, 113–44. Albany: State University of New York Press.
———. 2002. "Mencius and a Process Notion of Human Nature." In Chan, *Mencius*, 72–90.
Ames, Roger T., ed. 1998. *Wandering at Ease in the Zhuangzi*. Albany: State University of New York Press.
Ames, Roger T., and David L. Hall. 2003. *Daodejing—Making This Life Significant—A Philosophical Translation*. New York: Ballantine.
Angle, Stephen C. 2009. *Sagehood: The Contemporary Significance of Neo-Confucian Philosophy*. Oxford: Oxford University Press.
Andreini, Attilio. 2006. "The Meaning of Qing 情 in the Texts of Guodian Tomb no. 1." In *Love, Hatred, and Other Passions: Questions and Themes on Emotions in Chinese Civilization*, ed. Paolo Santangelo and Donatello Guida, 149–65. Leiden: Brill.
Annas, Julia, and Jonathan Barnes, trans. 2000. *Sextus Empiricus: Outlines of Scepticism*. Cambridge: Cambridge University Press.
Ariew, Roger, and Daniel Garber, eds. and trans. 1989. *Leibniz: Philosophical Essays*. Indianapolis, Ind.: Hackett.
Augustine. 1960. *The Confessions of St. Augustine*. Trans. John K. Ryan. New York: Doubleday.
———. 1993. *On Free Choice of the Will*. Trans. Thomas Williams. Indianapolis: Hackett.

Barnes, Jonathan, ed. 1984. *The Complete Works of Aristotle*. 2 vols. Princeton, N.J.: Princeton University Press.
Behuniak, James. 2004. *Mencius on Becoming Human*. Albany: State University of New York Press.
———. 2008. "Confucius on Form and Uniqueness." In Jones, *Confucius Now*, 49–57.
Bergson, Henri. 1946. *The Creative Mind*. Trans. Mabelle Andison. New York: The Philosophical Library.
Billeter, Jean François. 2006. *Contre François Jullien*. Paris: Editions Allia.
Bloom, Irene. 2002. "Biology and Culture in the Mencian View of Human Nature." In Chan, *Mencius*, 91–102.
Boodberg, Peter A. 1952/53. "The Semasiology of Some Primary Confucian Concepts." *Philosophy East and West* 2: 317–32.
Brindley, Erica Fox. 2006. "Music and Cosmos in the Development of 'Psychology' in Early China." *T'oung Pao* 92.1–3: 1–49.
———. 2010. "'The Perspicuity of Ghosts and Spirits' and the Problem of Intellectual Affiliations in Early China." *Journal of the American Oriental Society* 129.2: 215–36.
Brindley, Erica Fox, Paul Goldin, and Esther Klein, trans. 2013. "A Philosophical Translation of the Heng Xian." *Dao: A Journal of Comparative Philosophy*, 2.12: 145–51.
Brooks, E. Bruce, and A. Taeko Brooks. 1998. *The Original Analects*. New York: Columbia University Press.
———. 2002a. "The Nature and Historical Context of the Mencius." In Chan, *Mencius*, 242–81.
———. 2002b. "Word philology and text philology in Analects 9:1." In Van Norden, *Confucius and the Analects*, 163–215.
Cáo Fēng 曹峰. 2006. *Shànghǎi chǔjiǎn sīxiǎng yánjiū* 上海楚簡想研究. Taibei: Wanjuanlou.
Chan, Alan Kam-Leung. 2002. "A Matter of Taste: Qi (Vital Energy) and the Tending of the Heart (Xin) in *Mencius* 2A2." In Chan, *Mencius*, 42–71.
Chan, Alan Kam-Leung, ed. 2002. *Mencius: Contexts and Interpretations*. Honolulu: University of Hawai'i Press.
Chan, Shirley. 2009. "Human Nature and Moral Cultivation in the Guodian 郭店 Text of the *Xing Zi Ming Chu* 性自命出 (Nature Derives from Mandate)." *Dao: A Journal of Comparative Philosophy* 8: 361–82.
Chan, Wing-tsit. 1963a. *A Sourcebook in Chinese Philosophy*. Princeton, N.J.: Princeton University Press.
———. 1963b. *The Way of Lao Tzu*. New York: Bobbs-Merrill.
Chén Dàqí 陳大齊. 1954. *Xúnzǐ xuéshuō* 荀子學說. Taibei: Zhonghua wenhua chuban shiye weiyuanhui chubanshe.
———. 1980. *Mèngzǐ dàijiě lù* 孟子待解錄. Taibei: Taiwan shangwu yinshuguan.
Chén Gǔyìng 陳鼓應. 1983. *Zhuāngzǐ jīnzhù jīnyì* 莊子今注今譯. Beijing: Zhongguo shuju.
———. 1988. *Lǎozǐ zhùyì jí píngjià* 老子註譯及評價. Beijing: Zhonghua shuju.
———. 2013. *Dàojiā de rénwén jīngshén* 道家的人文精神. Beijing: Zhonghua shuju.
Chén Lái 陳來. 2008. *Gǔdài sīxiǎng wénhuà de shìjiè: Chūnqiū shídài de zōngjiào, lúnlǐ yǔ shèhuì sīxiǎng* 古代思想文化的世界：春秋時代的宗教，倫理與社會思想. Beijing: SDX Joint Publishing.

———. 2009a. *Gǔdài zōngjiào yǔ lúnlǐ: Rújiā sīxiǎng de gēnyuán* 古代宗教與倫理：儒家思想的根源. Beijing: SDX Joint Publishing.

———. 2009b. *Tradition and Modernity: A Humanist View.* Trans. Edmund Ryden. Leiden: Brill.

———. 2009c. *Zhúbó Wǔxíng yǔ jiǎnbó yánjiū* 竹帛《五行》與簡帛研究. Beijing: SDX Joint Publishing.

Chen, Ning. 1994. "The Problem of Theodicy in Ancient China." *Journal of Chinese Religions* 22: 51–74.

———. 1997a. "Concept of Fate in Mencius." *Philosophy East and West* 47.4: 495–520.

———. 1997b. "Confucius' View of Fate (Ming)." *Journal of Chinese Philosophy* 24.3: 323–59.

———. 1997c. "The Genesis of the Concept of Blind Fate in Ancient China." *Journal of Chinese Religions* 25: 141–67.

———. 2002. "The Ideological Background of the Mencian Discussion of Human Nature: A Reexamination." In Chan, *Mencius*, 17–41.

———. 2003. "Mohist, Daoist, and Confucian Explanations of Confucius's Suffering in Chen-Cai." *Monumenta Serica* 51: 37–54.

Chén Qíyóu 陳奇猷. 1984. *Lǚshì chūnqiū xīnshì* 呂氏春秋新釋. Shanghai: Shanghai guji chubanshe.

———. 2000. *Hánfēizǐ xīn jiàozhù* 韓非子新校注. Shanghai: Shanghai guji chubanshe.

Chén Wénhào 陳文浩. 2008. *Xúnzǐ de biànshuō* 荀子的辯說. Beijing: Huaxia chubanshe.

Cheng, Chung-ying, and Franklin Perkins, eds. 2010. *Chinese Philosophy in Excavated Early Texts. Journal of Chinese Philosophy* Supplement (37.S1).

Chong, Kim-Chong. 2002. "Mengzi and Gaozi on *Nei* and *Wai*." In Chan, *Mencius*, 103–25.

Cook, Daniel J., and Henry Rosemont, Jr., eds. and trans. 1994. *Writings on China.* Chicago: Open Court.

Cook, Scott. 1997. "Xunzi on Ritual and Music." *Monumenta Serica* 45: 1–38.

———. 2010. "'*San De*' and Warring States Views on Heavenly Retribution." In Cheng and Perkins, *Chinese Philosophy in Excavated Early Texts*, 101–23.

Cook, Scott, ed. 2003. *Hiding the World in the World: Uneven Discourses on the Zhuangzi.* Albany: State University of New York Press.

Cooper, John M., ed. 1997. *Plato Complete Works.* Indianapolis, Ind.: Hackett.

Cottingham, John, Robert Stoothoff, and Dugold Murdoch, eds. and trans. 1985. *The Philosophical Writings of Descartes*, vol. 2. Cambridge: Cambridge University Press.

Coutinho, Steve. 2004. *Zhuangzi and Early Chinese Philosophy: Vagueness, Transformation and Paradox.* Burlington, Vt.: Ashgate.

Crandell, Michael. 1983. "On Walking without Touching in the Ground: 'Play' in the Inner Chapters of the Chuang-tzu." In Mair, *Experimental Essays on Chuang-Tzu*, 101–24.

Creel, Herrlee G. 1932. "Was Confucius Agnostic?" *T'ung Pao* 29: 55–99.

———. 1960. *Confucius and the Chinese Way.* New York: Harper Torchbooks.

———. 1970. *What is Taoism and Other Studies in Chinese Cultural History.* Chicago: University of Chicago Press.

Cua, Antonio S. 1985. *Ethical Argumentation: A Study in Hsün Tzu's Moral Epistemology*. Honolulu: University of Hawai'i Press.
Curley, Edwin, trans. and ed. 1994. *A Spinoza Reader: The Ethics and Other Works*. Princeton, N.J.: Princeton University Press.
Csikszentmihalyi, Mark. 1999. "Mysticism and Apophatic Discourse in the *Laozi*." In Csikszentmihalyi and Ivanhoe, *Religious and Philosophical Aspects of the Laozi*, 33–59.
———. 2002. "Confucius and the Analects in the Han." In Van Norden, *Confucius and the Analects*, 134–162.
———. 2004. *Material Virtue: Ethics and the Body in Early China*. Leiden: Brill.
Csikszentmihalyi, Mark, and Philip J. Ivanhoe., eds. 1999. *Religious and Philosophical Aspects of the Laozi*. Albany: State University of New York Press.
Csikszentmihalyi, Mark, and Michael Nylan. 2003. "Constructing Lineages and Inventing Traditions through Exemplary Figures in Early China." *T'oung Pao* 89: 59–99.
Deangelis, Gary D., and Warren G. Frisina, eds. 2008. *Teaching the Daode Jing*. Oxford: Oxford University Press.
Defoort, Carine. 2004. "Mohist and Yangist blood in Confucian Flesh: The Middle Position of the Guodian Text 'Tang Yu zhi Dao.'" *Bulletin of the Museum of Far Eastern Antiquities* 76: 44–70.
Deleuze, Gilles. 1988. *Bergsonism*. Trans. Hugh Tomlinson and Barbara Habberjam. New York: Zone Books.
Derrida, Jacques. 1981. *Dissemination*. Trans. Barbara Johnson. Chicago: University of Chicago Press.
Dīng Sìxīn 丁四新. 2000. *Guōdiàn chǔmù zhújiǎn sīxiǎng yánjiū* 郭店楚墓竹簡思想研究. Beijing: Dongfang chubanshe.
Dīng Wèixiáng 丁為祥. 2008. "Mengzi's Inheritance, Criticism, and Overcoming of Mohist Thought." Trans. Franklin Perkins. *Journal of Chinese Philosophy* 38.3: 403–19.
Dīng Yuánzhí 丁原植. 2000. *Guōdiàn chǔjiǎn: Rújiā yìjí sìzhǒng shìxī* 郭店楚簡儒家佚籍四种釋析. Taibei: Taiwan guji.
Duàn Yùcái 段玉裁. 1988. *Shuōwén jiězì zhù* 說文解字注. Shanghai: Shanghai guji chubanshe.
Dubs, Homer H. 1927. *Hsüntze: Moulder of Ancient Confucianism*. London: Arthur Probsthain.
———. 1958. "The Archaic Royal Jou Religion." *T'oung Pao* 46.3–5: 217–59.
Eno, Robert. 1990a. *The Confucian Creation of Heaven: Philosophy and the Defense of Ritual Mastery*. New York: State University of New York Press.
———. 1990b. "Was There a High God *Ti* in Shang Religion?" *Early China* 15: 1–26.
———. 1996. "Cook Ding's Dao and the Limits of Philosophy." In Kjellberg and Ivanhoe, *Essays on Skepticism*, 127–51.
———. 2002. "Casuistry and Character in the *Mencius*." In Chan, *Mencius*, 189–215.
Epictetus. 1983. *The Handbook (The Encheiridion)*. Trans. Nicholas White. Indianapolis, Ind.: Hackett.
Fàn Zhòngyān 范仲淹. 2002. *Fàn Zhòngyān quánjí* 范仲淹全集. Chengdu: Sichuan daxue chubanshe.
Flanagan, Owen. 2008. "Moral Contagion and Logical Persuasion in the *Mozi*." *Journal of Chinese Philosophy* 38.3: 473–91.

Fraser, Chris. 2006. "Zhuangzi, Xunzi, and the Paradoxical Nature of Education." *Journal of Chinese Philosophy* 33(4): 529–42.
———. 2008. "Mohism and Self-Interest." *Journal of Chinese Philosophy* 38.3: 437–54.
———. 2010. "Mohism." In *The Stanford Encyclopedia of Philosophy (Summer 2010 Edition)*, ed. Edward N. Zalta. plato.stanford.edu/achives/sum2010/entries/mohism.
———. 2012. "Skepticism and Value in the *Zhuāngzǐ*." *International Philosophical Quarterly* 49.4: 439–57.
Fraser, Chris, Timothy O'Leary, and Dan Robins, eds. 2011. *Ethics in Early China*. Hong Kong: Hong Kong University Press.
Gadamer, Hans-Georg. 1994. *Truth and Method*. Trans. Joel Weinsheimer and Donald G. Marshall. 2nd ed. London: Continuum.
Gāo Hēng 高亨. 1980. *Shījīng jīnzhù* 詩經今注. Shanghai: Shanghai guli chubanshe.
———. 1998. *Zhōuyì dàchuán jīnzhù* 周易大傳今注. Jinan: Qilu shushe.
Gasché, Rodolphe. 2009. *Europe, or the Infinite Task: A Study of a Philosophical Concept*. Palo Alto, Calif.: Stanford University Press.
Gerhardt, C. J., ed. 1978. *Die Philosophischen Schriften von Gottfried Wilhelm Leibniz*. Hildesheim: George Olms Verlag.
Girardot, Norman J. 1985. "Behaving Cosmogonically in Early Taoism." In Lovin and Reynolds, *Cosmogony and Ethical Order*, 67–97.
———. [1983] 2008. *Myth and Meaning in Early Taoism*. Reprint, Magdelena, N.M.: Three Pines Press.
Goldin, Paul. 1999. *Rituals of the Way*. Chicago: Open Court.
Graham, Angus C. 1989. *Disputers of the Tao: Philosophical Argument in Ancient China*. Indianapolis, Ind.: Open Court.
———. 2001. *Chuang-Tzu: The Inner Chapters*. Indianapolis, Ind.: Hackett.
———. 2002. "The Background of the Mencian Theory of Human Nature." In Liu and Ivanhoe, *Essays on the Moral Philosophy of Mengzi*, 1–63.
———. 2003a. "Chuang Tzu's Essay on Seeing Things as Equal." In Roth, *A Companion to Angus C. Graham's Chuang Tzu*, 104–29.
———. 2003b. "How Much of *Chuang Tzu* Did Chuang Tzu Write?" In Roth, *A Companion to Angus C. Graham's Chuang Tzu*, 58–103.
———. 2003c. "Textual Notes to *Chuang Tzu: The Inner Chapters*." In Roth, *A Companion to Angus C. Graham's Chuang Tzu*, 5–57.
Gray, John. 2003. *Straw Dogs: Thoughts on Humans and Other Animals*. New York: Farrar, Straus and Giroux.
Gù Xiégāng 顧頡剛 and Liú Qìyú 劉起釪. 2005. *Shàngshū jiào shì yì lùn* 尚書校釋譯論. Beijing: Zhonghua shuju.
Guess, Raymond, and Ronald Speirs, trans. 1999. *The Birth of Tragedy and Other Writings*. Cambridge: Cambridge University Press.
Guō Qìngfán 郭慶藩. 1978. *Zhuāngzǐ jíshì* 莊子集釋. Beijing: Zhonghua shuju.
Guō Yí 郭沂. 2001. *Guōdiàn zhújiǎn yǔ Xiānqín xuéshù sīxiǎng* 郭店竹簡與先秦學術思想. Shanghai: Shanghai jiayu chubanshe.
Hagen, Kurtis. 2007. *Xunzi: A Philosophical Reconstruction*. Chicago: Open Court.
Hall, David L., and Roger T. Ames. 1987. *Thinking Through Confucius*. Albany: State University of New York Press.
Hàn shū 漢書. 1983. Beijing: Zhonghua shuju.

Hansen, Chad. 1983. "A Tao of Tao in Chuang-tzu." In Mair, *Experimental Essays on Chuang-Tzu*, 24–55.
———. 1992. *A Daoist Theory of Chinese Thought*. Oxford: Oxford University Press.
———. 2003. "Guru or Skeptic? Relativistic Skepticism in the *Zhuangzi*." In Cook, *Hiding the World in the World*, 128–62.
Hé Níng 何寧. 1998. *Huáinánzi jíshì* 淮南子集釋. Beijing: Zhonghua shuju.
Hegel, Georg Wilhelm Friedrich. 1952. *Phänomenologie des Geistes*. Hamburg: Verlag von Felix Meiner.
———. 1955. *Ästhetik*. 2 vols. Frankfurt am Main: Europäische Verlagsanstalt.
Heidegger, Martin. 1993. *Heidegger: Basic Writings*. Trans. David Farrell Krell. Bloomington: Indiana University Press.
———. 1996. *Hölderlin's Hymn "The Ister."* Trans. William McNeill and Julia Davis. Bloomington: Indiana University Press.
Hendrischke, Barbara. 1991. "The Concept of Inherited Evil in the Taiping Jing." *East Asian History* 2: 1–30.
Henricks, Robert G. 1999. "Re-exploring the Analogy of the Dao and the Field." In Csikszentmihalyi and Ivanhoe, *Religious and Philosophical Aspects of the Laozi*, 161–74.
———. 2000. *Lao Tzu's Tao Te Ching: A Translation of the Startling New Documents Found at Guodian*. New York: Columbia University Press.
———. 2008. "The Dao and the Field: Exploring an Analogy." In Deangelis and Frisina, *Teaching the Daode Jing*, 31–47.
Hill, Jason D. 1999. *Becoming a Cosmopolitan: What It Means to Be a Human Being in the New Millennium*. Lanham, Md.: Rowman and Littlefield.
Horstmann, Rolf-Peter, and Judith Norman, eds. 2001. *Beyond Good and Evil*. Cambridge: Cambridge University Press.
Hú Shì 胡适. 2003. *Zhōngguó zhéxuéshǐ dàgāng* 中國哲學史大綱. Beijing: Dongfang chubanshe.
Huāng Huī 黃暉. 1990. *Lùnhéng jiàoshì* 論衡校釋. Beijing: Zhonghua shuju.
Hume, David. 2007. *Dialogues Concerning Natural Religion and Other Writings*. Ed. Dorothy Coleman. Cambridge: Cambridge University Press.
Hutton, Eric. 2000. "Does Xunzi Have a Consistent Theory of Human Nature?" In Kline and Ivanhoe, *Virtue, Nature, and Moral Agency*, 220–36.
Inwood, Brad, and L. P. Gerson, eds. 1988. *Hellenistic Philosophy: Introductory Readings*. Indianapolis, Ind.: Hackett.
Ivanhoe, Philip J. 1988. "A Question of Faith: A New Interpretation of Mencius 2B.13." *Early China* 13: 153–65.
———. 1991. "A Happy Symmetry: Xunzi's Ethical Thought." *Journal of the American Academy of Religion* 59: 309–22.
———. 1996. "Was Zhuangzi a Relativist?" In Kjellberg and Ivanhoe, *Essays on Skepticism*, 196–214.
———. 1999. "The Concept of *de* ('Virtue') in the *Laozi*." In Csikszentmihalyi and Ivanhoe, *Religious and Philosophical Aspects of the Laozi*, 239–57.
———. 2000. "Human Nature and Moral Understanding in the *Xunzi*." In Kline and Ivanhoe, *Virtue, Nature, and Moral Agency*, 237–49.
———. 2002a. *Ethics in the Confucian Tradition: The Thought of Mencius and Wang Yang-Ming*. 2nd ed. Indianapolis, Ind.: Hackett.

———. 2002b. "Whose Confucius? Which Analects?" In Van Norden, *Confucius and the Analects*, 119–33.

———. 2007. "Heaven as a Source of Ethical Warrant in Early Confucianism." *Dao: A Journal of Comparative Philosophy* 6: 211–20.

Ivanhoe, Philip J., and Bryan W. Van Norden, eds. 2005. *Readings in Classical Chinese Philosophy* (2nd ed.). Indianapolis, Ind.: Hackett.

Jì Xùshēng 季旭昇, ed. 2003. *Shànghǎi Bówùguǎn zàng Zhànguó Chǔzhújiǎn II dúběn* 上海博物館藏戰國楚竹簡 (II) 讀本. Taibei: Wanjuanlou tushu fufen.

———. 2004. *Shànghǎi Bówùguǎn zàng Zhànguó Chǔzhújiǎn I dúběn* 上海博物館藏戰國楚竹簡 (I) 讀本. Taibei: Wanjuanlou tushu fufen.

———. 2005. *Shànghǎi Bówùguǎn zàng Zhànguó Chǔzhújiǎn III dúběn* 上海博物館藏戰國楚竹簡 (III) 讀本. Taibei: Wanjuanlou tushu fufen.

Jiāo Xún 焦循. 1987. *Mèngzǐ zhèngyì* 孟子正義. 2 vols. Beijing: Zhonghua shuju chubanshe.

Johnson, David G. 1980. "Wu Tzu-hsu Pien-wen and Its Sources." *Harvard Journal of Asiatic Studies* 40.1: 93–156 (part 1); 40.2: 465–505 (part 2).

———. 1981. "Epic and History in Early China: The Matter of Wuzi Xu." *Journal of Asian Studies* 40.2: 255–71.

Johnston, Ian. 2010. *The Mozi: A Complete Translation*. New York: Columbia University Press.

Jones, David, ed. 2008. *Confucius Now: Contemporary Encounters with the* Analects. Chicago: Open Court.

Kaltenmark, Max. 1969. *Lao Tzu and Taoism*. Trans. Roger Greaves. Stanford, Calif.: Stanford University Press.

Kant, Immanuel. 1900. *Kants gesammelte Schriften*. Berlin: German Academy of Sciences.

Karlgren, Bernhard. 1944. "Glosses on the Siao Ya Odes." *Bulletin of the Museum of Far Eastern Antiquities* 16: 25–169.

———. 1946. "Glosses on the Ta Ya and Sung Odes." *Bulletin of the Museum of Far Eastern Antiquities* 18: 1–198.

———. 1950. *The Book of Documents*. Stockholm: Museum of Far Eastern Antiquities.

Kirkland, Sean D. 2012. *The Ontology of Socratic Questioning in Plato's Early Dialogues*. Albany: State University of New York Press.

———. Forthcoming. "Tragic Time." In *The Returns of Antigone: Interdisciplinary Readings*. Ed. Sean D. Kirkland and Tina Chanter. Albany: State University of New York Press.

Kjellberg, Paul. 1996. "Sextus Empiricus, Zhuangzi, and Xunzi on 'Why be Skeptical?'" In Kjellberg and Ivanhoe, *Essays on Skepticism*, 1–25.

Kjellberg, Paul, and Philip J. Ivanhoe, eds. 1996. *Essays on Skepticism, Relativism, and Ethics in the* Zhuangzi. Albany: State University of New York Press.

Klein, Esther. 2010. "Were There "Inner Chapters" in the Warring States? A New Examination of Evidence about the *Zhuangzi*." *T'oung Pao* 96.4-5: 299–369.

Kline, T. C., III. 2000. "Moral Agency and Motivation in the Xunzi." In Kline and Ivanhoe, *Virtue, Nature, and Moral Agency*, 155–75.

Kline, T.C., III, and Philip J. Ivanhoe, eds. 2000. *Virtue, Nature, and Moral Agency in the* Xunzi. Indianapolis, Ind.: Hackett.

Knoblock, John, trans. 1988, 1990, 1994. *Xunzi: A Translation and Study of the Complete Works*. 3 vols. Stanford, Calif.: Stanford University Press.

Knoblock, John, and Jeffrey Reigel, trans. 2000. *The Annals of Lü Buwei: A Complete Translations and Study*. Stanford, Calif.: Stanford University Press.

Kohn, Livia, and Michael LaFargue, eds. 1998. *Lao-tzu and the Tao-te-ching*. Albany: State University of New York Press.

Krell, David Farrell. 2005. *The Tragic Absolute: German Idealism and the Languishing of God*. Bloomington: Indiana University Press.

LaFargue, Michael. 1992. *The Tao of the Tao Te Ching*. Albany: State University of New York Press.

———. 1998. "Recovering the Tao-te-ching's Original Meaning: Some Remarks on Historical Hermeneutics." In Kohn and LaFargue, *Lao-tzu and the Tao-te-ching*, 255–75.

———. 2008. "Hermeneutics and Pedagogy: Gimme that Old-Time Historicism." In Deangelis and Frisina, *Teaching the Daode Jing*, 167–92.

Lau, D. C. 2000. "Theories of Human Nature in *Mencius* (孟子) and *Xunzi* (荀子)." In Kline and Ivanhoe, *Virtue, Nature, and Moral Agency*, 188–219.

Lau, D. C., trans. 1963. *Tao Te Ching*. New York: Penguin.

———. 1970. *Mencius*. New York: Penguin.

———. 1979. *Confucius: The Analects*. New York: Penguin.

———. 1994. *Tao Te Ching: Translation of the Ma Wang Tui Manuscripts*. New York: Alfred A. Knopf.

Lee, Janghee. 2005. *Xunzi and Early Chinese Naturalism*. Albany: State University of New York Press.

Legge, James, trans. 1985. *The Chinese Classics*, Vol. 3, *The Shoo King, or the Book of Historical Documents*. Taibei: Southern Materials reprint.

———. 1970. *The Works of Mencius*. New York: Dover.

Lǐ Díshēng 李滌生. 1979. *Xúnzǐ jíshì* 荀子集釋. Taibei: Xuesheng shuju.

Lǐ Líng 李零. 2002. *Guōdiàn chǔjiǎn jiàodújì* 郭店楚簡校讀紀. Beijing: Peking University Press.

Lǐ Ruì 李銳. 2004. "Guōdiàn Chǔjiǎn *Qióngdá yǐ shí* zàikǎo" 郭店楚簡〈窮達以時〉再考. In *Xīn chūtǔ wénxiàn yǔ gǔdài wénmíng yánjiū* 新出土文獻與古代文明研究, ed. Xiè Wéiyáng 謝維揚 and Zhū Yuānqīng 朱淵清. Shanghai: Shanghai daxue chubanshe, 268–78.

———. 2009. "Lùn Shàngbó jiǎn *Guǐshén zhī míng* piān de xuépài xìngzhì—jiān shuō duì wénxiàn xuépài shǔxìng pàndìng de wùqū" 論上博簡《鬼神之明》篇的學派性質—兼說對文獻學派屬性判定的誤區. *Húběi dàxué xuébào (Zhéxué shèhuìbǎn)* 湖北大學學報(哲學社會版) 36.1: 28–33.

Lǐ Tiānhóng 李天虹. 2003. *Xìng zì mìng chū yánjiū* 《性自命出》研究. Wuhan: Hubei jiaoyu chubanshe.

Liáng Tāo 梁濤. 2008. *Guōdiàn zhújiǎn yǔ Sī Mèng xuépài* 郭店竹簡與思孟學派. Beijing: China People's University Press.

Liào Míngchūn 廖名春. 2006. "Dú 'Shàngbó wǔ · Guǐshén zhī míng' piān zhájì" 讀《上博五·鬼神之明》篇札記. Confucius 2000 website. www.confucius2000.com/admin/list.asp?id=2250.

Liú Bǎonán 劉寶楠. 1990. *Lúnyǔ zhèngyì* 論語正義. Beijing: Zhonghua shuju.

Liú Xiàogǎn 劉笑敢. 1995. *Classifying the Zhuangzi Chapters.* Trans. Donald Munro. Ann Arbor: University of Michigan Press.

———. 1999. "Naturalness (Tzu-jan), the Core Value in Taoism: Its Ancient Meaning and its Significance Today." In Kohn and LaFargue, *Lao-tzu and the Tao-te-ching,* 211–30.

———. 2006. *Lǎozǐ gǔjīn* 老子古今. Beijing: Zhongguo shehui kexue chubanshe.

Liu Xiusheng. 2002. "Mengzian Internalism." In Liu and Ivanhoe, *Essays on the Moral Philosophy of Mengzi,* 101–31.

Liu Xiusheng and Philip J. Ivanhoe, eds. 2002. *Essays on the Moral Philosophy of Mengzi.* Indianapolis, Ind.: Hackett.

Liú Zhāo 劉釗, ed. 2003. *Guōdiàn Chǔjiǎn jiàoshì* 郭店楚簡校釋. Fuzhou: Fujian renmin chubanshe.

Lóu Yǔliè 樓宇烈, ed. 1999. *Wáng Bì jí jiàoshì* 王弼集校釋. Beijing: Zhonghua shuju.

Louden, Robert B. 2002. "'What Does Heaven Say?' Christian Wolff and Western Interpretations of Confucian Ethics." In Van Norden, *Confucius and the Analects,* 73–93.

Lovin, R., and F. Reynolds, eds. 1985. *Cosmogony and Ethical Order: New Studies in Comparative Ethics.* Chicago: University of Chicago Press.

Lowe, Scott. 1992. *Mo Tzu's Religious Blueprint for a Chinese Utopia.* Lewiston, N.Y.: Edwin Mellen.

Loy, David. 1996. "Zhuangzi and Nagarjuna on the Truth of No Truth." In Kjellberg and Ivanhoe, *Essays on Skepticism,* 50–67.

Loy, Hui-chieh. 2008. "Justification and Debate: Thoughts on Moist Moral Epistemology." *Journal of Chinese Philosophy* 38.3: 455–71.

Mǎ Chéngyuán 馬承源, ed. 2004. *Shànghǎi Bówùguǎnzàng zhànguó Chǔ zhújiǎn III* 上海博物館藏楚竹簡III. Shanghai: Shanghai guji chubanshe.

———. 2005. *Shànghǎi Bówùguǎnzàng zhànguó Chǔ zhújiǎn V* 上海博物館藏楚竹簡, V. Shanghai: Shanghai guji chubanshe.

Machle, Edward. 1993. *Nature and Heaven in the* Xunzi: *A Study of the Tian Lun.* Albany: State University of New York Press.

Mair, Victor, ed. 1983. *Experimental Essays on Chuang-Tzu.* Honolulu: University of Hawai'i Press.

Mair, Victor, trans. 1990. *Tao Te Ching: The Classic Book of Integrity and the Way.* New York: Bantam.

———. 1994. *Wandering on the Way: Early Taoist Tales and Parable of Chuang Tzu.* Honolulu: University of Hawai'i Press.

Major, John S., Sarah A. Queen, Andrew Seth Meyer, and Harold D. Roth, trans. 2010. *The* Huainanzi: *A Guide to the Theory and Practice of Government in Early Han China.* New York: Columbia University Press.

Makeham, John. 1996. "The Formation of the Lunyu as Book." *Monumenta Serica* 44: 1–24.

———. 1998. "Between Chen and Cai: *Zhuangzi* and the *Analects.*" In Ames, *Wandering at Ease in the Zhuangzi,* 75–100.

Malebranche, Nicholas. 1980. *Dialogue Between a Christian Philosopher and a Chinese Philosopher on the Existence and Nature of God.* Trans. A. Dominick Iorio. Washington, D.C.: University Press of America.

Martin, Bill. 2008. *Ethical Marxism: The Categorical Imperative of Liberation*. La Salle, Ill.: Open Court.
Mei, Yi-pao. 1934. *Mo-tse, the Neglected Rival of Confucius*. London: Probsthain.
Meineck, Peter, and Paul Woodruff, trans. 2003. *Sophocles: Theban Plays*. Indianapolis, Ind.: Hackett.
Moeller, Hans-Georg. 2006. *The Philosophy of the Dao De Jing*. New York: Columbia University Press.
——. 2007. *Dao De Jing*. Chicago: Open Court.
——. 2009. *The Moral Fool: A Case for Amorality*. New York: Columbia University Press.
Neiman, Susan. 2002. *Evil in Modern Thought: An Alternative History of Philosophy*. Princeton, N.J.: Princeton University Press.
Nienhauser Jr., William H., ed. and trans. 1995. *The Grand Scribe's Records*. Bloomington: Indiana University Press.
Nietzsche, Friedrich. 1988. *Kritische Studienausgabe*. Ed. G. Colli and M. Montinari. Berlin: de Gruyter.
Nivison, David S. 1978–79. "Royal 'Virtue' in Shang Oracle Inscriptions." *Early China* 4: 52–55.
——. 1996a. *The Ways of Confucianism*. Ed. Bryan W. Van Norden. Chicago: Open Court.
——. 1996b. "Replies and Comments." In *Chinese Language, Thought, and Culture: Nivison and His Critics*, ed. Philip J. Ivanhoe, 267–341. Chicago: Open Court.
——. 2002. "Mengzi as Philosopher of History." In Chan, *Mencius*, 282–304.
Nussbaum, Martha C. 1986. *The Fragility of Goodness: Luck and Ethics in Greek Tragedy and Philosophy*. Cambridge: Cambridge University Press.
Olberding, Amy. 2008. "Slowing Death Down: Mourning in the *Analects*." In Jones, *Confucius Now*, 137–49.
Páng Pǔ 龐朴. 1999. "Zhúbó Wǔxíng piān jiàozhù" 竹帛五行篇校注. Jianbo/Bamboo Silk website. www.bamboosilk.org/pangpu/Zhuanzhu/Wuxing/Jiaozhu1.htm.
——. 2005. *Wénhuà Yīyú* 文化一隅. Zhengzhou: Zhongzhou guji chubanshe.
Pankenier, David W. 1995. "The Cosmo-Political Background of Heaven's Mandate." *Early China* 20: 121–76.
Paolucci, Anne, and Henry Paolucci, eds. and trans. 1962. *Hegel on Tragedy*. New York: Harper and Row.
Parkes, Graham. 1983. "The Wandering Dance: Chuang Tzu and Zarathustra." *Philosophy East and West* 33.3: 235–50.
Parkes, Graham, trans. 2005. *Thus Spoke Zarathustra*. Oxford: Oxford University Press.
Péng Guóxiáng 彭國翔. 2007. *Rújiā chuántǒng: zōngjiào yǔ rénwén zhǔyì zhījiān* 儒家傳統：宗教與人文主義之間. Beijing: Peking University Press.
Perkins, Franklin. 2004. *Leibniz and China: A Commerce of Light*. Cambridge: Cambridge University Press.
——. 2007. *Leibniz: A Guide for the Perplexed*. London: Continuum Press.
——. 2008. "The Moist Criticism of the Confucian Use of Fate." *Journal of Chinese Philosophy* 35.3: 421–36.
——. 2009. "Human Motivation and the Heart (*xin*) in the *Xing Zi Ming Chu*." *Dao: A Journal of Chinese Philosophy*, 8.2: 117–31.
——. 2010a. "Of Fish and Men: Species Difference and the Strangeness of Being Human in the *Zhuangzi*." *The Harvard Review of Philosophy* 17: 118–36.

———. 2010b. "Recontextualizing *Xing* 性: Self-Cultivation and Human Nature in the Guodian Texts." In Cheng and Perkins, *Chinese Philosophy in Excavated Early Texts*, 16–32.
———. 2011a. "No Need for Hemlock: Mengzi's Defense of Tradition." In Fraser, Robins, and O'Leary, *Ethics in Early China*, 65–81.
———. 2011b. "Wandering beyond Tragedy with Zhuangzi." *Comparative and Continental Philosophy* 3.1: 79–98.
———. 2013. "The Spontaneous Generation of the Human in the 'Heng Xian.'" *Dao: A Journal of Comparative Philosophy*, 12.2: 225–240.
Pines, Yuri. 2002. *Foundations of Confucian Thought: Intellectual Life in the Chunqiu Period, 72–453 B.C.E.* Honolulu: University of Hawai'i Press.
Poo, Mu-chou. 1998. *In Search of Personal Welfare: A View of Early Chinese Religion.* Albany: State University of New York Press.
Puett, Michael J. 2001. *The Ambivalence of Creation: Debates Concerning Innovation and Artifice in Early China.* Stanford, Calif.: Stanford University Press.
———. 2002. *To Become a God: Cosmology, Sacrifice, and Self-Divinization in Early China.* Cambridge, Mass.: Harvard University Asia Center.
———. 2003. "'Nothing Can Overcome Heaven': The Notion of Spirit in the *Zhuangzi*." In Cook, *Hiding the World in the World*, 248–262.
———. 2004. "The Ethics of Responding Properly: The Notion of *Qing* 情 in Early Chinese Thought." In *Love and Emotions in Traditional Chinese Literature*, ed. Halvor Eifring, 37–68. Leiden: Brill.
———. 2005. "Following the Commands of Heaven: The Notion of Ming in Early China." In *The Magnitude of Ming: Command, Allotment, and Fate in Chinese Culture*, ed. Christopher Lupke, 49–69. Honolulu: University of Hawai'i Press.
Raphals, Lisa. 1996. "Skeptical Strategies in the Zhuangzi and Theaetetus." In Kjellberg and Ivanhoe, *Essays on Skepticism*, 26–49.
Roberts, Moss. 2001. *Laozi Dao De Jing: The Book of the Way.* Los Angeles: University of California Press.
Robinet, Isabelle. 1999. "The Diverse Interpretations of the *Laozi*." In Csikszentmihalyi and Ivanhoe, *Religious and Philosophical Aspects of the Laozi*, 127–59.
Robins, Dan. 2001. *The Debate over Human Nature in Warring States China.* Ph.D. diss., University of Hong Kong.
———. 2008. "The Moists and the Gentlemen of the World." *Journal of Chinese Philosophy* 38.3: 385–402.
———. 2011a. "It Goes Beyond Skill." In Fraser, Robins, and O'Leary, *Ethics in Early China*, 105–24.
———. 2011b. "The Warring States Conception of *Xing*." *Dao: A Journal of Comparative Philosophy* 10.1: 31–51.
Rosemont, Henry, Jr., and Roger T. Ames. 1998. *The Analects of Confucius: A Philosophical Translation.* New York: Ballantine.
Roth, Harold D. 1998. "The Laozi in the Context of Early Daoist Mystical Praxis." In Kohn and LaFargue, *Lao-tzu and the Tao-te-ching*, 59–96.
———. 2003a. "Bimodal Mystical Experience in the 'Qi Wu Lun 齊物論' Chapter of the *Zhuangzi* 莊子." In Cook, *Hiding the World in the World*, 15–32.
———. 2003b. "Colophon: An Appraisal of Angus Graham's Textual Scholarship on the *Chuang Tzu*." In Roth, *A Companion to Angus C. Graham's Chuang Tzu*, 181–219.

Roth, Harold D., ed. 2003. *A Companion to Angus C. Graham's Chuang Tzu.* Honolulu: University of Hawai'i Press.
Sato, Masayuki. 2003. *The Confucian Quest for Order: The Origin and Formation of the Political Thought of Xun Zi.* Leiden: Brill.
Schneewind, J. B. 2005. "Globalization and the History of Philosophy." *Journal of the History of Ideas* 66.2: 169–78.
Schwartz, Benjamin I. 1985. *The World of Thought in Ancient China.* Cambridge, Mass.: Harvard University Press.
Shào Hóng 邵鴻. 2007. *Zhāngjiāshān hànjiǎn "Hé Lú" yánjiū* 張家山漢簡〈盧〉研究. Beijing: Wenwu chubanshe.
Shaughnessy, Edward. 1993. "Shang shu 尚書 (Shu ching 書經)." In *Early Chinese Texts: A Bibliographical Guide.* ed. Michael Loewe, 376–89. Berkeley: University of California Press, 1993.
———. 2006. *Rewriting Early Chinese Texts.* Albany: State University of New York Press.
Shih, Joseph. 1969/70. "The Notion of God in Ancient Chinese Religion." *Numen* 16/17: 99–138.
Shih, Vincent Y. C. 1963. "Metaphysical Tendencies in Mencius." *Philosophy East and West* 12.4: 319–41.
Shun, Kwong-loi. 1997. *Mencius and Early Chinese Thought.* Stanford, Calif.: Stanford University Press.
Sīmǎ Qiān 司馬遷. 1959. *Shǐ jì* 史記. Bejing: Zhonghua shuju.
Slingerland, Edward. 1996. "The Conception of Ming in Early Confucian Thought." *Philosophy East and West* 46.4: 567–81.
———. 2003. *Confucius Analects, with Selections from Traditional Commentaries.* Indianapolis, Ind.: Hackett.
Stalnaker, Aaron. 2006. *Overcoming Our Evil: Human Nature and Spiritual Exercises in Augustine and Xunzi.* Washington, D.C.: Georgetown University Press.
Sūn Xīdàn 孫希旦. 1988. *Lǐ jì jíjiě* 禮紀集解. Beijing: Zhonghua shuju.
Sūn Yíràng 孫詒讓. 2001. *Mòzǐ xiángǔ* 墨子閒詁. Beijing: Zhonghua shuju.
Tan, Sor-hoon. 2008. "Three Corners for One: Tradition and Creativity in the *Analects*." In Jones, *Confucius Now*, 59–77.
Táng Jūnyì 唐君毅. 1958. *Zhōngguó rénwén jīngshén zhī fāzhǎn* 中國人文精神之發展. Hong Kong: Rensheng chubanshe.
Tseu, Augustinus. 1965. *The Moral Philosophy of Mo-tze.* Taibei: Fu Jen Catholic University, Graduate School of Philosophy.
Tucker, Mary Evelyn, and John Berthrong, eds. 1998. *Confucianism and Ecology: The Interrelation of Heaven, Earth, and Humans.* Cambridge, Mass.: Harvard University Press.
Van Norden, Bryan W. 1996. "Competing Interpretations of the Inner Chapters of the Zhuangzi." *Philosophy East and West* 46.2: 247–68.
———. 1999. "Method in the Madness of the Laozi." In Csikszentmihalyi and Ivanhoe, *Religious and Philosophical Aspects of the Laozi*, 187–210.
———. 2000. "Mengzi and Xunzi: Two Views of Human Agency." In Kline and Ivanhoe, *Virtue, Nature, and Moral Agency*, 103–34.
———. 2007. *Virtue Ethics and Consequentialism in Early Chinese Philosophy.* Cambridge: Cambridge University Press.

———. 2008. *Mengzi, with Selections from Traditional Commentaries*. Indianapolis, Ind.: Hackett.
Van Norden, Bryan W., ed. 2002. *Confucius and the Analects: New Essays*. New York: Oxford University Press.
Waley, Arthur, trans. 1958. *The Way and Its Power: A Study of the Tao Te Ching and Its Place in Chinese Thought*. New York: Grove Press.
———. 1989. *The Analects of Confucius*. New York: Vintage.
———. 1996. *The Book of Songs: The Ancient Chinese Classic of Poetry*. New York: Grove Press.
Wáng Guówéi 王國維. 1997. *Wáng Guówéi wénjí* 王國維文集. 4 vols. Ed. Yào Gánmíng 姚淦銘 and Wáng Yān 王燕. Beijing: Zhongguo wenshi chubanshe.
Wang Huaiyu. 2008. "Care and Reverence: Exploring the Origin of Early Confucian Thinking." *Journal of Chinese Philosophy* 35.1: 139–57.
Wáng Kǎ 王卡. 1997. *Lǎozǐ Dàodéjīng Héshànggōng* 老子道德經河上公章句. Beijing: Zhonghua shuju.
Wang, Robin R. 2005. "Dong Zhongshu's Transformation of Yin-yang Theory and Contesting of Gender Identity." *Philosophy East and West* 55.2: 209–31.
———. 2012. *Yinyang: The Way of Heaven and Earth in Chinese Thought and Culture*. Cambridge: Cambridge University Press.
Wáng Xiānqiān 王先謙. 1988. *Xúnzǐ jíjiě* 荀子集解. Beijing: Zhonghua shuju.
———. 2008. *Zhuāngzǐ jíjiě* 莊子集解. Beijing: Zhonghua shuju.
Watson, Burton, trans. 1967. *The Basic Writings of Mo Tzu, Hsün Tzu, and Han Fei Tzu*. New York: Columbia University Press.
———. 1968. *The Complete Works of Chuang Tzu*. New York: Columbia University Press.
Weber, Max. 1964. *The Religion of China: Confucianism and Taoism*. Trans. Hans Gerth. New York: Macmillan.
Wong, Benjamin, and Hui Chieh Loy. 2004. "War and Ghosts in Mozi's Political Philosophy." *Philosophy East and West* 54.3: 343–64.
Wong, David B. 2000. "Xunzi on Moral Motivation." In Kline and Ivanhoe, *Virtue, Nature, and Moral Agency*, 135–54.
———. 2002. "Reasons and Analogical Reasoning in Mengzi." In Liu and Ivanhoe, *Essays on the Moral Philosophy of Mengzi*, 187–220.
Wood, Allen, and George di Giovanni, trans. 1998. *Religion within the Boundaries of Mere Reason, and Other Writings*. Cambridge: Cambridge University Press.
Wú Jìn'ān 吳進安. 2003. *Mòjiā zhéxué* 墨家哲學. Taibei: Wunan tushu chuban.
Xú Fùguān 徐復觀. 1969. *Zhōngguó rénxìnglùn shǐ* 中國人性論史. Taibei: Taiwan shangwu yinshuguan.
Yáng Bójūn 楊伯峻. 1990. *Chūnqiū Zuǒzhuàn zhù* 春秋左傳注. Beijing: Zhonghua shuju.
———. 2002. *Lúnyǔ yìzhù* 論語譯註. Beijing: Zhonghua shuju.
———. 2003. *Mèngzǐ yìzhù* 孟子譯註. Beijing: Zhonghua shuju.
Yearley, Lee H. 1980. "Hsun Tzu on the Mind: His Attempted Synthesis of Confucianism and Daoism." *Journal of Asian Studies* 39: 465–80.
———. 1983. "The Perfected Person in the Radical Chuang-tzu." In Mair, *Experimental Essays on Chuang-Tzu*, 125–39.
———. 1985. "A Confucian Crisis: Mencius' Two Cosmogonies and Their Ethics." In Lovin and Reynolds, *Cosmogony and Ethical Order*, 310–27.

———. 1988. "Toward a Typology of Religious Thought: A Chinese Example." *Journal of Religion* 55.4: 426–43.
———. 1990. *Mencius and Aquinas: Theories of Virtue and Conceptions of Courage.* Albany: State University of New York Press.
———. 1996. "Zhuangzi's Understanding of Skillfulness and the Ultimate Spiritual State." In Kjellberg and Ivanhoe, *Essays on Skepticism,* 152–82.
Zhāng Zǎi 張載. 1978. *Zhāng Zǎi jí* 張載集. Beijing: Zhonghua shuju.
Zheng Jiadong (鄭家棟). 2005. "The Issue of the 'Legitimacy' of Chinese Philosophy." *Contemporary Chinese Thought* 37.1: 11–23.
Zhōu Zhènfǔ 周振甫. 2002. *Shījīng yìzhù* 詩經譯注. Beijing: Zhonghua shuju.
Zhū Xī 朱熹. 2003. *Sìshū zhāngjù jízhù* 四書章句集注. Beijing: Zhonghua shuju.
Ziporyn, Brook. 2003. "How Many Are the Ten Thousand Things and I? Relativism, Mysticism, and the Privileging of Oneness in the 'Inner Chapters.'" In Cook, *Hiding the World in the World,* 33–63.
———. 2009. *Zhuangzi: The Essential Writings, with Selections from Traditional Commentaries.* Indianapolis, Ind.: Hackett.
———. 2012. *Ironies of Oneness and Difference: Coherence in Early Chinese Thought, a Prolegomena to the Study of Li.* Albany: State University of New York Press.

Index

acceptance, 60, 121, 125, 126, 135, 139, 153, 159, 171, 175, 176, 220. *See also* harm: acceptance of
actions, 12, 16, 21, 23–24, 31, 32, 33, 34, 38–39, 47, 52, 54, 55, 60, 66, 72, 77, 78, 80, 85, 87, 91, 102, 106, 112, 121, 126, 127, 129, 130, 133, 138, 140, 143, 149, 153, 157, 171, 184, 187, 188, 189, 194, 195, 198, 205, 207, 208, 212, 214, 221, 232n54, 237n28, 241n60, 244n86, 244nn88–89, 250n46, 250n53, 251n63, 258n50, 260n69, 265n3, 266n15; bad, 19, 38–39, 74, 139, 185, 204; consequences of, 76, 85, 88, 99; deliberate, 40–41, 89, 109, 193, 206–207, 267n34; efficacy of, 8, 28, 35, 40, 45–46, 62, 65, 79, 83, 98, 102–103, 105, 114, 116, 172, 173, 185, 186–87; good, 5, 6, 23, 40–41, 52, 59, 64, 74, 96–103, 131, 139, 147, 204; of heaven, 67, 71, 89, 118; motivation for, 59, 77, 128; non-action, 42, 76, 91, 103, 104, 105, 114, 172; power of, 31, 35, 83–84, 89, 98; spontaneous, 41. *See also* Ru: and human actions
affirmation, 42–43, 154, 174
afterlife, 26, 65, 220, 231n35
agency: of heaven, 65, 126; of humans, 76, 88, 138, 244n93
ài 愛 (care), 55, 84, 90–91, 131, 135, 142, 143, 170
Ames, Roger, 90, 93, 231n33, 235n10, 237n26, 240n50, 241n65, 248n24, 249n40, 250n53, 251nn58–59, 251n64, 252n68, 252n74, 253n76, 258n48
amorality, 13, 25, 37, 100, 157, 187, 199–200, 202, 207, 214, 217, 220
Angle, Stephen C., 227n2
anthropocentrism, 35, 36, 45, 73, 82, 92, 93, 98, 99, 115, 142, 152, 165, 170, 178, 180–81, 183, 199, 212, 214, 220–21, 224
anthropomorphism, 17, 28, 29, 32, 37, 45, 51, 63–64, 72, 73, 86, 87, 92, 95, 96, 98, 105, 117–18, 123, 142, 145, 153, 180, 188, 198, 199, 212, 237n25, 247n22, 249n39, 250n49, 253n3
anxiety, 15, 24, 26, 30–31, 43, 51, 53, 54, 60, 114, 125, 162–63, 164, 165, 167, 173, 178, 185, 199, 215, 237n26
appropriation, 201–202, 208, 214, 217
Aristotle, 5, 41, 181, 267n30

assistance, 18, 56, 108, 111–12, 114, 145, 187, 250n48, 252nn74–75, 253n78, 260n70
Augustine, 3, 38, 42, 109, 233n71, 268n47
authority, 5, 27, 63, 67–68, 69, 77, 215, 216, 262n32, 269n49; of the heart, 168, 169; moral, 47, 49; political, 13, 69
Axial Age, 16

Bacon, Francis, 199
Bayle, Pierre, 180
Behuniak, James, 92, 141, 241n65, 253n3, 255n15, 256n26, 256n33, 257n37
bēi 悲 (sadness). *See* sadness
benefit, 20, 47, 53, 56–57, 59, 66, 68, 70, 71, 73–74, 83, 84, 87, 88, 91, 97, 102, 104, 129, 133, 134, 136, 148, 149, 154, 190, 192, 193, 195, 196, 200, 201, 238n36, 239n44, 258n47, 260n73, 267n32; calculation of, 132, 195, 213, 265n13; and harm, 23, 170, 171, 174, 185; from heaven, 73, 82, 105, 112, 243n76; and humaneness, 62, 166; long-term, 189, 195, 206; of nature, 72, 104–106; for oneself, 60, 65, 78, 136, 238n41, 239n44; for others, 63–65, 73; of the way, 106–107, 212. *See also* humaneness: and benefit; *lì* 利 (benefit)
Bergson, Henri, 107, 227n5
bì 蔽 (conceal), 135, 210, 211, 216, 268nn40–41
Bǐ Gàn, 22–24, 27, 103, 151, 230n19
Bó Yí, 4, 22–25, 28, 90, 103, 105, 151
Brindley, Erica, 244n86, 244n88, 256n33
Buddhism, 1, 46

Cáo Jǐnyán, 76, 244n85
causality, 3, 15, 31, 39, 41, 109, 251n64
Chan, Alan, 259n65
Chan, Wing-tsit, 15, 92, 93, 249n40, 250n49
cháng 常 (regularity), 86, 105, 184, 185, 204, 246n9. *See also* regularity
chaos, 48, 50, 56, 64, 98, 100, 125, 126, 128, 129, 141, 192, 223, 224. *See also* disorder
Chén Dàqí, 118, 124, 127, 199, 203, 204, 253n3, 254n5, 256n28, 267n31
Chén Gǔyìng, 88, 92, 167, 230n24, 246n8, 247n21, 248n25, 250n49, 252n73, 261n18, 263n38

285

286 | Index

Chén Lái, 16, 28, 31, 231n38, 232n53, 260n69
Chen Ning, 11, 231n35, 231n38, 236n15, 254n10, 255n18, 258n48
chéng 成 (complete), 86, 110, 168, 170, 193, 201, 204, 211, 252n68
Chéng Xuányīng, 23, 162, 167, 261n18
Chéngzhī wenzhī 成之聞之 (Completing it, hearing it) 51, 86, 236n22, 267n28
Christianity, 1, 3, 12, 13, 42, 142, 199, 235n4, 238n35, 241n57, 242nn70–71, 267n33
Chǔ state, 17, 18, 19–20, 21–22, 25, 80, 119, 120, 188, 245n103, 254n8
Cicero, 258n50
conformity, 79, 81, 131, 158, 159–60, 163, 164, 165, 174, 181, 204, 242n70, 252n66, 266n16; nonconformity, 161
Confucianism, 1, 4, 11, 14, 46, 142, 157, 227n7, 228n3, 235n4, 257n43, 264n48. *See also* Kǒngzǐ; Ru (Confucians)
Confucius. *See* Kǒngzǐ
consequences, 62, 68, 76, 78, 83, 85, 88, 99–100, 102, 105, 140, 157, 172, 180, 183, 192, 208, 268n36. *See also* actions: consequences of
constancy, 30, 85–87, 88, 104, 113, 211, 237n28, 243n83, 247n11; of heaven, 51, 86–87, 203, 267n28. See also *héng* 恆 (constancy)
contingency, 43, 63, 85, 208, 251n64
continuity, 2, 14, 16, 40, 105, 141, 143, 157, 203, 228n6; discontinuity, 14, 228n6
control, human, 12, 21, 29, 31, 35, 45, 54, 56, 61, 62, 63, 68, 76, 77, 84, 85, 87, 103, 110, 113, 119, 121, 124, 125, 127, 138–40, 172, 186, 187, 188, 196, 198, 202, 217, 233n61, 237n26, 240n50, 247n13, 251n57, 258n51; of nature, 38, 114, 198, 215, 220; self-control, 135, 140
correctness, 89, 96, 102, 165, 245n98, 247n19
Coutinho, Steve, 156–57, 263n38
Crandell, Michael, 176, 263n44
Creel, Herrlee, 92, 99, 235n5, 240n50
Csikszentmihalyi, Mark, 11, 235n5, 235n7, 240n50, 250n52, 260n69
culture, 1–2, 3–4, 13, 47, 51, 67–70, 72, 92, 100, 108, 154, 198, 201, 203, 204, 208, 213, 215, 217, 218, 219, 223–24, 236n15

dá 達 (success, reach to), 21, 91, 121, 185. *See also* success
dào, 50, 63, 76, 83, 87, 93–96, 97, 99, 103–104, 107, 109–10, 112, 113, 115, 128, 131, 132, 139, 152, 157, 168, 193, 194, 195, 198, 245n98, 247n22, 248n29, 249nn33–34, 250n51, 251n57, 251n64, 266nn15–16. *See also* way, the

Dàodéjīng 道德經, 5, 6, 8, 22, 25, 63, 72, 76, 82–88, 90, 91–101, 102–103, 105–107, 108–10, 111–12, 114–15, 116, 127, 129, 134, 143, 145, 148–49, 152–53, 159, 170, 171, 173, 175, 179, 184, 185, 187, 190, 221, 223, 224, 228n12, 230n21, 230n25, 239n43, 244n89, 245n100, 247n22, 248n30, 249n36, 249n39, 250nn49–53, 251n56, 251n65, 252n69, 260nn70–71
dé 德 (virtue), 24, 25, 30, 47, 52, 85, 86, 93, 96–97, 103–104, 110, 147, 148, 158, 161, 164, 171, 185, 230n21, 243n82, 251n59. *See also* virtue
defiance, 42–43, 128, 182–83, 215
Defoort, Carine, 236n22
Deleuze, Gilles, 107, 227n5
Derrida, Jacques, 81, 277n1, 245n101
Descartes, René, 3, 42, 69, 109
desires, sensory, 38, 129, 134, 135, 190, 197, 207, 265n13
determinism, 41, 138. *See also* fatalism
Dīng Wèixiáng, 234n1, 242n66
disorder, 9, 21, 25, 33, 40, 41, 55–58, 65, 75, 79, 108, 116, 117, 118, 125, 140, 185–88, 194, 204, 207, 214, 222, 230n26, 232n53, 251n60, 255n21. *See also* chaos; government: disordered; order
divination, 6, 28, 65, 85, 228n9, 241n59, 265n4
divine, the, 25, 29, 30, 45, 49, 51, 64, 65, 69, 242n69; and humans, 1, 16, 66, 82, 198; views of, 20, 28, 32, 34, 46, 49, 249n39; and the world, 11, 12, 37, 220
divine forces, 12, 13, 29, 32, 63, 66, 71, 76, 77, 96, 149, 156, 198, 266n17
divisions: between heaven and human, 8, 14, 15, 52, 116, 139, 141, 155, 187, 198, 206–207, 208, 225; social, 201–202, 204, 214. See also *tiānrén zhīfēn* 天人之分 (division between heaven and human)
Dǒng Zhòngshū, 228n5
dú 獨 (singularity). *See* singularity
Dubs, Homer, 11, 140, 236n20, 269n49

è 惡 (bad), 40, 187, 200. *See also* evil; *wù* 惡 (hate)
education, 40, 46, 57, 67, 121, 208, 230n23, 268n38
efficacy, human, 20, 64, 76, 85, 86, 87, 88, 89, 96, 97, 103, 104, 126, 173, 188, 198, 199, 249n34, 249n40, 250n53. *See also* actions: efficacy of
emotions, human, 8, 95, 130, 146, 147, 157, 167, 169, 183, 191, 257n40. See also *qíng* 情 (genuine feelings)

emulation, 8, 59, 122, 140, 161, 162, 232n45, 238n40, 239n43, 242n68, 263n36
Enlightenment, 17, 70, 198, 199, 212, 214
Eno, Robert, 11, 50, 157, 189, 232n52, 235n11, 238n38, 244n91, 246n104, 254n4, 265n3, 268n36
Epictetus, 239n46
Epicurus, 21, 35, 229n17
ethics, 8, 12, 17, 35–36, 43, 74, 82, 87, 102, 128, 141, 153, 170, 184, 220, 222, 241n60; Confucian, 14; humanistic, 46, 66, 74; Mohist, 64; Ru, 117, 197; virtue, 2
Europe, 1, 3, 4, 5, 10–11, 13–17, 34, 35, 36, 37–38, 41, 43, 46, 87, 98, 107, 114, 198–99, 214, 222, 223, 225, 227n1, 228n1. *See also* philosophy: European; tradition: European
evil, 11, 13, 24, 25, 32, 39–40, 43, 109, 115, 121, 200, 203, 228n1, 229n17; metaphysical, 38; moral, 17, 33, 35, 38, 39, 214, 223, 224, 233n70, 240n47, 250n52; natural, 17, 33, 38, 214, 220, 223, 224; problem of, 4, 8–9, 11–12, 13, 15, 17, 19, 21, 24, 26, 27, 29, 31, 34–38, 40, 41–43, 49, 66, 74–75, 81, 87, 90, 97, 98, 101, 103, 105, 116, 117, 118, 120–21, 136, 140, 141, 151, 152, 153, 157, 164, 171, 180–81, 184, 196, 197, 198, 214, 219–20, 222, 223, 224, 228n9, 233n58, 233n69, 236n19, 239n44, 254n4, 264n46; radical, 35, 39–40, 214. *See also* è 惡 (bad)
external, the, 58, 59–60, 61, 62, 83, 91, 96, 121, 122, 131, 134, 146–47, 190, 198, 215, 229n10, 237n26, 240n48, 253n78, 257n38; external things, 23, 26, 53–54, 57, 62, 130, 151, 169. *See also* internal, the; rightness: externality of

failure, 12, 20–21, 23, 25–26, 54–55, 56, 57, 60, 61, 62, 77, 84, 88, 101, 106, 121, 141, 171, 172, 175, 176, 181, 182, 184, 185, 188, 198, 201, 237n31, 240n55, 245n97. *See also* qióng 窮 (failure, limit)
family, 15, 19, 30, 42, 55–56, 70, 72, 91–93, 131, 134, 142, 192, 238n35, 238n41, 258n46
fatalism, 8, 17, 45, 51–52, 54, 57–59, 61, 62, 63, 66, 77, 83, 106, 116–17, 125, 137, 171–72, 176, 186, 237n26, 239n45, 240n48. *See also* Ru (Confucians): and fatalism
fate, 4, 22, 24, 25, 29, 30, 31, 34, 46, 48–50, 51, 52, 53, 54, 56–59, 60–61, 62, 64, 76, 77–79, 80, 83–86, 116, 118, 122, 123, 125, 135, 137–40, 141, 151, 153, 158, 171, 172, 177, 183, 185, 186, 188, 202, 205, 230n18, 237n32, 240nn50–51, 245n97, 255n17, 256n27, 258n48, 258nn51–52, 265n6; blind, 34, 45, 56, 123, 236n15, 254n10; correct, 137–40, 230n18, 258n49, 258n51. *See also* mìng 命 (fate)
fēi 非 (wrong), 133, 154, 166–67, 174. *See also* shì 是 (right)
Flanagan, Owen, 238n40, 242n68
fortune, 87, 89, 240n55; good, 20, 22, 30, 47, 51, 63, 75, 85, 89, 247n15, 247n19, 250n53, 258n47, 265n4. *See also* misfortune
Fraser, Chris, 238n35, 242n66, 242n74, 243n75, 245n98, 263n37, 268n41
free will, 2, 3, 15, 38–39, 41, 108, 109, 199, 214
fú 福 (fortune). *See* fortune
fǔ 輔 (assist), 111, 252nn74–75, 260n70

Gadamer, Hans-Georg, 176
Gāo Hēng, 232n56, 248n25
Gàozǐ, 129, 134, 142, 144, 146–47, 200, 257n38, 262n32
gentlemen, 23, 25, 26, 51, 53, 54–55, 59, 60–61, 66, 68, 77, 87, 110, 116, 119, 123, 134–35, 139, 140, 142, 148–49, 159, 162, 188–89, 195–96, 197, 198, 202, 204, 206, 210, 216, 231n33, 237n26, 237n29, 240n48, 241n64, 258n52, 265n13, 266n15
ghosts, 6, 16, 21, 45, 46, 65–66, 71, 74, 75–76, 79, 231n35, 235n7, 237n32, 240n55, 241nn58–61, 243n76, 243n78, 244nn93–94. *See also* spirits
Girardot, Norman, 95, 251n61
God, 11, 12, 13, 17, 21, 31, 34, 35, 36–39, 41–42, 44, 46, 50, 64, 69, 74, 98–99, 180, 199, 220, 225, 233n58, 240n56, 242nn70–71
gods, 14, 16, 21, 28, 29, 34, 36, 64, 166, 182, 217, 229n17, 232n53, 232n55, 233n66, 234n86, 236n15
Goldin, Paul, 203, 265n4, 266n16
governing, 29, 58, 60, 63, 78, 100, 108. *See also* government
government, 12, 20, 58, 76, 100, 106, 205, 247n20, 249n34, 261n18; disordered, 188; heavenly, 207, 268n36; humane, 119, 134; kingly, 120; meritocratic, 56; sagely, 104. *See also* governing
Graham, A. C., 11, 79, 152, 160, 167, 174, 233n61, 234n1, 244n94, 249n35, 253n79, 256n29, 257n40, 261n9, 261n17, 262n21, 262n23, 262n26, 263n38, 263n40, 267n31
Gray, John, 179
Guǐshén zhī míng 鬼神之明 (Discernment of ghosts and spirits), 6, 21, 23, 75, 230n26, 244n88
Guō Xiàng, 23, 152, 156, 164, 165, 167, 171, 256n31, 261n10, 263n33

Guōdiàn, 6, 228n12; texts, 51, 52, 81, 83, 86, 90, 91, 92, 96, 131, 134, 228n5, 246nn3–4, 246nn6–7, 246n9, 247n10, 247n22, 248n23, 248n29, 248n31, 249n36, 252n68, 252nn72–74, 255n23, 256nn32–33, 257n38, 259n66, 260n70, 265n5, 265n10, 266n22, 267n28, 267n34

Hagen, Kurtis, 211
Hall, David, 93, 235n10, 240n50, 241n65, 248n24, 249n40, 250n53, 251n58, 251n64, 252n68, 252n74, 253n76
Hàn dynasty, 4, 7, 20, 21, 46, 106, 222, 228n5, 229n10, 229n16, 234n2, 246n2, 255n14, 258n51, 261n6
Hánfēizǐ, 67, 122
Hánfēizǐ 韓非子, 26, 90, 106, 111, 240n55, 247n13, 247n19, 252n75
Hansen, Chad, 93, 236n21, 238n40, 243n83, 245n95, 245n99, 249n40, 250n50, 251n63, 253n79, 257n43, 262n31
harm, 20, 23, 25, 30, 32, 38, 40, 47, 55, 57, 62, 64, 78, 84–85, 88–89, 103–104, 106, 107, 112, 132, 135, 146, 147, 149, 154, 158, 162, 167, 170, 173, 174, 176, 185, 189, 200, 201, 207, 211, 221, 222, 238n36, 238n41, 239n46, 250n47, 260n68, 260n73; acceptance of, 101, 171; avoidance of, 86, 99, 101–102, 136, 173; causes, 105, 118
harmony, 14–15, 41, 50, 55, 65, 73, 85, 91, 96, 101, 102, 114, 145, 147, 152, 174, 180, 193, 197, 200, 203, 205, 222, 224, 228nn5–6, 261n13, 267n32; of heaven and human, 26, 116, 150, 155, 156; organic, 99, 100, 220, 250n46, 253n78; of social order, 148, 202
heart, 48, 61, 62–63, 86, 91–92, 94, 96, 100, 108, 129, 130, 132, 135, 136–37, 140, 141, 142, 143, 145, 146, 154, 155, 159, 167, 169, 187–88, 189–90, 193–94, 196, 200, 207–208, 210, 212, 235n4, 245n102, 257n34, 257n43, 258n52, 260n69, 262n29, 262n32, 263n33, 265n11, 267n34, 268nn37–38; of affirming and negating, 133, 154, 257n34; completed, 110, 167–69, 180, 184, 208; constant, 121; deliberations of, 194, 206–208; empty, 208, 211, 224, 268n46; responses of, 168, 177; of shame and aversion, 133–34, 147, 191; unmoved, 60, 146
heaven. See tiān 天 (heaven)
Hegel, Georg Wilhelm Friedrich, 14, 42, 43, 182
Heidegger, Martin, 12, 69, 227n1, 242n70
hell, 12, 39
héng 恆 (constancy), 86–87, 90, 105, 246n9, 260n68. See also constancy

Héng xiān 恆先 (Constancy first), 40, 87, 95, 107, 143, 246n9, 248n30, 259n56
Henricks, Robert, 246n3, 247n22, 249nn39–40, 251n57
Héshànggōng, 88–89, 106, 246n8, 247n13, 247n15, 247n19, 248n24, 252n66, 252n68, 252n73
Hill, Jason, 227n4
honor, 51–52, 53, 58, 59, 74, 80, 103–104, 110, 140, 185, 189, 191
Hú Shì, 19, 92, 98, 199, 203, 204, 230n27, 243n84, 260n71, 266n17
Huáinánzǐ, 229n10, 249n37
Huì Shī, 73, 221, 243n84
human nature, 15, 39, 59, 128, 141, 158, 162, 184, 189, 190, 191–93, 200, 209, 223, 235n6, 239n43, 257n43, 268n39. See also xìng 性 (nature/disposition)
humaneness, 22, 25, 46, 53, 66, 91–92, 96, 118, 120, 121, 125, 126, 133, 134, 142, 144, 145, 148–49, 154, 163, 164, 166, 198, 229n14, 235n6, 241n62, 246n3, 248n24, 254n11, 259n62; and benefit, 62, 170; and feelings, 131, 134; and heaven, 31, 117, 142
humanism, 9, 15–17, 31, 34, 38, 45–46, 57, 61, 66, 69, 70, 74, 77, 82, 95, 97, 101, 114, 118, 122, 129, 143, 153, 155, 181, 197, 198, 199, 218, 228n3, 229n8, 235n7, 236n23, 250n49
Hume, David, 35, 141, 198, 233n64; Philo, 35, 37, 180
huò 禍 (misfortune). See misfortune
Hutton, Eric, 265n3, 266n15, 268n40

immanence, 14, 145, 149, 259n63
impartiality, 72, 161, 243n79; of heaven/nature, 73–74, 104, 105, 156, 159, 170, 175, 178, 202, 213, 220, 221, 222
inclusive caring, 51, 55, 60, 62, 72, 79, 136, 141, 174, 220, 243n84, 258n46
inhumanity, 118, 121, 178, 179
injustice, 35, 45, 48, 202. See also justice
internal, the, 25, 59–60, 61, 62, 83, 91, 96, 99, 101, 121, 131, 133–34, 140, 147, 148, 153, 171, 237n26, 250n53, 257n38. See also external, the
Ivanhoe, Philip, 117, 142, 156–57, 203, 205, 241n62, 242n74, 243n78, 243n80, 253n3, 255n14, 257n43, 263n37, 268n48

Jaspers, Karl, 16
jí 吉 (propitious), 187–88
Jiāo Xún, 124, 254n8, 255n14, 255n23, 255n25, 257n40, 258n49

Jié (emperor), 28, 58, 62, 64, 172, 185–87, 190, 197, 198, 241n58, 255n21
jié 節 (moderation, order), 112, 131, 159, 189, 190, 261n17
Johnston, Ian, 241n62, 242n74, 243n78, 243n80, 243n82
judgment: the heart's, 207–208; heaven's, 29, 231n35; human, 12, 41, 74, 130, 159, 161, 168, 169, 175, 180, 211, 215; individual, 69, 70, 212, 213, 216–17; moral, 154, 264n51
jūnzǐ 君子. See gentlemen
justice, 38, 65, 79; desire for, 12; divine, 32, 38, 41, 47, 74, 76, 99, 233n59. See also injustice

Kant, Immanuel, 5, 38–39, 108, 233n70, 242n70
karma, 12
kě 可 (acceptable), 159, 168, 194–95, 207, 265n11, 265n13
kings, 18–20, 22, 30, 71, 99, 103, 118, 119, 120, 122, 123, 125, 145, 148, 216, 229n14, 232n52, 244n92; Chéng, 32; Fū Chāi, 18; Gōu Jiàn, 18–19, 229n14; Hé Lú, 18–19, 229n14; Huì, 80, 120, 132, 245n103; Kuài, 122, 126; Píng, 17–18, 19–20; Tài, 119, 186, 254nn6–7; Tāng, 28, 58, 62, 64, 120, 255n21; Wén, 22, 27, 28, 29, 30, 47, 64, 106, 122–23, 186, 246n9, 254n6; Wǔ, 22, 27, 29, 58, 64, 123; Xuān, 121, 122–23, 161; Yǎn, 120, 254n8; Yōu, 33. See also Jié (emperor); sageliness: sagely kings; Shùn (emperor); Yáo (emperor); Yǔ (emperor); Zhòu (emperor)
Kirkland, Sean, 227n3, 264n50
Knoblock, John, 185, 189, 260n73, 265n3, 265n12, 266n15, 266n19, 267n33, 268n36, 268nn39–40
knowledge, 43, 50, 69, 86, 107, 108, 135, 166, 167, 170, 208–10, 211, 212, 213, 244n86, 250n50; accumulation of, 206, 208, 212, 213
Kǒngzǐ, 7, 8, 16, 17, 21, 24, 25–26, 31, 34, 49, 50, 53, 54, 55, 60, 61, 62, 67, 73, 77, 82, 90, 120, 128, 139–40, 143, 144, 151, 153, 158–59, 162, 163, 169, 172–73, 175, 178, 188, 196, 197, 227n7, 229n13, 230n28, 230n31, 231n32, 234n2, 235nn6–7, 235n9, 235n11, 236nn19–20, 237n26, 240nn50–51, 241nn64–65, 243n79, 247n14, 254n11, 255n25, 260nn1–2; attitude toward heaven, 46–48, 50–51, 63, 66, 239n45, 241n63, 253n3; sayings of, 50, 52, 80, 91, 110, 171. See also Ru (Confucians)
Krell, David Farrell, 42

LaFargue, Michael, 83, 94, 99, 245n100, 250n45, 250n53, 251n65, 253n78, 253n80

Lǎozǐ, 73, 92, 98, 109, 113, 158–59, 163, 250n46, 251n63; Laoists, 247n22, 250n46
Lau, D. C., 61, 91, 194, 240n48, 249n40, 253n76, 255n14, 255n19
Leibniz, Gottfried Wilhelm, 1, 11, 16, 36, 38, 41, 46, 50, 107, 115, 180, 221, 233n64, 235n4, 258n50
lǐ 禮 (ritual) 102, 133, 222. See also rituals
lǐ 理 (patterns) 86, 123, 155, 156, 186, 192, 204, 206, 209, 211, 267n27, 267n28, 267n29
lì 利 (benefit), 53, 56, 70, 78, 102, 104, 105, 134, 136, 137, 154, 170, 189, 190, 258n47. See also benefit
Lǐ Dísheng, 201, 265n3, 265n12, 268n39
Lǐ jì 禮記 (Record of Rituals), 16, 91, 228n12, 244n92, 245n102
Liáng Tāo, 248n26, 255n24, 258n46
Liú Bǎonán, 80, 240n52
Liù dé 六德 (Six virtues), 257n38, 265n5, 266n22
Liú Xiàogǎn, 88, 99, 105, 113, 114, 152, 228n13, 246n9, 247n20, 250n46, 250n49, 251n64, 252nn71–72, 253n78, 262n26
Lowe, Scott, 241n59
Loy Hui-chieh, 242n66, 245n98
Lǔ state, 48, 71, 122, 158, 229n13, 239n45
lù 祿 (prosperity), 63, 240n55
luck, 52, 57, 62, 85, 86, 201, 202, 214, 240n52, 240n55, 247n18
Lùnhéng 論衡, 4, 237n28, 255n14. See also Wáng Chōng
Lúnyǔ 論語, 5, 26, 46, 47, 48, 49–54, 57, 61, 62, 66, 80, 81, 83, 90, 105, 117, 129, 178, 188, 230n31, 234n2, 236nn19–20, 237n33, 239n45, 240n51, 243n79, 249n36, 254n11, 258n48
Lǔshì chūnqiū 呂氏春秋, 3, 19, 27, 28, 73, 77, 106, 109, 149, 190, 191, 197, 221–22, 229n11, 237n28, 239n44, 254n7, 255n21, 265n8, 265n13, 266n20

Malebranche, Nicholas, 3
Mandate of Heaven, 9, 29, 30, 31, 32, 34, 45, 48, 49, 57, 87, 97, 114, 116, 119, 120, 122, 123, 125, 126, 145, 232n53
Mǎwángduī, 83, 147, 228n12, 246n2, 246n4, 246nn6–7, 246n9, 247n10, 249n36, 251n55, 251n58, 259n66
Mèngzǐ, 3, 5, 7, 46, 19, 22, 50, 60, 67, 83, 116, 117, 119–20, 129, 136, 137, 142, 146–48, 154, 155, 176, 177, 189, 196, 197, 198, 216, 227n7, 239n45, 240n47, 244n92, 253n1, 254n6, 254n8, 255n20, 255n21, 255nn24–25, 256n32, 258n47, 259n65, 262nn31–32; and fate, 62, 116, 137–38; and heaven, 20, 49, 117–18, 122, 123–28, 142, 148–50, 153, 164, 186, 222, 223, 253n3, 254n4,

264n48, 267n32; and humaneness, 118, 126, 134, 142; and humans, 62, 64, 82, 139, 143, 154, 155, 162, 167, 168, 169, 177–78, 179, 181, 182, 190, 191, 257n34, 257n43, 262n29; and nature, 145, 153, 161, 178, 222, 259n63, 260nn70–71; and virtue, 120–21, 122–23, 129, 134, 148, 184; and *xìng*, 129–30, 131–34, 135, 140, 141, 142, 143, 144, 222, 223. See also *Mèngzǐ* 孟子

Mèngzǐ 孟子, 5, 6, 8, 50, 53, 57, 62, 66, 89, 91, 92, 95, 116, 118–19, 120, 121, 127, 128, 132, 134, 136, 138, 141, 143, 144, 145, 147, 148, 153, 154, 155, 158, 159, 164, 171, 188, 200, 224, 231n35, 231n44, 236n17, 236n19, 237n29, 237n33, 239nn44–45, 243n79, 249n36, 253n1, 253n3, 254n4, 254n6, 256n32, 257n38, 258n51, 260n70. See also Mèngzǐ

míng 命 (fate), 4, 25, 29, 30, 31, 34, 45, 46, 48–49, 51–52, 54, 56–57, 59, 62, 77–78, 79, 81, 85, 88, 103, 116, 117, 118, 123, 126, 127, 129, 134–35, 138–40, 141, 151, 153, 171–72, 187, 188, 189, 238n38, 239n45, 240n48, 240n50, 244n91, 244n93, 246n6, 246n8, 247n14, 265n6

ministers, 17–20, 21–22, 28, 29, 47, 48, 51, 55, 58, 61, 65, 69, 76, 86, 96, 118, 122, 126, 127, 132, 134, 139, 172, 203, 239n45

misfortune, 22, 23, 41, 51, 63, 68, 75, 85, 89, 98, 99, 185, 187–88, 200, 211, 240n55, 247n15, 265n4

Moeller, Hans-Georg, 92, 247n13, 249n34, 249n40, 250n53, 251n58, 252nn70–71, 265n7

Mohists, 65, 67–70, 76, 77, 79, 81, 86, 90, 93, 100, 101, 102, 103, 105, 114, 117, 118, 121, 123, 133, 136, 143, 152, 163, 174, 184, 186, 187, 188, 192, 213, 223, 229n8, 231n35, 234n1, 236n22, 237n33, 238n35, 238nn38–41, 239n44, 240n56, 241nn58–59, 241n61, 243n76, 244n89, 244n91, 244n94, 245n95, 245n98, 255n21, 258n46, 260n71; and benefit, 56, 190; ethics, 64; and fate, 4, 57, 78; and ghosts/spirits, 75–76; and heaven, 8, 17, 26, 37, 45, 49, 51, 56, 63–64, 66, 67, 70, 74, 79, 82, 89, 96, 98, 105, 142, 148, 153, 221, 234n1, 237n32, 240n52, 243n81, 245n97; and humans, 45, 57, 65, 70, 74, 184, 187, 239n43; and inclusive care, 55, 62, 141; and nature, 73, 220, 242n66, 242n74; and Ru, 40, 46, 48, 60–62, 66, 73, 77, 80–81, 82, 236n22; terms, 90, 104, 130, 134, 154, 170, 246n3; and Xúnzǐ, 191, 197

morality, 8, 11, 12, 13, 20, 24, 27, 29, 33, 40, 66, 68, 82, 89, 91, 93, 96, 102, 103, 117, 133, 156, 161, 171, 175, 187, 195, 199, 201, 207, 217, 222, 231n39, 233n61, 233n70, 238n35, 241n60, 242n74, 244n86, 248n24, 255n20, 257n43; moral codes, 163, 223, 239n43, 242n74, 266n21, 268n37; moral judgments, 154, 264n51; moral qualities, 33, 121. See also amorality; authority: moral; evil: moral; judgment: moral; nature: moral indifference of; norms: moral; order: moral

motivation, 11, 42, 53, 54, 59, 61, 62, 77, 79, 81, 100, 105, 116, 128, 129, 131, 134, 135, 137, 143, 171, 190, 191, 192, 193, 195, 196, 197, 206, 221, 227n6, 238n41, 239nn43–44, 260n69, 264n50, 265n11, 265n13, 267n25

Mòzǐ, 3, 7–8, 20, 34, 45, 50–51, 56, 65–68, 69–70, 71, 74–80, 82, 83, 102, 103, 122, 143, 178, 198, 210, 213, 236nn20–21, 237n33, 238n34, 238n36, 238n41, 241n57, 241n59, 242n71, 243nn83–84, 244nn88–89, 245n103, 253n3. See also Mohists; *Mòzǐ* 墨子

Mòzǐ 墨子, 5–6, 12, 19, 23, 26, 45, 52, 55, 64, 74, 75–76, 78, 80, 81, 82, 83, 84, 85, 89, 90, 91, 92, 98, 105, 116, 129, 134, 152, 153, 159, 166, 171, 174, 184, 213, 220, 230n25, 231n35, 232n47, 234n1, 237nn32–33, 238nn38–39, 241n59, 242n67, 242n74, 243n82, 244n88, 244n94, 245n95, 245n103, 246n104, 249n36, 253n2, 269n2. See also Mòzǐ

music, 54, 64, 79, 131, 162, 191–92, 197, 217, 238n37, 257n38

naturalism, 37, 40, 46, 92, 94, 95, 102, 143, 186, 214, 219, 224, 245n97, 250n49, 266n14

nature, 37–39, 44, 69, 72–74, 92, 93, 94–95, 96, 98, 101, 103, 104, 106–107, 109, 111, 113, 114–15, 125, 129, 152–54, 155, 156, 161, 170, 171, 175, 177, 179, 180–81, 187, 198, 200–201, 211, 215, 217–18, 221–22, 236n21, 240n56, 243n76, 247n22, 248n29, 249n34, 251n60, 252n71, 253n77, 263n38, 266n17, 266n19, 267n31, 268n43; aberrations in, 33, 64; generative forces of, 97, 103, 105, 134, 144, 145–46, 148, 221, 222, 260n71; and heaven, 14, 20, 32; and humans, 1, 11, 14, 15, 34, 37, 41, 43, 70, 99, 113, 128, 142, 143, 150, 155, 173, 178, 181, 184, 199, 202–10, 212, 214, 222–24; moral indifference of, 37, 220; order of, 39, 41, 204, 215; patterns of, 8, 32, 34, 65, 66, 67, 69, 82, 89, 98, 99, 101, 102, 111, 114, 116, 128, 141, 142, 149, 152–53, 198, 203, 204, 241n63; power of, 39, 97, 144–46, 148, 212, 260n71; state of, 243n74, 248n28. See also benefit: of nature; control, human: of nature;

Index | 291

impartiality: of heaven/nature; Mèngzǐ: and nature; Mohists: and nature; regularity: of nature; *shēng* 生(grow, live)
Neiman, Susan, 4, 10, 12, 17, 34, 228n1
Nietzsche, Friedrich, 41, 42–43, 107, 149, 153, 181, 182, 221, 222, 251n59
Nivison, David, 239n43, 254n12, 255n24, 268n37
norms, 66, 70, 153, 159, 160, 161, 163, 165, 168, 178, 242n74, 243n75, 263n36; moral, 118, 264n51
Nussbaum, Martha, 42, 43, 233n66, 264n49

optimism, 17, 26–27, 41–42, 50, 104, 126, 153, 181, 264n48. *See also* pessimism
order, 20, 40, 56–58, 59, 65, 67–68, 69, 79, 82, 83, 84, 87, 107, 112, 117, 128, 141, 180–81, 185–87, 189, 194, 197, 202–205, 207, 221, 222, 248n24, 266n20; cycles of, 125, 140, 223; ethical, 8; human, 202, 203, 204, 205, 215, 250n51; moral, 87, 215; natural, 15, 41, 86, 87, 123, 250n51; political, 45, 59, 93, 200, 201, 204, 248n28; responsibility for, 31, 118; social, 65, 99, 100, 148, 153, 197, 218; of universe, 12, 267n25; of world, 29, 36, 56, 58, 92, 124, 149, 171, 201, 202, 206, 209, 212, 240n51, 264n46. *See also* disorder; nature: order of

Páng Pǔ, 127, 256nn26–27, 267n34
passivity, 59, 77, 189, 244n93
Péng Guóxiáng, 16, 228n3
Péng Zǔ, 163, 170, 262n24, 263n36
pessimism, 42, 43, 53, 84, 117, 119, 181, 196, 200. *See also* optimism
philosophy, 5, 7, 13, 42, 179, 227n5, 233n64; Arabic, 1; comparative, 1–6, 227n4; European, 1, 2, 3, 4, 9, 10, 13, 14–15, 40, 41, 107, 109, 181, 199, 219, 220, 221, 225, 227n1, 249n35; global, 227n2; Greek, 1, 258n50; history of, 2, 5, 8, 10; medieval, 1; philosophers, 74, 77, 81, 199; philosophical problems, 4, 12, 28, 36, 38, 39, 219; philosophical systems, 15, 45; philosophical theology, 81; political, 76; Roman, 1; Western, 1, 2, 13, 130
piety, filial, 55, 96, 100, 102
Pines, Yuri, 11, 20, 34, 233nn59–60, 233n63
Plantinga, Alvin, 233n69
plants, 101, 112, 143, 144–46, 202, 260n70
Plato, 42, 69, 80, 81, 242n69
pleasures, sensory, 143, 190, 191–92, 197, 200, 209, 239n43
politics, 12, 22, 62, 83, 98, 99, 126, 167, 172, 173, 174, 175, 184, 222, 231n39, 244n91, 249n34;

262n20; political failure, 49, 60, 236n19; political leaders, 67, 68, 69, 118, 119, 216, 217, 230n23; political office, 48, 173, 260n5; political philosophy, 76; political power, 122; political problems, 3, 69; political relations, 61; political success, 119, 126; political systems, 76. *See also* order: political
Pope, Alexander, 13
potentiality, 110, 130, 168, 170, 174, 257n37
poverty, 21, 25, 31, 53, 54, 57, 58, 59, 60–61, 65, 101, 121, 128, 140, 171, 194, 200
power, 2, 36, 68, 104–105, 112, 125, 126; of heaven, 31, 47, 49, 187, 214, 241n63; human, 26, 35, 39, 43, 52, 57, 65, 70, 96–97, 118, 120, 122–23, 127, 148, 171, 184, 185, 188, 196, 198–99, 201–202, 214, 216–17, 222, 224, 249n40, 253n77, 256n27; will to power, 107, 149, 221, 251n59. *See also* actions: power of; nature: power of; rulers: power of
prosperity, 23, 28, 51, 52, 53, 55, 56, 57, 58, 59, 63, 65, 74, 80, 84, 100, 104, 140, 152, 171, 187, 240n55
psychology, 12, 54, 60, 108, 122, 127, 130, 136, 140, 161, 211
Puett, Michael, 14, 43, 118, 155, 203, 227n6, 228n10, 228n6, 232n54, 234n86, 236n16, 243n81, 253n77, 257n34, 263n43, 264n48, 264n51
punishment, 11, 16, 23, 27, 28, 29, 38, 39, 41, 47, 49, 56, 57, 59, 65, 68, 71, 79, 98, 101, 106, 121, 140, 160, 171, 231n35, 234n1, 239n43, 240n52, 244n89, 261n18, 262n25, 267n23; of the bad, 32, 37, 49, 62, 72, 74, 75–76, 88, 147, 158–59, 163, 184, 187, 216, 220; escaping, 12, 24, 76, 79; by ghosts, 21, 76, 79, 243n78; by God, 38–39, 74; by heaven, 31, 32, 63–64, 66, 68, 71, 158, 232n53, 239n45, 241n58, 243n78, 244n89, 255n13

qì 氣 (vital energy), 24, 95, 110, 129–30, 144, 146–48, 149, 169, 170, 249n37, 252n66, 256n32, 259n65
Qí state, 18–19, 25, 119–21, 122–23, 125–26, 161–62, 163, 191, 229n13, 239n45, 244n92, 254n8
qíng 情 (genuine feelings), 24, 60, 129–31, 133, 145, 157, 158, 163, 164, 166–67, 171, 186, 190, 191, 193–94, 206, 209, 213, 256n32, 257n36, 257n40, 257n42. *See also* emotions, human
Qīng dynasty, 80, 240n52, 255n15, 258n52
qióng 窮 (failure, limit), 21, 24, 25, 26, 55, 121, 172, 175, 185, 198, 263n41. *See also* failure

Qióng dá yǐ shí, 6, 20, 21, 25, 51, 52, 54, 58, 61, 66, 77, 89, 121, 125, 156, 172, 185, 198, 228n5, 238n39

Qū Yuán, 22

regularity, 89, 189; of heaven, 31, 187, 204; of nature, 86–87, 203; of the universe, 185. See also *cháng* 常 (regularity)

religion, 6, 11, 31, 37, 65, 77, 228n3, 232n45, 233n58, 234n1, 236n23; popular, 45, 63, 66. See also Buddhism; Christianity; skepticism: religious; theism

rén 仁 (humaneness), 90–92, 93, 117, 133, 222, 235n6, 248n23, 248nn25–26. See also humaneness

responsibility, human, 30–31, 39–40, 54, 57, 65, 81, 114, 117, 184, 187, 222, 224, 239n44. See also order: responsibility for; *yōuhuàn yìshí* 憂患意識 (sense of responsibility and anxious concern)

reward, 38–39, 57, 65, 98, 140, 231n35; from ghosts, 21, 76; of the good, 37, 41, 72; from heaven, 64, 68, 90, 117; hopes for, 11, 79; from nature, 198. See also virtue: rewards of

rightness, 25, 26, 53, 63, 64–65, 66, 68, 70, 74, 86, 118, 121, 125, 129, 133, 134, 136, 137, 139, 144, 145, 146–48, 154, 155, 163, 166, 172, 185, 189, 190, 192, 193, 195, 201, 229n14, 238n41, 242n66, 242n74, 255n25, 258n52, 262n30, 263n39, 266nn21–22, 268n37; externality of, 91, 131, 146, 257n38; and humaneness, 164, 170, 241n62, 246n3; lack of, 61, 64–65, 139; and ritual, 196, 198, 200, 202, 204, 206, 257n39, 268n39; and the way, 131, 146

rigidity, 112, 113–14, 224

rituals, 16, 20, 25, 51, 63, 67, 79, 90, 91, 100, 126, 131, 132, 133–34, 137, 139, 148, 166, 188, 191, 192, 195–98, 200–202, 203–204, 206, 213–15, 217, 222, 223, 232n54, 244n91, 257nn38–39, 268n39, 268n48; mourning, 102, 192; ritual propriety, 102, 133, 134, 137, 139, 148. See also *lǐ* 禮 (ritual); sacrifices, ritual

Robber Zhi, 24–25, 28, 35, 136, 196, 197, 198, 221, 222, 230n26, 260n1

Roberts, Moss, 90, 246n8, 248n25, 249n39, 252n73

Robinet, Isabelle, 109, 250n50

Robins, Dan, 237n32, 238n35, 249n33

Rosemont, Henry, 90, 237n26, 258n48

Ru (Confucians), 4, 8, 15, 16, 17, 25, 26, 35, 40, 46, 49–51, 52, 53, 54, 56, 57, 58–62, 66–67, 73, 74, 79, 81, 82, 84, 88, 91, 98, 103, 114, 116, 126, 140, 141, 142, 163, 172, 177, 178, 192, 197, 198, 223, 227n7, 228n5, 236n20, 236n22, 237n25, 241n64, 242n68, 244n93, 246n104, 248n23, 254n7, 258n46, 265n5; ethics, 117, 197; and fatalism, 80, 176, 186; and fate, 50, 60, 76–77, 125, 138, 153, 158, 240n50; and heaven, 46, 77, 117, 236n23; and human actions, 84, 97; and humaneness, 91, 134; and humanism, 16–17, 77, 97, 197; and Mohists, 80, 82, 238n40; Ru way, 93, 131, 142, 153, 184, 192, 195–96, 217; terms, 21, 85, 162, 231n33, 246n3; texts, 22, 46, 48, 51, 52, 62, 80, 94, 142, 188, 192, 235n8, 236n22, 240n48, 244n92, 253n1; tradition, 17, 31, 77, 82, 121, 188, 216; and virtue, 102, 117, 133, 166

rulers, 20, 29, 30, 31, 32, 40, 52, 53, 55, 61, 65, 68, 70, 76, 79, 83, 84, 92, 104, 111, 114, 117, 118, 119, 120, 121, 122, 125, 126, 132, 145, 148, 164, 213, 238n38, 240n51, 243n76, 250n47, 254n10; bad, 32, 33, 79, 101, 107, 216, 232n53, 247n19; good, 45, 79, 122; power of, 79, 84, 250n47; sagely, 113, 203; success of, 29, 79, 125

sacrifices, ritual, 28, 32, 33, 65–66, 70–71, 102, 126, 169, 188, 231n35, 235n7, 241n61, 243nn79–81, 253n2

sadness, 129, 162, 165, 173, 179, 181

sageliness, 21, 23, 51, 54, 66, 68, 75, 84, 86, 87, 89, 90, 97–98, 100, 104–105, 106, 108, 110, 111–12, 113–15, 128, 135, 145, 147, 155, 163, 166, 167, 171, 174, 175, 176, 182, 184, 190, 196, 203, 206, 207, 209–10, 213, 217, 221, 247n17, 248n24, 250n48, 251n54, 252n69, 252nn73–74, 253n78, 258n52, 263n43, 268n48; sagely kings, 27, 57, 64, 67, 71, 75, 78, 213

Sān dé 三德 (Three virtues), 63, 87, 231n35

Schneewind, J. D., 2

scholars, 23, 35, 61, 62, 82, 93, 118, 119, 121, 128, 144, 203, 230n23, 252n67, 254n11, 257n34, 259nn58–59, 269n50; scholar-officials, 66, 239n44

Schopenhauer, Arthur, 200

Schwartz, Benjamin, 95, 109, 250n49, 251n61

science, 76, 99, 179, 198–99, 203, 243n84, 266n17

self-control, 135, 140

self-cultivation, 39, 60, 116, 124, 130, 131, 134, 144, 196, 197, 205, 213, 237n26, 244n93, 251n54

self-interest, 153, 189, 221, 222

self-preservation, 152

self-sacrifice, 239n44

self-so. See *zìrán* 自然 (self-so/spontaneity)

Sextus Empiricus, 180, 229n17, 263n37

shame, 84, 99–100, 117, 133, 134, 147, 163, 164, 167, 185, 189, 191, 222

shàn 善 (good), 40, 89, 136, 257n34
Shàng dynasty, 22, 27–28, 29–31, 58, 231n38, 232n54, 268n48
Shàng shū 尚書 (Book of Documents), 27, 29, 30, 31, 32, 33, 52, 96–97, 114, 122, 230n21, 232n47, 238n38
Shàngdì, 28–29, 30, 31, 33, 63, 71, 98, 243n76, 247n11
shēn 身 (body), 92, 110, 166–67
shēng 生 (grow, live), 73, 103, 105, 107, 129, 144, 251n59, 259n57, 259n59, 265n12. See also nature: generative forces of
shí 時 (timing), 20–21, 24, 52, 58, 85, 124, 125, 128, 172, 186, 187, 233n60, 237n28
shì 是 (right), 154, 166, 167, 170, 174. See also fēi 非 (wrong)
shì 士 (scholar, scholar-official). See scholars
Shī jīng 詩經 (Book of Odes), 24, 32, 43, 219, 245n103, 269n2
Shū Qí, 4, 22–23, 24, 90, 151
Shùn (emperor), 28, 52, 124–25, 126, 127, 136, 161, 162, 167, 172, 243n79, 253n2, 255n25, 262n22
shùn 順 (follow along with), 51, 114, 125, 247n15
Sīmǎ Qiān, 4, 20, 22–23, 24, 90, 229n13
singularity, 14, 159, 209, 225, 241n65; of individuals, 40, 164, 165; of things, 156, 159–60, 163, 169–70, 173, 180
skepticism, 7, 34, 50, 68, 101, 157, 180, 212–13, 250, 261n12, 263n37, 268n45; religious, 45, 47, 51, 56, 237n32
Slingerland, Edward, 90, 237n26, 244n93
Socrates, 69, 80, 233n66, 242n69
Sòng dynasty, 31, 46, 88, 228n5, 250n52, 260n70
Sòng state, 18, 25, 47, 119, 120, 139, 151, 237n26, 254n8
Sòngzǐ, 59, 191, 210
Spinoza, Baruch, 3, 39, 54, 107, 141, 221–22
spirits, 6, 14, 16, 21, 28, 31, 33, 34, 37, 45, 46–47, 51, 56, 65–66, 71, 75–76, 79, 86, 106, 143, 148, 161, 166, 170, 171, 188, 232n54, 235n7, 240n55, 241n59, 241n61, 243n76, 243n79, 244n93, 249n36, 253n2. See also ghosts
Spring and Autumn Period, 11, 19, 20, 31, 34, 116, 187, 230n27, 233n59, 233n63, 237n32, 238n38
Stalnaker, Aaron, 39, 190, 203, 215–16, 265n11, 267n25, 268n37, 268n47
stillness, 85, 86, 130
Stoicism, 59, 140, 239n46, 240n17
Sū Zhé, 88, 248n25
success, 4, 11–12, 20–21, 23, 25, 26, 50, 51, 52–53, 54, 56, 57, 59, 62, 64, 78, 84, 87, 88, 98, 99–100, 101–102, 103, 106, 118, 119, 121–23, 125, 126, 141, 152, 171, 172, 173, 184, 185, 188, 195, 201, 209, 212, 229n10, 237n28, 247n19, 250n53, 255n18. See also dá 達 (success, reach to); rulers: success of; tōng 通 (succeed, commune)
suffering, 9, 12, 14, 19, 21, 24, 25, 29, 32–33, 34, 38, 42, 43, 50, 60, 75, 112, 116, 117, 120–21, 124, 125, 126, 139, 140, 150, 151, 170, 173, 180, 196, 212, 230n31, 232n53, 236n19, 239n44, 240n47, 264n46, 265n13; of bad people, 45; of good people, 22, 23, 89, 103, 188
supernatural, the, 20, 39, 46, 63, 199, 224, 229n15

Tàipíngjīng 太平靜, 231n35
Tàiyī shēng shuǐ 太一生水 (Great unity generates water), 86, 95, 111, 198, 248n30
Táng dynasty, 23, 162, 265n3
Táng Jūnyì, 1, 17
Táng Yú zhī dào 唐虞之道 (Way of Táng and Yú), 51, 236n22, 255n23
teleology, 50, 73, 130, 145, 203, 256n29, 257n37, 259n63
Téng state, 119, 120, 122, 254n8
theism, 42, 46, 51, 69, 77, 92, 236n20, 240n56
theodicy, 11, 180, 228n4, 231n35, 231n38
tiān 天 (heaven), 1, 29, 31, 33, 49, 51–52, 57, 62–63, 72, 95–96, 117–18, 123, 129, 141, 142, 152, 153, 156, 180, 185–86, 187, 198, 200–201, 206, 208, 232n52, 232n55, 235n8, 235n11, 240n56, 242n71, 243n76, 249n36, 249n39, 253n3, 266n17, 266n19
tiānrén héyī 天人合一 (unity of heaven and human), 8, 14, 16, 116, 228n5
tiānrén zhīfēn 天人之分 (division between heaven and human), 14, 116, 155, 188, 198, 228n5. See also divisions: between heaven and human
timing. See shí 時 (timing)
tōng 通 (succeed, commune), 21, 24, 25, 26, 172, 177, 185, 198. See also success
tradition, 3, 10, 15, 27, 51, 59, 66–67, 68, 78, 118, 198, 208, 213, 215, 217, 218, 227n2, 241n65, 266n14, 268n48; European, 39, 43, 69, 181, 182. See also Ru (Confucians): tradition
tragedy, 35, 41–44, 181–83, 264n50
transcendence, 2, 14, 37, 170, 205, 220
Tseu, Augustinus, 234n1, 241n57, 242n71

uniqueness, 159–60, 180, 241n65, 251n64, 261n17; of humans, 40–41, 129, 143, 160, 199, 223, 224 unity, 13, 95, 152, 165, 202, 228n5, 267n33; of heaven and human, 8, 14–16, 116

Van Norden, Bryan, 50, 143, 239n43, 245n95, 250n50, 255n14, 255n19, 257n41, 258n47, 259n62
vice, 19, 27–28, 29, 39
violence, 39, 44, 101, 102, 106, 112, 153, 163, 166, 175, 215
virtue, 2, 12, 17, 20, 22, 24, 25, 26, 27–28, 29–31, 32, 35, 41, 47, 52–53, 54, 59, 72, 90, 92, 96–97, 103, 118, 119–20, 121–23, 125, 126, 129, 131, 133–35, 137, 140, 142, 144–45, 147–48, 158, 164, 166–67, 171, 185, 187, 189, 196, 211, 230n21, 237n29, 238n39, 242n69, 243n82, 249n40, 251n56, 252n67, 254n7, 257n40, 257n43, 265n13; of heaven, 51, 87; rewards of, 78, 140, 184, 191, 198, 201, 203, 219, 254n10. See also *dé* 德 (virtue); Ru (Confucians): and virtue

Wáng Bì, 84, 85, 88, 102, 111, 246nn8–9, 247n13, 247n15, 247n17, 247n20, 248n24, 250n47, 252n66, 252n68, 252n70
Wáng Chōng, 4, 21, 47, 52, 229n10, 229n15, 230n18, 230n26, 239n45, 240n55, 252n75, 258n47, 258n51, 260n70. See also *Lùnhéng*
Wáng Guówéi, 43
Wang Huaiyu, 234n88
Wáng Ní, 153–54, 155, 170, 182, 261n11, 263n38
Warring States Period, 1, 4–5, 6, 11, 27, 30, 33, 51, 63, 73, 75, 78, 82, 95, 96, 106, 151, 190, 219, 222, 225, 229n10, 229n16, 231n35, 234n2
water, 54, 95, 104, 112, 123, 143, 144–47, 149, 162, 188, 201, 202, 214, 248n31, 259n63
Watson, Burton, 167, 189, 241n62, 242n74, 243n78, 243n80, 262n21, 263n34, 263n38, 265n3, 268nn39–40
way, the, 19, 24, 25–26, 31, 49–50, 53, 54, 58, 66, 83, 85–86, 88, 91, 92, 95–98, 100–101, 102, 103–106, 107–13, 114–15, 121, 125, 129, 131, 146, 148, 160, 168, 169, 170, 172, 174, 175, 182, 185, 187, 189, 191, 195, 196, 198, 209, 211, 212, 214, 215, 221, 249n35, 250n53, 251n54, 251n65, 253n77, 257n43, 266nn15–16, 267n25, 268n46; enactment of, 48, 60, 61, 84, 138, 139, 140, 218, 234n88, 258n49; following of, 99, 105, 212; of heaven, 87, 88, 90, 135, 147, 156, 198, 233n59, 235n6, 247n15, 249n32. See also *dào*
wealth, 53–54, 56, 59, 63, 102, 107, 121, 124, 188, 240n48, 241n58, 258n47; accumulation of, 153, 164, 197, 200, 239n45; extreme, 101, 103

Weber, Max, 11, 14, 254n10
wisdom, 20, 27, 42, 46, 52, 56, 57, 91, 96, 133–34, 148, 163, 166, 171, 172, 188, 194, 211, 223, 238n39, 257n34, 258n52
Wolff, Christian, 46
Wong, David, 265n11
writing, 7, 8, 67, 80–81, 245n101, 246n104
wú 無 (non-being), 61, 248n30
wù 惡 (hate), 104, 200. See also *è*
Wú Jìn'ān, 240n50
Wú state, 18–19, 20, 21, 25, 229nn13–14
Wǔ xíng 五行 (Five actions), 7, 81, 96, 147, 206, 228n12, 259n66
Wǔ Zǐxū, 17–22, 24, 28, 43, 52, 75, 151, 229n11, 229n16, 230n24, 230n26
wúwéi 無爲 (non-action). See actions: non-action

Xià dynasty, 27, 28, 58, 126
xiào 孝 (filial piety). See piety, filial
xīn 心 (heart). See heart
xìng 幸 (luck). See luck
xìng 性 (nature/disposition), 26, 108, 116, 117, 128–31, 133–35, 140–45, 149–50, 155, 158, 162, 164–66, 169, 191, 193–94, 197, 200–201, 206–107, 222–23, 235n6, 246n8, 256nn29–31, 257nn36–37, 257n40, 259n57, 259n59, 260n70, 265n12
Xìng zì mìng chū 性自命出, 7, 40, 81, 94, 131–32, 135, 141, 148, 158, 169, 192, 193, 228n12, 244n92, 248n31, 252n66, 256n30, 257n40, 257n42, 263n33, 266n22, 268n38, 268n48
xiōng 凶 (unpropitious), 85, 187–88. See also misfortune
Xú Fùguān, 15, 30–31, 34, 49, 54, 231n35, 233n63
Xúnzǐ, 5, 8, 11, 27, 39, 46, 49, 53, 67, 86, 129, 130, 142, 155, 184–206, 208–20, 222–23, 263n44, 264n1, 265nn3–4, 265nn10–11, 266n14, 266nn16–17, 266n21, 267nn25–26, 267n31, 267nn33–34, 268nn37–39, 268n43, 268nn47–48
Xúnzǐ 荀子, 4, 5–6, 8, 51–52, 116, 127, 141, 147, 158, 184, 185, 187–89, 192, 195, 196, 199, 203–204, 207, 208, 210–11, 213, 216, 222, 223, 224, 231n32, 241n61, 249n32, 256n30, 264n1, 265n4, 265n10, 266n16, 267n23, 267n31, 267n34, 269n2

Yān state, 122–23, 125, 244n92, 255n24
Yán Huí, 25, 48–49, 50, 53–54, 88, 128, 153, 162, 169, 175, 239n45, 247n14

Yáng Zhū, 152, 170, 221
Yáo (emperor), 28, 51, 126–27, 161, 162–63, 172, 187, 243n79, 255n25, 262n22
Yearley, Lee, 11, 49, 157, 179, 236n17, 240n47, 253n3, 254n4, 255n16, 257n43, 261nn14–15, 263n44, 265n11, 268n45
yì 義 (rightness). *See* rightness
yōu 憂 (anxious). *See* anxiety
yōuhuàn yìshí 憂患意識 (sense of responsibility and anxious concern), 30, 43, 54, 114, 199. *See also* responsibility, human
yù 遇 (meet), 52, 122, 189
Yǔ (emperor), 28, 64, 126–27, 128, 145, 185–86, 216, 235n7, 241n63, 255n23, 255n25
Yǔ cóng 語叢 (Collected sayings), 40, 91, 131, 134, 139, 156, 248n30, 249n36, 259n62

Zhāng Ěrqí, 258n52
Zhāng Zǎi, 228n5
Zhào Qí, 255n14, 255n17, 255n25, 257n40, 257n42, 258n51
zhèng 正 (correct). *See* correctness
Zhōng yōng 中庸 (Doctrine of the Mean), 91, 130, 257n36
Zhòu (emperor), 22, 27, 28, 30, 58, 64, 172, 190, 238n38, 241n58
Zhōu dynasty, 15, 16–17, 22, 27–30, 32, 34, 36, 45, 47, 57, 67, 97, 116, 123, 231n38, 232n45, 232n52, 254n6, 268n48
Zhōu yì 周易 (Book of Changes), 30, 85, 87, 107, 111, 188, 228n9, 235n3, 258n47
Zhū Xī, 49, 123, 135, 144, 235n7, 236n13, 252n67, 254n7, 254n11, 257n36, 257n40, 257n42, 258n49, 260n70
Zhuāngzǐ, 3, 5, 73, 152, 155–57, 165, 166–67, 171–72, 176–79, 181–83, 184, 198, 210, 211, 213, 218, 220, 222, 229n8, 244n94, 260n3, 261n6, 261n12, 261n14, 262n20, 262n32, 263n37, 263n44, 264n51, 265n3, 268n45
Zhuāngzǐ 莊子, 5–6, 8, 13, 23, 24, 26, 37, 38, 40, 43, 44, 72, 73, 74, 90, 95, 96, 97, 101, 106, 108, 110, 115, 127, 128, 151–53, 155–58, 161, 163–65, 167–76, 177, 178, 179–81, 182, 183, 191, 198, 200, 201–202, 208–209, 211, 212–13, 218, 220, 221, 222, 223, 224, 230n31, 239n44, 246n8, 250n53, 251n65, 254n7, 256n31, 261n7, 261n14, 263n37, 264nn49–50, 268n36, 269n3
Zǐgòng, 26, 51, 53, 229n13, 239n45
Zǐlù, 46–48, 50, 51, 55, 61, 66, 80, 230n28, 235n9, 258n51
Ziporyn, Brook, 167, 261n13, 262n19, 262n21, 262n27, 263nn37–39, 263n41, 268n43
zìrán 自然 (self-so/spontaneity), 40, 95, 99, 109, 111–12, 113, 156, 165, 167, 190, 193, 248n24, 250n46, 250n48, 252n74, 253n78, 260n70
Zǐsī, 147, 216
Zǐxià, 51–52, 54, 237n26
Zōu Yǎn, 229n8
Zūn dé yì 尊德義 (Honoring virtue and rightness), 236n22, 248n31
Zuǒ zhuàn 左傳, 229n11, 230n21, 231n44, 256n31

FRANKLIN PERKINS is Professor of Philosophy at DePaul University. He is author of *Leibniz and China: A Commerce of Light* (2004) and *Leibniz: A Guide for the Perplexed* (2007).

www.ingramcontent.com/pod-product-compliance
Lightning Source LLC
Chambersburg PA
CBHW030608230426
43661CB00053B/1893